DON'T MENTION THE WAR

DON'T MENTION THE WAR
Northern Ireland, Propaganda
and the Media

David Miller

Pluto Press
LONDON • BOULDER, COLORADO

First published 1994 by Pluto Press
345 Archway Road, London N6 5AA
and 22883 Quicksilver Drive, Sterling, VA 20166-2012, USA

www.plutobooks.com

British Library Cataloguing in Publication Data
A catalogue record for this book is available from the British
Library

Library of Congress Cataloging in Publication Data
Applied for

ISBN   0 7453 0835 X hardback
ISBN   0 7453 0836 8 paperback

Printed on demand by Lightning Source

For my father, Robert Miller, who would have approved.

To those journalists who have asked the right questions.

Contents

Acknowledgements

In writing this book I have accumulated many debts, most of which I will probably never be able to repay. A myriad of people helped by sharing their time, expertise and knowledge and by helping to trace information and people. For help with cuttings, press releases, obscure speeches and other documentation thanks to John Conway for allowing me access to the BBC cuttings library in Belfast, Anne Crilly, John Foster at the NUJ, Michael Goodall of the Public Records Office of Northern Ireland, Ted Howell and Pat O'Hare of the Sinn Féin Foreign Affairs Bureau, Oliver Kearney, Marian Laragy and Helen Dady at the Irish Information Partnership, Bill McGookin of the RUC, Paddy and Barra McGrory, Niall Meehan, Fr. Raymond Murray, Michael Ritchie at the Committee on the Administration of Justice, Bill Rolston, Mike Tomlinson, the Ulster Information Service, Robin Wilson, Jane Winter, George Woodman, the Librarian at Stormont. For asking questions in the House and finding other bits of information, thanks to Mike Brown MP, Frank Dobson MP, George Galloway MP, Kevin McNamara MP and Tom Lyne. The Northern Ireland Information Service were also very helpful, at least in the early stages of the research. Special thanks to Liz Curtis and Aly Renwick for access to the voluminous Information on Ireland archive and to Liz for endless conversations, tips and information. Thanks to David Maguire for his encyclopaedic (and pedantic) knowledge of Irish history. Gerard McLaughlin helped immensely with introductions and contacts as well as providing accommodation .in the McLaughlin guesthouse *The Cheapest Place in Town*. Thanks also to Cahal McLaughlin in Belfast and Jim Curran in Derry for recording local news bulletins. For help in tracking down British propaganda materials and other pieces of information overseas thanks to Pat Doherty, Jack Holland, Fr. Sean McManus, Rita Mullan and Aogan Ó Maolchatha.

No researcher with a genuine interest in the Northern Ireland conflict can ignore the wealth of materials housed in the wonderful political collection at the Linenhall library in Belfast. The contents of the collection and the immense helpfulness of Robert Bell, Bern Kane and their colleagues have been essential to the completion of this book. Every major city should have its own version. Unfortunately it seems that some elements of the Republican Movement do not share my admiration: in early January 1994 the IRA placed fire bombs in the Library, which narrowly avoided destroying the entire collection.

Understandably many of those who helped did so on the condition that they would remain anonymous. My thanks to all of those journalists, activists and civil servants who supplied me with information and views, especially those who spoke openly when they might have chosen not to.

For help with the organisation of audience discussion groups thanks to Kate Phillips, George Greig and Bob Turner at the WEA, Kathy McMaster at SACRO, Malcolm Thwaite at Glasgow School of Art, Jane Miller, Robert Miller, Jeanne Barsby in Chislehurst, Janis Anderson in Harrow, John Hunter of Hammersmith police station, Lt. Col. P.N.P. Watts of the Royal Military College of Science in Swindon, Major David Magee and Major J. P. Hannan, RAEC, Redford Barracks, Edinburgh and the Ministry of Defence for allowing me access to the soldiers. In Belfast thanks to Roisin McDonough, Maggie Bowers at Dee Street Community Centre, Hazel Bruce of the Shankill womens group, Mr Bahman at Farset, Dr Jack Spence of Suffolk Community Services Group, Stevie Johnston at the Falls Community Council. Thanks also to Phil Radcliffe at Manchester University for the American groups. Lastly thanks very much to all those who participated in the audience discussion groups, for putting up with my questions.

I am indebted to my colleagues at the Glasgow University Media Group for their criticisms and advice on early drafts of the material contained here. Thanks to John Eldridge, Lesley Henderson, Jenny Kitzinger, Greg McLaughlin, Jacquie Reilly and especially to Greg Philo.

I typed most of this myself, but thanks to Kathleen Davidson for typing the first draft of Chapter 5 and especially to Joanne Yuill for coping so good humouredly with endless 'extra bits' and changes.

Thanks to Pressdram Ltd for permission to reproduce the cover of *Private Eye*, Colin Wheeler for permission to reproduce his cartoon from the *Independent* and the *Los Angeles Times* for permission to reproduce the Wasserman cartoon from the *Boston Globe*. Thanks are also due to the Deputy Keeper of Records, Public Records Office of Northern Ireland and the Copyright Officer, Public Records Office, Kew, for permission to publish from Crown papers and to the BBC for permission to publish from papers held at the Written Archives Centre.

Lastly, my love and thanks to Emma Waddell and to Caitlin Miller, who was born days after the first draft of what follows was finished.

David Miller
Glasgow, August 1994

Abbreviations

BBC	British Broadcasting Corporation
BBCNI	BBC Northern Ireland
BIS	British Information Services
BSC	Broadcasting Standards Council
CAB	Cabinet files (PRO/PRONI)
CAJ	Committee on the Administration of Justice
COI	Central Office of Information
CPGB	Communist Party of Great Britain
CPI	Communist Party of Ireland
DG	Director-General (BBC)
DPP	Director of Public Prosecutions
DUP	Democratic Unionist Party
FCIC	Force Control and Information Centre
FO	Foreign Office files (PRO)
FCO	Foreign and Commonwealth Office
HO	Home Office files (PRO)
IBA	Independent Broadcasting Authority
IDB	Industrial Development Board
INLA	Irish National Liberation Party
IRA	Irish Republican Army
IRD	Information Research Department (FCO)
ITC	Independent Television Commission
MoD	Ministry of Defence
NIIS	Northern Ireland Information Service
NIO	Northern Ireland Office
NITB	Northern Ireland Tourist Board
OVIS	Overseas Visits and Information Studies Division (COI)
PACE	Police and Criminal Evidence Act
PMG	Postmaster-General
PREM	Prime Minister's Office files (PRO)
PRO	Public Records Office
PRONI	Public Records Office of Northern Ireland

PTA   Prevention of Terrorism Act
RUC   Royal Ulster Constabulary
SACHR   Standing Advisory Commission on Human Rights
SACRO   Scottish Association for the Care and Resettlement of
        Offenders
SDLP   Social Democratic and Labour Party
UDR   Ulster Defence Regiment
UFF   Ulster Freedom Fighters
UUP   Ulster Unionist Party
UVF   Ulster Volunteer Force
UWC   Ulster Workers Council
WAC   Written Archives Centre (BBC)

Introduction

BASIL FAWLTY (to Polly) Listen ... Don't mention the war ... *I* mentioned it once, but I think I got away with it all right ... (He returns to his guests.) So it's all forgotten now and let's hear no more about it. So ... that's two egg mayonnaise, a prawn Goebbels, a Herman Goering and four Colditz salads ... no, wait a moment, I got a bit confused there, sorry .... (from *Fawlty Towers*, BBC Television, in Sadler and Hallyar 1985)

This book emerges from wide-ranging empirical research conducted between 1988 and 1993. It is an attempt to examine the process of mass communication from the genesis of media strategies, through the production of news and other factual accounts of the Northern Ireland conflict, to the content of press and television reporting. It also attempts to examine the impact of the media on public opinion and belief.

The research for this book draws on over 200 interviews with both sources and journalists. Amongst the former were serving and former Information Officers and administrative civil servants in the Northern Ireland Office, Royal Ulster Constabulary, Ministry of Defence, Foreign and Commonwealth Office, Central Office of Information, Northern Ireland Tourist Board, Industrial Development Board and Fair Employment Agency, together with press officers or representatives of the Democratic Unionist Party, the Ulster Unionist Party, the Social, Democratic and Labour Party, Sinn Féin and a range of civil liberties and human rights organisations such as Amnesty International, Liberty, Committee on the Administration of Justice, the Standing Advisory Commission on Human Rights, etc. Amongst the journalists were representatives of all British national papers, all Belfast- and Dublin-based papers, both BBC TV and ITN reporters, together with numerous current affairs and radio journalists and senior broadcasting management in both London and Belfast. I also inter-

1

viewed a selection of foreign correspondents and a range of US journalists.

There are very few recent studies which analyse media coverage together with its interpretation by audiences (although see Corner et al. 1990; Morley 1980; Philo 1990; Schlesinger et al. 1992). By contrast there has been a huge explosion of research on the television audience which tends to downplay or ignore media messages and concentrate simply on audience interpretation. Much of this has been concerned with demonstrating audience 'activity'. Texts are seen as having no fixed meanings and audiences may (to some extent at least) pick and choose the meanings they take from a given message.

However, 'the most important thing for audience research to focus on' (Corner 1991: 275) is the relationship between media content and public belief. If we want to understand media content, it is also crucial to examine the production of media messages and the strategies used by sources to influence the media. Framing all these processes are, of course, the prevailing economic relations of media production. Yet surprisingly there are very few other studies which have taken in such a broad sweep from source strategies to audience belief. The arguments about the influence of the media on public belief presented here are the result of extensive empirical research with groups of people living in Britain and Northern Ireland, together with serving British soldiers.

British Policy

The guiding light of British policy over the last seventy-five years has been to try and push Ireland to the margins of British politics. This was managed quite successfully until 1968, when the North exploded on to television screens around the world. Since then, British policy has been directed to containing the 'troubles' and attempting to reduce the killing to what one government minister called 'an acceptable level of violence' (*Sunday Times* Insight Team 1972: 309). It borders on the heretical even to describe what is happening in Northern Ireland as a 'war'. Yet, in one of the many confusions surrounding British policy, public relations strategy has consistently emphasised the criminality and 'evil' of the Irish Republican Army (IRA), thus raising the news value of a conflict which successive governments have otherwise tried so hard to keep out of the spotlight. In this 'war' over 3,000 people have died out of a population of 1.5 million in a part of Ireland about the same size as Wales. The conflict costs in excess of £2 billion a year and has dragged on for over a quarter of a century. Millions of words have been spoken and written about it. Yet Northern Ireland has been very low on the political agenda. Northern Ireland ministers are exiled to a British Siberia and very few return to job promotion. Political parties do not prioritise Northern Ireland – indeed, they have tended to agree on many aspects of policy. At general elections the issue has not intruded into the hysteria of canvassing. So low is the profile of Northern Ireland that during the 1992 election, the last cabinet or shadow cabinet ministers to appear on TV news were either those that their parties were embarrassed about – Gerald Kaufman or John Gummer – or their Northern Ireland spokespersons – Peter Brooke and Kevin McNamara (Billig et al. 1993).

But debate, argument and negotiation about the war in Ireland are crucial if the conflict is to be brought to an end: this book is written in opposition to those who would prefer debate to be stifled or permitted only so long as it contributes to governmental objectives. Thus Paul Wilkinson, the 'doyen' (Gearty 1991: 14) of British terrorism studies, has suggested that debate about the meaning and use of the term 'terrorism' may simply be a device to obstruct 'anti-terrorist' policies:

> The problems of establishing a degree of common understanding of the concept of terrorism have been vastly exaggerated. Indeed, I suspect that some have tried to deny that any common usage exists as a device for obstructing co-operation in policies to combat terrorism. (Wilkinson 1990: 27)

For such writers the only worthwhile argument concerns how to increase the effectiveness of 'anti-terrorist' policies. Should we choose to question the assumptions in such an approach, the ideological policing of the counterinsurgents will label us as fellow travellers of the 'terrorists'. But in truth there is no universal agreement on the causes of the Northern Ireland conflict and the term 'terrorism' is not unambiguous in its meaning and use.

Definitions of Terrorism

For Western governments, 'terrorism' is an illegitimate form of violence which is a dangerous threat to liberal democracies. There is an 'alternative' view, which emphasises the rhetorical and ideological functions of the term terrorism. In this view Western governments and counterinsurgency writers label only their enemies as terrorists and ignore their own 'terrorist' actions and those of their allies or friends.

Almost all writers are agreed that 'terrorism' is the 'systematic' use of 'murder' or other physical violence for political ends. In particular, there is substantial agreement that 'terrorist' violence is either 'indiscriminate' or mostly targets civilians or both (e.g. Gearty 1991; Thackrah 1987; Wilkinson 1978, 1990; Wright 1991). Were we to use the killing of civilians as a criterion and apply it literally to the Northern Ireland conflict, we would be unable to label the IRA unequivocally as 'terrorist', since a minority (37.4 per cent) of victims of the IRA between 1969 and June 1989 were civilians. On the other hand, the army and the police in Northern Ireland would be categorised as 'terrorists', since a majority (54.4 per cent) of the people they have killed were civilians (Irish Information Partnership 1990). Of course, the 'security forces' would claim that they do not kill civilians deliberately, but then so would the IRA. Indeed, the IRA routinely apologises when it does kill civilians 'by mistake'.

The degree of discrimination in targets is not, however, a reliable guide to the organisations described as 'terrorist' in the writings of 'counterinsurgency' theorists. Writers such as Wilkinson do not apply their definitions with any rigour. The IRA are referred to as 'terrorist' not according to their targets, but whatever they do. Counterinsurgency theorists have already made up their minds about the groups they think of as 'terrorist'. They then manage to define 'terrorism' so that it fits with their own preconceptions. For example, Paul Wilkinson writes that:

> Terrorism can be briefly defined as coercive intimidation or more fully as the systematic use of murder, injury, and destruction or threat of same to create a climate of terror, to publicise a cause, and to coerce a wider target into submitting to its aims. (Wilkinson 1990:27)

In principle this could fit any form of political violence, including state violence. So could the definition written into British law in the Prevention of Terrorism Act: "Terrorism" means the use of violence for political ends and includes any use of violence for the purpose of putting the public or any section of the public in fear' (cited in Walker 1992: 7). But in practice it is only the violence of non-state groups, or non-Western states, to which these definitions refer. Even those who write from a civil liberties perspective, such as Conor Gearty, are vulnerable to polemical uses of the term.

Gearty's concern is to narrow the definition to make it less partisan, as well as to tease out the subtleties of meaning in writing on 'terrorism'. This leads him to set out a definition of 'pure' or 'core' terrorism which he regards as sufficient for the task:

> Acts of violence which we consider unambiguously terrorist have certain characteristics in common. They uniformly involve the deliberate infliction or ... the threatened infliction of severe physical violence; killing and maiming are the trademark of the true terrorists. Such acts are not in themselves rare in contemporary society. Despotic governments may do the same, but, unlike the practitioner of subversive terror, they have the authority of the state to enforce and legitimate their actions. (Gearty 1991: 8)

Unfortunately even this is not free from polemical implications. When his definition does not work, Gearty manipulates it to distinguish groups of which he apparently approves (the African National Congress is referred to as a 'genuine' liberation movement [1991: 98]) from those of which he disapproves. This is especially clear in the case of Northern Ireland where, in order to call the IRA 'terrorists', he redefines 'pure' terrorism – from the 'deliberate infliction' (1991: 8) of indiscriminate violence, it is violence which is 'for all practical purposes indiscriminate in its effect' (1991: 126). It should also be noted that he explicitly omits state violence, making his definition a good deal more partisan than that given by either Wilkinson or the Prevention of Terrorism Act. The problem which this points up is, though, common to counterinsurgency theory as well. Despotic governments are excluded because 'they have the authority of the state to legitimate their actions'. But the legitimacy of even 'democratic' states such as the 'United Kingdom of Great Britain and Northern Ireland' (to give it its full title) is not definitively established. The legitimacy of British rule of the 'six counties' of Northern Ireland is precisely the point of contention between the IRA and the British government. It is hardly neutral to accept the claim of one side to be the legitimate rulers and define 'terrorism' so that it fits only the actions of the other side.

The most fundamental problem with trying to define 'terrorism' is that it is contested. Noam Chomsky illustrates this by citing St Augustine:

> St. Augustine tells the story of a pirate captured by Alexander the Great. 'How dare you molest the sea?' asked Alexander. 'How dare you molest the whole world?' the pirate replied. 'Because I do it with a little ship only, I am called a thief; you, doing it with a great navy, are called an emperor.' (Chomsky 1991a: 9)

Were a non-partisan definition possible, then either it would be ignored by those who have the power to define it in world politics, or a new term of abuse would be found. But as things stand 'terrorism' is pejorative and is only used to describe violence of which the user disapproves. In contemporary debate the use of the term can mainly be explained 'in terms of Western interests and policy, not by the actions and plans of the "terrorists"' (Herman and O'Sullivan 1991: 39). If 'terrorism' consists of either 'strategic' or 'indiscriminate' attacks in which the victims are civilian, then why are the bombings of Dresden, Hiroshima and Vietnam or of the Greenpeace ship *Rainbow Warrior* by the French Secret Service, not defined as 'terrorist'? And why was the 'carpet bombing' of civilians in Iraq during the Gulf War not terrorism? Why are the killings on Bloody Sunday in Derry 1972, when thirteen civilians were shot dead by the Paratroop Regiment, or the killings of civilians John Downes by plastic bullet in 1984, taxi driver Ken Stronge in 1988 and over 300 other civilians by the British Army and RUC not described as 'terrorism'? Because, as George argues, the term '"terrorism" has been virtually appropriated to signify atrocities targeting the West' (George 1991b: 1).

The labelling of one organisation or action as 'terrorist' is intimately related to questions of power and influence. The attempt to label an opponent as 'terrorist' is not a question of more and more exactly separating the actions which qualify as terrorist from those which don't. Defining opponents as 'terrorists' represents an active pursuit of legitimacy. Such legitimation strategies are central to the operation of all governments, whether they are dictatorships or liberal-democracies.

The Legitimacy of the State

The fundamental dispute in Northern Ireland is around the legitimacy of the state. In the official view armed opposition to the state is illegitimate since conditions of democracy prevail. Yet the definition of the political entity itself is what is contested. The official British view acknowledges that the civil rights protests in the late 1960s against the systematic discrimination, gerrymandering and repression of the Unionist government had some justification. But it sees the introduction of direct rule in 1972 as having fundamentally reformed the Northern Ireland state, thereby removing the causes of the conflict; any subsequent manifestations of unrest can only be explained as initiating from 'extremists'. The IRA is held to be a criminal conspiracy similar to organised crime networks such as the Mafia (hence the use of the term 'godfathers' in some official propaganda). It is also presented to some audiences as part of an international network of 'terrorists', and has been linked variously with Marxist revolutionaries in Europe, with anti-Western feeling in the Middle East, particularly Libya, and with the global ambitions of the former Soviet Union.

The role of the British Army and RUC in all this is seen as being to counter the 'terrorist threat' and keep the peace between the warring factions. The governmental apparatus exists solely to oversee a return of 'normality'. Thus we have seen media coverage of a large number of attempts by the British to 'facilitate' a negotiated settlement between the two communities. When these fail, the responsibility rests, in the official version, solely with the deep and irreconcilable historical antagonisms that bind the unionist and nationalist communities in conflict.

But there are other views. The most widely held of these stresses that Britain is not 'above' the conflict but is actually an intimate part of it. The conflict in Ireland is seen as rooted in the creation of the statelet of Northern Ireland in 1921. The creation of Northern Ireland is itself seen as a breach of democracy in that the last elections in Ireland overwhelmingly returned a Sinn Féin government. The parliament in the north was created purely on the basis of a sectarian head count to ensure a Protestant majority in perpetuity. In this view, the idea that there is democracy in a state which is gerrymandered from the atart is fundamentally flawed. The maintenance of the border is seen as being guaranteed by both the presence of British troops and the funding of the current administrative set-up by the British government. (The cost of this British subvention to Northern Ireland in 1988/9 was £1.9 billion; see Gaffikin and Morrissey 1990: 49.) Versions of this view are held by many politicians in the South of Ireland, the Social, Democratic and Labour Party (SDLP) in the North as well as by some politicians in Britain. It is also current in some parts of the media. The *Daily Mirror*, for example, routinely put this view between 1978 and 1991. Following the collapse in the summer of 1991 of the latest round of talks sponsored by the NIO, the *Mirror* repeated its opinion that the conflict continues because it is funded and underwritten by Britain:

> Once again, a well-meaning attempt by the British government to solve the unsolvable in Ulster has ended in failure. It will always be so. The Northern Ireland Secretary, Peter Brooke, as so many decent men before him, tried to win from the leaders of the Protestant majority and the Catholic minority an agreement on some measure of power sharing. He was doomed to failure, as were all the other Government Ministers who have tried before him. The Protestant Unionist leadership will never concede an inch to the Catholic republicans as long as

they believe they have a Big Brother in Britain to protect and finance them. The nationalists will remain obstinate while they believe the Dublin Government is always in their corner. (*Daily Mirror*, 5 July 1991)

Arguments like these recognise that there is no military solution to a conflict which is essentially political. Contrary to the logic of much *public* official thinking, some senior figures in the British establishment also accept that this is the case. General Sir James Glover, the former commander-in-chief, UK Land Forces, who had previously served as an intelligence officer in Northern Ireland, [1] has said:

> In no way can, or will, the Provisional IRA ever be defeated militarily ... The long war will last as long as the Provisional IRA have the stamina, the political motivation – I used to call it the sinews of war – the wherewithal to sustain their campaign and so long as there is a divided island of Ireland. (BBC1 *Panorama*, 29 February 1988)

At the time of the revelation of British contacts with Sinn Féin in November 1993 a 'key British source' made a striking departure from the public official position. The source told the *Observer* that the IRA

> was imbued with an ideology and a theology. He then added ... that its ideology included an 'ethical dimension' – that members would not continue killing for the sake of it ... The Provisionals did not kill 'for no purpose', and that if that purpose was removed, there was no reason why they should not stop killing. (*Observer*, 28 November 1993)

Clearly, there is a recognition in some official circles that the problem in Ireland is political, yet publicly the government adheres to its depiction of a conflict caused by 'terrorism'.

Some Unionists in Northern Ireland also question the idea that Britain is neutral in the conflict. Many are distrustful of the motivations of British policy and often suspect that their interests are being ignored or that they will be 'sold out' to the South. This was one of the main loyalist objections to the Anglo-Irish

Agreement of 1985. As a result of such uneasy feelings, some unionists now advocate either an independent Northern Ireland or closer integration with Britain in order to lessen the chances of being 'cut loose'.

Perhaps the most perplexing question is why the British have remained in Northern Ireland for so long. The simple truth is that it is easier to stay than to go. In addition there has been some benefit to the army in that Northern Ireland provides training in combat and allows it to defend some measure of resource allocation. There is no 'objective necessity' for British forces to remain in Ireland. Indeed, it has been argued that there has been very little strategic reason for around thirty years, well before the demise of the Soviet Union (Bew and Patterson 1985). But this is only to say that the monolithic inertia of the British state is moved in new directions only when the interests of the state are seen to override the difficulties of a change in policy or when opposition is unstoppable. The opposition to British policy has never been strong enough to force withdrawal since British forces left the twenty-six counties over fifty years ago. Added to this is the historical legacy of the Conservative Party's links with the Unionists and the occasional usefulness to tottering governments (Labour or Conservative) of the Unionist block vote. It seems likely, in these circumstances, that the impetus for a British withdrawal will only become strong enough when the cost (or potential cost) to the British exchequer becomes great enough to worry an insecure government.

Structure of this Book

The first chapter of this book examines the limits imposed on media coverage by the economic context of media production, government intimidation, the use of the law and direct censorship. It traces the mounting pressures on the public space for dissent and assesses the relationship between broadcasting and the state. It reveals, for the first time, the government threat, in the 1950s, to vet all programmes on nuclear weapons and the BBC's subsequent agreement not to make programmes which discussed the effects of radiation. Also for the first time, it tells the story of the senior BBC official who was sacked in 1988 because of his criticisms of senior management decisions on the coverage of the killings in Gibraltar.

Chapter 2 examines the public relations strategies of official and unofficial sources in Northern Ireland. It starts by looking at contending definitions of 'propaganda', then describes changing propaganda strategies between the early 1960s and 1993. Finally it assesses the veracity of official public relations and their relationship to British policy in Ireland. It argues that official disinformation did not stop in the mid-1970s with the disbanding of the black propaganda 'Information Policy' unit at army HQ. Both the RUC and the army continue to give false information to journalists in order to protect security forces personnel from the due process of law and, more importantly, legitimise otherwise unlawful killings by the state.

Chapter 3 includes a detailed examination of the resources available for PR activities and the uses to which they are put. Even though official sources have a huge inbuilt advantage in terms of resources, they do not always succeed in managing the media exactly as they would wish. However, they have been remarkably successful in some areas in shaping media agendas. This chapter reveals the covert propaganda role of the little-known London Radio Service. Operated by the British government, the service places news stories in radio news bulletins around the world – including the United States, in contravention of US criminal law.

Chapter 4 surveys international coverage of the conflict in Northern Ireland and then presents a detailed comparison between US and British press and television coverage. It argues that the US media are significantly more open and diverse than the British, showing that British media coverage could be different. It also examines the substantial variations between different types of actuality coverage.

Chapter 5 presents the results of my own audience research. It focuses on public responses to media coverage of the Gibraltar killings and suggests that, unless they have an alternative source of information, people in Britain are inclined to believe the distorted picture of life in Northern Ireland presented by television and newspaper reports. In particular, a large proportion of my sample believed official misinformation about the killings to be true. The Gibraltar killings are a striking illustration of the way in which official misinformation can have a powerful effect on public belief.

Chapter 6 reviews the major debates about the effects of media coverage of the conflict, examining counterinsurgency theory, 'active' audience research and other approaches. It concludes by assessing the role of the media in the struggle for definition, arguing that media information can have a powerful impact on public opinion and on the ability of the state to carry on regardless.

The Propaganda War

Competing definitions of the legitimacy of political and military action in Northern Ireland are actively pursued. The constant definitional struggle over language is central to the conflict. The importance of the mass media is that they provide an arena in which such battles are fought. Alongside, but intimately connected with the bombings and shootings, the torture and the beatings, runs another conflict. It is waged from the offices of the Secretary of State for Northern Ireland at Stormont Castle to the Republican Press Centre on the Falls Road; from the offices of the *Irish Times* in Dublin, and in *The Times* in London, to the *New York Times* in the USA; from living-rooms in Protestant East Belfast and Catholic West Belfast to the English home counties; and from the offices of the British government in Whitehall to diplomatic missions around the world.

This is the propaganda war. It attracts much less attention than its shooting counterpart, but is arguably the more crucial part of the conflict – the battle for hearts and minds. This book examines the struggle for legitimacy as it is waged in the pages of the press and on television screens across the world.

1

Policing the Media:
Secrecy, Intimidation and Censorship

> On paper, the Government of the day has the power to veto any BBC broadcast. The BBC – and this is the important point – has the right to broadcast that this veto has been exercised. In the whole history of the BBC no Government – not even in war time – has made use of this power in connection with any particular programme or item and it is now pretty well politically unthinkable that it ever could be made use of.
> (Sir Hugh Greene, *The Third Floor Front*, 1969, p. 69)

> The power to require the BBC to refrain from broadcasting particular material is the famous 'unused' veto. This arouses immense suspicion in the minds of those visitors to Britain, who are not accustomed to the force of convention in British society. The fact that the power exists leads them to suspect that it must be used, or that its use must, at times, be threatened in order to secure desired objectives. This is simply not the case.
> (Sir Charles Curran, *A Seamless Robe*, 1979, p. 64)

In fact, the threat of the veto to secure desired objectives has been threatened by governments on several occasions. However, the use of the veto is not the only indicator of the degree to which broadcasting is independent of the state. In Britain, there is an identifiable 'tradition' in the relationships between broadcasters and the state. The veto has rarely been used both because it has not been necessary to use it and because successive governments have recognised the immense value of an apparently independent broadcasting system. Broadcasting in Britain is centrally legitimated by its claim to be independent of the state. Maintaining the appearance of independence is crucial to the broadcasters and it is this that can allow the government to exert pressure for informal and 'voluntary' agreements with the media. The history of the relationship is one of government pressure and 'voluntary self-restraint' or 'responsibility' by the broadcasters. This has been tempered by the occasional willingness of BBC and independent television management to display their 'independence' by refusing to accede to government 'requests' or threats.

This chapter explores the 'policing' of the media by examining four main limits on media coverage. These are, first, the economic context of media production, second, indirect censorship via pressure, intimidation and the use of the law, third, direct censorship imposed under the Broadcasting Ban in 1988, and fourth, the limits imposed by the broadcasters on themselves – that is, self-censorship.

A key argument is that none of these limits, including the law, is hard and fast, rather, the way in which the powerful use the techniques at hand (indeed the techniques which are available) and the way in which the broadcasters react are related to an ongoing process of contest and to changing political and economic circumstances.

'Responsibility' versus 'Independence'

An early example of the 'responsible' approach was the General Strike, during which there was pressure for the government to take over the BBC. In the event it decided not to. But as Lord Reith, the first Director-General of the BBC, recorded in his diary, 'The Cabinet decision is really a negative one. They want to be able to say that they did not commandeer us, but they know that they can trust us not to be really impartial' (Stuart 1975: 96).

In the 1939-45 war, the BBC saw itself as having a central role in fighting the enemy. It was subject to strict control of all news bulletins by the Ministry of Information, although it was not simply the mouthpiece of the government. During the Suez crisis in 1956 the BBC came under very heavy government pressure. Prime Minister Eden regarded Suez as a war situation and expected internal criticisms of the government to be suppressed. When the BBC gave the opposition the right to reply to ministerial broadcasts and refused to excise critical comments from its overseas bulletins the government made threats of financial cuts and planted a Foreign Office liaison officer in Bush House to vet the external services. [1] The BBC was able to resist government pressure partly because Suez was not a national emergency, but also because there was a deep division in the press and in politics, stretching to the cabinet itself. [2]

The credibility of British broadcasting was a key reason for the reluctance of the government to take over the BBC. This thinking was shared by the broadcasters. In the aftermath of Suez, Postmaster-General Charles Hill argued this point with the Cabinet:

> In my view, the gain to Britain from the BBC's high reputation is immense, far outweighing any confusion which may occur through failure to understand its relationship to government. The independence which the corporation has should always be kept inviolate. Once this issue was decided little more was heard of the agitation to destroy or to reduce the BBC's independence. (Hill 1964: 188)

In 1958, the crisis in Cyprus and the possibility of Archbishop Makarios being interviewed on a visit to London prompted the Foreign Secretary, Selwyn Lloyd, to write to the BBC expressing his concern. Charles Hill, who by then was the Chancellor of the Duchy of Lancaster, went to visit Harman Grisewood, Chief Assistant to the Director-General, for what he called 'one of our informal chats' (*Irish Times*, 2/3 January 1989). Grisewood resisted the attempt to keep Makarios off the air, but nevertheless Hill 'was left with the impression that ... if they did put Makarios on, they would make it the occasion for severe hostile questioning of the gentleman' (PREM 11/2226, 16 June 1958).

In August 1956, over two months before the Suez crisis came to a head, the BBC had already come under pressure from Eden, who objected to an Egyptian major being interviewed. The BBC rejected his complaints. Eden's press adviser, William Clark, then wrote to the Prime Minister advising on the powers that could be used against the BBC. Clark noted that every dispute with the BBC had been 'settled by persuasion so far' (*Guardian*, 2 January 1987). Charles Hill also advised Eden that 'while the powers of formal intervention remain so limited, it is only by informal contact and discussion that programme content can be influenced' (HO 256/360, 20 August 1956).

During the Falklands episode the broadcasters again found it difficult to admit critical or oppositional views to news programmes, and they were attacked for being 'traitorous' when they did. In 1956, the BBC had managed to resist government pressure, but it is clear that during the Falklands crisis much news was shaped to support government policy (Glasgow University Media Group 1985). During the Gulf conflict of 1991 the broadcasters' obsession with 'surgical strikes' and 'precision killing' meant that civilian casualties were ignored and there was little criticism which questioned the rationale for the war (Kellner 1992; Mowlana et al. 1992; Philo and McLaughlin 1992; Pilger 1992).

Threatening the Veto

Contrary to the official view, the threat of the veto arose as early as 1935 in the case of *The Citizen and His Government*, a series of talks that was to have included contributions from Oswald Moseley of the Fascists and Harry Pollitt of the Communist Party as well as representatives from the other parties. The Foreign Office wanted to stop the programmes because of the embarrassment they would cause. After some argument the BBC agreed to cancel the series only 'if they were authorised to state that "they had been given to understand that the broadcasting of these talks would be an embarrassment to the Government" or something similar'. Foreign Secretary Anthony Eden tried to get the BBC to say instead that the government felt that the talks 'were not in the national interest'. In the event, after further pressure from the government, the BBC cancelled the talks without mentioning the government intervention. The force of the government pressure was underlined by the Cabinet's decision to authorise the Postmaster-General 'if necessary, to make quite clear that the Government would not permit these broadcasts' (Briggs 1979: 198–201; Scannell and Cardiff 1991: 72–8).

For government ministers and information managers, the quiet chat is a less overt and more effective way of managing coverage. In the post-war period 'informal consultation' seems to have produced some remarkably effective results – so effective that they don't even feature in the history books. It is notable that Briggs' many volumes on the history of the BBC (Briggs 1965, 1970, 1979; cf Cockerell 1989) contain no mention of an informal arrangement between the BBC and the government on one of the most controversial issues of the time – nuclear weapons.

The BBC and the Bomb

The introduction of nuclear weapons in Britain and the build-up of the British 'independent deterrent' have been shrouded in secrecy from the very beginning:

> The War Cabinet never discussed the atomic bomb in the period leading up to 1945; the (Labour) Deputy Prime Minister was told nothing about it; and the Labour Cabinet as a whole, after the 1945 election, never discussed Britain's own bomb. From then until now every effort has been made to discountenance public debate on the subject. (Downing 1986: 167) [3]

By late 1954 BBC producer Nesta Pain was researching a possible programme on nuclear weapons. Her preliminary explorations with scientists and others came to the attention of the government, prompting a pre-emptive letter from the Postmaster-General (PMG) to the Chair of the BBC, Sir Alexander Cadogan. Earl De La Warr's letter was a crude attempt to vet all programmes on nuclear weapons by threatening the veto:

> The wide dissemination in a broadcast programme of information about thermo-nuclear weapons might well raise important issues of public policy. Indeed this is a subject on which the public interest might in certain circumstances require the issue of guidance or directions to the Corporation in pursuance of Section 15(4) of the Corporations Licence. I am therefore writing to ask you to let me see in advance the script of any programme, whether for broadcasting or for television, which contains information about atomic or thermo-nuclear weapons. (BBC WAC R34/997, 18 December 1954)

Since Cadogan was out of the country at the time, the Director-General, Ian Jacob, raised the letter at the board of management meeting on 20 December, where it was felt that 'it was not in accordance with precedent to submit scripts to the PMG' and that 'it would be more appropriate if the government would give the BBC general guidance in the matter'. [4] Around the same time Sir Ben Barnett of the Post Office had phoned the Director-General to threaten the use of Clause 15(4) against a planned programme called 'The Spirit in Jeopardy'.

Cadogan raised both these issues in a stinging four-page reply to the PMG in January 1955. He queried 'whether the government is interested from the point of view of security or from the point of view of wider questions such as the effect on public morale'. The letter from the PMG, together with the phone call from Ben Barnett, 'seem to indicate' wrote Cadogan 'that the Government desires to exercise a measure of control over BBC output which would be unprecedented in peacetime'. He rejected the threat in the PMG's letter and more or less challenged him to introduce a notice or back down:

> Experience over a good many years seems to show ... that the corporation cannot agree to accept and follow Government guidance over particular fields of output except where security is concerned. To do so would be to abdicate from responsibilities given to the Governors by the Charter. (BBC WAC R34/997, Cadogan to De La Warr 24 January 1955)

Cadogan concluded by asking for 'enlightenment on the thinking that has inspired these communications ... with sufficient precision to enable the Governors to decide what their attitude should be'. However, at the board of management meeting later that day the Director-General ruled that until they got more information from the government that 'no programmes should be broadcast about atomic weapons' (Minute 49, Board of Management meeting 24 January 1955).

Enlightenment came in the shape of an informal meeting at the Ministry of Defence between Cadogan and Jacob of the BBC and the PMG, the Minister of Defence and two officials. By all accounts the mood was much calmer than it had been in the earlier exchange of letters. According to the BBC account of the meeting the Minister of Defence explained that government anxiety had been sparked by the 'mistaken impression that the BBC was proposing to do a programme about Thermonuclear weapons and their effects before the publication of the Government's white paper on Defence Policy'. According to this account, the government's concern here was not one of national security, but rather a simple desire to manipulate public opinion:

> The government had been giving anxious consideration to the extent of the information that should be made public about the hydrogen bomb and its effects, and to the way in which this information should be presented. On the one hand they did not desire to keep the public in entire ignorance; on the other hand they did not want to stimulate the feeling so easily accepted by the British people because it agreed with their natural laziness in these matters, that because of the terrible nature of the hydrogen bomb there was no need for them to take part in home defence measures (Ian Jacob, 'Note of meeting held at the Ministry of Defence' 15 February 1955).

Having tried to assure the BBC that the target of the governments action was the lazy British people rather than the independence of the BBC, the Minister of Defence went on to suggest that the PMG's rather intemperate letter and Cadogan's reply be quietly forgotten about and that they start afresh:

> The Minister of Defence felt that these two communications should now be put away in the files and that the matter should be handled on a more informal basis. He assumed that there would be no difficulty in close touch being maintained between the Ministry of Defence and the Corporation on this matter, and this would enable both parties to exchange information and views without hampering documents. (Ian Jacob, 'Note of meeting held at the Ministry of Defence' 15 February 1955)

The BBC response was one of relief and it quickly agreed that quiet chats were a better way of proceeding: 'The Chairman entirely agreed with the Minister's proposal and confirmed that the Corporation had no desire to embarrass the Government in this very delicate matter' (Ian Jacob, 'Note of meeting held at the Ministry of Defence' 15 February 1955). Ian Jacob then explained that discussions of the white paper on defence would simply take their agenda from the government's concerns set out in the paper itself:

> I explained to the Minister that we should be under the necessity of having programmes expounding and discussing the White Paper on Defence but that naturally these would be founded on the information contained in that paper. I did not foresee any immediate desire on the part of the corporation to mount programmes about the effects of the hydrogen bomb. There did not seem to be any immediate point in doing so. (Ian Jacob, 'Note of meeting held at the Ministry of Defence' 15 February 1955)

A public interest in such programmes was perhaps not considered reason enough.

Following this the Director-General prepared a paper on nuclear weapons and broadcasting, which was discussed inside the corporation on 4 March. In it he emphasised that certain types of discussion of nuclear weapons which furthered the 'national interest' should be made 'with no hesitation':

> To further the national interest in this case will be to give full exposition to the facts given in the White Paper, and to the theories expounded in it by the Government. But there are many conclusions founded on these facts and theories which call for full discussion. For example, should Britain make hydrogen bombs? Could there be a greater partition of the defence effort between us and our allies? What role should the TA play? and so on. ('Thermo-Nuclear Weapons and Broadcasting', A note by the Director-General 28 February 1955)

On the other hand there were other topics which were a 'more difficult problem', such as 'the symptoms induced by the "fall-out", the degree of radioactivity in the atmosphere which may prove harmful, and so on'. Such topics had to satisfy much stricter criteria, such as whether there was 'a worth-while object to be achieved by the programme, which would outweigh the horrific impact'. As we have seen, Jacob had already told the Minister of Defence that there seemed to be 'no immediate point' in such programmes. In a draft letter to Prime Minister Winston Churchill, following the meeting with Jacob and Cadogan, the PMG was flushed with success:

> We finally agreed that the Corporation should keep in close touch with the Ministry of Defence on all matters relating to the presentation of the hydrogen bomb to the public. We all thought that this was a more satisfactory and practical solution than that the Government should try to lay down precise rules in writing. I hope you agree that this arrangement should give us the results we want. (PRO DEFE 13/71)

Churchill was also pleased, and congratulated Jacob for 'standing up' for self-censorship:

> I realise how great your difficulties are. The responsibility for the use of the vast machinery of radio and TV is at once formidable, novel and perpetual. In this case I think there would have been no trouble if the topic had been part of a rather high-grade programme like the Third programme. What vexed me was the millions of humble homes affected. I am very glad you are standing up against the idea of anticipating the Parliamentary debate on the H bomb. (Churchill to Jacob 20 February 1955)

Thus is the intemperate language of vetting and censorship translated into cooperation, consultation and responsibility.

This informal arrangement seems to have worked for some years and was regarded as something of a success in Whitehall. Some eighteen months later the PMG advised the government that informal consultation was the best way to control the BBC. In his support he cited the nuclear weapons agreement as a 'major question' on which 'informal consultation has had some success' (HO 256/360, Hill to the Prime Minister 20 August 1956). However it seems that the agreement was not still operating in 1965 when Peter Watkins' celebrated film, *The War Game*, was banned by the BBC following government pressure (see Tracey 1982; Briggs 1979: 121–3).

What is the Veto for?

The power vested in the government was originally interpreted as being for use only in time of national emergency. The problem for the broadcasters has been that the agreement on this interpretation has always been informal and interpretation by the government and by the civil service has been uneven, depending partly on whether it suits them.

In 1932 the government succeeded in getting the BBC to cancel an interview with a German former U-boat commander by threatening, though without using, the power of veto. In a letter of complaint the Chairman of the BBC said that they had been assured by the Postmaster-General in 1927 that the veto would only be exercised 'in time of national emergency'. The PMG, however, denied all knowledge of this informal arrangement and stated that 'there was no such limitation in the licence' (Briggs 1979: 193–4).

During the Suez crisis, the Prime Minister sought the advice of the Post Office on what powers were available to influence the BBC. The civil service advice was that 'these wide powers had never been used for the purpose of suppressing individual programme items. They were really designed to suit conditions of national emergency.' [5] Following the attempt to keep Archbishop Makarios off the air during the Cyprus crisis, the Chancellor of the Duchy of Lancaster, Charles Hill, wrote to the Prime Minister that 'there is no power to prevent such an appearance either on the BBC, or ITA'. [6]

It is curious that Hill should give this advice since only three years previously, as Postmaster-General, he had issued two directives to the broadcasters prohibiting certain 'matters' from being broadcast.[7] One interesting possibility is that the government interpretation of the PMG's power to limit 'matters of any particular class' did not include banning individuals from being interviewed. This would, of course, be in contrast to the Home Office interpretation in Douglas Hurd's directive of October 1988, banning direct appearances by eleven named Irish organisations.

However, it does seem more likely that the decision to threaten the use of the power or to pretend that the power is not available is related more to government information strategies. The acknowledgement that the power exists places responsibility for censorship squarely in the hands of the government, whereas if it is believed that the government has no power in this area then the responsibility rests rather more heavily on the shoulders of the broadcasters. In fact, the law tends to be used in ways that suit the powerful, which will, of course, vary over time. In the spring of 1988, for example, the *Daily Telegraph* reported that 'Powers to ban press and television contact with terror organisations like the IRA have been discussed by senior ministers but there are no plans at present for legislation to introduce such a wide-ranging curb on press freedom' (28 March 1988). Yet following the BBC's *Spotlight* programme on the Gibraltar killings, Whitehall sources told the *Independent* that 'the reserve power could only be used as "an ultimate weapon"'. [8]

The next section describes the organisational, legal and economic contexts within which the media operate. Taken together these factors further limit the space available for critical or alternative perspectives on the conflict in Northern Ireland. There is a particular emphasis on the period from 1979 onwards, partly because previous developments are recounted elsewhere (Curtis 1984a; Curtis 1986; Schlesinger et al. 1983, Schlesinger 1987) and partly because the pressures have so intensified (Garnham 1986; Elliot 1982; Thornton 1989; Hillyard and Percy-Smith 1988; Ewing and Gearty 1990).

The Economic Context

The ownership and control of media institutions provides the context within which journalists work. In Britain the press is very largely in the hands of a small number of media corporations. The newspaper industry is first and foremost a business enterprise. The politics of the press are dictated by a collection of diverse judgements, foremost among which is the need to maintain or increase readership. This does not mean that all of the press is on the right politically. There is an extent to which newspapers target particular audiences because of their assessment of the market for

23

non-conservative coverage. Such judgements are also influenced by the state of the market, competition with other titles, and by political circumstances, which will in turn affect the size of the market. These factors also inform the judgement of media barons such as Rupert Murdoch and Lord Rothermere. The extent to which they intervene in the running of a particular newspaper or the kind of intervention will not simply be related to their personal political alliances and commitments, but also to wider economic factors.

However, it is clear that political intervention does occur. For example, in 1988, the *Daily Telegraph*, under editor Max Hastings, had pursued a more liberal line on Northern Ireland, for example in coverage of the Gibraltar killings (see Chapter 4). In 1989, however, proprietor Conrad Black exerted more direct control over the *Daily Telegraph* and *Sunday Telegraph*, complaining publicly about Hastings' 'flirtation with incorrect thinking about Ulster and about South Africa' (cited in Curran and Seaton 1991: 90).

In fact newspapers do not have strictly bounded ideologies which are insulated from the market or from political circumstances. The content of British newspapers cannot be explained simply by the personal prejudices or occupational ideologies of journalists, editors or even proprietors.

Segmentation

In Britain there has been an increased segmentation of newspaper audiences by region. The content of news reports in those regions will vary according to the audience being targeted by the particular edition. The *Sunday Times*, for example, has a separate Northern Ireland section. This segmentation is related to competition with the strong national and regional press in Scotland and Northern Ireland respectively. The constant hunt for more readers can mean that papers place different stories on different pages to appeal to different types of reader or on occasion different stories in the same place in different editions. Following the killing of three would-be robbers in west Belfast by undercover soldiers, the editorials in the London and Dublin editions of the *Daily Star* were as follows:

IT'S IRA WHO SHOOT TO KILL
(London)

Undercover troops shot dead three men robbing a betting-shop in West Belfast. The robbers were brandishing replica guns indistinguishable from the real thing. Whining do-gooders – joined by Sinn Fein, the political wing of the IRA – immediately jumped on the left-wing bandwagon, and demanded to know whether our security forces are operating a shoot to kill policy. The three villains -- all with records as long as your arm -- were dressed in IRA 'uniform' of black balaclavas and black woollen gloves. The Army must not waste time on a ridiculous inquiry into these absurd allegations. Anyone who tries to commit a robbery in Northern Ireland carrying weapons – or lifelike replicas – can hardly expect to be welcomed with tea and scones. And do people have to be reminded: it is the IRA who STARTED the shoot-to-kill policy.

WE WANT THE FACTS
(Dublin)

No one is above the law. And that includes the security forces in the North. Last Saturday in Belfast they shot dead three raiders outside a betting shop in what can only be described as strange circumstances. Taoiseach Charles Haughey rightly said that his Government had 'serious disquiet and misgivings' about the incident. But yesterday in the House of Commons Ulster supremo, Peter Brooke, refused demands from MPs to hold an independent inquiry. Not good enough, Mr Brooke. Surely you cannot dismiss so lightly reports of eye-witnesses who said that even after the raiders had stopped, further shots were fired into their bodies. The Government here must not let the matter rest. They must insist that all the facts are brought fully into the open. Nothing else will satisfy decent people. (Source: reprinted in *UK Press Gazette*, 29 January 1990.)

Cross-promotion

The direct influence of economics on news coverage is of course not the only way in which the ownership and control of the media impacts on the content of the news. Ever increasing concentration of ownership and the formation of multimedia conglomerates, symbolised in Britain by Rupert Murdoch, have opened up many opportunities for cross-promotion as well as the possibility of attacking the opposition in one sphere (say broadcasting) with media in another sphere (the press). The most cited example of this in Britain is the cross-promotion of BSkyB satellite television by Murdoch-owned newspapers. The practice is so well known that in the late 1980s the satirical magazine *Private Eye* introduced a feature titled 'Eye-sky' which offered readers 'the usual £10' for 'Sky-plugs masquerading as news items in Murdoch papers'. The major attacks on public service broadcasting in relation to the coverage of Northern Ireland are also to be found from the mid-1980s in the Murdoch press. It was the *Sunday Times* that started the ball rolling in the *Real Lives* affair, and it was the *Sun* and *Sunday Times* that were consistently to the fore in the attacks on 'Death on the Rock' and the attempt to shore up the official version of the Gibraltar shootings (Bolton 1990; Miller 1991). In the latter case there was a strong economic interest in destabilising public service broadcasting as Sky television is engaged in a protracted battle with terrestrial television over the viewing audience. The Conservative government's auction of television franchises, which has further destabilised public service programming, was encouraged by the onslaught on 'Death on the Rock'.

Television

Television is more heavily regulated than the press and is bound by law to standards of 'impartiality' and 'objectivity'. This does not, however, mean that broadcasting is immune to market pressures. The fact that independent television is funded by advertising revenue means that it is audiences themselves rather than television programmes which 'are the primary commodity. The economics of commercial broadcasting revolves around the exchange of audiences for advertising revenue.' (Golding and Murdock 1991: 20). So the need to secure large audiences promotes the production of familiar programming and limits the production of innovative or risky programmes. 'Hence', as Golding and Murdock argue, 'the audience's position as a commodity serves to reduce the overall diversity of programming and ensure

26

that it confirms established mores and assumption far more often than it challenges them' (1991: 20). The auctioning of televisions franchises in 1992 resulted in a dilution of a public service commitment amongst television companies and, because of the high cost of some franchises, has led to a concern with maximising audiences and keeping programme budgets down. One indication of this is the debate about the historically guaranteed peak slots for both current affairs and news programmes. The opening up of the BBC to commercial forces will also inevitably have the effect of minimising critical programming, either by the hunt for audience figures or by the retreat of the BBC to minority broadcasting status. Arguments about whether television should attract high audiences or whether it should inform are once more on the agenda, accompanied by a move away from conceptions of broadcasting as a 'right to information' to notions of the right to be entertained and reassured.

The ownership and control of media organisations, together with the legal regulation of broadcasting, provide the context within which the media report the world. Of course, this context is affected and indeed managed by the state. The level of the licence fee for the BBC and the regulatory apparatus of independent television are set by the government. State control over the legislative context of broadcasting allows government to exert leverage in relation to the content of broadcasting. Such leverage has in fact been a routine part of the relationship between broadcasting and governments of all complexions since the founding of the BBC. For example, Tom McNally, adviser to Labour Prime Minister James Callaghan, has revealed:

> In 1978, the Government had been going through a rough patch and had been getting some pretty rough treatment from television ... particularly from BBC Newsnight, and at the Labour Party conference in Brighton that year, I came face to face with Brian Wenham, then head of BBC2, and I eyeballed Brian in the way of Mohammed Ali and looked [at] him squarely and said ... 'Hell will freeze over before you get a licence fee increase unless we get a better deal out of you'. (*World in Action*, 1988)

Such pressure forms the backdrop to routine political relationships

27

between broadcasters and the government. However, when the government has more specific objectives in mind a range of other tactics for pressurising the broadcasters come into play.

Intimidation and Pressure

Rex Cathcart, the historian of the BBC in Northern Ireland notes that 'Until 1951 the BBC [in Northern Ireland] sought to portray a society without division: the very mention of "partition" was precluded' (1988: 7). It wasn't until the Civil Rights Association took to the streets in 1968 that Northern Ireland began to feature extensively on British network TV screens. The pattern of relationships between the broadcasters and the state was set in 1971. Although the press has periodically been involved in conflicts with the government it has been the broadcasters, and particularly the BBC, which has born the brunt of government intimidation. This is partly because of the perceived national role of the BBC, but also because the government has more cards in its hand when dealing with a publicly regulated system than it does with the press. Television is also perceived by government to be more important because of its immediacy and the large audiences it attracts.

Following the entry of the Provisional and Official Irish Republican Armies into armed conflict with the British Army in 1971 and the introduction of internment in August of that year, the BBC came under mounting criticism. The Minister for Posts and Telegraphs, Christopher Chataway, let it be known, in a speech in November, that broadcasters were no longer required to strike an even balance between the IRA and the Unionist government, nor between the army and the 'terrorists'. [9] Lord Hill, the Chair of the BBC, wrote to the Home Secretary later that month, agreeing that 'as between the British Army and the gunmen the BBC is not and cannot be impartial'. [10] The Independent Television Authority's Lord Aylestone put it even more directly: 'As far as I am concerned, Britain is at war with the IRA in Ulster and the IRA will get no more coverage than the Nazis would have done in the last war' (cited in Curtis 1984a: 10). This definition of the role of the broadcaster fitted well with the view of the state. Since 1971, this has

28

remained the view of the broadcasting establishment, although editorial policy has been repeatedly tightened in the intervening years, as we shall see.

Within the BBC, however, it was the events of the following month, December 1971, which were to pass into the institutional memory as the key example of the ability to resist government pressure. *The Question of Ulster*, a two and a half hour current affairs programme, came under direct and public pressure from the Home Secretary Reginald Maudling and sections of the press, even though no IRA members were to be interviewed. The fact that the BBC resisted such open pressure is still vividly remembered in the corporation. [11] At the time Sir Charles Curran said that *The Question of Ulster* was 'the central example in my time of the BBC's insistence on editorial independence' (cited in Schlesinger 1987: 217).

However, at that time it would have been very difficult for the BBC to back down, since the price would have been a considerable injury to perceptions of their independence from the state. As we saw in the course of the row over nuclear weapons, informal arrangements and 'responsibility' are much favoured over open intimidation. By the 1980s the political climate had changed and more overt intimidation was both increasingly likely and increasingly successful.

Legislation

From the early 1970s we can see an increasingly tight system of internal and external control on coverage of Northern Ireland. Perhaps the most dramatic indication of this is the large body of legislation which has been enacted.

While some laws, such as the Special Powers Act, which had very sweeping provisions, have been abolished or, at least temporarily, fallen into disuse (Ó Maoláin 1989: 19), many more have been introduced. According to Ó Maoláin (1989: 18), between 1970 and 1986 some seventy pieces of 'emergency' legislation were applied in all or part of Ireland, although not all of these restrict media practice. In addition there are a number of laws which apply in Britain and were not solely enacted to deal with the Irish conflict. Some of these predate the current conflict, whilst others represent the drift to the strong state since the late 1970s, particularly under successive Conservative governments.

From Fighting Terrorism to Policing the Media

Some legislation which was never intended for use against the media has subsequently turned in a useful few laps in the cause of government secrecy or censorship. The most important provisions that affect journalists covering Northern Ireland are the Official Secrets Act (and the associated 'D' Notice committee), the Prevention of Terrorism Act and the Emergency Provisions Act.

The Official Secrets Act 1911 (revised in 1920, 1939 and 1989) is supposed to function to protect national security, especially against espionage and spying. It can also be used against media organisations. The main provision affecting the media has been section 2, which prevents unauthorised communication or receipt of official information. The government brought in an amended Act in 1989, claiming that it would liberalise the provisions of the previous law. It has, however, been described as 'even more repressive' (Ó Maoláin 1989: 80) and as imposing 'tighter controls than ever before in peacetime' (Ponting 1990: 79).

The revised Act makes it an offence for any member or former member of the security or intelligence services (or anyone associated with security or intelligence activities) to disclose any information about those activities. Journalists who publish such information having grounds to believe it has been disclosed without permission may also be prosecuted as accessories. It is also an offence to disclose other kinds of government information where damage is caused, or likely to be caused, by unauthorised disclosure. Information conveyed to other governments and then leaked overseas is also protected under the Act (McBride 1990: 138–9). Section 5 makes it an offence to publish information known to be protected by the Act and having cause to believe that publication would be damaging to the national interest. There is no provision for a public interest defence or protection for exposing wrongdoing or illegality by the government or security services. There is, however, a 'no damage' defence which would allow journalists to report the words of a former member of the

30

security services or other information so long as it did not harm national security.

The 'D' notice, or Defence, Press and Broadcasting Committee, is closely associated with monitoring potential breaches of 'national security'. It issues notices on subjects on which it is deemed too sensitive to report. However, the notices have no legal force and the committee, on which representatives of the media sit, operates on the basis of a 'voluntary' agreement. The major notices in relation to Northern Ireland cover the activities of the intelligence services, the photographing of government installations and discussion of telephone tapping and surveillance operations. Under the 1989 Official Secrets Act prior clearance by the 'D' notice Committee is no defence against prosecution. Nevertheless, the committee remains in operation and is evidently seen as worthwhile by some sections of the MoD (see Campbell 1980; Palmer 1984; Robertson and Nicol 1992: 435–7).[12]

The Emergency Provisions (Northern Ireland) Act 1978 prohibits the collection of information which is likely to be of use to terrorists and although its 'overt purpose is to punish espionage' the Act is broad enough to 'cover normal journalistic activities' (Robertson and Nicol 1992: 443–4). The Act also prohibits soliciting or inviting support for an illegal organisation such as the IRA or the UDA (Ó Maoláin 1989).

The Prevention of Terrorism Act started life, as did the Official Secrets Act, with a hurried passage through Parliament. Introduced by Home Secretary Roy Jenkins as 'draconian' in the aftermath of the 1974 Birmingham pub bombings, the Act was not tested until five years later. In the meantime, it was amended in 1976 to make it an offence under Section 11 not to pass information to the police about any future act of terrorism or about people involved in terrorism without 'reasonable excuse'. It was further amended in 1984 to apply to non-Irish 'terrorism', an extension of 'emergency' powers to the wider polity which were until then premised on the conflict in Ireland.

Also in 1984, the Police and Criminal Evidence Act extended police powers to seize material, powers only previously available in relation to Northern Ireland. Following the seizure of film from the BBC and ITN in March 1988, the government was reported to be considering introducing the powers under PACE to Northern Ireland (*Financial Times*, 24 March 1988). In 1990 the circle was completed with the implementation of the PACE (NI) 1989 Order. This represents the reimportation to Northern Ireland of exceptional powers first introduced because of the conflict and now 'normalised' in British legislation. PACE grants police officers who are lawfully on any premises the power to seize anything found there if they have reasonable grounds 'for believing that it has been obtained as a result of an offence, or that it is evidence in relation to any offence, and that seizure is necessary in order to prevent it being concealed, lost, damaged, altered or destroyed' (Dickson 1990: 20–1).

Similar powers were written into the PTA in 1989. The objective of this additional provision was said to be uncovering funding for paramilitary organisations. Clause 17, Schedule 7 allows the police access to privileged documents such as medical records, so long as the police say that the documents are needed in connection with a 'terrorist investigation' (see Bunyan 1977: 291; Ó Maoláin 1989; Curtis 1984a; Dickson 1990).[13]

Practice and Precedent: the Law and Selective Communication

It is often assumed that the law is simply an impermeable and unchanging limit on journalism and public debate. In fact, it tends to be interpreted and used according to the prevailing political climate (Downing 1986). The policing of the media by censorship, secrecy, court orders and police pressure does not only work to exclude certain representations or information; it helps to allow the powerful to communicate as and when they want (Kuhn 1988). As David Leigh has memorably put it: 'The obverse side of the secrecy coin is always propaganda' (Leigh 1980).

Historically legislation has been introduced under the rubric of national security which has included provisions for policing the media. On occasion the legislation is ostensibly not intended to apply to the media, but once in place it is quickly put to use in the service of the media police. The Official Secrets Act of 1911 was rushed through Parliament on the understanding that it applied only to those covered in the previous Act. But applying the Act to the press was a covert preoccupation of the government and in their view fell within the terms of the new Act. On the basis of advice from the Department of Public Prosecutions one civil servant argued that:

In certain circumstances the Act could be used against a newspaper. We have a note on our official papers to the effect that the speedy passage of the Act was due to a general understanding that the new measure was not directed against any new class, but against that which the former Act was aimed, viz. the spy class, and that to use it against a newspaper merely for publishing news useful to an enemy would amount to a breach of faith with Parliament. But there is no record to this effect in the official version of the debates. (cited in Palmer 1984: 235)

The way the law is used can owe more to the political priorities of the government and the state than to actual breaches of legislation. For example, changes to the PTA in 1989 which allow the police to seize previously privileged materials were said to be intended to clamp down on alleged paramilitary fund-raising. Yet by early 1992 this provision had been used on two occasions against media organisations. It is clearly much easier to legitimate repressive laws for purposes which are unambiguously 'anti-terrorist', than those which impact upon freedom of the media.

Furthermore, according to some commentators, the 1989 Official Secrets Act has 'turned out to be something of a damp squib' (Dorrill 1993: 3). Emphasising the selectivity with which the law is enforced, several books have now been published which are in clear breach of the Act and no prosecutions have followed – for example, Fred Holroyd's account of his activities with MI6 in Ireland in the 1970s (Holroyd with Burbridge 1989). It seems likely that the government is not keen to have a re-run of the *Spycatcher* affair, in which government lawyers chased Peter Wright's book halfway round the world.

On the other hand, there is some evidence that the Act has had some effect on broadcasting. The BBC's editorial policy meeting has debated the impact of the Act on who could be interviewed on radio and television. The confidential minutes show that ex-intelligence operatives such as Colin Wallace and Fred Holroyd were considered out of bounds:

to allow Colin Wallace to speak on air would be in breach of Section 1; but it remained unclear as to whether a journalist reporting on him would be safe under Section 5. Robin Walsh

(ACRB (NCA)) said Fred Holroyd had been making himself available for interviews in the regions. Anne Sloman (Ed SCAP) said they were not worth the trouble; they had been interviewed for over an hour for 'My country – Right or Wrong?' and the results had been unbroadcastable. (Minute 79, EPM 16 May 1989: 3)

They also decided that there were some individuals who were not technically covered by the Act but whom it would be difficult to interview. The prohibition on ex-members of the intelligence services was deemed also to apply to civil servants such as Clive Ponting. BBC solicitor John Coman said that 'there was a difficulty over the definition of who was, or had been, a member of the security forces. Clive Ponting had not been a member in fact, but had been considered to be as good as' (Minute 79, EPM 16 May 1989: 3). Here we can see the clear effect of secrecy legislation on British broadcasting.

Although there was no explicit reference to the media in the Prevention of Terrorism Act in 1974, it made the IRA illegal in Britain. This, together with the Home Secretary's view that he would 'personally regard' IRA interviews as 'wholly inappropriate' (cited in Curtis 1984a: 161) was interpreted by broadcasters as making interviews with the IRA illegal or at least effectively impossible (Schlesinger et al. 1983: 126). Certainly, there were no further interviews with active republican paramilitaries until 1979. The INLA interview on *Tonight* was the first interview with any republican paramilitary for four and a half years. Just as IRA interviews ceased when the IRA was made illegal in Britain, so did INLA interviews: the INLA was made illegal in the same week as the interview was broadcast, effectively stopping further appearances. Since then there have been no interviews with active professing republican paramilitaries on British television. [14]

Mrs Thatcher asked the Attorney-General to consider taking legal action against the BBC for the INLA interview. Section 11 of the PTA was considered for the first time. This was a 'completely new departure in the relationship between broadcasting and the state' (Schlesinger et al. 1983: 127). The Carrickmore affair followed hot on the heels of the INLA interview. In the course of compiling a report on the IRA, a *Panorama* crew filmed an IRA roadblock in the village of Carrickmore in Northern Ireland. [15] There was an outcry in parliament and in the press, with Mrs Thatcher calling on the BBC to 'put its house in order'. The police seized – again for the first time – a copy of the untransmitted film under Section 11 of the PTA (Curtis 1984a: 164–72).

In August 1980 Attorney-General Sir Michael Havers issued the official view of the PTA, arguing that there was enough evidence to prosecute the BBC under Section 11 for both incidents. He did not do so, according to the *Guardian*, because 'he clearly decided that a court case would have caused an embarrassing row about press freedom' (cited in Curtis 1984a: 171). Such an intimidatory use of the law against the broadcasters was not envisaged when the PTA was brought in. Havers' legal judgement remains untested by the courts.

The row around the INLA interview and the outcome of the 'Carrickmore' affair represent a turning point in the coverage of Northern Ireland in two distinct senses. They signalled the willingness of the government to use the full force of the law against the broadcasters, a precedent for escalating further hostilities. And they indicate the relative success of the government in their battle to keep the voice of armed republicanism off the screen. However, this victory was quickly followed by a further problem: the rise of Sinn Féin. It was therefore fitting that the next major row should be about the portrayal of Sinn Féin politician Martin McGuinness.

Real Lives

The legacy of the Carrickmore affair, the 1979 assassination of Airey Neave, and the 1984 Brighton bombing (in which Mrs Thatcher herself narrowly escaped death), coupled with the major rows over the Falklands and the coverage of the miners' strike in 1984/85, set the context for government relations with the broadcasters. In the summer of 1985, the government was at a critical stage in Anglo-Irish negotiations [16] and there had been much controversy about the way in which US television had covered the hijack of a TWA plane. The networks were accused of favouring the hijackers by interviewing them and televising their demands. Referring to the hijacking Mrs

Thatcher suggested, in a speech in the US, that the media had supplied the 'terrorists' with the 'oxygen of publicity'.

The details of the row over *Real Lives* are well known. The *Sunday Times*, sensing a story in the forthcoming programme, started the ball rolling by asking Mrs Thatcher (who was in the USA at the time) a hypothetical question about how she would react to a television interview with the Chief of Staff of the IRA. It also sought comments from the Home Secretary, the Northern Ireland Secretary and at least two of the BBC's governors, both of whom had not been previously aware of the programme. The *Sunday Times* report prompted the Home Secretary to issue a press statement and a day later, at the insistence of the BBC, reluctantly to write a formal letter of complaint. Leon Brittan insisted that he was not writing in his capacity as Minister for Broadcasting, for that would be censorship. 'I do on the other hand also have a ministerial responsibility for the fight against the ever present threat of terrorism', he wrote.

The programme would give 'an immensely valuable platform' and would 'in my considered judgement materially assist the terrorist cause'. The film had already been referred to senior management but after the *Sunday Times* story it was viewed and passed by the entire board of management (except the Director-General, who was on holiday and had also not been aware of the programme). Delaying of the programme until the Director-General returned from holiday was difficult since 'At the edge of the Union' was the cover story in that week's edition of the *Radio Times* (Milne 1988: 187). Relations between the governors and management had been unsettled over the previous year and the governors were put out at not having known about the programme. [17] They broke with the usual practice, insisted on viewing the film and banned it. Apparently, only after their statement had been drafted were the words 'in its present form' added (Leapman 1987: 315).

The Prime Minister and the Home Secretary congratulated the BBC. A deep division was opened up between the governors and the board of management, with the public implication that the judgement of the management was lacking. At a further meeting of the governors, at which the management tried to have the decision reversed, the ban was confirmed. A twenty-four-hour strike, on the day the programme was to have been screened, followed and included journalists from throughout broadcasting, not just from the BBC. The Director-General considered resigning and the Controller Northern Ireland did, but was persuaded to change his mind.

'At the edge of the Union' featured two elected representatives from Derry – Gregory Campbell, a member of Ian Paisley's DUP and Sinn Féin's Martin McGuinness. The cameras followed them as they went about their daily tasks. Both men were seen in political and domestic settings, both talked of their support for political violence. There was no commentary and no hostile questioning. To that extent the programme was marked out from routine news and current affairs coverage, and qualified more as a documentary. In another respect, though, it had all the classic hallmarks of 'balance' between the 'two extremes'. In a sense, the appearance of Gregory Campbell was a side issue in the row. The question which 'At the edge of the Union' threw into sharp relief was the coverage of Irish republican politicians. In the early 1980s Sinn Féin members stood for and were elected to council seats across Northern Ireland. [18] This increased the democratic legitimacy of Provisional republican politics, and consequently the difficulties for the government in removing the voice of armed republicanism from the screen. From the start, the broadcasters treated Sinn Féin councillors differently from those of other political parties. On the one hand they were democratically elected members of a legal political party, and hence 'legitimate' with a right to access to the media. On the other hand, they were public supporters of the armed struggle and, potentially at least, covert members of the Provisional IRA and so 'illegitimate' with no right of access. Indeed Martin McGuinness had been alleged in the *Sunday Times* to be a past Chief of Staff of the IRA.

Rather than try to wean Sinn Féin from the IRA, government strategy has been to try to marginalise the party as part of the wider attempt at 'containing' the troubles. This has all been done under the guise of 'fighting terrorism'. In the official view, Sinn Féin is simply a 'front' for the Provisional IRA and as such no more deserve airtime than the IRA themselves. Television programmes that feature Sinn Féin politicians are therefore expected to be clearly hostile. The BBC's internal referral procedures had anticipated this problem in 1980, giving the Director of News and Current Affairs the job of deciding which people 'are or may be associated with' 'terrorism'. The problem with *Real Lives*, from the official perspective, was that it allowed McGuinness to appear as a legitimate politician. The scene that aroused the most ire was one in which McGuinness was shown at home with one of his children sitting on his knee. For Stuart Young, Chair of the Board of Governors, who seems to have been less inclined to ban it than some, the film 'made them out to be nice guys, bouncing babies on their knees', while for Daphne Park, who was more inclined to ban it, it was a 'Hitler loved dogs' film (cited in Milne 1989: 188 and 190). To portray McGuinness as a rational human being who lived in many deeply familiar and ordinary ways was beyond the pale of acceptable coverage. In the *Real Lives* affair the government came closer than ever before to direct censorship.

Recent Developments

Between 1974 and 1988, the Prevention of Terrorism Act had been used to seize material from broadcasters on one occasion. Since then there have been numerous legal threats against both the press and television. The powers under PACE seem to have been first used to seize photos and film from press photographers and local television companies following the riots in Bristol in 1986. [19] Since then the powers have been used following the clashes between police and pickets outside Wapping in January 1987, once in 1988, four times in 1989 and eight times in the first ten months of 1990 (Birt 1990: 18), including, notably, after the anti poll tax demonstration that year. [20] According to John Birt, the BBC's then Deputy Director-General, there are now routine requests to the BBC from the police for footage of disturbances, most commonly to regional BBC offices following trouble at football matches. In the main these requests are refused and the police do not apply for a court order (Birt 1990).

The Andersonstown Killings

At the funeral of the Gibraltar dead in Milltown cemetery, West Belfast, a loyalist paramilitary launched a gun and grenade attack on the mourners, killing three people and wounding more than fifty. Three days later, at the funeral of one of the Milltown dead, a car drove at high speed towards the cortege. Fearing another loyalist attack mourners surrounded the car, dragged its occupants out, beat them and carried them off. The two occupants were members of the British Army; both were armed and one fired a shot. They were later killed by the IRA. The approach of the car, the initial surge to surround it and the firing of one of the soldier's guns were captured on television and stills cameras and broadcast around the world that night. Pictures of the soldiers' stripped, battered and bruised bodies filled the front pages of many British newspapers,[21] while news reports revealed a widespread sense of revulsion amongst media personnel. On Monday 22 March the RUC Chief Constable, Sir John Hermon, 'requested' that the BBC, ITN and RTE (the national broadcasting channel in the Republic of Ireland) hand over untransmitted film of the attack. The broadcasters refused, unless faced with a court order. In parliament the next day Mrs Thatcher set out the options for the broadcasters in straightforward terms:

> I believe that everyone, the media included, has a bounden duty to do everything they can to see that those who perpetrated the terrible crimes, which we saw on television, which disgusted the whole world, are brought to justice. Either one is on the side of justice in these matters, or one is on the side of terrorism. (BBC2 *Newsnight*, 22.50, 22 March 1988)

Although all three television companies initially refused to hand over their film, Mrs Thatcher's attack was entirely directed against the BBC. The BBC's initial refusal cited staff safety: 'Our policy on requests for untransmitted material, including requests from the RUC, is that we do not make such material available. This policy is to protect our film crews – to protect the lives of our staff.' (*Daily Mail*, 22 March 1988).

By the next day, there were signs that other factors, such as press reporting and comments in parliament allied to perceptions of public opinion, were starting to have an effect. David Nicholas of ITN echoed the BBC line on staff safety, but went on to add 'Saturday's events were heinous crimes, and I understand why people are saying "why aren't you helping the police?"' (*Independent*, 23 March 1988). The pressure on the broadcasters mounted as negotiations with the RUC continued during the day.

The next evening around 6.30 p.m. senior RUC officers arrived at BBC and ITN headquarters in Belfast and, saying that they were acting under the Prevention of Terrorism Act, the Emergency Provisions Act and the Criminal Law Act 1967, demanded copies of untransmitted material. The BBC's Controller Northern Ireland, Colin Morris, was told that, if he refused, the Editor, News and Current Affairs, John Conway, would be arrested. The BBC and ITN complied. The next day RTE too handed over its untransmitted footage. The BBC's Director-General said 'the BBC has never set itself above the law' (*Daily Telegraph*, 24 March 1988). This was the second time that police had seized film material under the PTA.

However, there remains some doubt as to the applicability of Section 11 to seizing media materials. As with the seizure of the Carrickmore film and the later 1980 opinion of the Attorney-General, the legality of the RUC action was *de facto*. The power has still not been tested in the courts. ITN's Editor, David Nicholas, emphasised that ITN 'does not consider itself above the law and it is open to the authorities to use the due process of the law in its enquiries' (*Guardian*, 23 March 1988). But the due process in this case does not involve a court order. When the RUC raided the Belfast offices of BBC and ITN they were not acting with any kind of search warrant or court order, they simply threatened to arrest senior broadcasters. Unlike the Police and Criminal Evidence Act there are no provisions under the PTA which specifically relate to the seizure of film or other media material, and consequently there are no safeguards. It is an offence under Section 11 to withhold information without 'reasonable excuse'. The definition of 'reasonable excuse' is unclear. More importantly it remains unclear that a prosecution under Section 11 would necessarily allow the RUC access to the information, since the PTA only gives the power to prosecute for the withholding of evidence, not the power to seize that evidence. It seems that this point was acknowledged in government circles prior to the film being handed over. The *Daily Express* reported an off-the-record briefing in which 'a senior cabinet minister' acknowledged that 'the legal position over the film was obscure ... The minister said that if the case failed in the courts, then Northern Ireland Secretary Tom King would take a fresh look at the Prevention of Terrorism Act, and how it applied to possible evidence held by the media' (*Daily Express*, 23 March 1988). According to the *Independent*'s legal corespondent any 'prosecution could not be used to force the media to surrender the unstransmitted footage and would require a wide interpretation of the word "information"' (*Independent*, 23 March 1988). Thus if the BBC, ITN and RTE had refused to release the footage under threat from the RUC, it is not certain that any case could have been won on the basis of the PTA. This is perhaps why the RUC constructed the legal cocktail of the PTA backed up by the Emergency Provisions Act and the Criminal Law Act. Once BBC personnel had been threatened with arrest under Section 11, the RUC still needed to find some power to seize the film material. Its officers quoted Section 13 of the EPA 1978, which states that a constable may seize 'anything which he suspects is being, has been or is intended to be used in the commission of a scheduled offence'. The scheduled offence in this case is the refusal to hand over the film. This emergency power was then backed up with the threat under the non-emergency Criminal Law Act 1967 of arrest for failing to disclose information requested by a police officer.

The American magazine *Newsweek* ran into trouble later in the year when it published an interview with 'a staff officer in the Northern Command' of the IRA (Foote 1988). In Australia on 5 August, Mrs Thatcher had observed: 'the IRA is a proscribed organisation in Britain and anyone who interviews them should expect to be committed for an offence' (*Independent*, 25 October 1988). In the light of this the Crown Prosecution Service examined whether the article contravened Section 11 of the Prevention of Terrorism Act. It ruled that the interview was not illegal and a 'well placed Whitehall source' told the *Independent* that Mrs Thatcher 'had been wrong' (25 October 1988). Nevertheless, here was a further warning for the British media. In 1989 the PTA was used to seize untransmitted film of Fr. Patrick Ryan from Thames television (Bolton 1989). The *Daily Telegraph* was forced to hand over photographs under the Police and Criminal Evidence Act in October 1989, although the BBC defeated an RUC court order later in the month arguing that the PACE legislation did not then apply to Northern Ireland. [22] In 1991 the new clause 17, introduced in 1989, was used for the first time against Channel 4 (see below) and at the beginning of 1992 it was used against American network ABC in relation to the Lockerbie bombing.

Gibraltar

The *Real Lives* affair was followed by increasing government pressure on the BBC, and the relationship between the governors and management seems to have deteriorated even further. The Tebbit attack on the BBC's coverage of the US bombing of Libya, the BBC's libel payout to two Conservative MPs, the 1987 sacking of Director-General Alasdair Milne by the governors and the Special Branch raid on BBC Scotland the following weekend left the BBC weak and demoralised (Leapman 1987; Milne 1988). Meanwhile, government policy on independent broadcasting had been on the move. In 1988 the government widened its attack to both broadcasting systems. This time the controversy did not arise because of interviews with members of Sinn Féin or the IRA. Television reporting on the Gibraltar killings touched that other especially tender nerve: the conduct of the British military and intelligence services.

At approximately 3.41 p.m. on the afternoon of Sunday 6 March 1988, three members of the IRA, Mairead Farrell, Dan McCann and Sean Savage, were shot dead in Gibraltar. The killings occurred in a main street of the tiny British colony at the southern tip of Spain. First reports suggested a reasonably straightforward story. Three armed members of the IRA were shot dead by Gibraltar police after planting a massive car bomb and, in some reports, engaging in a gun battle. Later that evening the MoD changed its account, acknowledging that military personnel had been involved in the killings (Miller 1991).

However, at around 3.30 the next afternoon, Foreign Secretary Geoffrey Howe said in the House of Commons that no bomb had been found and that the three IRA members were unarmed. Roger Bolton, the editor of *This Week*, Thames television's networked current affairs programme, describes his reaction to the story:

> I had a late lunch and when I came back to the office sat down with Julian Manyon and Chris Oxley (respectively reporter and producer of 'Death on the Rock') ... They thought me somewhat preoccupied with Ireland so, rather playfully,

asked me if I was going to do anything about the shootings. 'No, there's nothing left to say.' Almost at that moment Oracle updated its report on Gibraltar quoting the Foreign Secretary's statement to the House of Commons ... I drew in my breath. Well, that put a very different perspective on the whole matter. (Bolton 1990: 191)

Bolton set a team to work on researching a programme almost immediately.

Death on the Rock

Following the deaths at Milltown and Andersonstown, after which hostilities between broadcasters and the state were renewed, 'there were now', according to Roger Bolton, 'even more compelling reasons to continue the story' (1990: 203). The *This Week* team uncovered new evidence about the shootings, though without any cooperation from official sources. In London 'Death on the Rock' was guided through internal politics at Thames as well as the referral system. Senior management at Thames were kept informed and Bolton told the IBA that he thought the film would be a 'sensitive one' (Bolton 1990: 224). The IBA indicated that they would want to preview the film. It was passed by the Thames hierarchy and dispatched to the IBA for approval at 6 p.m. on 26 April.

The government had been aware that the programme was being made because of regular requests from the Thames team to official sources for guidance. It had also been given an indication of the 'likely shape' of the programme over a week before transmission. A special cabinet subcommittee had coordinated government responses to the shootings, particularly information management. According to Roger Bolton the activities of the Thames journalists had been reported to the committee at regular intervals (Bolton 1990: 223).

One hour before Thames dispatched a copy of the programme to the IBA the Foreign Secretary personally telephoned Lord Thomson, the Chair of the IBA, saying that he was concerned that the programme might prejudice the inquest on the killings. Howe asked Thomson to postpone the programme until after the inquest in Gibraltar. Thomson said he would look into the matter.

IBA staff viewed the programme the next day and asked for three changes to be made in the commentary. According to Bolton:

> senior staff in the Programme Division, together with the IBA's officer for Northern Ireland, felt that the programmes summing up suggested too strongly that the coroner's Inquest would be unable to establish the truth, and that the Gibraltar police evidence would be unreliable. I accepted these two points but the IBA accepted my arguments on the third point which concerned the Prime Minister's prior knowledge of the detection of an IRA unit in Spain. (Bolton 1990: 228)

Inside the IBA, the programme was referred up to the most senior personnel, via the Director of Television to the Director-General and the Chairman, all of whom viewed and passed the programme successively on the evening of 27 April. Legal advice sought by the IBA indicated that the programme would not prejudice the forthcoming inquest because the programme was broadcast in a different jurisdiction. This was the end of what Windelsham and Rampton were to call the 'tortuous process' of referral (1989: 75). The next morning the IBA informed Geoffrey Howe's private secretary of their decision and then the Cabinet was informed. At around noon Howe again phoned the IBA, this time speaking with David Glencross, the Director of Television. This time he raised the issue of contamination of evidence and referred to the Salmon Report on the law of contempt, which states:

> The Press, Television and Radio have always considered that once any type of tribunal has been appointed it is inappropriate for them to conduct anything in the nature of a parallel inquiry and they have never done so. We regard it as of the utmost importance that this restraint should continue to be exercised. (cited in Windelsham and Rampton 1989: 136)

However, neither a tribunal nor an inquest had at that stage been appointed or scheduled. It is worth noting here that neither of the objections of the Foreign Secretary had the slightest legal basis. [23] What is more important, for the government, is the appearance of legalistic legitimacy. Shortly after Howe's second phone call, the Foreign Office invited lobby correspondents to a press conference in which it revealed the contact with the IBA. [24] Thomson responded with a statement that afternoon and the programme went ahead as planned at 9 p.m. that evening. This left the IBA at the centre of what the *Daily Telegraph* described as its 'greatest crisis since it was set up in 1954, just at a time when the government is preparing the most radical restructuring of commercial television for 30 years' (30 April 1988). [25]

The account given by 'Death on the Rock' directly contradicted the official version, which was based on Geoffrey Howe's statement to parliament on 7 March and developed in unattributable briefings to papers such as the *Sunday Times* (Miller 1991; *Private Eye* 1989). Howe claimed that the IRA personnel had been

> challenged by the security forces. When challenged they made movements which led the military personnel, operating in support of the Gibraltar police, to conclude that their own lives and the lives of others were under threat. In the light of this response, they were shot. Those killed were subsequently found not to have been carrying arms. (*Hansard*, 7 March 1988, Col. 21)

However, eyewitnesses interviewed for 'Death on the Rock' alleged that there had been no challenge and that the IRA members had made no movements, simply putting their hands up as if in surrender. [26] Their testimony raised the possibility that the killings were simply extra-judicial executions. [27]

As well as fitting conveniently with wider policy initiatives on broadcasting, it should be remembered that the government reaction to the programme was part of a wider attempt to win the symbolic and legal battle to present the killings as lawful. As we have noted, a Cabinet subcommittee was set up specially to deal with this problem. Consequently we can see government strategy in this area as operating at a number of levels. [28] Attacking the broadcasters serves as a tool for disciplining journalists, undermining public service broadcasting, hastening policy objectives on broadcasting and publicly legitimating the actions of British military forces. The furore over 'Death on the

Rock' also had the result of diverting attention from arguments about what actually happened in Gibraltar on 6 March 1988.

Government strategy in relation to perceptions of the killings took two main forms. The first was to say nothing about the events of 6 March in public, while the second involved unattributable briefings given to selected journalists. Misinformation was also used in order to undermine the credibility of those who contradicted the official account. We will return to the information management aspects of these approaches in later chapters, but for present purposes it is the attacks on 'Death on the Rock' which are of interest.

Both the Home Secretary and the Northern Ireland Secretary called the programme 'trial by television' and Mrs Thatcher, when asked if she was furious, commented that it was 'deeper than that'. In a television interview in Japan she said:

> Trial by television or guilt by accusation, is the day that freedom dies ... Press and television rely on freedom. Those who do rely on freedom must have the duty and responsibility and not try to substitute their own system for it. (cited in the *Daily Telegraph*, 30 April 1988)

In its response the IBA neatly turned Mrs Thatcher's phrase the 'oxygen of publicity', back on her: 'The IBA believes that to postpone the programme until after an inquest which is apparently a long time away would give the IRA more 'oxygen of publicity' and would certainly not prevent it being shown elsewhere.'

The government kept up the pressure all through the summer until the inquest in September. When one of the Thames witnesses appeared to retract his testimony during the month-long proceedings, knives were unsheathed in the press and the government more or less obliged Thames to hold some form of inquiry into the programme. The inquiry took on a quasi-legal form in order that it might gain some credibility and it was carried out by a privy councillor (who was also a former Conservative Northern Ireland minister) and a QC, who were felt to have the authority to gain access to the relevant evidence (Trethowan 1989: vii-viii). Windelsham rejected the criticisms of the Foreign Secretary on prejudice and contamination and largely cleared the programme, making only a small number of minor critical points:

> The programme makers were experienced, painstaking and persistent. They did not bribe, bully or misrepresent those who took part. The programme was trenchant and avoided triviality. Despite the various criticisms which we have noted in our report, we accept that those who made it were acting in good faith and without ulterior motives. (Windelsham and Rampton 1989: 144)

Spotlight

BBC Northern Ireland also made a programme on the killings to fill its *Spotlight* current affairs slot. Revealed by the press on 4 May, the BBC press office maintained that 'a programme is under consideration, but has not yet been finalised. It is in its early stages and we don't have a transmission date or details of its possible content' (*Irish News*, 4 May 1988). The day before, a senior NIO official had phoned the BBC in Belfast to enquire about 'the timing and subject matter of the programme' (*Belfast Telegraph*, 4 May 1988). A spokesperson said that if the BBC decided to show the programme 'clearly the same criticism could be levelled at them as was levelled at Thames TV – that of prejudicing a coroner's inquest' (*Irish News*, 4 May 1988). At this stage the programme had still to receive clearance from the BBC hierarchy.

Foreign Secretary Geoffrey Howe phoned the Chair of the BBC Governors, Marmaduke Hussey, at around noon on Wednesday 4 May in an attempt to stop the programme being shown. He used the same arguments as had been used against 'Death on the Rock' and sought assurances that interviews with witnesses to the shootings would not be broadcast. A Foreign Office spokesperson told the *Independent* (5 May 1988): 'we are not objecting to documentaries on the Gibraltar shootings. We are concerned that interviews with eyewitnesses could prejudice the inquest.' In contrast to the *Real Lives* affair, the Chair of the Governors deflected the request on to the Director-General, Michael Checkland. Hussey commented: 'I pointed out to the Foreign Secretary that programme making matters must be dealt with by the Director-General, who is now considering the matter with Northern Ireland management. Once full information is available, he or

I will be able to respond to the Foreign Secretary' (*The Times*, 5 May 1988).

A rough cut of the programme was viewed by the editor of the programme, Andy Coleman, the Editor News and Current Affairs John Conway, and the Head of Programmes Arwel Ellis Owen on the evening of 4 May (*The Times*, 5 May 1988). They passed the programme for transmission and referred it up to Controller Colin Morris, who viewed it later that evening, also recommending that it be shown. The next day the programme was apparently sent down the line to London, where a collection of senior management, including the Director-General, watched it the next day. The decision to broadcast was taken during the day of 5 May and announced less than two hours before transmission. In line with the convention, broken during the *Real Lives* crisis, the governors did not view the film, relying on the judgement of the Director-General and his senior staff. Emphasising this, the reply to Geoffrey Howe's telephone call came from Director-General Michael Checkland and not from Marmaduke Hussey, to whom Howe had originally spoken.

It is interesting to note the different ways in which the BBC and the IBA/Thames dealt with the government pressure over their respective programmes on Gibraltar. The special position of the BBC in relation to the government and to international perceptions means that it is easier for the government to move the BBC in the direction that it wants. Another factor is that there are a variety of different ITV companies as well as the regulatory body, the ITC (then the IBA). The degree of centralised control that is possible with the BBC is less easy to maintain over the ITV companies.

BBC management was in a 'tight corner' (Bolton 1990: 246) over *Spotlight*. It is very unusual for decisions about programmes broadcast only in Northern Ireland to be taken out of the hands of local management and referred up through the BBC hierarchy (Owen 1989). This is because BBC Northern Ireland (BBCNI) is assumed to be a safer pair of hands than 'outside' journalists covering Northern Ireland. Journalists from Britain are required to keep BBCNI management informed of programmes concerning Northern Ireland at all stages. In this case, there was some feeling among senior executives in London that there had been a breakdown of referral procedures. Consequently there was some dismay at the lack of time that remained to check the programme adequately, although there was apparently time for a total of five editorial viewings of the programme on 4 and 5 May. During the discussions on 5 May – which involved Northern Ireland staff, as well as the Head of Regional programming Geraint Stanley Jones, the Controller Editorial Policy John Wilson and the DG – there was apparently some suggestion that the script should be changed and that the programme be delayed for a week (*Irish News*, 6 May 1988). There was a corresponding feeling in BBC Northern Ireland that the referral system was overweening and unnecessary. Alex Thomson, the reporter on the programme, is reported to have said that he believed the BBC had an 'over-managed' editorial system. 'To take five editorial viewings to get it on the air is ridiculous', he said (*Irish News*, 6 May 1988). Thomson himself was apparently denied access to the meeting at which it was finally decided to show the documentary. There was some lobbying for network transmission, which according to Bolton would 'usually' have been the case. However, Alex Thomson was apparently told 'look, you've won one battle, don't push your luck' (Bolton 1990: 246). Almost at the last minute the decision was taken to broadcast the programme largely intact. Some in BBC Northern Ireland felt that the extended referral process masked a chronic indecision on the part of senior management. Others suggested that BBC executives were vulnerable to pressure from the Prime Minister. This seems to have been the view of even some of the management in BBCNI.

In this view, the decision to broadcast hinged on Mrs Thatcher's performance at Prime Minister's question time that afternoon. According to one BBC insider, the perception among some BBC staff was that 'If she [Thatcher] had made an outcry in particularly strong terms the impression was that they may well have shelved it' (telephone interview, February 1990). The Prime Minister was noticeably less forthright at question time that day. There was no repetition of the legal threat of contempt via prejudice. Indeed, Mrs Thatcher seemed to acknowledge that there was no legal case, but simply a custom or convention: 'Trial by television was not so much a matter of the specific rules, but rather a dependence on customs and conventions that had been referred to by Lord Justice Salmon' (*The Times*, 6 May 1988).

After the programme went out the feeling inside the BBC was that heads would have to roll. Alex Thomson apparently had his 'head on the chopping block', but by that time he had already been offered another job. The axe does seem to have fallen on a more senior neck, that of Arwel Ellis Owen. On the day following transmission, Owen gave a radio interview in which he criticised the BBC's caution in the face of governmental attack. In particular he is said to have alleged that the transmission of the programme hinged on the tone of Mrs Thatcher's comments at question time. [29] The interview came to the attention of senior management when it was proposed that it should be transmitted on Radio 4's *PM* programme. It was then pulled on the instructions of the Director-General, and staff were instructed not to refer to it in public. Hints of criticism can be found in a public lecture delivered by Owen almost a year later in Oxford. Asking why the decision on *Spotlight* was taken in London, he argued:

> When a government quotes 'national security' as its reason for expressing an interest in say, the two programmes I have mentioned ('Death on the Rock' and *Spotlight*) – the Corporation slips easily into its role as a 'national institution' – protecting the public interest – locally and nationally – as well as protecting its own independence and credibility. The lessons of *Real Lives* were fully understood. (Owen 1989: 28) [30]

Owen was, by the time *Spotlight* was broadcast, already scheduled to take up an appointment for a sabbatical year as the first Guardian/Nuffield Fellow at Oxford University in October 1988. He was then supposed to return to the BBC, where insiders say he was tipped to get a more senior job in BBC Wales. Certainly Owen appears to have expected to return to the BBC following the scholarship. He started his Nuffield lecture by saying he was indebted to the BBC 'for releasing me for a sabbatical year. I look forward to rejoining my colleagues at the BBC' (Owen 1989: 2). This, however, was not to be. In effect, and very quietly, he was sacked, or as senior management at the BBC prefers to put it 'eased out'. [31] It is a mark of the great sensitivity of this story that until now this information has never been published.

'The Committee'

The representation of the forces of law and order was also the focus of the next major confrontation between the media and the state. On 2 October 1991 Channel 4 transmitted a programme in its *Dispatches* series made by independent company Box Productions. [32] Titled 'The Committee', the programme alleged a secret conspiracy between members of the Protestant business community, loyalist paramilitaries and members of the 'security forces'. Citing the Prevention of Terrorism Act the RUC demanded that the company reveal the identity of the main source of the programme; when Box and Channel 4 refused, the RUC took them to court. The moves seem to have originated with the RUC and continued with the aid of the Metropolitan police in London. In roughly comparable previous cases such as Carrickmore, the use of the Prevention of Terrorism Act was only considered after the political row had erupted, as part of a strategy of intimidating the broadcasters. In the Andersonstown case, considered above, the broadcasters complied with RUC threats following press and government pressure. In this case, though, there was no great political row and no manufactured controversy in the press of the sort usual on these occasions. Indeed, the fact that the RUC was taking Channel 4 to court was kept secret for around six months following Channel 4's lawyers' interpretation of the new powers contained in the 1989 update of the Prevention of Terrorism Act.

After the programme was broadcast both Sir Hugh Annesley, Chief Constable of the RUC and Peter Brooke, the Northern Ireland Secretary asked Channel 4 to hand any evidence they might have to the RUC. The day after, Annesley took the unusual step of issuing a four-page press statement 'utterly rejecting' the programme as an 'unjust and unsubstantiated slur' on the RUC. [33] Channel 4 responded that it was regrettable that the Chief Constable had dismissed the film without 'investigating it or awaiting the additional evidence which he knows Channel 4 is providing'. On 7 October Channel 4 provided the RUC, the Special Branch and the NIO with a dossier of information on the alleged 'committee'. However, on 31 October the RUC, through the Metropolitan police, applied for production orders under schedule 7, paragraph 3 of the PTA, requiring Channel 4 and Box Productions to reveal the identity of their sources, particularly source 'A'. Following this, 'further material not included in the original dossier was handed over' (C4 *Press Release*, 29 April 1992). Channel 4 and Box, who had not been present at the initial hearing, applied to discharge or vary the orders and then to clarify their ambit. Finally the television companies appeared before the court on 21 January 1992 and stated that they could not fully comply with the orders. The RUC then referred the matter to the Attorney-General, who, on 29 April, obtained leave to commit C4 and Box for contempt of court. Let us remember that this entire legal procedure was conducted in secrecy. Only when the Attorney-General obtained leave to commit the broadcasters did the story become public. The contempt case opened towards the end of July 1992, with the possibility that Channel 4 could be subject to unlimited rolling fines or even sequestration of assets, as in the case of the National Union of Mineworkers during the pit strike of 1984/5.

In the face of closing down one of Britain's four television networks, the court opted for a pragmatic judgement. It found in favour of the RUC, but limited the fine to a one-off amount of £75,000 plus 'not insubstantial' costs. Recognising that closing Channel 4 down would not be likely to change the 'moral' position of its directors or to achieve the disclosure of the information, Lord Justice Woolf stated: 'the court in my judgement must accept the reality of the situation' (Woolf and Pill 1992: 20). But, evidently viewing his judgement as a precedent, Woolf indicated that part of the reason for his pragmatism was that

> I have particularly in mind the fact that it may not have been appreciated by the companies in this case the dangers which were implicit in giving an unqualified undertaking [of confidentiality to their sources], although ... this should have been in their mind. This will not apply to the future but is a compelling factor in the present situation. (Woolf and Pill 1992: 20)

This judgement has the effect of warning journalists what will happen if they are ever again tempted to put the public interest above the law.

The C4/Box case was a further departure in the use of legal powers over the media in two distinct ways. Firstly, the case was kept secret. Second, it was the first use of an additional provision of the 1989 version of the PTA. Section 17, schedule 7 confers powers to obtain information including material which would otherwise be excluded under the Police and Criminal Evidence Act (in this case journalistic material). The criteria for gaining access to this material is that 'there are reasonable grounds for believing that the material is likely to be of substantial value' in a 'terrorist investigation' and that it is in the public interest (see Woolf and Pill 1992). This provision, the objective of which was originally said by the government to be uncovering funding for paramilitary organisations, has now emerged as a severe limitation on media reporting of Northern Ireland. [34] In the High Court, the import of this was made clear by Lord Justice Woolf:

> I, of course, appreciate that the companies [C4 and Box] would say that 'A' would never have co-operated but for the undertakings and without his co-operation there would have been no programme. As it was in the public interest the programme be broadcast, so the public interest required them to give the undertaking. However, this in law is an impermissible approach for the companies to adopt. (Woolf and Pill 1992: 16–17)

In other words, in the view of the law, broadcasters should not make programmes about Northern Ireland using (non-official or unauthorised) confidential sources.

The key issue is to what extent can the rule of law remain inviolate in relation to journalistic activity when the wrongdoing which is being alleged by journalists is centrally coordinated by agencies of law and order themselves:

> Even if they decided improperly to adopt this approach they should have at least tried to secure 'A's' co-operation by qualified undertaking or sought advice of the highest level of government which should have been available in view of Channel Four's standing as to the propriety of the action they were proposing. (Woolf and Pill 1992: 17)

As Liz Forgan of Channel 4 then argued, 'presumably' this would be 'with an eye to indemnity if the appropriate official agreed with the thrust of the programme. But what, she continued, 'if it were the behaviour of a government agency that a journalist was seeking to expose? And since any guarantee has to be given before the witness tells his story, let alone before it can be checked, it is hard to see how any government figure could take the proposition seriously' (Forgan 1992b).

The RUC did not let the matter rest there. Chief Constable Hugh Annesley again took the unusual step of issuing a seven-page press release, alleging that Channel 4 had been the subject of a hoax by a loyalist intent on discrediting the RUC. As with 'Death on the Rock' there then followed a series of stories based on official briefings attempting to discredit the programme. These appeared in the *Daily Telegraph*, the *Sunday Times* and the *Sunday Express*. [35] Among them was the predictive suggestion on 9 August 1992 that the RUC was considering taking Channel 4 to court for a second time in relation to the *Dispatches* programme. On 29 September the police did take action, arresting the *Dispatches* researcher Ben Hamilton at 6.30 in the morning and charging him with contempt. The nature of the charges were never officially spelt out and were eventually dropped when the case came to trial.

Direct Censorship

The skirmishes and rows over Northern Ireland that started in 1971 had meant a continual tightening of the broadcasters internal procedures, so that by 1980 the voice of armed republicanism had successfully been banished from the screen. The challenge to government policing of the media which the rise of Sinn Féin represented, exacerbated the already increasing attempts at control under successive Thatcher administrations. If in 1985 *Real Lives* was the furthest the government had gone stopping short of direct censorship, 'Death on the Rock' proved to be the furthest they could go. The logic of the attempt to remove republican views from the screen was to stop Sinn Féin from being interviewed at all, but since it is a legal political party, it would be very hard to legitimate such a step in the international community. This left the government in a bind. It had already gone as far as it was able, unless a way could be found to separate Sinn Féin as 'politicians' from Sinn Féin as 'terrorists'.

In all the controversy around the *Real Lives* affair, this dilemma remained relatively obscure. But there is evidence that some top broadcasters were thinking this issue through to its logical conclusions. For example, BBC Assistant Director-General Alan Protheroe (1985: 6) had recognised the tendency:

> Does the government therefore wish to prevent the expression on the air of views with which it disagrees from democratically elected supporters – at local council, Assembly or parliamentary level? Or does it wish to say, 'You can use Sinn Féin people on the air if they're talking about the drains in the Bogside or the state of the pavements in West Belfast – but you can't use them if they mutter a word about the need for the maintenance of the armed struggle'?

In the event the government opted for the more restrictive former option some three years later when introducing a ban on direct interviews with Sinn Féin and others. The ban is an unprecedented intervention in peacetime. It is the only piece of direct censorship legislation operating in Britain. The British Home Office notice prohibits the broadcasting of 'any words spoken ... by a person who ... represents or purports to represent' a listed organisation or 'the words support or solicit or invite support for such an organisation'.

The precise meaning of the text of the notice was not immediately clear to the broadcasters, and much time was spent in drawing up guidelines followed by consultations with the Home Office. The Home Office then set out its own interpretation 'so that the BBC would be left in no doubt' (BBC 1989b: Appendix V). For example, there was much confusion about the precise definition of 'represent' in the notice and whether Sinn Féin spokespersons could be held to 'represent' their party twenty-four hours a day, whatever they said. The Home Office interpretation was that 'A member of an organisation cannot be held to represent the organisation in all their daily activities'. The crucial distinction, therefore, is in which capacity a speaker appears.

BBC television news made use of this definition of 'represent' for the first time on 16 February 1989, when it interviewed Gerry

Adams about jobs in West Belfast. Thirty seconds of sound on film was broadcast in Northern Ireland, with Adams speaking as MP for West Belfast rather than Sinn Féin MP for West Belfast. The *Media Show* took this definition of 'represent' to its logical conclusion when it interviewed Sinn Féin councillor Jim McAllister about his role in Ken Loach's film *Hidden Agenda*. McAllister was representing himself as an actor rather than as a Sinn Féin councillor, even though his acting role in the film is that of a Sinn Féin councillor (8 May 1990). However, following the Home Office letter, there continued to be occasions on which the broadcasters disagreed among themselves about the 'representativeness' of a particular statement (BBC news and ITN have made a number of opposite decisions on particular news events) and there has been criticism of the broadcasters for censoring comments which were spoken by Sinn Féin members acting in other capacities.

The clearest result of this uncertainty has been that broadcasters have routinely erred on the side of caution in editorial decision making, thus extending the ban well beyond the letter of the notice. At the BBC a decision was taken at the corporation's bi-weekly editorial policy meeting to ban subtitles from news bulletins. According to one BBC executive this was because 'It looked so dramatic – It looked like we were seeking to make a point' (Miller 1990). In the climate of government hostility at the time, the last thing the BBC were interested in was making a point. Perhaps the most widely known extension of the notice was the IBA's banning of the Pogues song 'Streets of Sorrow/ Birmingham Six'. The song proclaims the innocence of the Guildford Four and the Birmingham Six, jailed for IRA bombings in the 1970s. It followed a widespread campaign to expose what the campaigners saw as miscarriages of justice. The IBA, however, believed that the song contained words which 'support or solicit or invite support' for one of the listed organisations because of their 'general disagreement with the way in which the British government responds to and the courts deal with the terrorist threat in the UK' (*Observer*, 20 November 1988). Ironically the courts then went on to accept that both the Guildford Four and the Birmingham Six were wrongly convicted. The most far reaching extension of the ban was the subtitling of Bernadette McAliskey, the former MP and civil rights activist, on a BBC discussion programme. Asked her view on political violence in the cause of Irish republicanism she said:

> Well, I have to put it in context. Quite honestly, if I supported it fully, if I could justify it, I would join the IRA. But since I am not a soldier, since I cannot within myself justify it, then I'm not. But I can understand it, I can explain it, I can articulate it and I can offer what I believe to be a rational way out of it, which is discussion and negotiation, wherever it is in the world.

Her first eight words were broadcast and then the rest of her contribution to the programme was subtitled, because it was deemed by BBC lawyers to be supportive of the IRA. The atmosphere of caution in the BBC had now reached the pitch that understanding the actions of the IRA could now apparently be construed as support for it (Miller 1993c). Prior to this the BBC guidelines on what was covered by this part of the notice maintained that 'Generalised comments about or even in favour of terrorism in Ireland or about Irish republicanism are not prevented' (BBC 1989c: 40). Following the McAliskey episode, the Controller Editorial Policy rewrote the guidelines, although he has maintained that 'I will continue to apply the guidelines as narrowly as I reasonably can'. [36]

The effect of the confusion and caution on news reporting has been a dramatic drop in Sinn Féin interviews in the five years following the ban. In the year immediately after its introduction Sinn Féin interviews on British television network news declined by 63 per cent compared with the year before. In addition the interviews which were carried were shorter and less informative (Henderson et al. 1990). With the emergence of the 'Hume–Adams' peace process, in which Sinn Féin was a leading player, the basics of political reporting required interviews with Sinn Féin representatives. In a departure from the ban Sinn Féin leaders were interviewed at length on television news programmes in late 1993. This led Conservative MP Dame Jill Knight to complain (inaccurately) that broadcasters were breaching the ban. As a result John Major said that a review would be instituted to see if the ban needed to be tightened (Miller 1993e). However, within weeks, official sources were letting it be known that the ban could be lifted quickly pending progress of the peace process.

What emerges from the series of confrontations between broadcasters and government over the past twenty-five years is a picture in which the tendency is to ever greater restriction on the arena for public comment. This has functioned in tandem with a tendency within broadcasting organisations to operate tighter and tighter editorial procedures in order to pre-empt government intervention. We have already seen how this operates in times of controversy. Let us now look at the effect of such pressure and intimidation on broadcasting guidelines that govern routine reporting.

Self-censorship

According to Anthony Smith, 'caution has grown over broadcasting like lichen over standing stones' (cited in Briggs 1979: 246). Indeed, it can be argued that the conflict in Northern Ireland has resulted in a substantial chill factor throughout the whole media system in Britain.

The Reference Upwards System

The development of an internal system of control whereby journalistic activities are increasingly subject to scrutiny by top management – the reference upwards system – was set in motion in 1971. This followed the attacks on the broadcasters and the agreement on the part of both the BBC and ITA that they were against the 'terrorists'. The system has two main components: first, the referral procedure through which all programmes on Northern Ireland have to go; and second, the more specialised rules on interviewing members of republican organisations. The BBC's *News Guide*, produced in 1972, laid down that all reports on Northern Ireland should be referred to the Controller, Northern Ireland or other senior Belfast staff and that interviews with the IRA must be referred to Editor News and Current Affairs in London. The federated structure of the ITV network has meant that referral is in the first instance internal to the various television companies, with advice being sought from Ulster

Television. The ITC (formerly the IBA) has the final say, however, and there have been many examples of the IBA overruling individual programme companies since the 1970s.

The BBC standing instructions were reissued and tightened following the Carrickmore incident, strengthening the role of the Controller Northern Ireland (see Curtis 1984a). They were tightened again following the *Real Lives* episode. In an agreed statement the boards of management and governors stated that 'the Director-General has reinforced to all staff the vital importance of these procedures being strictly observed at all times' (cited in Rudin 1985: 288). The guidelines were reissued in 1987 and included a number of changes in relation to Northern Ireland.

In the 1980 guidelines 'all programme proposals having a bearing on Ireland as a whole and on Northern Ireland in particular' (BBC 1980b: 45) must be referred to the Controller Northern Ireland. By 1987 this had been tightened further to include 'all programmes and items' with the added rider that 'Programme proposals and responses to them should be confirmed in writing' (BBC 1987: 55).

The major development in the period between 1980 and 1987 was the evolution of the guidelines to deal with the rise of Sinn Féin in electoral politics. In 1980 proposals to interview members of 'terrorist organisations and those who are or may be associated with such organisations' had to be referred up to the head of department and from there to senior management for approval by the Director-General. There was though, a problem of definition which was to be resolved by reference to the Director of News and Current Affairs, Richard Francis, who would decide who he 'deemed' to be closely associated. Gerry Adams of Sinn Féin was deemed closely associated in 1981 and permission had to be sought from the DG to interview him (Curtis 1984a: 180). This system rapidly became untenable with Sinn Féin's electoral success in 1982 and the 1983 election of Gerry Adams to the Westminster parliament. Thus by 1987 the BBC had evolved a two-tier system of referral for different categories of republican interviewee. In the case of members of Sinn Féin [37] the 'Head of Department must make a fundamental judgement' about the status of the interviewee and then follow either the established referral procedure to the Director-General or the alternative. This latter procedure is for elected representatives 'who are to be interviewed in connection with their legitimate activities' (BBC 1987: 56). These interviews need only be referred to the Editor, News and Current Affairs, Northern Ireland, although 'when in doubt', journalists are advised to consider referring to senior management and to the Assistant Director-General (BBC 1987: 57). By 1989, the guidelines had developed to cover the preferred hostile style with which members of Sinn Féin are to be interviewed: 'Generally whenever interviews are allowed they should be used sparingly, short clips often being more appropriate than long extracts. Challenging questions should be used to get valid contributions to the examination of the issues' (BBC 1989a: 79).

At the end of the 1980 and 1984 guidelines there is a paragraph which claims that the purpose of the revision of the reference procedures: 'is not to inhibit the proper pursuit of journalism, but to clarify procedures in the light of case histories studied by News and Current Affairs Editors since the Standing Instructions were first written in 1971. These directions should not therefore be read as restrictions' (BBC 1980b: 47; 1984: 53).

By 1987 even this modest statement is gone. A further change seems to be related to the BBC's embarrassment over the *Real Lives* case, to which the *Radio Times* had devoted its cover story only to find the programme pulled at the last minute. It requires that even publicity for BBC programmes be referred up: 'Because the public perception of a programme can be significantly affected by the way it is promoted – in the press, in *Radio Times* and over BBC airwaves – the promotion of programmes affecting Northern Ireland must be referred ... Some instances will require specific clearance by Managing Directors' (BBC 1987: 55).

In the 1987 guidelines there is a one-page section dealing with terrorism in general in which it is noted that the 'BBC is opposed to terrorism'. It is also noted that 'some terrorist activity enjoys virtually no popular support and is totally reprehensible'. But 'it is also true that sometimes yesterday's terrorists have become today's prime ministers and that one man's [sic] terrorist may be another man's freedom fighter' (BBC 1987: 81). The guidelines then go on to demonstrate this last statement in practice by indicating that BBC guidelines have different procedures for interviewing 'terrorists' in the UK context than for those overseas. In the latter case referral to the news editor or head of department is acceptable. By 1989, all proposals to interview 'terrorists' from anywhere in the world required to be referred through senior line management and the Controller, Editorial Policy, John Wilson. This development apparently occurred under the direction of John Birt on the grounds that maintaining a separate editorial policy on Northern Ireland left the BBC in an anomalous position. [38] It has however, raised the difficulty of how to define a 'terrorist' rather more sharply, especially given the changing international status of groups such as the ANC and the PLO.

In December 1989 the BBC's guidelines were published for the first time, doing away with the odd status of the News and Current Affairs Index. [39] The new guidelines exhibit a further tightening of rules and some further extension of their scope. Referral is now to be conducted not only at the planning stages of a programme but for the duration of the production process.

> Staff outside Northern Ireland must without fail seek advice from and discuss with local staff their programme plans affecting Northern Ireland, *at all stages ... It is very important that the BBC in Belfast is kept aware of the evolution of projects, including the inevitable changes which take place as ideas are developed.* (BBC 1989c: 38, original emphasis)

In 1987, the guidelines covered *interviews* with 'terrorists'. By 1989 they had widened to cover all 'terrorist' *appearances*.

> Publicly evident events like gunshots at gravesides and other demonstrations at funerals are common in Northern Ireland. As part of the political scene they should be reported when relevant. There are other managed events of a surreptitious kind over which special care must be taken: restricted news conferences, demonstrations of manpower such as road blocks, or training sessions. Sometimes reporters will be invited to such events, perhaps at instant notice. Sometimes the BBC will be supplied with material, maybe a video. *Referral is always necessary in these cases although occasionally it will be after the event because of pressure of circumstances.* (BBC 1989c: 81, original emphasis).

Following the funerals resulting from the Gibraltar killings there had been some debate about outlawing media coverage of paramilitary funerals, and especially military salutes and other ceremonies. These debates have obviously had their effect.

The internal rules of referral for ITV companies have also been strengthened. Both the 1979 and 1985 versions of the guidelines require that producers should not plan to interview members of a proscribed organisation without 'previous discussion' with the company's top management. The proposal then has to be referred to the IBA if it · is decided to go ahead (Independent Broadcasting Authority 1979; 1985: 8.1[i]). In the 1991 ITC programme code, which replaced the guidelines, a producer needs to gain 'the specific consent of the licensee's chief executive or most senior programme executive' (Independent Television Commission 1991: 5.2). In addition all commercial television companies are 'required' to consult the ITC on interviews with members of proscribed organisations. Along with alterations in the BBC guidelines, cited above, the ITC now requires (from 1991) that film of 'a volley of shots or a show of arms by men in hoods' be referred to the most senior programme executive or designated alternative within the company before they are included in programmes.

BBC guidance on Northern Ireland increased from three paragraphs in 1972 to just over four pages in 1980, four and a half pages in 1984, just over five in 1987 and finally to nearly eight in 1989. In 1980, 1984 and 1987, the guidelines included one page on 'Terrorism'. By 1989, this had increased to nearly six pages. The IBA guidelines, simply headed 'Crime, Anti-social Behaviour, etc.' in 1985 were two pages in length. By 1991 the additional word 'terrorism' had been added to the heading and the guidelines were three and a half pages in length.

There is a long history of broadcasters agreeing with the official definition of the republican opposition. Lord Hill's declaration that 'as between the British Army and the gunmen the BBC is not and cannot be impartial' (Hill 1974: 209), set the pattern. Echoing this David Nicholas, editor of ITN, objected to the introduction of the broadcasting ban on the grounds that ITN interviews with Sinn Féin were conducted 'responsibly':

Because we all understand what these extremist organisations stand for is abhorrent to many people. British public opinion has never been more resolute than it is now, in my opinion, in defeating terrorism and that owes a lot to the full and frank reporting that we've been able to conduct on Northern Ireland over nineteen years. (ITN 22.00, 19 October 1988)

Here Nicholas claims to act 'responsibly' in the name of 'public opinion' – opinion which, he maintains, the broadcasters have helped to create with their 'full and frank' coverage.

Some journalists who have argued that the ban is counterproductive implicitly agree with supporters of the ban that the main object of covering Sinn Féin and the IRA is not to explain the conflict but to discredit the republicans as part of the campaign to defeat 'terrorism'. Their difference with supporters of the ban is that they see it as a means of 'inhibiting' the exposure of Sinn Féin.

The close coincidence of the views of the broadcasters and the state on 'terrorism' has meant that Sinn Féin have never been allowed them what Douglas Hurd called an 'easy platform'. On the contrary, much coverage has been directed at discrediting the party as part of the campaign to defeat 'terrorism'. One of the objections of the broadcasters has been that they no longer have control over their part of the battle. In part, the caution of the broadcasters is not simply about being intimidated by the government; it also includes a strategy to defend their legitimacy to the outside world. Thus broadcasters are opposed to the notice. But they are not in favour of free reporting. They would prefer that the government trust them not to be really impartial.

Conclusion

The legitimation of government activity rests centrally on its claim to be democratic and thus to have the monopoly control over the means of legitimate violence. Attempts to reconstitute the impulse to censorship as 'restrictions' in the interests of 'national security' are therefore a central feature of government rhetoric. During the *Real Lives* controversy Mrs Thatcher argued:

The BBC, in my view – because we don't censor, never do, we request sometimes – should never show things which help anyone who wishes to further their cause by the use of violence. And that is why we said, have a look at it again. The BBC and the Governors who are ultimately responsible to the public did have a look at it again, and have made their decision, and I am very pleased with it. (Cited in *World in Action* 1988)

This legitimation was returned to again during the attempt to prevent the broadcast of 'Death on the Rock'. In his letter to Marmaduke Hussey, Foreign Secretary Howe emphasised that 'there is no question of the Government seeking to muzzle the media. There is no thought of ministers challenging the constitutional independence of the broadcasting authorities' (*Independent*, 7 May 1988).

The tendency on the part of the government has been to try to incorporate and coopt the media as part of a national security design – as simply another weapon in the 'fight against terrorism'. This strategy has met with some success in that, as we have seen, broadcasters have tended on the whole to accept the state definition of the conflict in Ireland as 'terrorism' versus 'democracy'. However, this has in some ways damaged the position of the broadcasters.

In Northern Ireland there was a souring of relations between the republican movement and the media in the late 1980s (Hearst 1989; Bolton 1990; *Journalist* 1991). In Britain, BBC executives now complain of 'a fundamental change of attitudes in the crowds' (Birt 1990: 14) towards the cameras. John Birt has argued that this is related to a perception that camera crews are on the side of the police:

During the Trafalgar Square [poll tax] riot there were cries of 'Maggie's Boys'. At Bournemouth it was 'police narks' and 'You're on their side'. What this suggests – and this is the firm conviction of BBC crews with long experience on the ground – is a growing perception among crowds that all film shot during public disturbances can and will be used against them, in court cases; that broadcasters are no longer there simply to observe and report; that we are in effect gatherers of evidence and – by only one remove – an extension of the arm of authority. (Birt 1990: 14–15)

For their part the media are legitimated precisely by their apparent distance from the state. It is of crucial importance that the broadcasters can present themselves as having different concerns from those of the state, even where these result in them taking a public position in alliance with the state. In fact, even within this perspective, there can be a real divergence of interest between broadcasters and the government. Broadcasting is not a simple instrument of government, nor on the other hand is it an open door for the powerless. The extent to which the broadcasters can present themselves as independent of the government depends partly on their collusion with state views of the conflict in Ireland, but also, importantly, on the continued interrogation of the actions of both the state and the insurgents. The ability of broadcasting to provide an intelligible account of the conflict depends on the extent to which such interrogations continue to be broadcast. We will assess some of the other sources of resistance to the complete closure of the media system in later chapters. For the present let us note that what remains of public service broadcasting in Britain can still muster significant resources to investigate and critique government policy, albeit that, in practice, such critiques tend to be hemmed in by formidable limits and restrictions. If broadcasters go too far they are very likely to be subject to attacks from government and sections of the press. One result of this is that programmes are not made, or are censored before they can be shown. Between 1959 and 1993 over 100 programmes on Northern Ireland were banned, censored or delayed (Jempson and Curtis 1993).

Government strategy has been to limit and preferably eliminate any hearing for its enemies in Ireland, while at the same time ensuring that its activities are portrayed as favourably as possible. By 1979 the government had largely succeeded in excluding republican paramilitaries from television. It is worth remembering that the last republican paramilitary was interviewed in 1979 and that the last British television interview with a member of the IRA was in 1974. The rise of Sinn Féin created new problems for both the government and the broadcasters. The most important reason for objections to the *Real Lives* was that Martin McGuinness, who, in the conventional register, is an 'extremist', was portrayed as an elected politician who appeared at the domestic, personal and political levels as 'ordinary' and 'rational'.

By the late 1980s the British government had been relatively successful in excluding analysis of Irish republicanism and its armed variety from the British broadcasting system. Active members of the IRA were not interviewed and coverage of Sinn Féin was minimal and generally hostile. However, in government circles, success was thought to be only partial. The desire to remove the legal political part of the Provisional republican couplet from television altogether resulted in the most direct and extensive interference with freedom of expression in the history of British broadcasting. The use of the law, intimidation and direct censorship do not exhaust the information management repertoire of the government. The next two chapters explore the tactics used in public relations strategies.

2

The Development of
Propaganda Strategies

Although the same channels of communication are available to those involved in protecting the existing order, they seldom manipulate them so skilfully as their opponents. (Brigadier Frank Kitson 1971: 17)

Let us assume Section 31 has been lifted and an RTE reporter is free to interview Gerry Adams in the wake of the Enniskillen atrocity ... I believe that by manipulating the concept of consensus the Provos can always draw and often win any such interview even if the interview takes place within minutes of the most appalling atrocity. (Eoghan Harris, RTE television producer, November 1987)

The terrorists, working through their political wings and their own often highly experienced propagandists, can also relatively easily get some of their general propaganda into the mass media. Such propagandising does not necessarily involve infiltrating fully trained terrorist activists into media organisations. The terrorists can readily find useful idiots to latch on to cryptoterrorist propaganda and parrot its slogans in the name of radical and critical comment. According to these trendy journalists and left-wing politicians, Northern Ireland is a brutally repressive, colonial society ... With independent journalists like this, the Provisional Sinn Féin hardly needs to conduct a political campaign to change mainland opinion. (Paul Wilkinson 1990: 31)

Information versus Propaganda

Journalists covering Northern Ireland routinely refer to the 'propaganda war' which accompanies the conflict. Some of the participants in the conflict are keen to distance themselves from such a label. In a policy statement some years ago the Northern Ireland Information Service drew a distinction between 'propaganda', which is the 'manipulation of facts and non-facts in such a way as to achieve an objective which is basically to mislead', and 'Information', which:

> is the dissemination of facts which are designed to inform and educate. It is very important to draw this distinction when looking at the problems faced by the public service in its task of – and responsibility for – informing the public. (Reproduced in Hardy 1983)

The NIO, so the argument goes, is automatically disadvantaged in a propaganda war because it has to fight fair. The Director of Information at the NIO, David Gilliland, argued this point to an American journalist in 1981:

> A government cannot win a propaganda war. Terrorists and their spokesmen can say or do anything they like and the perception becomes the fact. We can only hammer away at telling the truth, but the truth gets overwhelmed in the sea of propaganda. (Hickey 1981: 13)

In practice, the term propaganda is applied almost exclusively to the media strategies of 'terrorists'. But in the contemporary literature there is almost no direct investigation of the 'terrorists'' media strategies (e.g. Alexander and Latter 1990; Alexander and Picard 1991; Alali and Eke 1991). Some writers analyse the activities of 'terrorists' without so much as speaking with any member of the organisation they seek to comment on. Joanne Wright's study of the propaganda activities of the IRA and Rote Armee Fraktion (RAF) entirely lacks, as far as can be seen, any contact with members or former members of the republican movement. Part of her research, she says, was undertaken in the Linenhall Library in Belfast (Wright 1991: vii), itself only a ten-minute taxi ride from the Republican Press Centre in the Falls Road.

The Power of Propaganda

The importance of defining an organisation as propagandist is that propaganda is widely assumed to be very powerful. Its effects are seen as insidious and unconscious. In this view, government officials, academics and journalists need to be constantly on their guard lest they be unwittingly subverted by 'propaganda'. According to Paul Wilkinson, terrorist propaganda is especially worrisome:

> We should never underestimate their skill in disseminating ... illusions among the public and among politicians and other influential groups. At its most subtle and effective, this form of propaganda campaign may more than compensate for the military weaknesses and security failures of a terrorist organisation. If government, faced with these more sophisticated challenges, do not succeed in dealing effectively with the terrorists' political and psychological subversion, they may indeed be on the slide to disaster. (Wilkinson 1990: 30)

Amongst counterinsurgency writers and politicians in Britain 'terrorist propaganda' organisations are held to be highly effective in their use of the media. This perception can fairly be called the orthodox position. On the other hand, there is also a diametrically opposed view to be found on the left and in some Irish republican writings. In this view it is the 'British propaganda machine' which is able to 'use' the media almost at whim in order to dominate news agendas.

Defining Propaganda

It is perhaps wise to pause here to consider some definitional aspects of propaganda. It is plain that in common usage, the term propaganda is pejorative. Some writers are quite happy to apply the term only to those groups of which they disapprove. Thus there is a large body of writing in English on the propaganda of enemies of Western nations, such as the Soviet Union or the 'terrorists'. It is worth looking briefly at the definitions of propaganda used in such writing in order to reveal the assumptions behind it. Both Wright (1991: 73) and Tugwell (1987: 409) use the definition established by NATO: 'Any information, ideas, doctrines or special appeals disseminated to influence the opinion, emotions, attitudes or behaviour of any specified group in order to benefit the sponsor either directly or indirectly.' This is clearly not in principle a partisan definition, but in the work of the counterinsurgency theorist it is only applied to the enemies of the West. Such writers are apparently unable to conceive that Western governments might also engage in 'special appeals' to their own benefit and so discussions of the media strategies of governments as propaganda are sparse indeed. The activities of Western governments are referred to (in passing) as 'counter-propaganda' (Wright 1991: 207; Alexander and Latter 1990: 24). Indeed the suggestion that governments may engage in propaganda is seen by some as perilously close to swallowing the 'propaganda' of the 'terrorists'; Wilkinson argues that one of the 'key propaganda themes' of 'terrorists' is 'to undermine all claims to legitimacy on the part of the incumbents ... It is no longer they who are legitimate and whose authority and word you should believe, but we the terrorist organisation' (Wilkinson 1990: 30). But, it is clearly demonstrable using official definitions, that the British government and its agencies have engaged in overt and covert propaganda in Northern Ireland.

On the other hand there are some writers who use the term propaganda to refer only to the activities of the British government in Northern Ireland. This is overly simplistic. The British government does engage in propaganda activities in Northern Ireland which are not matched by any of the other participants, but it is too simple to call the rest of the propaganda simply the dissemination of information. The differences in methods and tactics that do exist are identifiable. These relate to such factors as resources, cultural capital and the legal framework rather than simply whether an organisation has links with 'terrorism' or the government. We should remember that there are a myriad contending organisations competing for media space. In addition to the institutions of the British government, the republican movement and the loyalist paramilitaries, there are a range of political parties, pressure groups, trades unions, religious organisations, community groups, etc. which routinely compete for space in the media. Recognising this is a first step towards thinking in more complex ways about media strategies.

Towards a Neutral Definition?

Some critics have argued that the term propaganda should be used in a non-pejorative or 'neutral' sense. One widely cited definition is that of Jowett and O'Donnell: 'Propaganda is the deliberate and systematic attempt to shape perceptions, manipulate cognitions, and direct behaviour to achieve a response that furthers the desired intent of the propagandist' (Jowett and O'Donnell 1992: 4).

This is not very different from the NATO definition used by the counterinsurgents and cited above. It is, however, hard to resist the temptation to use the term pejoratively, especially when the authors go on to contrast the manipulative intent of the propagandist with the 'free and open exchange of ideas' (1992: 8). Such an exchange, guaranteed, they argue, by the First Amendment in the US, is 'in the long run ... the greatest deterrent to the misuse of propaganda' (1992: 271). A society without propaganda would evidently be one with no serious divisions of interest in which disputes were adjudicated on by free, fair, and above all rational, debate. In the real world, however, things are not so agreeably simple. The central problem with attempts at workable definitions of propaganda is that the question of who is the propagandist is always contested. The identification of a propagandist in the real world is a matter of political argument which is linked to specific interests and ideologies. This does not mean that there are not, in principle, ways of evaluating the information (or propaganda) for accuracy or of deciding between competing versions of reality on the basis of the available evidence.

In the present work it is recognised that propaganda is a 'matter of the politics of information' (Robins et al. 1987: 8). This reminds us that propaganda is only a small part of the media and information strategies of governments. As we have seen, the entire apparatus of government secrecy and the intimidation and regulation of media institutions are the ever-present companions of the media strategies of the powerful. The capacity of non-governmental organisations to pass laws and regulate media institutions is obviously limited. [1]

The next section examines changes in official British policy on Northern Ireland and relates these to changes in information management and organisation. I will suggest that these changes came about partly as a response to the political problems of pursuing a strategy of containment. Thus the scaling down of army responsibility both operationally and in terms of information strategy occurred partly because it was a way of trying to manage deep divisions within the state apparatus. The gradual and uneven increases in PR sophistication and the increasing priority given to media management has been a response both to events within Northern Ireland and to struggles within political organisations over the importance of information work.

Changes in information strategies since the 1960s

The unionist Prime Minister Basil Brooke created a Cabinet Publicity Committee in 1943 and the Information Service as a separate entity came into existence in 1955. But it was not until the mid-1960s that 'modern' ideas about marketing and image entered Northern Ireland politics under the impetus of Finance Minister Terence O'Neill. [2] In 1962 former *Belfast Telegraph* journalist Tommy Roberts was appointed as Public Relations officer at the Ulster Office in London by O'Neill, in the face of Cabinet Office objections. His job was to remedy the 'bad industrial press' which O'Neill thought that Northern Ireland was getting (O'Neill 1972: 38). In 1963 O'Neill became Prime Minister and Roberts, while remaining based in London, operated informally as his press secretary on his almost annual visits to the US (O'Neill 1972: 88).

On the election of O'Neill's successor James Chichester-Clark as Prime Minister, some members of the Cabinet decided that the new Prime Minister needed a press secretary. Information Officer David Gilliland was offered the newly created post. A New York public relations firm was also appointed in 1970. Its official function was 'promoting economic investment in Northern Ireland'

(*Stormont Hansard*, 12 February 1970: 158). However, less than a week after this announcement, it issued a statement headed 'For your information only and not for publication'. It alleged that civil rights marches: 'must be viewed in their true context – [as] a calculated political offensive by self-styled disciples of Lenin, Mao, Castro and other idols of international extremism' (*Irish Times*, 18 February 1970). Much to the government's embarass-ment, this background briefing was promptly published in the Dublin and Belfast press.

The Coming Crisis

As the conflict over civil rights mounted in the late 1960s the pressure to explain what was happening in the North intensified and the potential contradictions of the unionist public relations approach of trying to show the positive side of 'Ulster' became more and more exposed. The first and major problem that the government faced in the aftermath of the police attack on civil rights marchers in Derry, on 5 October 1968, was the realisa-tion amongst journalists that something very odd had been happening. Twenty years later Mary Holland of the *Observer* recalled that:

> even allowing for all that's happened in between, the shock of what happened in Derry on October 5th still sears the memory. As far as we were concerned this was a British city and these were British police. In 1968 I'd never seen a policeman use a baton let alone charge a crowd of demonstra-tors, trapped in a narrow street, with such naked eagerness. (*Irish Times*, 3 October 1988)

Jon Snow, now of *Channel 4 News*, has recounted that:

> All of us who went to Northern Ireland for the first time in the early seventies were absolutely shattered by what we saw. We were shocked by the housing, we were shocked by the poverty, we were shocked that this was part of Britain that appeared to be 50 years behind what we had grown up amongst. ('Pack up the Troubles', *Critical Eye*, Channel 4, 24 October 1991)

Lack of Policy

Although there was pressure for reform from the Labour government at Westminster (Callaghan 1973), the Unionists decided that the problem in the North was one not of substance but of image. Five days after the RUC batoned civil rights marchers on the streets of Derry on 5 October 1968 the American Consul-General in Belfast visited the Stormont Cabinet Secretariat and was briefed by the Prime Minister and senior officials on the situation. According to his reports to Washington the government did not appear to have any plans to deal with the substance of the civil rights grievances. Instead they were acting to try and improve the perception of Northern Ireland (Cronin 1987: 284–5). In the words of one information officer who worked at Stormont at the time: 'At that time there was no actual message that could [be] put out other than to say that the Unionist government was a happy band of brothers who were doing the best they could to stamp the Catholics in the face because they were very difficult. But there was no line of policy at all' (personal interview, Belfast, August 1989). In these circumstances, on 23 January 1969 the Northern Ireland Information Service issued a long press release stressing not 'what is wrong with Northern Ireland' but 'what is right in Ulster' (Cronin 1987: 289–90). As the American Consul-General reported back to the USA:

> The government feels that the Ulster image is vital to the province's economic progress ... Stormont has always placed a primary emphasis on attracting industry to this area. Its trump has been the stable and peaceful social and political environment as well as initial financial incentives. The government has voiced its apprehension that continued bad publicity will hurt the province's chances for economic growth. (cited in Cronin 1987: 289)

Inexperience of PR

The lack of clear policy and the concentration on image by the government put a heavy burden on the information service. As the media deluged Belfast and Derry the Government Information

Service at Stormont was overwhelmed by demands for information. Stormont had moved quickly in late 1968 to appoint a UTV producer, Bill McGookin, in a part-time position as the first RUC press officer. In March 1969 the appointment was made full-time and a press office was set up staffed by McGookin and one police officer. [3] The army PR department at the Lisburn HQ had been a quiet backwater. In 1968 a new PRO, Colin Wallace, was appointed and he was to accompany the British army into Derry on that first day in August 1969. For the RUC the media, especially the non-local media, were an oppositional force. Maurice Tugwell has written: 'In the RUC "PR" itself was a completely new idea. At first there was a tendency in the RUC to hostility towards a news media that seemed to be implacably biased against the force' (Tugwell 1980: 247). This is partially confirmed by RUC press officer Bill McGookin:

> Believe it or not, when this trouble first erupted in Northern Ireland the RUC had no guns, it had no information at all ... with the result that when the world fell in, so to speak, and the news media of the world descended on them ... the RUC simply didn't have the structure of the means of explaining its position, and the result was that the RUC received a very very severe jugging from local, national and international opinion. And it took long years to retrieve the situation. (cited in Hamilton-Tweedale 1987: 292)

More staff joined the Stormont Information Service during 1969, but they were still overwhelmed with around five information officers. As one *Guardian* reporter, writing in 1970, put it:

> The cultural shock of the mass descent of Fleet St is still not over. In the early days the whole machinery of official information was disastrously geared to the requirements of the occasional facility trip. It certainly was not built to withstand the Attila like assault it got after the first riots in Londonderry. (*UK Press Gazette*, 6 July 1970)

The historical insulation of Northern Ireland from the world meant that public relations techniques were woefully inadequate. As David Gilliland has acknowledged, at that time he was simply 'inexperienced' (*Belfast Telegraph*, 21 May 1987). Prior to the civil rights agitation little government advertising or promotional publicity had been issued. *Ulster Commentary*, a local freesheet, first published in March 1946 (*Newsletter* 1 July 1975), was still being produced and in December 1968 the current issue was ridiculed by the *Irish Times* for claiming that Northern Ireland was 'one of the most peaceful countries in the world' (*Irish Times*, 17 December 1968).

One indication of the inexperience in official PR was that in September 1970 the *Belfast Telegraph* complained that the Information Service was releasing press statements without a phone number on the releases for journalists to ring back (*Belfast Telegraph*, 30 September 1970). The method for putting across the message about the image of Northern Ireland was also not particularly sophisticated. As one information officer recalled: 'In those days I don't think any of us realised that there was a great deal more to dealing with journalists than just pouring them gallons of drink and being a hail-fellow-well-met' (personal interview, Belfast, August 1989).

The Role of the Media

Although both local and national news had reported the growing unrest in Northern Ireland from the Divis riots in 1964, it was not until the 5 October demonstration in Derry that the North really took off for the national and international media (Butler 1991; Cathcart 1984). Before 1968 very few networked current affairs programmes had covered the political situation in Northern Ireland and two that were made were not shown in Northern Ireland after UTV vetoed them. The British press also seems to have largely ignored Stormont (Downing 1982: 128 and 131). Mary Holland, who was then writing for the *Observer*, has recalled her scepticism about the existence of discrimination; it was only after persistent phone calls from Gerry Fitt MP that she was persuaded to cover civil rights activist Austin Currie squatting in a council house allocated to a young single Protestant. She thought it was a good story but even then 'the enormity of what I was seeing still didn't really hit me' (*Irish Times*, 3 October 1988). Fitt persuaded her 'reluctantly' to go to Derry the week before the 5 October demonstration. Back in London at an editorial conference she described what she had seen and learnt of discrimination in housing and gerrymandering in Derry: 'The people around the table listened with absolute incredulity. David Astor, the editor of the *Observer*, cut me short. "Write it", he said "Take as much space as you like, just write it"' (*Irish Times*, 3 October 1988).

The widespread sympathy for the civil rights protesters among the British media was to change after the IRA campaign began in earnest in 1971. Chibnall argues that 'press ideology is profoundly *liberal*' (1977: 19; original emphasis) and so:

> As long as extra-parliamentary opposition was restricted to civil rights campaigning it could be treated as a legitimate area of controversy about which sensible and responsible people could hold different opinions. But as soon as the relatively peaceful protester gave way to the petrol bomber and then the gunman, and opposition became insurrection, responsible debate had to be restricted to the discussion of the most effective means of eradicating the behaviour. (Chibnall 1977: 19)

This attributes too much of the change in coverage to the concept of press ideology. It is a 'media centric' (Schlesinger 1990) account which assumes that changes in journalistic practice can be explained as emanating more or less directly from changes in ruling-class ideology. In this version, the government and the forces of law and order don't have to *do* anything to convince journalists. The mere presence of the British army is enough to secure a kneejerk response from the media. However, it is clear that there was a major change in the public relations of the British government between 1969 and 1971. At least part of the explanation must relate to the *source* organisations which supply journalists with information. The Government Information Service at Stormont were overwhelmed, the RUC had only just appointed its first press officer and both organisations had little credibility and authoritativeness for journalists. After all, civil rights demands for reform were being echoed by the Westminster government. [4] Once the army moved in, the ideological resources of the British state were tied closely to the defence of that position. While the Information Service at Stormont expanded quite rapidly, army HQ moved much faster. The army's experience in fifty-three 'operations of the counter revolutionary type' (Ministry of Defence 1969) between 1945 and August 1969 meant that it gave a much higher priority to PR than did either the Northern Ireland government or the RUC. The army press office had increased in size from just two staff in 1968 to forty by 1971. It also began twenty-four-hour operations (Foot 1990: 9), something which the NIO did only during crisis situations. The massive expansion of the army press office meant that it rapidly became the most prominent source for journalists. To be sure, there were many journalists whose kneejerk response was to support the army, but in explaining changes in coverage by reference to 'press ideology', the huge increase in army public relations activity is assumed to be inconsequential.

When the army was brought in its attitude to the problem relied heavily on past experience of counterinsurgency campaigns. The tarnished public image of the police, together with the fact that it was overstretched and understaffed, partly conditioned its relationship with the army. In the view of one information officer at Stormont at the time:

> You've got to remember that the army were very much in the driving seat in those days. They were the hard men, they had the numbers. The RUC were seen as a bunch of wankers. The Northern Ireland Office were just wets who didn't know what time of day it was. The army felt that they were the people who knew how to handle a situation of this sort, they'd done it in Malaya and they'd done it God knows where. And they were being held back in Northern Ireland by all these wets and incompetent policemen. (personal interview, Belfast, August 1989)

But by 1971 many in the army felt that the propaganda war against the IRA was beginning to be lost, especially in the aftermath of internment. [5] The response was the setting up of the Information Policy Unit in late 1971. Officially its role was to supplement the work of the army press office in releasing information to the media. In fact, this was a cover for its real function, which was 'psychological operations' (psyops), otherwise known as disinformation. Information Policy worked closely with the intelligence community and the Foreign Office. Hugh Mooney of the Information Research Department at the Foreign and Commonwealth Office joined Information Policy in November 1972. IRD was itself closely involved with MI6 and had experience of disinformation work in previous colonial type conflicts. But Information Policy also worked with MI5 and army intelligence against a background of institutional rivalry and conflict. According to Duncan Campbell:

> The intelligence scene in Northern Ireland in 1973 was a nightmare. The MoD ordered a new head of army information services to take joint control of both public relations and Psyops. Whitehall wanted propaganda in the province under control. But the Psyops unit was also working with and to the instructions of MI5 and Secret Intelligence Service (SIS or MI6) officials in the North, who were openly at war with each other as well as, often, the civil ministries. (Campbell 1990: 16)

The effect of such divisions on the credibility of the Army Information Service was quite severe. David McKittrick (1990: 5) of the *Independent* summed it up in the following terms: 'It came to be regarded as probably the most unreliable of the many agencies involved in the conflict earning itself the nickname of "the Lisburn Lie machine". The IRA was found to be more truthful than the army.'

According to some writers, this state of disarray was not matched on the republican side. Maurice Tugwell [6] has written that the problem was that 'normal army public relations' staffs were only skilled in dealing with the press in 'a society free of mass indoctrination. This was not the same as bearing the brunt of a sophisticated propaganda attack' (Tugwell 1980: 247) such as Sinn Féin were alleged to have carried out. However, the Republican Press Centre only came into existence in 1970 *after* the NIO, RUC and army had increased their PR operations. By contrast with official PR it was not formally organised and statements were delivered by hand to news rooms. Sinn Féin was not the large political organisation it is today and its contacts with journalists tended to be informal. In that temporal sense it was the IRA whose activities were counter-propaganda. The public relations skills of some leading IRA members were also, to say the least, embryonic. According to Simon Winchester of the *Guardian*, IRA press conferences were 'usually marked by considerable confusion'. He has described a meeting between the press and IRA leader Seamus Twomey, in 1972:

> This was a great cloak and dagger operation with people arriving at staggered times, and ostensibly going to see a homeless family's relief centre. Unfortunately for the IRA, the word got out, and so the hall was besieged with reporters, making it quite obvious to any passing army patrol what was going on. Mr Twomey arrived very late, and seemed not quite aware of what he was supposed to do. (cited in Curtis 1984a: 264)

Following the introduction of direct rule and the return of the Labour government in late 1974 it is clear that tensions between the army and the NIO became greatly exacerbated with Merlyn Rees's tenure as Secretary of State. The existence of the 'black propaganda' unit at army HQ in Lisburn on occasion caused difficulties for the NIO in the sense that the unit operated against the NIO and in terms of its more general negative impact on the credibility of the British government in Northern Ireland (Foot 1990; Miller 1993b).

Ulsterisation, Criminalisation, Normalisation and the Primacy of the Police

Following the Ulster Workers Council (UWC) strike through which the strikers brought down the power-sharing executive, the British government resigned itself to the containment of the conflict and set about trying rigorously to redefine the conflict in Northern Ireland in military and law and order terms rather than as a political problem. This meant a shift in the day-to-day running of security matters from the army to the police under a policy known as the primacy of the police. The army's presence was gradually scaled down and, officially at least, its only role was to support the police. This had the result of ensuring that a greater proportion of those killed in Northern Ireland would be RUC officers and UDR soldiers, and a lesser proportion from

British army regiments. At the same time the policy of criminalisation was adopted in relation to paramilitary organisations, pre-eminently republican groups. Secretary of State William Whitelaw had granted paramilitary prisoners special category status in 1972, which meant that they were effectively treated as prisoners of war. This was now withdrawn.

Both Ulsterisation and criminalisation were consistent with the British attempt to normalise the conflict by labelling the armed actions of the IRA as simply criminal and by claiming that these criminals were dealt with by means of the civil law (albeit with extensive emergency additions). Republican claims that they were engaged in a war to end the British occupation of the six counties were thus less easy to sustain than when the British had more or less acknowledged the war situation by allowing special category status.

During the UWC strike army information officers had regularly undermined the Secretary of State, Merlyn Rees (Miller 1993b) and so attempts were made to curtail the activities of the Army Information Service. The introduction of the policies of Ulsterisation and criminalisation meant the radical pruning of the army press office. The NIO set up a committee which it claimed was to coordinate information policy. It was, according to one NIO official, 'the beginning of putting the brakes on the army' (personal interview, Belfast, August 1989).

The army stopped twenty-four-hour operations in 1977, reducing to eighteen and then twelve hours. By 1983 the press office closed at 6 p.m. with one press officer on call. In February 1976 the army had more than forty press officers; by 1981 there were twenty-one including seven at HQ in Lisburn (Curtis 1984a: 253). By 1989 the army press office was down to a total of three press officers in headquarters. The RUC's press operation was correspondingly expanded. The army was now instructed to refer all questions about security matters to the police. Following the removal of Colin Wallace from Information Policy for allegedly leaking classified information,[7] the army was also instructed that statements about security incidents must be passed to the NIO so that 'a view' could be taken on them. [8] But the RUC was not above suspicion and the ruling that security statements on serious issues be checked by the NIO was also applied to the police.

The ending of active psychological operations in Northern

Ireland had much to do with changes in British strategy. The shift to normalisation would not support an active disinformation policy. However, the curbing of the power of the army, which normalisation secured, can also be seen as an attempt by the Northern Ireland Office to resolve the serious internal divisions by gaining control over the army. The drive to reconstitute the conflict within social democratic norms required that the government appear to act within the civil law rather than in a manner more reminiscent of an anti-colonial counterinsurgency campaign. This is to say that Ireland was too close to home and too vulnerable to the spotlights of the international and British media to be treated in precisely the same way as previous colonial counterinsurgency campaigns. [9] My argument is, therefore, that the media themselves played a prominent role in spurring the search by the government for more 'legitimate' ways of describing the conflict.

The key pattern of public relations activities since the introduction of normalisation has been the gradual decline in the availability of security information. Starting with the army, the decline has continued with the police. By 1977: 'The "watchkeepers" who man the army press desk at Lisburn 24 hours a day, no longer volunteer blow by blow details of every attack and shooting incident. Instead they draw reporters attention only to the army's successes' (Ryder 1977). There was also a change in the language of public relations, shifting from the style of counterinsurgency to that of law and order and criminality: 'An incident that in the past would have been reported like this: "shots were fired at an army foot patrol in Belfast", might now be reported by the army like this: "There was an attempt to murder members of an army foot patrol in Belfast"' (Ryder 1977).

By 1980 this approach seems to have been proceeding quite effectively. According to Thames TV journalist Peter Gill:

> These obstacles are making it formidably difficult, sometimes impossible, to report on the Army's counter-insurgency role in a way that we would expect and rightly be expected to cover other people's wars ... New and unpublished restrictions on press coverage introduced earlier this year by army headquarters in Northern Ireland and the Royal Ulster Constabulary – restrictions dating from changes in command in both forces at

the turn of the year – mean that only the barest of information on incidents is released and little else ... There is in current force an overriding policy that Press attention on the army's role in Northern Ireland should be kept to an absolute minimum. No public justification for these restrictions has been offered, but the outlook seems to be that an absence of Press and particularly TV coverage may help in winding down the conflict. (Gill 1980)

Attempts at normalisation suffered a severe setback with the republican hunger strikes of 1980 and 1981. However, the attempt to normalise the conflict has continued ever since. In 1982 the RUC press office was merged with its Command Centre to form Force Control and Information Centre (FCIC). Uniformed police officers now answered calls from journalists as well as doing other tasks. This afforded less opportunity for journalists to get to know RUC spokespersons, giving rise to complaints from journalists who 'quickly renamed it the "Force Control *of* Information Centre"' (Ryder 1989: 233; original emphasis)

The new arrangement had the merit, from the point of view of normalisation, of centralising all operational information and making it more susceptible to control. It seems, however, that the reorganisation was also linked with the arrival of John Hermon as Chief Constable. In contrast with the previous Chief Constable, Sir Kenneth Newman, Hermon was very hostile to the media [10] and his instinct was to give out as little information as possible. In the view of some journalists, this defensiveness hampered the positive portrayal of the RUC.

In 1989 a special committee was set up to coordinate publicity for the twentieth anniversary in August of the redeployment of British troops. The Northern Ireland Information Strategy Group included representatives from Whitehall, the NIO, the RUC and the army. One of its major roles was 'to minimise the emphasis attached to the Army's involvement' (*Observer*, 13 August 1989). The army attempted to stay out of the picture, preferring to refer journalists to the NIO and the RUC. Requests for facilities and trips with army patrols were turned down.

In the late 1980s the RUC practice of detailing all security incidents ceased and the RUC adopted the policy of confirming some incidents only if journalists got to hear of them from other sources. This means that some security incidents are not reported at all and helps to foster the notion that Northern Ireland is 'getting back to normal'. In one example, a shooting incident in the Markets area of Belfast, which occurred in July 1990, was not reported in the local press. The RUC confirmed that the incident had taken place in response to an enquiry, a month later, from a journalist who had learnt of the incident from other sources. [11]

The Hunger Strikes and the Rise of Sinn Féin

In the 1940s and 1950s the Unionist government had spent many years trying to convince the British to employ an 'Ulsterman' in Washington or New York to counter republican propaganda. The British refused, but the H-Block prison protests were to awaken such interest in the US, some of it hostile to the British, that the Foreign Office finally appointed a press officer in New York in 1980. Three further appointments were made to British Information Service in New York by August 1981 (*Daily Telegraph*, 24 August 1981). Even then, the view in the civil service was that it was the British who lost the propaganda war on the hunger strikes (Gormally et al. 1993: 61). The propaganda campaign around the issue of criminalisation resulted in the biggest mass mobilisations since the civil rights marches. They also resulted in an increased spend on public relations at the NIO [12] and the distribution of a large number of pamphlets and leaflets world-wide (NIO 1980a, 1980b, 1981a, 1981b, 1981c, 1981d). Ironically, the H-Block protests were also a key spur for republican public relations.

As one commentator has put it, a consequence of the hunger strikes was that 'the IRA and Sinn Féin were immeasurably strengthened and gained a political cohesion which they never had before' (Smyth 1987: 188). According to leading Sinn Féin members, one key element that allowed for more effective public relations during the hunger strikes was the attempt by the government to close down the Press Centre and Sinn Féin newspaper *Republican News*. According to Danny Morrison, the then editor of *Republican News* and subsequently Sinn Féin's Director of Publicity, a new feature of 1981 was:

having a mass movement with a public leadership. Before 1978, if I had been doing an interview with you, I would never have given my right name. In 1978 when Roy Mason moved against the staff of the Republican Press Centre in Belfast and tried to get *Republican News* closed down, we all appeared in court charged in our own names with conspiracy and IRA membership. But his moving against us was so clumsy, it strengthened our position to such an extent that when the charges were dropped, we were all able to 'go public'. For the first time since Maire Drumm was killed in October 1976, [13] Sinn Féin had people standing up in public saying: 'I'm a member of Sinn Féin, the IRA is right, the armed struggle is legitimate, the Brits are wrong, the loyalists are wrong' and so on. This was a totally fresh approach. Before, our politics had always been talked about and sold beneath the counter. Now [they were] being put forward openly. (Morrison 1985: 88–9)

It was Bobby Sands' election to Westminster as the MP for Fermanagh/South Tyrone that launched Sinn Féin on to the electoral battlefield and demanded a much greater investment in media relations. In 1980 the Republican Press Centre in the Falls Road had only one full-time volunteer (Curtis 1984a: 273). In 1981, Richard McAuley told American journalist Neil Hickey 'Do you know the sum total of the famous republican propaganda machine everyone talks about? I'm it' (Hickey 1981: 26). By 1989 the Press Centre had three people in the press office plus Richard McAuley as Six-County Director of Publicity and Danny Morrison as national Director of Publicity. [14] Sinn Féin's Dublin office at this time included up to three people in the press office. In the early 1980s the centre apparently had no separate allocation of funds, and its phone bills were paid by *An Phoblacht/Republican News* (Curtis 1984a: 272). This was no longer the case by the early 1990s. [15] As a result of their entry into electoral politics many more Sinn Féiners came into contact with the media.

In the aftermath of the hunger strike there was a much greater emphasis in government public relations on promoting a positive image for Northern Ireland as part of the emphasis on the 'return to normal'. The Tourist Board became important in this regard, as did the Industrial Development Board, created in 1982. The task of the latter is the promotion of inward investment and job opportunities. From the beginning public relations was a major part of its function. The main objective in this area was 'to present a positive image of Northern Ireland and the IDB at home and abroad to enable IDB programmes to succeed in securing new employment opportunities' (IDB 1985: 14).

The Anglo-Irish Agreement

The signing of the Anglo-Irish Agreement was generally well received in the international media and in Britain and Dublin. Even right-wing papers like the *Sun* and the *Daily Express* supported the agreement, in opposition to unionist sentiment (Grattan 1988). It led, however, to a loyalist backlash and concerted criticism in parts of the local press, particularly the Unionist morning paper, the *Newsletter*. The opposition of loyalists to NIO policy meant a further shift in NIO public relations strategy. Now, there was heavy pressure on the *Newsletter* to change its policy on the agreement. This meant that *Newsletter* journalists were excluded from briefings and private dinners at Stormont. According to the editor of the *Newsletter*, Sam Butler:

> It means you're not invited to various receptions at Stormont and Hillsborough, you're not privy to the sorts of briefings that go on, and the Northern Ireland Office is particularly good at giving briefings to its friends. If you're not one of its friends then you don't get told basic information. (*Hard News,* Channel 4, 19 October 1989)

The key result of normalisation has not been that control shifted from the army to the RUC, but that the NIO became the lead department in all matters. This is reflected in the staffing of government information departments. In 1976 the army had forty press officers to the NIO's twenty-six. By 1981 it had around the same number (twenty-one in the army and twenty in the NIO). By 1989 the NIO had fifty staff, of whom more than twenty were information officers compared with three press officers in the army. The RUC meanwhile had sixty staff in FCIC, most of whom were police officers on rotation with the equivalent of seven and a half permanent civilian staff.

The Dual Strategy

The central approach of successive British governments in Northern Ireland has been one of containment. Home Secretary Reginald Maudling provided an early illustration of this when he memorably revealed that the aim of the British government was to reduce the violence to 'an acceptable level' (*Sunday Times* Insight Team 1972: 309). But, as O'Dowd et al. have pointed out, the strategy of containment is not simply about repression or counterinsurgency. When the British introduced direct rule to Northern Ireland in 1972 they followed a dual strategy in which they: 'Accelerated the drive for reforms and the reconstitution of the rule of law, while at the same time drawing upon the latest repertoire of counterinsurgency thinking and practices derived from colonial experiences elsewhere' (O'Dowd et al. 1980: 201). This strategy developed over time and has been inflected according to both the party in power and perhaps more importantly the balance of forces within the state. For example, the strategy of criminalisation adopted by the British state following the collapse of the power-sharing executive in 1974 stressed the essential criminality of the assault on the state by abolishing 'special category status' for political offences. During Roy Mason's term as Secretary of State, in the late 1970s, this was supplemented with an attempt to portray the problems of Northern Ireland as emanating not simply from 'terrorism' but also from the evils of unemployment. This compares with the approach of the Thatcher government, at least in the early 1980s, which introduced the rhetoric of self-reliance as well as cutbacks and increasing unemployment (O'Dowd et al. 1982). More recently there has been a much greater emphasis on social and economic matters and particularly on industrial regeneration and development. This priority runs in tandem with the campaign against 'terrorism'.

Most research studies which have concentrated on the analysis of news coverage or on the production of news have tended to ignore or play down attempts to communicate the reform part of the NIO strategy. Nevertheless, it has assumed a very important role in the approach of the British government, which stresses two basic messages: on the one hand that the problem is the terrorist 'assault on democracy' (NIO 1989: 20) and on the other that the people of 'Ulster' are 'a community on the move' in which local 'entrepreneurial flair' and 'Ulster generosity' are 'rendering bigotry irrelevant' (NIO 1989).

In 1989 the NIO issued a publicity booklet which contains its analysis of the conflict. The booklet begins with a black and white photo of the bombed-out wreckage of the main street of a small town in Northern Ireland, juxtaposed with a colour image of the same street after reconstruction. The accompanying text reads:

This is one of the small towns in Northern Ireland targeted by terrorists during the past twenty years. But townspeople refused to give up. Within hours the windows had been replaced and it was business as usual. Within months, roofs were repaired, walls rebuilt and the scarred facades repainted. Such spirited resolve is the real story of Northern Ireland and its people; a community that is carving out international respect for its resilience, work ethic, enterprise and hospitality.

This 'true face' is then contrasted with that promoted by the media: 'More and more there is world wide acceptance that this, not the media image of the masked terrorist, is the true face of Northern Ireland.'

It would seem from this argument that the Northern Ireland Office is not too keen on the images of violence which routinely fill television reports on the conflict in the North. These images are blamed on the media and there is an implicit call for more 'responsible' or 'realistic' representations. Yet such images are not only purveyed by the media themselves. In fact, the image of the 'masked terrorist' (Figure 2.1) is taken from a Northern Ireland Office television commercial for the confidential telephone. Ironically the NIO attempted to use this image covertly to subtly influence viewers to use the confidential telephone. The IBA refused to pass the ad for broadcast until the NIO increased the length of the shot from four frames to eight to remove its subliminal character.

In 1993, the implicit contradictions of the government approach became open conflict. Officials at the Tourist Board

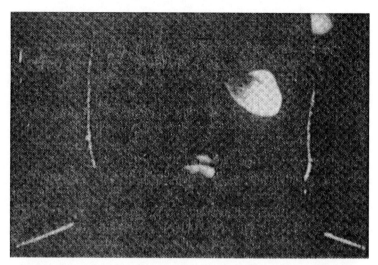

Figure 2.1 The 'media image of the masked terrorist'? An 'image of brief duration' from a Northern Ireland Office television commercial.

complained that a series of NIO confidential telephone ads were interfering with the Board's own television advertising campaigns. Tourist Board adverts showed idyllic scenes under the heading, 'The Northern Ireland you'll never know unless you go'. Meanwhile, the NIO ads, which could be seen by viewers in the South receiving Ulster Television, showed graphic images of political violence including killings. The Tourist Board's Chair, Hugh O'Neill, was reported as complaining that: 'The feedback we have had from the South is that the new TV commercial has had an adverse affect on our campaign' (Watt 1993).

While the NIO is anxious to promote images of a 'return to normality' and play down images of conflict, it is also involved in creating its own images of violence. This seeming paradox is the key to understanding the activities of 'official' sources in Northern Ireland. Some sections of the media apparently believe that the NIO produces information instead of propaganda. On the publication of the booklet referred to above, the *Belfast Telegraph* reported that:

> The book candidly admits and portrays the scale of the terrorist campaign which has gained Ulster such an adverse

reputation abroad ... This warts and all portrayal, aimed at improving international understanding of the province, may also be an effective counter to the more insidious propaganda as attention focuses on Northern Ireland during the forthcoming anniversary. (*Belfast Telegraph*, 28 July 1989)

The distinction is thus drawn between the honest 'warts and all' approach and the more sinister propaganda of, presumably, 'extremist' groups.

But is this characterisation of the Information Service justified? Does the publicity material it distributes contain only facts and undisputed information? Are such distinctions between truth and propaganda warranted, or are they themselves an integral part of the propaganda war?

Propaganda in Practice

The question of propaganda is more sharply raised by the credibility of government information. The official position is that the Government Information Service exists to provide the media and public with unvarnished facts. Yet on occasion information from official sources in Northern Ireland is simply false.

Even information on the conflict which is apparently merely factual can be distorted. The official statistics on the conflict are misleading in two ways. First of all, information about the absolute numbers of deaths is inaccurate. There is some evidence that, at least in the 1970s, the British army occasionally failed to acknowledge deaths of its personnel at the hands of the IRA, attributing them instead to accidental causes in Germany in order to boost military morale and deny it to the IRA (Morton 1989). Secondly, the compilation of statistics on conflict-related deaths do not distinguish between the deaths of paramilitaries and those of civilians. The RUC labels all of these deaths simply as civilian. This accords with the official view that the 'terrorists' are simply criminals, rather than an opposing (para)military force. It also allows British politicians to make statements attributing all deaths in the conflict to the IRA, ignoring the irony that many of these were actually IRA volunteers killed by British forces. For example Margaret

Thatcher has commented that: 'I hope Amnesty has some concern for the more than 2000 people murdered by the IRA since 1969' (*Guardian*, 1 April 1988).

Disinformation and the Protection of Life

It is now well established (and has been admitted by the government), that the task of the Information Policy branch of army headquarters in the early to mid-1970s was disinformation. False stories were spread in order to discredit the IRA as well as other enemies of the Intelligence services, such as loyalist politicians and the Labour government (see Curtis 1984a; Foot 1990). Information Policy was closed down in disputed circumstances in the mid-1970s and it seems that such a large-scale active disinformation operation has not existed since. However, the carefully drafted government statement acknowledging disinformation left a number of questions unanswered: 'It has not, since the mid-1970s, been the policy to disseminate disinformation in Northern Ireland in ways designed to denigrate individuals and/or organisations or for propaganda purposes' (*Hansard*, 30 January 1990: 111).

Later, Defence Secretary Tom King specifically drew attention to the wording of this statement, inferring that disinformation was still being used for other purposes: 'I did not say that it has not been the practice to use disinformation where it is necessary to protect lives, and for sound and absolutely honourable security reasons' (*Hansard*, 1 February 1990: 456).

Some might agree with Conservative MP Julian Amery that 'it is perfectly appropriate and right to use disinformation to protect ordinary military operations' (*Hansard*, 1 February 1990: 456), but they might be less sanguine if the object of the lies were simply to protect the image of the government, obstruct the due process of law and manipulate public opinion.

The use of disinformation in Northern Ireland is intimately connected with the use of force by the state. If the strategy of successive British governments since 1974 has been to redefine the actions of the 'security forces' as consistent with social democratic criteria, then it is essential that the police and the army be seen to act within the law. When this became difficult, the avenues taken have included changing the law, obstructing and controlling the justice system and lying to the media.

Allegations that the police and army have engaged in the illegal use of force are vigorously denied. The investigation in 1982, by Greater Manchester Deputy Chief Constable John Stalker, of six killings by undercover units of the RUC concluded, however, that:

> The circumstances of those shootings pointed to a police inclination, if not a policy, to shoot suspects dead without warning, rather than to arrest them. Coming, as these incidents did, so close together, the suspicion of deliberate assassination was not unreasonable. (Stalker 1988: 253)

Between 1969 and 1990, 'security forces' in Northern Ireland have been responsible for the deaths of over 350 people. Over half of these were uninvolved civilians (Irish Information Partnership 1990). In the early years of the troubles a pattern of public relations responses to such incidents emerged. The pattern was not changed by the closing down of the Information Policy unit in the mid-1970s. The cases of two of the civilians killed by the SAS in 1978 became widely known examples of army disinformation. In the first case, William Hanna, a Protestant civilian, was killed during an SAS ambush of three unarmed IRA members. 'Following the incident the army press office at Lisburn distributed versions of what had happened which some people at headquarters knew to be inaccurate, suggesting deliberate deception rather than mistakes made in haste' (Urban 1992: 61). The army statement on 21 June, the day of the shooting, alleged that: 'The men were challenged, and there was an exchange of gunfire. Four men were shot dead' (cited in Murray 1990: 221–2). The SAS soldiers also maintained that Hanna had 'moved as if to go for a gun' (cited in Murray 1990: 225).

The next month the SAS killed 16-year-old John Boyle, the day after Boyle had stumbled upon an arms cache in a local graveyard. He rushed home to tell his father, who phoned the police. It seems that Boyle returned to the graveyard the next day out of curiosity, whereupon he was shot by the SAS, who had the graveyard staked out:

The first statement [from the army] said a patrol spotted three men acting suspiciously and when challenged one pointed a rifle at them. One of the soldiers then fired five shots killing John Boyle. The second statement said only one man was present and he pointed a rifle at the soldiers when challenged; later two other men came to the scene [these were Boyle's father and brother] and they were arrested and handed over to the police. The third statement said no challenge was made to the man, that this was impracticable as he was 10 yards from them pointing a rifle in their direction. (Murray 1990: 232)

The army statement added that 'the rifle was later found with its magazine fitted and ready to fire' (cited in Curtis 1984a: 77). In fact, the Boyles had no paramilitary connections and the rifle was unloaded. The SAS men were tried and acquitted of murder, but the judge, Lord Lowry, declared that he was unable to decide if Boyle had picked up the rifle. Lowry stated that the SAS statement was 'self justificatory, and, in the context of the Boyle family's reputation, untrue' (cited in Urban 1992: 65).

These examples are good illustrations of the army's PR response when soldiers wound or kill civilians or paramilitary personnel. It is generally agreed by journalists and critics that RUC PR has been much more reliable than that of the army. But while it has not engaged in organised 'black propaganda' operations and its reputation and credibility for journalists has been relatively high (Curtis 1984a; Hamilton-Tweeddale 1987; Ryder 1989), when it comes to explaining deaths caused by its own personnel it has been less than reliable. As one NIO official sardonically observed: 'the RUC itself was not beyond reproach in these matters' (personal interview, Belfast, July 1990).

Perhaps the best known examples of RUC disinformation are the 'shoot-to-kill' operations of 1982, which resulted in six deaths and one wounding. In the first case IRA members Eugene Toman, Sean Burns and Gervaise McKerr were said to have been killed after their car had driven at speed through a checkpoint. The story changed the next day when the RUC said that the car had stopped briefly at the checkpoint before accelerating towards the policeman who had waved it down, knocking him over and driving off. The police statement continued: 'Other police opened fire on the vehicle which drove off in an attempt to escape. In doing so, it careered of the road, down a bank. When police arrived at the scene it was found that the three occupants were dead' (cited in Curtis 1984a: 78). But in fact no police officer was knocked down and the car was riddled with over 100 bullets, many of which had been fired from the front or side of the car rather than the back as would have been the case if RUC officers had fired from the alleged checkpoint. In addition, Toman stumbled from the car when it came to rest and was shot through the heart by a police officer (Curtis 1984a; Stalker 1988; Urban 1992). Within a few weeks the RUC also killed INLA members Seamus Grew and Roddy Carroll. The RUC press office again alleged that the INLA members had broken though a random police road block injuring a police officer. In fact Grew and Carroll had been under surveillance for some time and were waved down by police just after they had crossed the border into Northern Ireland. An unmarked police car pulled up behind them and an undercover police officer got out and 'walked towards the passenger side of the suspect vehicle, where Carroll was sitting. He fired his pistol through the window, killing the INLA man. Constable Robinson then walked around the front of the car, reloading his pistol as he went, and fired four times at Grew, slaying him as well. Neither of the INLA men was armed' (Urban 1992: 152). In between these killings the RUC also shot and killed 17-year-old civilian Michael Tighe and wounded his friend Martin McAuley. The official police story was that on a routine patrol an armed man had been seen entering a hayshed. The police approached and heard voices and the cocking sound of a rifle mechanism. Two warnings were shouted and then McAuley and Tighe were both seen pointing weapons at the RUC officers. The police later admitted that they had been keeping the hayshed under surveillance and they had seen no armed man. The guns recovered in the hayshed were pre-war Mauser rifles, but they were unloaded and there was no ammunition in the shed. According to McAuley, who survived, there was no initial warning and no chance to surrender (Stalker 1988). According to the RUC these cases were examples of honourable disinformation to protect informers (see Stalker 1988).

RUC disinformation has not, however, been confined to incidents in which informers might play a role. It has also consistently issued statements at variance with independent evidence in other situations. In the 1970s the RUC press office refused to acknowledge that suspects were being ill-treated in interrogation centres in Omagh, Gough barracks and Castlereagh (Taylor 1980). It also spread unattributable smears against a police surgeon who had worked at Castlereagh and had confirmed that he had seen between 150 and 160 suspects with injuries inflicted by police officers (Curtis 1984a: 63–7). The circumstances surrounding injuries and deaths as a result of plastic bullets have also be routinely disputed (Curtis 1982). One prominent example is the killing of John Downes in August 1984. American journalist Sally Belfrage was present on the internment commemoration march on 9 August 1984 and contrasts what she saw with the RUC statement on the death. After some stone-throwing and a police response with plastic bullets the march reached its destination:

> Gerry Adams' voice came amplified from the rostrum to plead for peace and calm. The police lowered their guns and the marchers dribbled back into the street ... Though depleted, the crowd still filled the square. The people had recovered in a second; even little children weren't sent home. Adams asked everybody to sit down to show their pacific intentions and to provoke no more reaction. They obeyed immediately and became a sea of sitting families, ringed entirely now by armed and helmeted police backed up by their vehicles. (Belfrage 1988: 58)

Adams went on to introduce Martin Galvin, the Noraid leader who had been banned from entering Northern Ireland by the government:

> As Galvin took the microphone, the police charged. They came in from all sides, ramming and running into people with armoured cars, bludgeoning them with truncheons, loosing hundreds of plastic bullets point-blank into the crowd. The air was full of puffs of smoke and cracking reports as spectators went down. There was nowhere for most of them to run, and they were beyond screaming: it was a matter of huddling in knots and praying and crying. Television cameras recorded the brutality. John Downes, attending the rally with his wife and

eighteen-month-old baby, was shot in the heart in full view of the lens of the man from the *Daily Mail*. The press people themselves were manhandled, threatened and hit ... In moments the square was still but for the police with their smoking guns and knots of hysterical, weeping people who were shot at if they tried to move. The injured lay bleeding everywhere. One man had a gaping hole in his cheek which spurted every time he breathed. A seven-year-old bled heavily from one ear; an elderly man lay unconscious, shot in the back of the head. Medics were frantically trying to revive John Downes, but he had already turned blue. (Belfrage 1988: 58–9)

The RUC statement was, according to Belfrage, 'so at variance with the witnessed, documented, photographed experience of the world's press that you could only wonder at the effrontery':

They [the police] were attacked and obstructed by groups within the crowd, which numbered in excess of 2,000, obviously determined to prevent Galvin's arrest and who had been instructed from the platform to do so. To protect themselves from those throwing missiles and to effect entrance to Connolly House, the door of which had been barricaded after Galvin had entered, a total of 31 plastic bullet rounds were discharged – a number of them in the air to disperse the crowds ... Initial reports indicate that 20 persons were taken to hospital, and a 22 year old man, who was identified as a rioter, was found dead on arrival at hospital. (cited in Belfrage 1988: 59)

Translated into the language of official public relations, this comes out as 'we are not required to lie down and let people walk all over us' (personal interview with senior RUC press officer, Belfast, July 1989).

The use of disinformation is not, however, just a matter of generic 'British lies'. Internal rivalries also have an important bearing on public relations tactics. Such rivalries can on occasion reveal that disinformation is used to cover mistakes. For example, after the first army statement on the killing of John Boyle in 1978, the RUC press office told journalists that the story was untrue. 'The RUC was furious with the army, which it considered to have behaved in an irresponsible manner' (Urban 1992: 64). Rivalries also seem to have been a factor in the PR response to the killing of Protestant civilian Kenneth Stronge. He happened to be in the vicinity when the IRA launched a mortar attack on North Queen Street police station in Belfast in July 1988. The RUC issued a statement claiming that Stronge was killed in crossfire. However, it was later confirmed he was killed by security force bullets (Irish Information Partnership 1990: 210–11). Statements also alleged that RUC officers had returned fire from within the station, but in fact the operation was run by the SAS. Their handling of the operation apparently allowed the IRA team to escape and greatly annoyed the RUC, who had themselves passed to the SAS the intelligence information that the station was about to be attacked. According to David Hearst of the *Guardian*:

> The commanding officer of the [SAS] team insisted on having full operational command of the station and turfed out the police reservist who operated the gold coloured levers which activated the steel doors. The plan was to leave the doors slightly ajar, so that when the [IRA] unit struck, the SAS would rush out and engage the car in rapid fire. When the attack came, the SAS pulled the wrong lever, closing the door instead of opening it. By the time they got out, it was too late. (cited in Murray 1990: 438)

It is not difficult to see that such treatment by the SAS might lead disgruntled RUC officers to talking unofficially to the press, while at the same time the RUC press office is supporting the official line that the 'terrorists' were to blame for the death of Mr Stronge.

One question which arises from these examples is: who knows about the lies? Merlyn Rees, for example, has claimed that he knew nothing of the Information Policy Unit when he was Secretary of State for Northern Ireland (*Hansard*, 1 February 1990: 450–2). At army HQ, Information Policy staff were aware that some of the material they produced was untrue, but it seems that at least some of the ordinary army press officers were not. John Stalker found that false stories about the 1982 killings were given to the CID officers who investigated the killings as well as to the media, and then 'finally and disastrously, the fabricated stories surfaced at the Crown Court' (Stalker 1988: 59). The stories originated not with the officers who carried out the killings but with 'a handful of Special Branch officers':

They were senior enough to carry a great deal of authority. After each operation, one or more of them gathered as a group with others, in what one of them described as a 'Chinese Parliament', which meant that everyone made a decision but no one was responsible for it. The prepared story would be refined to fit in with the events as they happened, and a jointly agreed account arrived at. A press statement was then prepared and released. (Stalker 1988: 59)

The drama-documentary *Shoot to Kill* shows a high-level RUC committee, including the head of the press office, as taking the decision to issue the press statement. The director of *Shoot to Kill*, Peter Kosminsky, has confirmed to me that this reconstruction was based on information from Detective Chief Superintendent John Thorburn, Stalker's deputy, who had in turn derived the information from interviews with members of the committee (telephone interview, May 1990). A BBC journalist and ex-member of the Royal Tank Regiment, Mark Urban, suggests that such killings were allowed to go unchecked because of a lack of real political control over the army and the police. According to Urban, during the 1980s at least, senior civil servants:

did not consider themselves to be in real control either of the RUC's or the army's special operations. The chief constable, as overall director of security operations succeeded in ruling specific discussion of undercover units and their activities off the agenda. A senior Stormont figure recalls, 'We just tended to hide behind the operational independence of the RUC. We couldn't be responsible for detailed operational matters, only for broad policy'. The result was one of those compromises, typical of British government, in which real power is exercised by those who are not responsible to Parliament or the electorate who, in return shield those who *are* responsible from painful decisions. (Urban 1992: 167–8, original emphasis)

We have already noted that from the mid-1970s, the army, and then the police press offices, were required to communicate statements on security incidents to the NIO for a 'view' to be taken on them. This system was still in place in 1982 and the false statements issued by the RUC were relayed to the NIO before being released to the media. According to a senior Information Service source:

I had become more and more suspicious of some of the facts or statements being issued from army and RUC sources and we had agreed at one of the meetings with the RUC and army information people that any statements to be issued had to be factual. For example 'three men were shot dead at a road check in Co. Armagh'. Until we knew what the facts were, the only statement that the RUC could issue – and I personally had to clear it – was that there had been a shooting incident ... They could say an incident had occurred, no security forces had been injured, three people were believed to have been hurt. Until it was absolutely and clearly established that those three people had been killed, nothing could be said except for those bare facts. Then subsequently, a statement would have to be issued which would say that the police had been involved in a road check, that an incident happened and three men had been killed but it had to be factual at all times. Now what actually happened was that I was telephoned about an incident ... it must have been well after midnight – and I was told the RUC intended to issue a statement that a policeman had been knocked down by a car, the police had opened fire on the car and I said 'are you absolutely certain that those are the facts? That somebody was placed in danger by this car and that the police did open fire on it and that as a consequence of that three men were killed?' 'Pretty sure.' So I said 'Not good enough. Go back and say nothing until you get the facts.' Quite clearly what then happened is people got together and created a statement to fit the consequences of the action. And so when they came back to me I said: 'you have checked with senior officers?' 'Yes.' 'And those are the facts?' 'Yes.' And so a statement was issued to that effect. But when one then saw the car, in which people were killed, it didn't quite gel with the statement. And so there was an example where the

Information Service was improperly used ... But there is a point beyond which you cannot go, because if you say 'are those the facts?' 'Yes.' 'And those have been approved and authorised by senior officers?' – well that's a point beyond which you can't go. (personal interview, Belfast, July 1990)

It seems clear from this statement that at least some senior NIO officials were aware that the RUC was releasing information to the media which was untrue, but it is possible that they did not know about it officially.

Since the 1970s it has become commonplace for killings to be followed by statements that the victims variously made suspicious movements, were armed, pointed a gun at the 'security forces' or opened fire. It is also important that statements imply that 'security forces' came across the suspects by accident rather than admitting foreknowledge. This is important both to protect informers and to deflect allegations of a deliberate ambush. Between 1982 and June 1991 there were at least sixty-seven killings by security forces in disputed circumstances:

A large proportion of the victims were unarmed when they were killed. Twenty-six, or 39%, had no weapons when shot while four were carrying imitation handguns or rifles. Of the 37 who had access to arms there were claims afterwards that nine were in no position to use weapons, mostly because they were on their way to arms dumps when killed ... Nearly two thirds had not been directly involved in violence when they met their deaths. (Moloney 1991b)

RUC and army press offices have regularly issued statements in which the victims of shootings are alleged to have caused injury to soldiers or police officers or have driven through a checkpoint (Armagh killings of Sean Burns, Eugene Toman, Gervaise McKerr, Seamus Grew and Roddy Carroll in 1982; killing of joyriders Karen Reilly and Martin Peake in 1990; Cullyhanna killing of Fergal Caraher and wounding of his brother Míceál, also in 1990), were armed (killing of Desmond Grew and Martin McCaughey in October 1990), made movements as if for a weapon or to detonate a bomb (1988 Gibraltar killings), were challenged (Michael Tighe and Martin McAuley, Armagh 1982;

Gibraltar killings, 1988), opened fire or were believed to have opened fire (1982 Armagh killings) or were believed to be on active service (Pearse Jordan, November 1992). Security sources have also regularly claimed that they had no foreknowledge and just happened to be in the vicinity by accident (Daniel Doherty and William Fleming, in Derry in December 1984; three would-be robbers carrying imitation guns at a bookmaker's on the Falls Road in January 1990; UVF member Brian Robinson, 1990; Gibraltar killings, 1988).

The issuing of manifestly false on-the-record statements by the RUC has become less common since the mid-1980s. The use of unattributable disinformation has, however, continued. This has been described by some as an increase in sophistication (Committee on the Administration of Justice, forthcoming). The advantage of unattributable 'steers' is that they can then be denied by the RUC press office. This might be thought to be acceptable were it only related to protecting informants or the lives of members of the security forces, but it is hard to see how some of the false stories emerging from official sources can be connected with either operational security or the public interest. Unless, that is, the concept of public interest is stretched to include automatic protection of state personnel from the due process of the law.

It is difficult to see, for example, how false stories about 'terrorist suspects' making movements, opening fire, breaking through road blocks, etc. could be calculated to protect the lives of informants. It is also difficult to account for false stories about the victims of plastic bullets, such as John Downes and others (Curtis 1982), in terms of operational security.

The purpose of 'honourable' disinformation is said to be to protect informers by pretending that encounters with 'terrorists' happen fortuitously. But when statements are issued in which details such as road blocks are fabricated, it is difficult to see how any IRA personnel involved in such an incident will be fooled, since they will actually be present when the shooting occurs and will know if there has been a road block. Such considerations do not of course apply if the IRA members are killed. It is repeatedly alleged that security personnel have 'finished off' wounded suspects by firing a series of single shots at their heads from close range. This would certainly be one way of ensuring that first-hand accounts of shootings do not reach the IRA.

It seems likely that in addition to the protection of informers and military lives there are two functions to such disinformation, both of which concern the legitimacy of state actions. First there is the immediate impact of official killing on public opinion, both in the nationalist community and internationally. It is here that media management is most important. Urban cites officers at Lisburn as 'readily' admitting to have misled the media. Various army and RUC officers privately acknowledge that 'it is not illegal to lie to the press' (Urban 1992: 77).

By the time any killing is investigated by the courts, the media tend to be less interested. The courts and the legal process are the second arena in which legitimacy is important for the government. The legal process has, however, been systematically eroded by successive governments and the inquest system to determine the circumstances of controversial deaths is regarded by civil liberties organisations as 'flawed from start to finish' (Committee on the Administration of Justice 1992):

> The role of the inquest in Northern Ireland has been radically curtailed by Government legislation in 1980 and extensive legal hearings since. The jury can no longer deliver a verdict nor add riders to its findings. Currently the sole function is to ascertain who died where and when, and how the death was caused. Thus the jury has been effectively precluded from making any comment on the actions of the security forces and in particular coming to a decision as to whether the death was lawful or unlawful. The inquest system suffers from a further major flaw: the coroner cannot compel any person to attend who may have been responsible for the death. (Committee on the Administration of Justice 1993)

The existence of the courts and the appearance of due process is, though, important for information management. According to Urban, senior army officers and politicians are

> aware of the importance of maintaining an appearance of the rule of law. Some believed that the best way to do this was to soothe nationalist unease after an incident by allowing inquests or outside police inquiries to proceed but to limit the damage which could be done by restricting the informa-

tion given to outsiders attempting to scrutinise sensitive operations. (Urban 1992: 76)

The public relations and court statements made by the security services are not only intended to protect informers, but also to preserve the 'myth of the "clean kill" – that IRA members lost their lives because they were encountered, armed and in the middle of an operation, when the security forces had no choice but to engage them' (Urban 1992: 200). Urban concludes that: 'As one incident has followed another, the ability of lawyers to examine them in the courts has been drastically reduced, the authorities have felt progressively less need to justify their actions by deliberate disinformation' (Urban 1992: 246).

Conclusions

It is clearly demonstrable that by their own definitions official agencies in Northern Ireland engage in propaganda. The type and extent of propaganda activities have not remained static, nor have they simply become more sophisticated. Instead, propaganda strategies have closely followed changes in British government policy. The use of disinformation did not cease with the closing down of the Information Policy Unit in the mid-1970s. Disinformation continues today. The government has claimed that its use is for 'absolutely honourable security reasons'. The evidence, however, is that disinformation is also used to protect 'security forces' personnel from the due process of law and to legitimise what would otherwise be regarded by the media, the public and the legal process as extra judicial executions. The next chapter considers the audiences approached in public relations strategies, the tactics and techniques used and assesses factors influencing the success and failure of public relations.

3

Public Relations
as a Propaganda Tactic

Organisations work with the media for various reasons and in various ways. A high profile in the media may be aimed at increasing membership, establishing a problem on the policy agenda, providing a morale boost to members, increasing monetary resources, putting pressure on an ally or an enemy, provoking or inhibiting the actions of others or any of a range of strategic objectives. Different objectives may require the targeting of different audiences and the use of different media. The media targeted in order to reach international opinion will be quite different from those used to communicate with supporters inside Northern Ireland. It is also clear that messages targeted at a particular audience in the mass media may also impact on other (intended or unintended) audiences. In recognition of this, some sources try to tailor information so that it speaks different messages simultaneously to different audiences.

It is possible for an organisation to regard a particular media strategy as a runaway success, while at the same time being convinced that the mainstream media are implacably biased against them. Furthermore, such perceptions need not be inaccurate. It is, in fact, quite possible to succeed in a particular media strategy despite the continued hostility of the media at large.

Targets and Audiences

Some organisations attempt to reach a very wide range of separate audiences via different channels. Others aim only to influence a very narrow group of people. Small organisations in the civil liberties and human rights fields tend only to target 'opinion formers' and the policy agenda. Thus, apart from local media, the Belfast-based civil liberties group, the Committee on the Administration of Justice, mainly deals with broadsheet newspapers such as the *Guardian*, *Independent* and *Irish Times*, and the London-based Irish Information Partnership saw its task as influencing 'opinion formers'. In the case of the CAJ, such a strategy recognises the weak position of human rights campaigners in relation to parts of the media. According to Michael Ritchie of the Committee:

> the tabloids in Britain are like a lost cause. They wouldn't be interested in the human rights situation in Northern Ireland ... If you try to impact on the debate in the BBC nationally you are probably doing as much as you can as far as mass national UK impact is concerned. (personal interview, Belfast, April 1992)

In general unionist public relations also targets a quite narrow range of audiences. The Democratic Unionist Party (DUP) targets perhaps the narrower range of the two major parties. According to DUP press officer Sammy Wilson:

> I think that probably we're fairly parochial, if there's a failing in our use of the media it is that we have ... used it more to appeal to people who already support us rather than trying to use it to appeal to people who either haven't made their minds up or are opposed to us and of course, that tends to colour the kind of things that you put to the media and the kind of phraseology you use and everything else. As far as views of people outside of Northern Ireland are concerned, I suppose it's part of just our insularity that we have felt that we can ignore them and I think that that's probably been a weakness. (personal interview, Belfast, June 1993)

Whereas DUP leaders such as Ian Paisley have their own contacts with the media in London, the party's publicity efforts predominantly centre on the local media within Northern Ireland. According to Wilson: 'If you look at our fax list, the one which is used most is the fax list for the local papers. We have a fax list with all of the English papers on; I think it's probably used about once a month, if that' (personal interview, Belfast, June 1993). The Ulster Unionist Party is more mindful of wider audiences, and does expend some effort in lobbying the US Congress, for example. By contrast Sinn Féin, the Social Democratic and Labour Party (SDLP) and the NIO have quite developed strategies for relating to the media.

The widest range of audiences are targeted by official sources. Some, such as the Northern Ireland Tourist Board (NITB) and Industrial Development Board (IDB), have specific sections of various communities in mind in their PR efforts. For the NITB the target is primarily potential holidaymakers and secondarily general images of Northern Ireland. The media are perceived as a particularly good method of communication: 'Almost 40 per cent of Northern Ireland's holiday-making visitors say they made the decision to come here after reading a positive magazine or newspaper feature on the province's attractions' (Northern Ireland Tourist Board 1990: 9). The aim of the IDB, on the other hand, is to shape business perceptions of Northern Ireland and more generally to alter public perceptions (Industrial Development Board 1990: 56).

The most sophisticated targeting of different audiences via different types of media is the practice followed by the Northern Ireland Office. The NIO is the lead department in matters of PR strategy. It attempts to oversee the activities of the Royal Ulster Constabulary (RUC), the army, the IDB, the NITB and the Central Office of Information (COI). This is not to say that such attempts at coordination work smoothly at all times, as we shall see below. The NIO operates what can be termed a 'hierarchy of access'. This general hierarchy, however, is traversed by media type, and by professional and personal relationships. For example, there have periodically been complaints from print journalists that better facilities are offered to broadcast journalists. Indeed, in late 1981 the then Northern Ireland Secretary Jim Prior was threatened with a news blackout by the National Union of Journalists if the practice continued (*Belfast Telegraph*, 30 September 1981; *Sunday World*, 1 November 1981). In addition there are clear differences within, as well as between, media types – for example, between news reporters and features writers or TV documentary makers. Journalists may move between different positions as their careers progress or they may simultaneously work in more than one capacity. The relationship of any given group of journalists with the NIO is also constantly in flux. Nevertheless, it is possible to categorise four main politico-geographical groups of journalists who are dealt with according to the hierarchy. In the lower part of the hierarchy are: (1) Dublin journalists and (2) local journalists, who work for regional newspapers, or broadcast outlets. The upper part of the hierarchy includes: (3) journalists for London-based media outlets (including both Belfast and London resident news reporters and TV current affairs and documentary makers) and (4) international journalists (both London- and home-based).

Dublin

Carrying on a tradition which goes back at least thirty years, Dublin journalists seem to be the least favoured of all those who cover the situation in Northern Ireland. This can perhaps best be illustrated by the treatment accorded to Garret Fitzgerald, the former Taoiseach (Prime Minister) of the Republic of Ireland, when he worked as a journalist. In 1960 the Northern Ireland Information Service (NIIS) was approached by Fitzgerald in his position as the Dublin correspondent of the *Financial Times* for information on economic affairs in Northern Ireland. The NIIS tried to exert pressure on the *Financial Times* to drop Fitzgerald in favour of their existing Northern Ireland correspondent, who worked for a unionist paper in Belfast. The Director of the NIIS wrote to the Cabinet Publicity Committee arguing that:

> Any Dublin writer wishing to become a commentator on Northern affairs should be discouraged as far as can tactfully be managed and no special arrangements should be made to supply him with press releases. The fact that Fitzgerald is a very able economist and writer and that he has got a firm foothold in the *Financial Times* and the *Economist* Intelligence Unit as well as a link with overseas papers makes it all the more important that we should keep our services to him to a minimum in an effort to restrict his scope to the South. Whatever about economics being non-political, Fitzgerald's viewpoint and sympathies are Southern and this must colour all his writings. (PRONI CAB9F/123/72, Memo from Eric Montgomery, 18 March 1960)

The publicity committee, chaired by Prime Minister Basil Brooke, agreed with the Director of Information and concluded:

'the Director should continue to provide only the basic minimum co-operation with Dublin writers as at present' (PRONI
CAB9F/123/72, Minutes of 97th Cabinet Publicity Committee
meeting, 23 March 1960).

In the last twenty years there have been many allegations
from Dublin journalists that they are denied information given
to others. When the Director of the NIIS tried to set up a
lobby system in the mid-1970s it was Dublin journalists who
were blamed for breaking it up. From the point of view of the
NIO, a group lobby system was impossible because while 'the
locals and to a great extent the Nationals obeyed the rules ...
there were others, particularly from the South of Ireland, who
simply didn't obey the rules and you got shopped' (personal
interview, Belfast, August 1989). The practice of the NIIS has
been shaped by the perception that Dublin journalists are more
likely to be critical of the NIO. They are, in effect, a lost
cause.

Local versus British Journalists

When journalists who work for media in the North of Ireland are
denied access by the NIO it is often in favour of those working
for British national outlets, particularly TV current affairs or
lobby journalists. I will therefore deal with local and British
journalists together. Because the audience for the local media is
by and large limited to Northern Ireland, a journalist on a local
paper is likely to be well down the hierarchy of access of the
NIIS. As one senior information officer related:

> Local journalists, with the best will in the world, are simply
> local journalists. Their interests are in the Northern Ireland
> scene and just occasionally they will ask, how is Northern
> Ireland going to be affected by nuclear legislation, or whatever
> and so briefings for local journalists were simply about the
> nitty gritty of everyday Secretary of State and ministerial life
> and there was never any deep political probing ... I haven't
> met one single Northern Ireland journalist who was worth five
> minutes of my time. (personal interview, Belfast, August 1989)

In an early example of the practice that goes with this view,

Secretary of State William Whitelaw's PR officer, Keith McDowall, attempted to exclude all but the correspondents of London papers.

> For several days towards the end of last week, Mr McDowall gave confidential 'lobby' briefings about what the Secretary of State had been doing during the day. But these were confined to English reporters only. No Belfast based papers were invited to send reporters, never mind Dublin based Irish dailies or evenings. (*Irish Times*, 6 April 1972)

Local journalists often resent this treatment. Some protest to the NIO about the facilities they are offered. The proximity of local journalists to the NIIS means that they are much more often in touch with it as a regular source than journalists who work for network current affairs or even television news programmes. Local daily news reporters tell of their daily routine involving the regular 'ring-round' of sources and half-hourly 'check calls' to the RUC press office. This means that the availability of a regular flow of news items is more crucial on a day-to-day basis.

When access is denied to local journalists, it may be in favour of London-based media outlets, with the emphasis on television current affairs programmes. In the hierarchy of access, media outlets that cover all of the 'United Kingdom' are more important for many messages. But public opinion in general may sometimes be an incidental target for image-conscious ministers. The suspicion of thwarted local journalists is that Northern Ireland ministers, none of whom are actually elected by Northern Ireland voters, can sometimes be more interested in their profile in government or in their own political party or constituency than in the content of the message. More importantly, the local media in the six counties of Northern Ireland are not read by the British establishment or the 'opinion formers' targeted by the NIIS.

Current affairs and documentary programmes are very high on the 'hierarchy of access' operated by official sources. This can allow the current affairs journalist more access to interesting and complex information and therefore the opportunity to interpret the information. It is precisely for this reason that official agencies attempt to elucidate the exact nature of queries and even of proposed programmes before permitting access. The access that is granted is heavily bounded by the interests of the sources, but in the end they are betting on slightly longer odds than with hard news stories, which have less space and time and are less likely to do investigative reports. Thus Bernard Ingham, Press Secretary to Mrs Thatcher during most of her time as Prime Minister, has described current affairs programmes as the 'main irritant' (Ingham 1991: 355) in relations between government and television. By the time he retired in 1990 Ingham:

> knew of no Departmental head of Information in Her Majesty's government who would trust current affairs television producers any further than he or she could throw them. It was impossible to have confidence in any agreement reached with them. (Ingham 1991: 356)

The differences I have identified between the various local and national media can be partly explained by the strategies and priorities of sources like the NIO.

International journalists

A final key area of interest for the NIO is international opinion. Information work for journalists from other countries involves additional tactics not used for British or Irish journalists, as well as messages that emphasise more heavily the 'positive aspects' of Northern Ireland.

Interest in overseas journalists is again subject to a hierarchy of access. Journalists from Western countries are seen as more important than journalists from what was the Eastern bloc or from the Third World. Indeed, journalists from Eastern Europe have, on occasion, even been refused official cooperation and prevented from setting foot in Northern Ireland. At the time of the H-Block protests in 1980, two Soviet journalists were told by the British authorities that they were: 'Unfortunately unable to make available the facilities for interviews at the time requested and, in these circumstances ... it was probably best that they should not make the trip' (*Irish Times*, 19 March 1980).

Even amongst Western journalists, degrees of access can depend on the importance to the British government of the country they are from. French and German journalists, for example, are higher up the priority list than their counterparts from Norway, Denmark, Sweden or Finland. When confronted with a Scandinavian TV crew, one information officer explained,

> That gave me a real pain in the head, because I had no interest in what Sweden or Norway thought. I really didn't care, because it wasn't going to affect the situation of HMG one little bit ... But Paris was different. French, Germans, in particular Parisian journalists, I used to make a fair bit of time for. (personal interview, Belfast, August 1989)

But the main target for information efforts overseas has long been the United States of America. This is because of the large Irish-American community in the US and its effect through elections and lobbying on US politics. America is an ally and can exert some influence on British government policy. It is also because the republican movement has many supporters in the US. One information officer explained the thinking of the NIIS:

> The prime target as far as I was concerned were American journalists. They were the people ... we had to get to ... because they really could influence policy in terms of [the] United Kingdom. Because here was the leading nation in the Western world [and] if the US government had thought that the United Kingdom was wrong in their policy towards Ireland ... then somehow one had to get the opinion formers onside. And so I devoted a great deal of my time to the American journalists ... to see if we couldn't possibly influence opinion there. And if you could influence the media then you could influence the senators, Congress and eventually perhaps, the White House. (personal interview, Belfast, August 1989)

In London the major targets amongst American reporters were the heads of bureaux because:

> I took the view that ... they were high flyers in their own papers and if one got to know them while they were in London and if you never sold them a bum steer – some day somewhere at some time you might get to see them in America when they were bigger guys ... And I must say that

proved a very effective thing to do. (personal interview, Belfast, August 1989)

The efforts of unofficial sources to influence international agendas have been more limited. However, there remains a clear contrast between the strategies of organisations such as Sinn Féin and the IRA and those of the UDA. Part of the rationale for IRA attacks is to keep the issue of Northern Ireland on the political agenda. As such IRA attacks have been described by Sinn Féin and IRA spokespeople as 'armed propaganda', as in this comment from Gerry Adams: 'The tactic of armed struggle is of primary importance because it provides a vital cutting edge. Without it the issue of Ireland would not even be an issue. So, in effect, the armed struggle becomes armed propaganda' (Adams 1986: 64).

But such tactics are blunt instruments in terms of reaching particular audiences. Bombings and killings capture the headlines to a greater or lesser extent. However, the reporting of killings by the IRA is difficult to target at one set of journalists rather than another. It is the development of Sinn Féin public relations that has meant a growing sophistication in media strategies. The growing politicisation of Sinn Féin and its involvement in politics meant that not only did strategies and audiences become more targeted, but there were new audiences to reach (i.e. potential voters) in the North and South of Ireland. According to Richard McAuley:

> There are different target audiences, there are different journalists speaking to those target audiences. Tonight, for example, we're issuing a statement [in Dublin]. It is a statement issued with the Southern media and audience in mind. The statement that is being issued in the North is with another audience in mind. (personal interview, Belfast, May 1991)

In the aftermath of the 1988 Broadcasting Ban, Sinn Féin launched a new International Publicity and Information Committee, which produced the *Ireland International News Briefing*, targeted at overseas, especially American, audiences. According to Gerry Adams:

> It is also worth mentioning our efforts to upgrade our own international work. Sinn Féin is, contrary to enemy propa-

ganda, a poor organisation with meagre material and financial resources, two essential and basic requirements of international work. However, we have in conjunction with those involved, started to modernise solidarity work in the USA, and in Europe, and we are currently reviewing this work in Britain, and, at a slower pace, Australia. (Adams 1990: 9)

The UDA, by comparison, has not regarded public relations as a central activity, largely confining itself to claiming responsibility for acts of violence. According to some sources, part of the objections to the former UDA leader Andy Tyrie was his perceived high media profile. According to David Adams of the Ulster Democratic Party, which took over the UDA's Ulster Information Service when the UDA was banned: 'Some of these people in the past became personalities in their own right and ... began to believe their own publicity and forgot they weren't actually there just for the sole purpose of appearing on television' (personal interview, Lisburn, June 1993).

The UDA's lack of concern for its media profile was illustrated when banned from television in 1988. Although it was said it opposed the ban, UDA spokespersons were remarkably sanguine about its impact. According to press officer Tommy Lyttle:

The ban doesn't affect us in the sense that the media, both television, radio and the press only carried the bad things, normally, about the UDA. Through our magazine and regular meetings, we communicate with our people and the ban has absolutely no effect ... We're a close-knit organisation, we're locally based. Our meetings take place at the local level ... So all in all our message continues. ('Politics', *Media Skills*, UTV, 2 February 1990)

How is the Message Delivered?

Information and impression management represent attempts to pursue definitional advantage – to shift perceptions in the direction of the information manager. Policing the information that reaches the public is the pre-eminent task of the information manager, but it involves much more than issuing or not issuing statements. Belfast City Councillor Sammy Wilson, press officer of the Democratic Unionist Party, explains:

> The first [thing] is a question of timing, making sure that statements go out on time for deadlines. The second thing is just having an eye for what kind of things the media are likely to pick up on ... The third is to build up a contact with particular journalists. (personal interview, Belfast, June 1993)

For Sinn Féin, innovation in PR is a key to gaining media attention. According to Richard McAuley:

> We are very conscious of the need to set the agenda or to impact onto the political agenda. You can best do that by being innovative, by issuing statements which are unusual. There is a limit to how far we can go in regard to that. We plan for it when it is possible to plan for it. (personal interview, Belfast, May 1991)

All parties to the conflict are consistently engaged in attempting to manage their own image and that of their opponents. For organisations such as Sinn Féin and the DUP, who tend to get a fairly bad press, this can be particularly important. According to Sammy Wilson:

> some of us were concerned that the media were presenting us as a kind of 'kick the Pope' party, you know, 'shoot the IRA', and that was about the limit of our involvement and we sat down and we planned out a series of press conferences. We did one about ... our view about pensioners, our view about housing and the economy and we steered, we deliberately because we felt it was something that we needed to do, we deliberately steered away from the kind of usual controversial constitutional or security issues. (personal interview, Belfast, June 1993)

Similarly for Sinn Féin:

> Although I'm aware of the dangers of being trapped in a reactive mode, the media reality for me is that much of the

stuff that we get carried tends to fall into reactive mode ... We need to snipe at their agenda while presenting our agenda, but doing it in a way where people aren't presenting Sinn Féin as being the begrudging party, or as being negative or as the wreckers. (personal interview, Belfast, May 1991)

Small alternative organisations may find it difficult to promote their own agendas in the media. Importing agendas already in existence elsewhere may then be one route to publicity. At the Committee on the Administration of Justice, Michael Ritchie argued: 'Northern Ireland is a small story in terms of UK news but if there is any way that we can get the issue raised in [a] forum [like] the UN Committee Against Torture ... then that does become more newsworthy' (personal interview, Belfast, April 1992).

Innovation and the development of public relations and campaigning skills are clearly seen as important by most organisations in gaining media attention. However, inventiveness can be supplemented by the ability to offer 'information subsidies' (Gandy 1980) such as media facilities.

Controlling Information

The ability to control media access is distributed unevenly among news sources. Official sources are the aristocracy of information supply. Organising media facilities for a 'positive' news story can bolster the image of an organisation. Thus the army is keen to lay on 'good news' stories about the things they do to 'help the community'. An opportunity to use military know-how or technology to help out with civilian tasks will be seen as the perfect opportunity for a media facility. According to a Lisburn press officer:

We don't get very many opportunities to do that, so when we do, we tend to pull out the stops a little bit because it is a means of showing that the army here was helping the community and not involved with the troubles or operations at all ... If you like it is a bit of cheap publicity. (personal interview, Lisburn, August 1989)

Alternatively, a pre-arranged opportunity to apparently surprise a Northern Ireland Minister or even the Prime Minister on a doorstep can be controlled so that journalistic cross-examination is very limited. Official information managers tend to maintain that these appearances by politicians to open shopping centres or inspect the troops are real events that the media have almost accidentally heard of. Bernard Ingham recalls that Mrs Thatcher's trips to Northern Ireland 'were planned in great secrecy. Number 10 and the NIO never confirmed them until they were underway. Nonetheless, reporters and cameramen always managed to follow her around in flocks' (Ingham 1991: 308).

This is disingenuous. It is true that ministerial visits are not confirmed until they are under way, but the itinerary of ministerial appointments is intimated to the media in advance under a mutual agreement that it will not be made public. [1] In addition, transport and other facilities are often laid on. Downtown Radio's political correspondent Eamon Mallie describes a typical visit:

> Journalists are managed from the moment Mrs Thatcher puts her foot on soil here. What happens is: there is a bus, the journalists are packed into the bus, herded, shepherded, brought to point A, B, C, D, etc., but very rarely given the opportunity to pose a question. She leaves here and we still don't get a chance to challenge her on whatever issue is current on the day. So that's a major, major problem for me as a practising journalist here. (*Hard News*, Channel 4, 19 October 1989)

Bernard Ingham has stated that he found 'press, radio and television in Northern Ireland, just about the most difficult to deal with in the whole of the United Kingdom' (1991: 308). He complains that:

> They had no compunction about forming a scrum around Mrs Thatcher, seething with indignation at the thought that she might have something better on her mind than talking to them. I could absolutely rely on interviewers to go on and on, to coin a phrase, in the hope of tripping her up.

On one occasion the scrum seems also to have formed around

Ingham himself. 'It was inevitable you would be knocked about', he says. 'And sure enough when I fought what became known as the War of Ingham's Buttock, by simply bouncing one or two marauders off my backside as they piled in with their microphones, complaints were registered' (Ingham 1991: 309). The journalists put it slightly differently, complaining that 'Mr Ingham used his elbows and shoulders to stop reporters talking to her and also knocked microphones away' (*Irish News*, 25 January 1983).

A similar pattern obtains on 'door-stepping' photo-opportunities for Northern Ireland ministers. Eamon Mallie has complained that:

> A pattern has emerged whereby the Secretary of State will take only one question from each news organisation. If he doesn't like the tone of the question he ignores it and refuses to answer, moving on to a question from the next broadcasting organisation. (*Guardian*, 14 August 1989)

The official response came in the form of a letter printed in the *Guardian* the very next day from the Director of the NIIS, Andy Wood: 'Absolute rubbish. There is no rationing – simply the constraints on time which apply to any Secretary of State' (15 August 1989).

But in less formal circumstances, the former head of the NIIS, David Gilliland, told a UTV schools programme about the problems for the Secretary of State:

> If he is trapped behind his desk with cameras staring at him and being pressed very hard on these particular issues he might find it very difficult indeed to escape looking shifty and dishonest, perhaps because he has to evade a number of questions which might effect peoples lives or deaths. So yes, it is contrived on occasions to put a minister on a doorstep in the open air so that when he [has] said as much as he deems to be in the public interest then he is able to say 'well I have another appointment. Thank you very much' and go. ('Politics', *Media Skills*, UTV, 2 February 1990)

Access to the scene of a shooting by republicans, loyalists or the 'security forces' is tightly controlled until it is advantageous to allow access. The RUC's Force Control and Information Centre (FCIC), monitors and controls all RUC radio traffic throughout Northern Ireland. The ability to monitor almost all security incidents in Northern Ireland from a central location obviously allows the RUC to gain an almost total monopoly on security information. The use made of this information has often been criticised. The comments of Edward Daly, Bishop of Derry, provide a useful example: 'After an incident in the North almost all information about it is controlled by the RUC through its press office. Access by reporters and photographers is refused until the RUC deems fit' (Daly 1989: 3).

This approach has the merit for the RUC that coverage can be allowed if it is advantageous and prohibited if it is not. Allowing coverage of the aftermath of an IRA attack is particularly likely. As one RUC press officer explained, 'We underline things which are positive for us and on the other side we ensure full reporting of horrific crimes and things which reflect badly on the terrorists' (personal interview, Derry, August 1989). Bringing in camera crews for close-up footage is recognised by the RUC as making television coverage of the aftermath of an IRA bombing more likely. If a bombing damages a religious building or civilian housing this will be a particularly good candidate for a media facility. The sight of Christmas decorations blowing in the ruins of a soldier's house was cited by this press officer as 'quite a powerful image' and thus suitable for a media facility.

Visits

Media facilities such as those above are mainly laid on for local and Belfast-based national journalists who are already covering Northern Ireland regularly. Organising an entire programme of briefings, meetings and events is aimed more at London and especially overseas journalists. Even small organisations in the civil liberties or human rights fields on occasion set up rounds of briefings for relevant opinion leaders or journalists. Sinn Féin will offer interested journalists the opportunity of staying for a few days in the home of a local nationalist family. But it is official sources who actually employ information officers exclusively to organise such trips. In addition the NIO, the COI, the FCO, the IDB and the NITB are all in a position to provide expenses-paid trips to Northern Ireland for appropriate journalists or other opinion leaders. On occasion expenses can even include intercontinental flights.

'Providing a Balanced View of Britain'? [2]

The Overseas Visits and Information Studies Division (OVIS) of the Central Office of Information organises and pays for visits to Britain and Northern Ireland by politicians, business people and 'influential media figures' (COI 1989: 23). The Information Service at Stormont has had a Visits Officer since at least 1965. In 1988 the NIO organised a total of 55 individual visits and 15 group visits – 172 people in total. Between January and early August 1989 a further ninety-five people had been on NIO visits. [3] The NITB and the IDB also organise a large number of visits for journalists and others. [4]

The NIO organises at least two types of visit to Northern Ireland. First there is the trip to show the nicer side of Northern Ireland and, second, there is the political tour, which includes briefings with politicians, civil servants, the army, police and others. Journalists in Northern Ireland tell apocryphal stories of the businessmen who were taken on the wrong trip round areas of high unemployment and poverty. In 1970 visits officer Stanley England described the routine of a visit to the *Newsletter*.

'The usual length of stay is three days. We try to pack in as much as we can in the time available', says Stanley. It is also part of Stanley's job to see that the visitors are made comfortable and entertained. The best hotels are used and each evening there is a dinner party at which guests can relax and converse informally with influential Ulstermen. (*Newsletter*, 27 November 1970)

Daily dinner parties would be complemented by a tour round:

'the other side of the picture, the progressive aspects of life – new industries, our advances in housing, education and agriculture' ... A typical tour would include visits to the Belfast shipyard, a linen factory, Craigavon, a dairy farm and the New University. (*Newsletter*, 27 November 1970)

More than twenty years later, sponsored visitors to Northern Ireland continue to be shown the 'progressive aspects of life' by the Facility Visits section of the NIIS, now staffed by two information officers. The itinerary of one tour for Japanese business people 'included stops at a couple of Japanese owned factories, where the local managers duly said no, they had never had any security worries – but yes, the labour costs were incredibly low' (*Economist*, 30 June 1990). Conducted by 'an irrepressible Mr Richard Needham, the minister for the economy' (*Economist*, 30 June 1990):

> the working day ends with a tour of Belfast. Mr Needham provides the commentary: 'You can have a quiet time here although we still have the occasional terrorist threat'. A security car drives at a discreet distance in front of the bus. Sectarian areas such as the Falls Road are avoided. (Burns 1990)

The tour 'wound up with a dinner in their honour in Stormont's parliament buildings' (*Economist*, 30 June 1990):

> Oysters, Irish stew and Irish coffee are on the menu. Mr Needham draws on the history of the Japanese and their tortured relations with the neighbouring Koreans to try to convey a sense of the complexity of it all. Few of the Japanese appear to understand the comparison. 'I would just like to correct the minister on one point: our civil war was 100 years ago' says Mr Yoki Okabe, senior managing director of the Sukimo bank in London. (Burns 1990)

Later: 'The evening allowed visitors and hosts to sing 'Danny Boy' with enough spirit to rival the Mitsubishi Heavy Industry male-voice choir' (*Economist*, 30 June 1990). One of the three British journalists present recounted what happened next:

> at the dinner Needham launched into a rendering of Danny Boy, which the Japanese just couldn't figure out at all, but we had all been given copies of a typed version of Danny Boy and were all expected to sing this together. I've never been so embarrassed in my life actually. (telephone interview, July 1992)

The second type of tour includes a programme of briefings and tours round other parts of Belfast not shown to business people whose investment is sought. Kevin Cullen of the *Boston Globe* has recounted his experience:

> I found that I was welcome and that there was a desire to possibly plan my entire itinerary while I was there ... In subsequent visits when I made it quite clear that it would be easier for me to arrange my own interviews and that I would appreciate the co-operation, with a couple of days notice, of having someone from the NIO at my disposal, I found that the co-operation wasn't as readily forthcoming. (untransmitted interview for *Hard News*, 19 October 1989)

One senior information officer told me that the NIO organised interviews for journalists with 'everyone except the Shinners' (i.e. Sinn Féin) (personal interview, Belfast, August 1989). Enquiring about itineraries can also be a useful guide to the type of story a journalist is likely to write. If a journalist indicates that a visit to the Republican Press Centre is planned it is not unknown for startled journalists to be offered a NIO escort up the Falls Road. Roy Greenslade was told that the tour he went on would be 'warts and all: we do *not* go in for "snow" jobs' (Greenslade 1993b). This has been translated by Edward Daly, Bishop of Derry and referred to as 'the carefully planned and guided tours organised by the NIO during which they meet all the nice, safe, intelligent and very respectable people' (Daly 1989: 7).

In practice journalists (and others such as politicians and academics) are briefed in two main areas corresponding to the two major strands of NIO public relations. The high quality of life and the marginality of the troubles are emphasised, together with briefings about the security situation. Greenslade describes the visit of ten Commonwealth journalists as including lessons in 'the lexicon of surreality':

> An official from the Belfast Development Office says in earnest: 'This place isn't what you think it is. It is vibrant, a good place to live and work, with a good quality of life.' All the problems are in the past. Housing is no longer an issue. Inward investment is booming. The city centre has been

regenerated. Night life is thriving ... 'Most people here have normal, happy lives. There is a high degree of normality', our man continued to insist. I noted the looks of bafflement [from the journalists]. Excuse me, asked one, but what about the IRA bombings? Belfast's champion publicist pointed to the new building opposite: 'There was a small bomb there recently. As you can see it's all been repaired. When they bomb we build them back bigger and better then before.' We boarded the coach for a tour of the city that, he said, 'is definitely *not* a war zone'. (Greenslade 1993b: 16)

But on a tour of the war zones descriptions of the troubles started to impinge:

When we reached West Belfast, like a sorrowful refrain form an Irish lament, came the word that was to impinge on every briefing thereafter: the troubles were 'unfortunate'. He said: 'There are, unfortunately, small pockets of unemployment'. Around a corner: 'That police installation unfortunately has to be a bit of a fortress'. Moments later: 'unfortunately there are a lot of stolen cars in this area'. (Greenslade 1993b: 16)

These themes are also elaborated in briefings given to journalists by government officials. But there are a number of ways of delivering such information.

Leaks, Briefings and Off-the-record Information

The institutionalised system of confidence and unattributable disclosure operated in Whitehall and in Northern Ireland exists for a variety of reasons. One advantage of giving information off the record is that it can then be denied. But there is another way in which disguising the source of information is important: that of promoting messages which apparently have no official fingerprints on them.

The lobby system and associated briefings are the well-known backbone of government information management (Cockerell et al. 1984; Hennessy 1987). There were a number of attempts to set up a lobby system in Northern Ireland. In the early 1970s the army operated a lobby-type briefing and Northern Ireland Secretary

William Whitelaw tried to introduce one in 1972 (*Irish Times*, 6 April 1972). There was a further attempt to introduce the system in the late 1970s and in 1983 Secretary of State James Prior, or the Minister for Information, Nicholas Scott, briefed journalists every week on lobby terms (*Irish News*, 16 April 1983). These systems broke down after a short time. It was an initiative from journalists that prompted the next attempt to set up a regular briefing on lobby terms. Belfast journalists instituted an informal monthly briefing session, called the Friday Club, in the late 1980s, to which they would invite relevant senior speakers on non-attributable and, it was hoped, less formal terms. The club met on a Friday for lunch, usually at the Europa Hotel. In 1988 and 1989 it was addressed by David Fell, Permanent Secretary of the Department of Economic Development, Peter Robinson MP of the Democratic Unionist Party, Bob Myers, the US Consul in Belfast, Archbishop Robin Eames and Bob Cooper of the Fair Employment Agency, amongst others. Gerry Adams of Sinn Féin was invited but declined on the grounds that it was against party policy to accept hospitality from journalists or give lobby-type briefings.

At one lunch, in June 1988, Northern Ireland Minister Brian Mawhinney suggested that the lobby be resurrected. This was opposed by at least three broadsheet journalists, who argued that it would make journalists over-dependent on official handouts. The response of one of the journalistic supporters of the proposal was: 'That only happens with lazy journalists.' Mawhinney himself offered to brief any lobby system personally. The proposal was, however, rejected, much to the apparent chagrin of the minister, who reportedly refused to shake hands with one of the journalists who had spoken against the proposal or to look him in the eye (personal interviews with Belfast journalists, August 1989; August 1990). Relationships between journalists and the NIO therefore remained on a less structured system of collective briefing.

Background Briefing Documents

'Official sources say', 'sources close to the NIO have confirmed' – these are the tell-tale phrases associated with off-the-record briefings. As well as face-to-face briefings with journalists, the NIO and the Foreign Office circulate written background material. [5] Between

1980 and 1993, at least 123 of these documents have been issued (see Appendix A for a list). Produced by the Information Department or the Foreign Office, they are regularly sent to selected journalists in plain brown envelopes. According to a senior information officer: 'We would stand over them but we don't particularly want them attributed to the NIO' (personal interview, Belfast, July 1990). Journalists working in Northern Ireland do not receive these briefings, which are mainly intended for use by overseas journalists.

Some sources in the NIO are sceptical about the value of this type of briefing document. In the view of one Stormont information officer, they are 'not worth a damn'. However, they have on occasion been reproduced unacknowledged in published material. Thus, volume one of David Barzilay's four-volume study, *The British Army in Ulster* (Barzilay 1973) includes large sections (on pp. 119–24) of the Information Research Department-produced briefing *The IRA: Aims, Policy, Tactics*. Once such writings are published, official sources can use them as impartial and independent commentaries. The authors themselves may then be called upon by journalists as 'experts' on 'terrorism'. In another example, in January 1988, one document, 'The Provisional IRA: International Contacts Outside the United States' (FCO 1988) was drawn on by counterinsurgency journalist Christopher Dobson (see *Irish Independent*, 2 May 1988 and *Daily Telegraph*, 3 May 1988; cf. Dobson and Payne 1982). Much of the information was inaccurate and, following legal action, the Foreign Office was forced to withdraw some of it. British author Liz Curtis was amongst those named in the document. However, the Foreign Office refused to remove her name from the briefing, thus labelling her as an 'international contact' of the IRA (*Guardian*, 11 May 1988; *New Statesman and Society*, 1 July 1988).

Planting Stories

Perhaps the most effective way of disguising the source of government information is to pretend that it is not government information. Official sources in Northern Ireland do this in two ways. First, they attempt to 'place' ready-made news stories or features in suspecting or unsuspecting media and, second, they try to use academics, journalists or others to promote their perspectives.

Both the NIO and the IDB employ staff whose function is to write and distribute good news stories. Such material is issued free of charge without copyright restrictions. Indeed, the features issued by the NIO do not state that 'Northern Ireland News Features' are produced by the British government; instead there is a contact address which mentions only the 'Northern Ireland Information Service (Features Section)'. Each of the regular packages are issued with the simple statement that 'The enclosed articles highlight some of the many positive aspects of life in Northern Ireland. You are welcome to use the material as you wish, and cuttings of what you publish would be appreciated.' A typical issue includes the following stories 'Belfast shows its other face', 'New life for Irish boglands', 'Peace village at folk museum' and 'University and Industry work together'.

The production and distribution of television items used to be quite important for public relations efforts. Started in the late 1950s under the control of the Unionist government, they were still important in the early 1970s. According to the Director General of British Information Services in New York, W.E.H. Whyte:

> We take a specimen radio newsline and check how many radio stations in the end actually have used it. If it is a good one – for example, a piece of two minutes by the Prime Minister -- we can get about 4,500 radio stations using it once or more across the USA ... We can do the same for TV clips, TV news briefs, TV news features that we disseminate. One can do this also with some precision for commercial publicity. We keep a score sheet of the number of press releases on new commercial products and processes which are published. The percentage over the last two years has been 100. (Commons Expenditure Committee 1973: 16)

However, the increasingly wide dispersion of television broadcasting and the comparatively well-resourced nature of US television has meant that television is no longer so widely used.

The London Radio Service

The most significant and least known of all the attempts to place material in overseas media involves the semi-covert use of radio news bulletins. The London Radio Service (LRS) provides verbatim transmission of ministerial speeches and press conferences as well as producing its own news reports, features and interviews, which it attempts to 'place' (COI 1989a: 2) in radio news programmes around the world. These reports and features are provided free and often the LRS provides the technical capacity to receive its products down phone lines for a nominal fee of about £25, which was described by one LRS news editor as 'peanuts' (personal interview, London, August 1990).

News and features are posted to British embassies and consulates on tape or, more directly, by telephone or satellite. They are provided in a variety of languages and the service is expanded 'to reflect FCO priorities' (COI 1989a: 2). For example, the Caribbean Service was established in the aftermath of the invasion of Grenada by the USA in 1984 (COI 1989a: 6–7). According to sources in the COI, the LRS has developed from an old style Pathé news-type propaganda outfit to supplying what is now called 'indirect propaganda'. In the 1970s:

> It was essentially still being run by civil servants with a strong Foreign Office input, therefore they would dictate policy and the result was that we tended to just pump propaganda. It was successful, but not as successful as it could have been. [But now] it has become a normal news service. So we're well away from propaganda to what I would call indirect propaganda ... The whole point is that you can't ... take the old approach by saying there's the good guys and the bad guys and the bad guys have to be shown as pretty nasty, bayoneting babies ... Now you have to be totally impartial, while still pushing the line. (personal interview, London, August 1990)

The speed of reaction is facilitated by the access the Information Service has to government ministers. On occasions, according to sources in the NIO, ministers have made statements on US radio within the hour of an event occurring: 'Long before anybody else could get in on the act' (personal interview, Belfast, August 1989). One example is Mrs Thatcher's condemnation of the London bombings in July 1982 (Simon 1982: 6).

The main interviewees on the LRS are the Prime Minister, Foreign Secretary, Chancellor of the Exchequer, Defence Secretary and Northern Ireland Secretary (COI 1989: 4). It is clear that government ministers are featured overwhelmingly and there are few, if any, interviews with critics of the British government or even with members of British opposition parties. On the rare occasions that the existence of the LRS has emerged in media reports, diplomats have been relatively upbeat about its success. Patrick Nixon, the head of BIS in 1982, related:

> We have a satellite link with the Central Office of Information in London, and when a government minister makes an important statement of policy, and we think that it's newsworthy for our customers, we can feed it, if necessary live, as we did on many occasions during the hunger strike ... direct through special lines into ten radio networks. These ten networks in turn service no less than 6,000 of the 9,000 radio stations in the country. And this means that we can put our policies right at the top of the news. (*File on Four*, BBC Radio 4, 23 November 1982)

One of the reasons that it is relatively easy for the LRS to place materials in radio schedules is that many radio stations are poorly resourced. This is well recognised by the COI; as one editor related: 'radio is the Cinderella of broadcasting. If it's free they'll take it' (personal interview, London, August 1990). Another valuable feature of LRS products, from the official point of view, is that there is no indication for radio listeners that the material originates with the British government: 'The distinguishing feature of COI radio as compared with other radio services is that material ... is then broadcast by a station as if it were its own' (COI 1989a: 1).

Some radio stations are themselves apparently not aware that the LRS is a semi-covert British government operation. But, because they get it free, many do not bother to ask questions. According to one news editor:

> A lot of stations are surprised that we're government. They don't put two and two together. Because we don't put an obvious government line across ... Four or five years ago I

was talking to people in broadcasting in the Middle East and they were stunned when I said 'No we're not BBC'. They thought we were BBC. They had their doubts because BBC have copyright. You can't touch or tamper with the content of the tape ... or the line of the tape, whereas with us, you can do what you like with it. At the end of the day someone could take the cut [interview] out and write a script around it which has the opposite effect. We find that most places don't do that because they haven't got time to do it. (personal interview, London, August 1990)

It is worth observing that this semi-covert approach is probably illegal in the US. Any information emanating from a 'foreign principal' is required under the Foreign Agents Registration Act to be identified as such. All written or printed information distributed by British Information Services in New York features a standard form of words indicating that 'This material is prepared, edited, issued or circulated by British Information Services ... which is registered under the Foreign Agents Registration Act as an agent of the British government.' Copies of all such material are required under the Act to be filed with the Department of Justice and available for public inspection. Not to do so is a criminal offence. However, the products of the LRS are not labelled as the product of the British government, nor are they filed with the Department of Justice.

Using Other People

Off-the-record briefings are useful in disguising the source of an official statement, but they still indicate that information emanates from official sources. Early NIO broadsheets and leaflets often used the words of public figures who might be thought to be independent, or critical, of the state. For example, the then director of British Information Services in New York said in 1973 that:

Some of the most effective material in this context comes from Dublin: from the statements of the last Prime Minister, Mr Lynch, the Cardinal, Cardinal Conway, and the former Irish Minister of Justice, Mr O'Malley, particularly on such matters as denouncing the support given in the USA to the IRA in way of funds. (Commons Expenditure Committee 1973: 18)

The philosophy of this approach was explained in the confidential planning notes of the film *Northern Ireland Chronicle*, which were leaked in 1981. They argued that statements about the criminality of those convicted for 'scheduled' offences would be 'far more cogently made by, say, a Catholic bishop than ... by any on-or-off-screen Government spokesman'. Interviewees from the British government might not be convincing, but unionist politicians too were out, particularly since the target audience for the film was the US. [6] The unionists:

are the people whom the film's target audience ... would be most inclined to reject. That Molyneaux would speak out against the IRA is obvious; that, say, John Hume or Bishop Daly would might be a revelation. These are the people who, in terms of the film, will carry the most authority and have the most 'muscle'. (cited in Curtis 1984a: 200)

On occasion the NIO will use journalists as proxies by distributing their writings, citing them in publicity material, inviting them to social events or even to act as witnesses in court cases. The Belfast journalist Martin Dillon has recounted the British government's invitation to him to give evidence in the US at court hearings held to consider the extradition of republican prisoner Joe Doherty. One 'classified' British government memorandum he received, while making a decision about whether to testify, revealed government strategy, outlined at a meeting in July 1983:

It would be prudent for the NIO during the period leading up to the defence's response to our depositions, to give thought to possible witnesses on the general situation in the Province at the time of Doherty's offences. It would be important for any such witness to be dissociated from the British Government, and for him to be able to paint a picture of declining violence and impartial law enforcement and judicial procedures. While such high profile figures as

Conor Cruise O'Brien, Lord Fitt or Robert Kee could be difficult to land, the bigger the 'fish' the better. (Dillon 1992a: xxvi)

In the event Dillon declined the offer and his place was taken by Professor Paul Wilkinson of St Andrews University.

The constant attention paid to the right message delivered by the right person is also influenced by the mode of delivery. Thus, 'for years the Foreign Office was criticised for failing to put across the government's case on Ulster, sending diplomats with plummy accents to defend the thesis that Ulster people really did want "the British to stay"' (Jenkins and Sloman 1985: 83). The solution was to send the press officer from the Department of the Environment in Belfast on a four-year secondment. Cyril Gray was clear about the advantages of not having a 'plummy' accent:

I find it quite remarkable the impact that an obvious Irish accent has on often very difficult Irish-American audiences. They may be many generations out from Ireland, they have a very imperfect, inaccurate knowledge of Ireland. Nonetheless, they do ask very detailed questions at all times and, to be frank, it's the only kind of detail you could know if you are yourself Irish and have been there. (cited in Jenkins and Sloman 1985:83)

Success of Propaganda: the Question of Resources

There is a profound inequality in the resources available to organisations to 'play' the media. Resources include the degree to which an organisation is institutionally secure, the amount of money and other financial resources it can call on and the cultural capital the organisation can command (Schlesinger 1990: 79–81).

The degree to which an organisation has a secure existence is centrally related to its ability to formulate and execute media strategies. Less institutionalised organisations are much more dependent on public support or the hard work of low-paid/unpaid committed activists. The NIO and RUC are heavily institutionalised, being central institutions of the state funded by taxation. The publication and circulation of information is for them a continuous, permanently important activity.

By contrast the least institutionalised organisations arise around specific issues or events on an *ad hoc* basis and have little or no funding. We can think of campaigns against plastic bullets or strip-searching or groups set up to challenge particular legal decisions. Recent campaigns to free victims of wrongful imprisonment, such as the Birmingham Six and the Guildford Four, started off in this way. Such informal groups may then disband if they are successful and their members may or may not join other campaigns. Groups that do not have fully secure institutional bases are especially vulnerable to disagreements and splits within their ranks or to the activities of other groups in the same area. In small organisations a split may result in two separate organisations emerging, each claiming to embody the 'real' spirit of the parent body. This happened a number of times with the Troops Out Movement in the 1970s and 1980s. Similarly, membership organisations can be fatally wounded if they lose out in the competition for members. Such factors are therefore important in the strategies of organisations. State institutions do not have to keep a watching brief on their membership.

In between the institutions of the state and the least secure *ad hoc* groupings are longer-term and broader-based organisations such as the well-established pressure groups (e.g. Amnesty International or Liberty) and the political parties of the North. The status of these will obviously change as new parties are founded (for example, the DUP and the SDLP are both products of the troubles) or as older established parties lose influence. The Ulster Unionist Party ran the Northern Ireland government for fifty years. It remains the single biggest party, but its power has waned considerably since the abolition of the Stormont parliament. However, the 'institutionalisation' of an organisation is affected by factors other than its closeness to the centres of political power.

The status of illegal and underground organisations is a case in point. The IRA is illegal in Britain and Ireland and yet there is a sense in which it is more institutionalised than many single-issue pressure groups. We might speak of the IRA as an institution within the nationalist 'community' of Northern Ireland, or as an oppositional institution. Such opposing forces and those associated with them are very vulnerable to the resources of the state. Thus it is that the Republican Press Centre was raided by the 'security forces' in 1978 and again in 1990. In the latter raid the police apparently 'wrecked' the centre by knocking down walls and lifting floorboards and also confiscated tapes, computer disks and contacts books (Farish 1990). Such vulnerability obviously affects the ability of an organisation to relate to the media. This includes some civil liberties groups whose strategies are planned with half an eye to their own security. The Irish Information Partnership was formally set up from an address in Belgium, partly because, according to Marian Laragy of the Partnership:

> there was a certain sense that no-one was quite clear how safe England was as a base to operate from in the sense that people tended to get arrested under the Prevention of Terrorism Act. Nobody knew whether material would be confiscated, whether there would be a need to send us elsewhere. (personal interview, London October 1991)

Finance

The institutions of the state command the largest budgets and spend by far the most on publicity and public relations. In 1989 the British government spent around £20 million on press and publicity work on Northern Ireland (Appendix B gives a compilation of available data on government PR spending).

By contrast the Republican Press Centre exists on a very insecure financial base. Sinn Féin press officers are not paid, and the main costs of the centre are telephone and fax bills. According to Sinn Féin's northern Director of Publicity, Richard McAuley:

> If they're really lucky and the party's feeling particularly generous, then they might get 50p for their lunch ... seriously. There would be a very small allocation of money set aside every week just for milk and tea bags and lunches and literally you're talking about a tenner. Outside of that, any other money that's spent on the office is spent on equipment, either in terms of phone bills, fax bills or buying computer disks. (telephone interview, October 1991)

According to McAuley, the fax and phone bills come to around £400 and £800 per quarter and spending on disks, paper, etc. comes to around £100 per month. Added to the money for lunches, etc., this makes an annual budget of under £7,000. Even supposing this is an underestimate by a factor of two, it is still less than the salary of a single government information officer. The availability of finance is crucial to the survival of alternative source organisations. The Irish Information Partnership, for example, was largely funded by the financial dealings of Chief Executive David Roche and sales of their publication *Irish Information Agenda*. Thus it was that the stock market crash in the latter half of the 1980s led to the closure of the Partnership.

Finance also has a central bearing on the employment of full-time personnel to deal with the media. Official organisations have the resources to employ large numbers of press officers and PR support staff. In 1989/90 official sources in Northern Ireland had, at the very least, 145 full-time posts in public relations. [7]

By contrast, the Unionist Party had one paid press officer for a short period in 1970 (Harbinson 1973). [8] The 1982 Northern Ireland Assembly, which returned very limited powers to an elected body in Belfast, meant that resources became available for the employment of press officers. Sammy Wilson of the DUP was first appointed press officer in this period. However, with the dissolution of the Assembly, the paid posts lapsed. More recently the SDLP employed a press officer on a three-year contract in the late 1980s. According to Jonathon Stephenson, who filled the post, the party: 'can't be absolutely certain that they have enough money for a permanent job and it certainly isn't a pensionable one' (personal interview, Belfast, August 1990).

Because of financial shortages, Stephenson's contract was not renewed. [9] In Northern Ireland none of the political parties are, at the time of writing, able to employ a paid full-time press officer. Such financial considerations have obvious implications for media strategies. In the view of Sammy Wilson, Press Officer of the DUP:

Time is the biggest problem. The second thing is that we're not very well resourced. I am contactable by fax and phone, people can get messages to me and I can get statements out on their behalf if they can't do it themselves but most of our spokesmen also find that there's a time constraint because they're maybe councillors as well and have got their jobs ... Really, the media require somebody who they can easily contact and very few politicians in Northern Ireland are easily contactable unless they're engaged full-time. (personal interview, Belfast, June 1993)

The DUP's main opponents for votes, the UUP, have more full-timers, by virtue of the fact that they have ten MPs compared with the DUP's three. According to Sammy Wilson: 'With having fewer people who're available to the press ... the range of people who you can get and promote in the media is that much more difficult' (personal interview, Belfast, June 1993). Levels of financial resourcing will tend to be positively related to the cultural and institutional resources of any organisation, but they are not a simple determinant of these more intangible but crucially important assets.

Cultural Capital

Organisations with considerable cultural resources are able to move in social circles and to influence agendas that are closed to less well resourced bodies. Correspondingly, the ability to move in such circles also gives a greater access to information and a certain invulnerability to the encroachment of the law or the police. Counterinsurgency writers such as Alan Hooper make much of the legal difficulties facing official sources when commenting on incidents such as shootings. The 'security forces', he says, 'so often have to wait for legal proof to underseal their credibility'. He goes on to specify that it is 'the law of libel and the rules of *sub judice*' which prevent the publication of information that would [enable] objective journalists to set the incident in context' (Hooper 1982: 139). However, it is clear that the army and the RUC have a long tradition of hiding behind *sub judice* at the same time as they are giving off-the-record unattributable briefings to favoured journalists. The reason given by Sir Geoffrey Howe in his 'request' that 'Death on the Rock' be postponed was a fear that it might prejudice the inquest. The MoD press office gave the same reason for refusing to brief the programme makers.

Yet at the same time they were briefing favoured journalists at the *Sunday Times*, *Sunday Telegraph* and other papers (Miller 1991).

The structural inequality in the resources available to source organisations does not necessarily doom a media strategy to failure. The level of resources at the disposal of an organisation is not static but can change. It can be deliberately or inadvertently enhanced or damaged by credibility-building strategies. In fact, all aspects of the strategies of organisations can affect its credibility and therefore the resources available to it.

In the 1970s, the army's authority as a source was compromised by some of its 'psyops' activities. Partly as a result of this the army was moved to a supporting role in the conflict and thus wound down their PR operation. That is to say that the balance of power within the state can heavily influence the financial resources available for PR. Resources can also be influenced by deliberate media strategies. Increased membership can bring more money and more credibility with government or with the media. The building of credibility is thus one of the central objectives of less well-off organisations. The Irish Information Partnership, for example, saw one of its tasks as compiling an alternative set of data on the conflict to the official RUC statistics. It was thus seen as crucial that the information was credible and authoritative. This meant that the Partnership refrained from analysis. According to Marian Laragy of the Partnership:

> we didn't always get to sit down and write up papers on the outcome of the stuff but we didn't see that as totally important ... We were very careful about that at the start. We would hardly string a sentence together on anything to draw up an analysis because when you are approached by someone in the media − if it was me, for instance, who took the call, immediately it was an Irish accent and immediately there was this kind of suspicion. (personal interview, London, October 1991)

In this case it was not only credibility in the eyes of the media that was important, but also credibility with other organisations active on Irish questions:

there was a lot of reaction from Irish people here in community organisations, about the fact that the Partnership was based in Belgium. One organisation put round the rumour that we were the CIA. It was great fun as far as they were concerned but it wasn't especially comfortable for us. (personal interview, London, October 1991)

Credibility-building strategies require the 'placement' of an organisation in a 'market niche'. The Committee on the Administration of Justice (CAJ) was formed in 1981 to monitor civil liberties issues in Northern Ireland. It is a sister organisation of Liberty (formerly the National Council for Civil Liberties) and has built itself into a formidable and respected campaigning body. In order to do that, it was seen as important that the CAJ avoid particular issues which would divide the cross community alliance. According to Michael Ritchie of the CAJ:

CAJ is quite a broad alliance and I think it is only because we have managed to kind of maintain that alliance that ... we have managed to be as successful as we have been. In order to maintain that alliance it is quite important that we do not, for example, take any position on the national question and that we do not involve ourselves in any other political question. (personal interview, Belfast, April 1992)

Taking up self-determination as a human right is problematic for the CAJ, as is the issue of abortion rights, as both might provoke fundamental splits among the membership.

Resources are important for small organisations. Without finance or the continued commitment of unpaid activists an organisation may disappear. The presence of full-time activists is also important for coordination and availability to the media or other organisations. However, the more credibility and respectability an organisation has the more effectively it can operate with fewer financial resources. On the other hand the strategies adopted by some groups may consciously avoid portraying themselves as 'respectable' in order to maintain principles and keep out of what are seen as the clutches of incorporation.

Internal Divisions

All organisations may have divisions on issues of policy or practice. Debates about the direction of the organisation are usually conducted in private, although on occasion they may overflow into the public arena of the media. Different factions may supply information to the media which embarrasses or compromises the opposing faction. Alternatively they may allow information that shows themselves in a good light to appear. Similar factors explain the relationships between organisations. The relative unity of different groups or organisations will influence their access to routine media coverage and potentially to the policy agenda. Unity may improve the coverage an organisation gets, although disunity, and especially competitive media strategies, may result in more coverage and a higher profile for a contested debate.

The rise of public relations in Britain since the 1940s and 1950s has been accompanied by a struggle by press officers for status, power and financial reward and by attempts to 'professionalise' the occupation. Administrative civil servants have often found their relationship with press officers difficult because of the short history and low status of press officers who may, however, be able to insist on access to confidential files or top meetings to which, traditionally, only senior civil servants had been allowed (cf. Cockerell et al. 1984; Ingham 1991; Harris 1990).

The NIO, like other government departments, consists of a variety of different professional groups (for our purposes here we can distinguish politicians, information officers and administrative civil servants), each of which have their own professional, political and personal agendas. When the Northern Ireland government started appointing press officers to the Northern Ireland departments in the 1960s this caused consternation amongst senior civil servants. In 1969 the first prime ministerial press secretary was appointed from amongst the ranks of press officers at Stormont. Ex-journalist David Gilliland accepted the new job on two conditions – that he should have immediate access to the Cabinet and that he should attend Cabinet meetings. The civil service was not happy with his demands. According to Gilliland, 'I think their first reaction was "What a cheek!"' (*Belfast Telegraph*, 21 May 1987). His demands were, however, eventually met.

Among administrative civil servants such perceptions were partly premised on a suspicion of the media. Journalists may be seen as prone to exaggeration, distortion and sensationalism, unable to resist a 'good story' and as favouring 'bad news' over good. This encourages an unwillingness to deal with the media and a preference for minimum disclosure. According to one NIO information officer: 'The civil service never believed, it still doesn't believe, that there is the slightest need to have press chaps running about telling the public what the government is doing and "God what business is it of the public's?"' (personal interview, Belfast, August 1989).

Many press officers come from a journalistic background, and this is often reason enough for civil servants to distrust them. John Oliver, former Permanent Secretary at Stormont, put this view in his memoirs:

> It is essential, absolutely essential, that the press officer be in the confidence of the senior officers and feel free to approach them with advice. This is not so easy for the administrator to accept as may appear on the surface, because the press officer is after all a journalist, he trades in news, he mixes with working journalists and editors and he is therefore extremely vulnerable to pressure and is a possible source of leakage of confidential information. (Oliver 1978: 149–50)

For information officers, civil servants like this are hopelessly naive. According to one director of the NIIS, it is more likely to be administrative civil servants who disclose unauthorised information:

> Actually some of the mainstream civil servants are far more guilty of leaking and briefing – far, far more guilty of doing it than information officers, because at the end of the day, to take a purely practical, pragmatic view of it, who is the bugger that gets rung up late at night when the first editions come out? It is the poor sodding press officer. It is not some twat sitting down in the bowels of the policy division who thinks it might be fun to have lunch with The *Guardian*. Look

back at the civil servants who have been prosecuted under the Official Secrets Act. Ponting and Sarah Tisdall – neither of them was an information officer. (personal interview, Belfast, July 1990)

In this view the role of the NIIS is to protect the department from unwanted disclosure, while maximising positive publicity, rather than acting as a conduit channelling information to the media. According to the same source, timing is a particularly important concern here:

It does happen that something comes barrelling along out of a clear blue sky and you think 'my God. If I had been asked about that or told about that, I would certainly have advised against publication on that day, perhaps' ... When you are working in a mainstream division or a research division, you get a very small overview of the whole office-wide activity. You tend to think that your particular report, your recommen- dations, whatever you are working on is the only thing that is vital and that matters, and you can lose sight of things which should be put in conjunction with this publication. Like is the minister going to face questions in the House of Commons that afternoon ... Is it judicious to put it out that very morning or the day before. Is there anything else going on in the department that you are not aware of which appears to run counter to it, which may appear to suggest that the department is split. (personal interview, Belfast, July 1990)

In short, the NIIS polices enclosure and disclosure and guards an image of the NIO as a unified organisation.

Similar organisational divisions occur in other bodies. In a political party like Sinn Féin, which has a centralised press office with a strong position within the republican movement, approaches from journalists to ordinary party members or even elected councillors are more likely to be referred to the Republican Press Centre. In contrast, the SDLP is, as its press officer puts it, very much a party of 'notables'. SDLP MPs or representatives each have their own media contacts and tend to conduct their own PR. According to Jonathon Stephenson this means that:

There is some opposition still in the party to the idea of a central structure, which I find a little bit difficult ... The party is not really used to having a central press operation. Its local constituent parts, particularly its MPs, very much do their own press work. The duty of a press officer is not necessarily to tell the press things all the time. It's sometimes the duty of the press officer to know what not to tell the press. It would be helpful to know what not to tell the press [more] than is sometimes the case in this party. (personal interview, Belfast, August 1990)

Tensions between civil servants and information officers in the NIO are regarded as 'old fashioned' in some Whitehall departments. In the NIO, information officers speak of administrative civil servants being 'very switched on' to the media. Nevertheless, tensions still exist. But, as we shall see, it is also clear that among the more 'switched on' civil servants, the protective role of the NIIS may well hamper active divisional or sub-department media strategies. Let us consider an example where administrative civil servants in an attempt to move forward a policy initiative by a carefully planned media strategy came up against attempts at enclosure from the 'Information' Service.

Closing Down the H-blocks

During the period of protests in the H-Blocks of the Maze Prison in the late 1970s and early 1980s, access for journalists was tightly controlled. The first republican prisoner started refusing to wear prison uniform in September 1976, but it was not until March 1979 that a small group of journalists was allowed in, although they were not allowed to speak to the protesting prisoners. During the 1980/1 hunger strikes journalists were simply not permitted to interview hunger strikers. When Bobby Sands stood for and was elected to parliament the NIO still refused access. Some journalists got in on ordinary visitors passes. 'But if their identity as journalists was discovered, they were required to sign a form saying they would not publish anything about the visit' (Curtis 1984a: 259). In the mid-1980s American journalist Sally Belfrage had to pretend she was a relative of a prisoner in order to gain access to the prison (Belfrage 1988).

Since the end of the 1981 hunger strike, journalists had periodically requested access to the prison. In the late 1980s the first newspaper correspondents were allowed access. The BBC's Paul Hamann had been trying to gain access to the Maze prison since the early 1980s (Dugdale 1990), but it was not until May 1990 that he was finally given permission to film inside the H-Blocks. This unprecedented access was advocated by the Prison Department of the NIO with a number of objectives in mind. According to the programme's producer, Steve Hewlett, there was a desire to pre-empt Sinn Féin's commemoration in the coming year of the tenth anniversary of hunger striker Bobby Sands' death (Dugdale 1990). There was also a move from within the NIO to close the prison down. A precondition for this was that the prison regime was no longer seen as a problem. BBC journalist Peter Taylor commented to me that: 'Once you have lanced the boil, if you like, demythologised the place, I think if you are an administrator, it creates a climate in which you can move rather more readily, without always worrying about what the media's going to say' (telephone interview, May 1991).

But the priorities of the Prison Department ran into conflict with those of the NIIS. Andy Wood, a former deputy of Bernard Ingham at Downing Street, was worried that the film would 'backfire' on the NIO. This was a particular concern, since both Taylor and Hamann had made programmes which had been banned or censored. Taylor's programmes on torture of suspects in interrogation centres caused rows in the 1970s (Taylor 1979) and Hamann had made the *Real Lives* programme 'At the Edge of the Union', which resulted in one of the most serious clashes between the government and broadcasters in the 1980s. According to Hamann:

> Andy Wood did everything he could to stop us getting in. He made it quite clear, in front of us, which surprised us, that this would backfire in an enormous way ... He thought Thatcher would go bananas. This programme, like 'Edge of the Union' – he said this – would be accused of giving succour to terrorism. (telephone interview, May 1991)

Eventually, though, the programme 'Enemies Within' was broadcast in November 1990. It was an important film made by two journalists with substantial experience of investigative reporting on Northern Ireland. In many respects the film was critical of the official perspective on Northern Ireland, in that it allowed republican and loyalist prisoners to explain their motivations and political philosophy (See Taylor 1990a; 1990b). It also showed that the prison authorities unofficially recognised republican and loyalist military command structures in the H-Blocks, which is contrary to the official position that the prisoners are simply criminals. Such coverage is rare on British television (see Chapter 4). But the key point for the Prisons Department was that the prison should cease to be popularly regarded as a blot on the landscape. Two days after the transmission of 'Enemies Within', the BBC reported that the NIO intended eventually to close the prison (*Fortnight* 1991a: 20). The NIO did not formally confirm this until 28 June the following year (*Fortnight* 1991b: 26), by which time there was little surprise or opposition. The important point for our present purposes is to note that a conventional textual analysis of the programme would have been unlikely to suggest that the programme was of benefit to the NIO. However, as we have seen, the strategy of the Prison Department in fact overrode such considerations and allowed the programme makers free access to the prison in order that they could 'lance the boil' of the prison's image. Here, a part of the bureaucracy was able to succeed in its specific media strategy by allowing current affairs journalists to make a programme that would otherwise have been likely to attract government antipathy.

Lack of Control

Information that may affect a source's image or credibility can reach the media in ways that are not part of any media strategy. One way this can happen is through a lack of internal control or communication within an organisation. Among official sources in Northern Ireland this is a particular problem for the RUC (and to a lesser extent the army), since these are the organisations whose operatives routinely come into contact with journalists at potential news events involving public order.

Chibnall, for example, looks at PR techniques in terms of the perceived aims of the 'control agency'. He then refers to 'harassment and repression' as being a control agency technique (Chibnall 1977: 182). However, while journalists and photographers are often harassed or indeed have been shot with plastic bullets by the army or RUC, [10] it seems clear that the role of the press office is not to coordinate such harassment but to deal with the fallout should the harassment be publicised. Thus in some circumstances army or RUC treatment of journalists can work against the image presented by the press office.

Similar tensions are evident in the republican movement, although they are compounded by the secrecy under which the IRA operates. Thus carefully planned Sinn Féin PR efforts may be compromised by IRA actions which, according to Richard McAuley: 'impact on our media strategy and political strategy. But it is not something we have any control over. It's a real headache, but it's a headache that we have had to learn to live with' (personal interview, Belfast, May 1991).

Mistakes

A second way in which unintended information can be disclosed is by straightforward human error. Sometimes official secrecy is maintained in order to prevent embarrassment for a government or political party. But details are not always released deliberately, even by sophisticated PR organisations.

One example is the case of British military incursions into the Republic of Ireland. Until the end of September 1988 the issue of incursions invariably brought protests from the Irish government. On 31 July 1988, for example, according to local people, and one security source, a helicopter 'hovered for some time directly over Monaghan, a town some four miles inside the border, before circling the area for ten minutes' (*Guardian*, 17 August 1988). At the time the army press office claimed that the helicopter had overflown the border by only 'several hundred metres' and that the incursion was a mistake: 'We know these have taken place. It is unfortunate, they are navigational errors. They are in no way deliberate. We would not have any clearance for that' (*Guardian*, 17 August 1988).

The *Guardian*, however, alleged that pilots had been told they could 'fly up to five nautical miles into the Republic' and that 'far from objecting to overflights, some of the recent sorties have been at the invitation of Irish security forces' (17 August 1988). The Dublin Department of Foreign Affairs dismissed the story as 'malicious rubbish' and, according to *Fortnight*, 'one normally suave Dublin official' subjected one of the *Guardian* journalists 'to a three hour going over' because of it (*Fortnight*, November 1988).

But unfortunately for the Department of Foreign Affairs, the new security minister at Stormont, Ian Stewart, let the cat out of the bag at an off-the-record lunch at Stormont. 'Of course there is an agreement on overflights', he blithely told journalists at a getting-to-know-you encounter at Stormont ... [leaving] the mouths of his officials agape. (*Fortnight*, November 1988) [11]

As David McKittrick pointed out, it 'appears that both governments have for some time been engaged in something of a pantomime' (*Independent*, 28 September 1988). The Irish government was then forced into acknowledging that there had been a secret agreement on overflights.

It is often assumed that official sources speak with one voice in Northern Ireland, but it is clear that there are important differences and contests between different branches of the state apparatus (for example the RUC and the army or the NIO). The rivalry and, at times, internecine warfare between the various intelligence organisations (MI5, MI6, Army Intelligence, RUC Special Branch) in Northern Ireland are a hardy perennial of Ireland-watchers. There have even been allegations that people have been killed as a result of some of these tensions (see Bloch and Fitzgerald 1983; Foot 1990; Holroyd with Burridge 1989).

These are long-term rivalries for spheres of influence which are overlaid by divisions about the most appropriate strategy for combating the IRA. Army concerns often centre on the constraints imposed on military action by politicians and civil servants, whose concerns are, in turn, more related to legitimising military action within the rule of law (Bew and Patterson 1985; Dorril and Ramsay 1991; O'Dowd et al. 1980; 1982; Urban 1992; Verrier 1983). It is occasionally useful for an organisation to further its aims by waging the rivalry, at least partially, in the media. The activities of the Information Policy Unit at Army HQ in Lisburn in the early 1970s often involved issuing false information or stories which would reflect badly on other official organisations. [12] But such activities are not confined to disinformation work; they are a regular part of the operation of official sources in Northern Ireland.

The raised public profile of MI5 in 1992 seems also to be related to particular policy objectives. The public naming of the new head of MI5 (an organisation which, until then, did not officially exist) was rapidly followed by the (unattributable) news that, following the collapse of the Soviet Union, MI5 was looking for new areas in which to operate. Thus stories appeared suggesting that MI5 wanted to take over all 'anti-terrorist' operations in Britain from the Special Branch. Most importantly, confidential minutes of a Metropolitan Police policy committee meeting were leaked to the *Irish Times* and then printed in British papers. These allegedly showed that the Met had 'little hard intelligence' on recent IRA activities in Britain. Such manoeuvring via the press seems to be clearly aimed at governmental audiences rather than the public at large, although it does result in a more visible public profile for the secret state. Shortly after this the government decided that MI5 would take over anti-terrorist operations within Britain from the Special Branch, thus securing a measure of resource and personnel allocation for MI5. [13]

'Leaking' of information to influence a particular and perhaps very small audience is a routine tactic in both official and alternative sources. In the case of MI5, the competition is with the Special Branch and the audience is government policy makers. In other cases the audience and the competitor may be the same. For example, the RUC report on the shooting of three would-be robbers by undercover soldiers in 1990 was leaked to the media shortly after it had been sent to the Director of Public Prosecutions for his decision. The report revealed that the RUC had recommended against prosecuting the soldiers and was seen as an attempt to pressure the DPP: 'The RUC's recommendation carries no legal weight but, since it is known, might make it difficult for the DPP to oppose without revealing a controversial division of opinion between him and the security forces' (Moloney 1990c). Such interdepartmental rivalries and attempts to influence other parts of the state apparatus are obviously premised on the view that the pressured part of the apparatus cannot be guaranteed to operate to the advantage of the leaker. [14]

Source Competition

Competition for credibility and legitimacy are central and conscious objectives of the major participants in the Northern Ireland conflict. Source competition may involve second-guessing an opponent, carefully timing a disclosure, selective release of information or any of a host of PR tactics and techniques. Different organisations have varying opportunities to use the range of tactics available and these will be partly conditioned by the resources or credibility of the organisation. Thus organisations which are less financially secure than the NIO cannot organise expenses-paid trips to Northern Ireland. The most obvious attempts to impose different understandings on the media and on public debate generally are the promotion of contending legitimations of the use of force. The use of the term 'terrorist' and the change in British government strategy in the mid-1970s to 'normalisation' and 'criminalisation' were *deliberate* attempts to ensure that the republican assault on the Northern Ireland state was shorn of all possible legitimacy. Similarly the republican contention that the border is the root cause of the conflict in Ireland sets out to undermine British claims to sovereignty and the right to the monopoly use of legitimate force. It is the active concern of both to label the other side as the *real* 'terrorists'. Counterinsurgency theorists bemoan 'terrorist propaganda' claims that all the problems of Ireland can be laid at the door of the British. We might also note that the strategy of official sources has been to try and attach all the blame to the IRA. Thus:

Since 1985 the RUC has maintained a policy of not commenting on individual allegations against those said to be police informers. In a standard prepared statement yesterday the RUC confirmed its policy: 'No inference is to be drawn from the RUC's silence in individual cases. Attention has often focused wrongly on whether a person was giving information to the police rather than on the fact that a person was brutally murdered by self-appointed executioners.' (*Guardian*, 19 July 1989)

Similarly, when John Hermon was appointed Chief Constable of the RUC his 'first order was to forbid police from disclosing the religion of terrorist victims, ostensibly because this was fuelling tit-for-tat retaliations' (Ryder 1989: 233). But, as Ryder has argued, this is hardly going to be effective in Northern Ireland, 'given that most Ulster citizens can be safely labelled by religion because of their name and address, given the rigid sectarian geography' (Ryder 1989: 233). It might be thought that the real impact of such a measure would be on the British public, who would henceforth be deprived of vital contextualising information, thus strengthening the perception that the conflict is incomprehensible. Moreover, since virtually all sectarian killings are of Catholics by loyalist paramilitaries, the absence of this information might reinforce the perception fostered by the British government that the root cause of the troubles is the IRA.

Competition, Cooperation and Agenda-building

There are also a variety of ways in which sources may seek to cooperate with each other in campaigning on a particular issue or in attempting to legitimise their own actions. The key to success in this area is credibility. Legitimising the activities of the RUC and British army in international human rights arenas can be difficult for the British government. Part of the reason for the formation of the Standing Advisory Commission on Human Rights (SACHR) in 1973 was its function in legitimating the British government's position that democratic checks and balances existed. In order to be effective in this way SACHR had to be set up as an 'independent' body. While appointments to the Commission are made by the government, SACHR is expected to monitor and criticise British policy on occasion. This then allows the government to point to SACHR as a check on the possibility of the over-enthusiastic exercise of police power. In practice the NIO tries to manage the public statements of SACHR and tends to ignore their findings. According to former Commission member Tom Hadden, the NIO:

> will be concerned not to have the Commission doing things which it views as damaging to its position, for example, the Chairman of the Commission was brought along to the Moscow meeting of the CSCE (Conference on Security and Cooperation in Europe). He delivered a statement at that meeting which I certainly wouldn't have made. That wasn't discussed. I thought it was a totally inappropriate statement given the Commission's experience. The statement says, in essence, here is an independent human rights commission which is doing a human rights job well. What it didn't say was that everything that we had said over the last five years had been ignored [by the government]. That was a case for the government using the existence of the Commission for its own ends. (personal interview, London, April 1992)

Similarly, the Committee on the Administration of Justice (CAJ) tries to influence the drafting of legislation by requesting meetings with the NIO. Such meetings may or may not bring results, but the experience of the CAJ is that the fact of the meetings may be used to legitimate government statements. As Michael Ritchie put it during the passage of the Emergency Provisions Act 1991:

> In the House of Commons, the fact the NIO had met with us was mentioned by them on two or three occasions, as if to say there was public debate about the Bill and they had engaged in consultations. I suppose the danger [is] you kind of get pulled into the argument about whether or not it was democratic consultation. We protested a wee bit strongly about that to them. That is the one thing that we have to watch – that we are not co-opted in some way. (personal interview, Belfast, April 1992)

However, the campaigning activities of civil and human rights activists can also make a real difference to the activities of official bodies, especially if allegations of human rights violations are published in the media (Whelan 1992).

Building credibility is crucial to an organisation like the Irish

Information Partnership and can enable it to 'bridge the gap' between campaigns on single issues like plastic bullets, strip-searching or miscarriages of justice and more institutionalised and credible organisations. By compiling the best available statistical information it could appear credible and independent to official organisations. This allowed extensive dealings with the Labour Party spokesperson on Northern Ireland, Kevin McNamara. According to Marian Laragy: 'We would have had a reputation with the campaigning people who gave us the information and with MacNamara. I think we were useful to him because all politicians need to be able to stand there and have the facts at their finger-tips' (personal interview, London, 16 October 1991). The work of the Partnership was also able to provide the factual information which journalists need and some will use: 'I think that the business of drawing attention to the killings by the security forces was important. I think to some extent we probably made it easier for other people in the world of journalism to open up' (personal interview, London, October 1991).

Media strategies are planned to deny any possible advantage to opponents. Following bombing incidents in Northern Ireland, the RUC seals off the area and controls all access to the site of the bombing. Television crews, especially, may be allowed access to the scene if it is felt that the footage will have positive results for the RUC or negative ones for the IRA. An explosion near a school, an old people's home, a hospital or a religious institution provides a particularly good photo opportunity illustrating the 'barbarity' of the IRA in threatening 'innocent' [15] and vulnerable civilians. However, for the RUC such publicity may be, in the words of an RUC press officer, 'a double-edged sword' (personal interview, Derry, August 1989). While it may deliver the desired message about the evils of the IRA to the public, it may also be perceived by the media or public as promoting fear. Furthermore, the graphic illustration of the damage which the IRA is able to wreak is in some ways a public illustration of the inability of the RUC to 'contain' the troubles, the result of which may be a boost to IRA morale. These worries also inform police and government information policy in combating the IRA campaign in England. On the one hand the government wants to emphasise the injury, destruction and disruption caused by bombings and bomb hoaxes, in order to discredit the IRA and to promote public vigilance. On the other hand it is anxious to play down the extent of the devastation and disruption in order to avoid handing the IRA a 'propaganda victory'. After the bombing of the City of London in 1993, it was reported that 'Ministers were yesterday ordered off TV and radio to avoid giving the IRA publicity. The decision – taken on advice from the security services – came despite world-wide coverage of the blast' (*Sun*, 26 April 1993). Concerns such as these lie behind calls from government ministers for journalists to report less of the violence and more of the 'real' side of Northern Ireland. However, this is one of the major contradictions of the strategies of all organisations engaged in force (including the IRA, the Ulster Defence Association (UDA)/Ulster Freedom Fighters (UFF) *and* the British government). It is a strategy that is often hindered by the routine operations of media institutions.

News Values

There is an important sense in which the priorities of journalists and those of the state are different. The professional imperatives of news journalism tend to make violence the main rationale for reporting Northern Ireland (Schlesinger 1987; Elliot 1977). It seems that in the early 1970s some newsdesks were so convinced (presumably, partly by their own prior reporting) that Northern Ireland was synonymous with violence, that they were reluctant to print stories which gave a different view. Simon Hoggart has related his experiences:

> Years ago I wrote an article about holidaying in Northern Ireland. I praised the gorgeous countryside, the friendly people, the opportunities for riding, fishing and boating and mentioned how – not surprisingly – it was wonderfully uncrowded. Sadly the *Guardian*, for which I then worked, refused to print it on the grounds that some things were so improbable that nobody would believe them even if they were endorsed by a team of notaries public headed by George Washington with his little axe. (*Observer Magazine*, 25 February 1990)

It has often been assumed by critics of the media that the concentration on violence indicated that there was a simple 'fit' between official definitions of the conflict and news reports. But it is clear from government statements that the coverage of violence is eschewed and, somewhat disingenuously, blamed on the media. Former Downing Street Press Secretary Bernard Ingham put it as follows:

> Against a background of continuing violence, the journalists' objectives and the Prime Minister's were diametrically opposed to each other. They wanted to accentuate the negative, the difficulties and the conflict, whereas Mrs Thatcher -- and I must say myself -- wanted to underline the positive achievements in Northern Ireland, to highlight the peaceful normality of life over most of the province and to encourage the public in their fight against terrorism. Once I raised with both the BBC and ITN the frustration felt in Belfast that a festival and parades there attended by the Mayors of Dublin and Belfast had passed off peacefully -- and without any coverage whatsoever. (Ingham 1991: 309)

However, official sources in Northern Ireland operate a dual strategy with regard to media coverage. It is not uncommon for the NIO, the RUC, or even officials promoting the government view on employment discrimination, to emphasise the deeds of the IRA, thereby painting a picture of Northern Ireland as a battle zone, where violence is endemic. Indeed, publicity material from the NIO prominently features such images in combination with an emphasis on the positive qualities of life in 'Ulster' (Miller 1993a).

The republican movement has similar problems. In order, at least partly, to counter 'normalisation' and the 'containment' (Rolston 1991) of the troubles, the IRA continues to plan attacks which 'expose' the inability of the state to control their struggle. At the same time Sinn Féin spokespersons routinely complain about the fixation of journalists with the activities of the IRA. If the perception is that Sinn Féin is simply a vehicle for championing the IRA, according to Gerry Adams:

> it is because that has been the issue on which the media has concentrated down the years. Eighty percent of all statements

issued through Republican Press Centres have been on social, economic or political issues in particular, most of which, incidentally, have been ignored. (cited in Morrison 1989: 8)

Some journalists do write committed articles consciously pointing out the positive side of Northern Ireland. This is especially the case with mid-range tabloid newspapers such as the *Daily Mail*, and was a feature of the coverage in *Today* under the editorship of Northern Ireland-born David Montgomery (Odling-Smee 1989). Nevertheless, violence remains the main rationale for coverage. It is the predominance of news values of this type that allows a contrast to be drawn between routine images of Northern Ireland and the 'other side of life'. Thus we can find a senior director of the Northern Ireland IDB writing for an American business audience under the title: 'Despite Its Bad Media Image, Northern Ireland Proves to be a Good Place to Do Business' (Walters 1984: 12).

But the NIO continues to promote this dual view in spite of its contradictions and the disadvantages as journalists, used to a diet of atrocity stories, are less than keen on good news. One such story was the delivery of aircraft ordered by the United States Air Force from Shorts manufacturers in 1984. The story was announced in a press release and, in cooperation with the NIO, some enthusiasm was drummed up amongst journalists. The BBC sent a camera crew and filmed the impressive array of dignitaries present, including a Northern Ireland minister, the US Ambassador, US generals and the USAF band. According to Shorts, 'the largest single contract ever received by Shorts, was won in the face of extremely stiff competition and has resulted in a substantial intake of new employees' (*Press Release*, 8 August 1984). This item seemed destined for the evening news until the IRA intervened. In County Derry a tour by Irish Northern Aid supporters featured an appearance by two armed and masked members of the IRA. Cameras were present and the incident made the television news that night (BBC1, 21.00, 8 August 1984). The story from Shorts, however, was dropped. The IRA, however, did not gain favourable publicity from this. The BBC reporter dismissed the incident as a publicity stunt. The issue is not the way in which the 'stunt' was covered, but simply that it was covered in preference to the 'good' news story. [16] It is clear that incidents like the appearance of two armed and masked IRA members contain a 'news value' that the Shorts story simply did not. However, it should be noted that this type of publicity stunt is not necessarily viewed as a success in the republican movement. According to Richard McAuley of Sinn Féin:

> I'm not sure that having armed IRA volunteers getting onto a bus with someone from Noraid is actually a constructive thing to do ... We certainly didn't know it was going to happen. The IRA in Derry decided for their own reasons it was an opportunity, they saw it as a publicity stunt and they did it. I think in the United States it probably was not something which should have been done. (personal interview, Belfast, May 1991)

According to McAuley, such stunts owe more to a lack of coordination between Sinn Féin and the IRA than to efficient public relations:

> It would have been seen primarily as something that was going to get some IRA volunteer in Derry onto television. Anything that gets IRA volunteers on television they would see as a good thing. But the linkage between Noraid and the IRA is politically not something that I think would work to our advantage. If one had had the opportunity to consider a proposal that that be done then my advice would have been no don't do it. Sensationalist news very rarely works to our advantage. Because it's tending to pander to the baser instincts of, particularly British public opinion, about what the IRA is, who they are and who supports them, and also about these crazy, sort of loony Irish Americans who come to Ireland so that the IRA can parade in front of them. (personal interview, Belfast, May 1991)

This is not to say that the image of the IRA as an efficient military force, keeping the might of the British army under pressure, is not regarded as good PR by Sinn Féin. The opportunity to film the IRA in action is more likely to be afforded to international film crews who are themselves more likely to be able to broadcast the resulting footage. The last such incident in Britain over filming in Carrickmore caused a major controversy (see Chapter 1). There is also a sense in which this image is useful to present to an international audience. According to McAuley:

> The hope is, presumably on the part of the IRA that the reports will reflect an analysis of the conflict at least in that part of the North where the IRA are in control, have territorial advantage, that the British are under pressure. The building of the hilltop forts and the closing of the border roads, all of that reinforces that image. That sort of film reinforces an image of the IRA having a political as well as a military advantage. (personal interview, Belfast, May 1991)

It is difficult to argue from this that journalists simply recycle or transmit the 'bureaucratic propaganda' of official sources or the 'terrorist propaganda' of the republican movement. There is a methodological point here, which is that it is possible to show that much of British mainstream coverage (as opposed to current affairs or features) is dominated by news about 'terrorism' and the evils of the IRA which is oriented towards the views of the powerful. At the same time we find that official sources are still not able to secure the prominence they would like for stories about the 'other side' of life in Northern Ireland. In the same way we find that even when alternative sources such as the IRA manage to secure news attention, it is still not the kind of attention necessarily desired by the Republican Press Centre.

The 'good news' part of British strategy meets with relatively little success in the news media, foundering on a contradiction within the strategy of official sources and on the rock of news values. Similarly, for the republicans, the problem is the contradictory elements of the Armalite and the ballot box strategies. Republicans want to get coverage for the political policies of Sinn Féin, but the violence of the IRA is more newsworthy.

Success and Failure

The measurement of 'success' is complicated by the fact that a given organisation may have a variety of aims. Thus a small and resource-poor group may be aiming simply to increase its membership. It may not get positive or even a great deal of coverage, but this might not be necessary for the successful completion of its strategy. Similarly, a resource-rich organisation may get lots of positive coverage but it may not be in the areas that it would wish. In that sense it could be said to be unsuccessful, while appearing to be successful in terms of its media profile.

In general there is a fair measure of agreement on who gets the good publicity. Thus we find the NIO's David Gilliland arguing that the NIO could have been given a much rougher ride by the media:

> Journalists are there to get the news and to print the news and they're not really there to take on a spoon everything that the government hands out. And so I think if there had been more drive and a more analytical approach to the information that was given by the journalists themselves, well then government would perhaps have come under greater cross examination. (*Hard News*, Channel 4, 19 October 1989)

Roy Greenslade found that the Commonwealth journalists he accompanied on an NIO tour almost all saw the conflict in colonial terms before they went:

> 'The British government doesn't want to give the people of Northern Ireland their rights and is trying to suppress them', says Khadija Riyami, from Tanzania. 'I don't condone the violence, but they have a cause.' It is the most common view. John Boyce, associate editor of the *Barbados Advocate*, says: 'The people are being deprived by the British government of some form of rights. There is a large colonial flavour to the dispute ... And how do they view the IRA? 'I won't call them terrorists' says Muhammed Ayub, a news editor in Lahore, Pakistan. 'We have a similar situation in Kashmir where people are struggling for their freedom from India.' (Greenslade 1993b: 16)

After their NIO-sponsored visit almost all had changed their minds:

> On the journey back, I discover that almost all have certainly changed their minds. No-one holds any more to the colonial theory. No-one views it as the Irish people fighting

for their rights. If there was little sympathy for the IRA before the trip, there was less after it ... One who was disabused of the colonialist scenario, John from Barbados, said: 'Originally, I thought the British Government were being unfair. Now I have a better grasp of it I see it as two communities and their political parties fighting among themselves.' Ayub, from Pakistan, was certain: 'No, I can't compare it with Kashmir, where the vast majority of the people are fighting against the government. Here there are two communities fighting each other with the government in between.' (Greenslade 1993b: 1)

From the point of view of the NIO, such trips seem to pay great dividends in shaping the perceptions of journalists from around the world.

There is also a widespread recognition that the republicans are not given sympathetic coverage. According to Jeffrey Donaldson of the Ulster Unionist Party:

Sinn Féin do get a fairly bad press. You get the occasional documentary from Channel 4 which we would argue is not helpful in that at times it tries to present Sinn Féin as a rational political organisation. But I think in general, John Hume and the SDLP get a very good press and I think in general, many sections of the media are broadly sympathetic to John Hume. (personal interview, Belfast, June 1993)

This is endorsed at the SDLP. According to Jonathon Stephenson, this is because Sinn Féin has:

a bigger mountain to climb than we have ... They are approaching a much more hostile media environment than we are. In a way I got a slight shock when I joined the SDLP straight from the TUC, because I was used to swimming against the tide of public opinion on almost every issue you care to mention. That the SDLP, in fact, on the nationalist side of this community, is the establishment party, representing a majority voice, has a lot of goodwill going for it among the media, that was a slight culture shock for me. (personal interview, Belfast, August 1990)

This type of coverage is enhanced by John Hume's good personal relationships with journalists. Stephenson says:

He will arrange for journalists to come and see him in Donegal. He kind of summons them to his cottage in Donegal. In fact I don't think that's a bad strategy at all. It puts them [journalists] at an instant disadvantage. He gives them a good time, mixes them a lethal cocktail, and they come back happy and Hume gets an extremely good press; (a) because he's very good and (b) because he does take time to develop good relations with individual journalists. (personal interview, Belfast, August 1990)

There is also widespread agreement that the unionist parties have a poor media image. According to Sinn Féin, the unionist protest campaign against the Anglo-Irish Agreement 'cost them dearly in PR terms and to the British public it has only emphasised the differences between the Six Counties and Britain' (Sinn Féin 1987: 4). Unionists too have acknowledged that they have a poor public image. According to Sammy Wilson, the image of the DUP is:

fairly bad as far as the general populace is concerned. I don't think it really matters too much with the people who support us. In fact I think that they'll come to expect that that should be the reaction and if the media are praising us you know they're going to wonder. I've had this all the time, 'what're you people at?' because there's something complementary said about you. (personal interview, Belfast, June 1993)

There is a perception here that the unionist parties are bound by their constituencies to repeating a message which may not be popular outside the confines of the unionist community. The cause of this poor image has been diagnosed by a wide range of unionist politicians and writers and there is considerable agreement across the spectrum of unionism that at least part of the problem is a failure of unionist public relations. Thus according to Jeffrey Donaldson, the Honorary Treasurer of the Ulster Unionist Party:

I think at times there is an attempt by those within the media to misrepresent some of the things that unionism does [but] I'm quite happy for unionism to share the blame with the media in terms of how our image is presented. It is not sufficient just to say it's all the fault of the media. That is not the case. Some of it's the fault of the media but a lot of it's also our own fault in the way that we have presented our case. (personal interview, Belfast, June 1993)

For Alan Wright of the Ulster Clubs, the Anglo-Irish Agreement was one result of the failure. The agreement was: 'the culmination of 50 years work by nationalists, not two years work in Dublin. Fifty years of lobbying right across the world. A 50-year PR job. We haven't been doing that and we have to learn that lesson' (interview in *Fortnight*, No. 233, 10 February 1986, cited in O'Dowd 1991: 168).

But the problem is that even now unionism has failed to mount a coherent PR campaign. In the words of John Oliver, former Permanent Secretary at Stormont:

The unionist philosophy has become disastrously stuck in a setting appropriate no doubt to earlier times, when intransigence was the response to continuing threat and exclusiveness justified by smouldering rebellion. It is largely for that reason that legitimate unionist governments from 1921 till 1972 remained tongue tied in so many important ways and that their energetic and expensive campaigns in Great Britain and North America were less than convincing. Spokesmen were hesitant, unsure and reticent because deep down they had no assurance that they could speak frankly for unionism. In so far as unionism had become in practice a defensive stance and in so far as it was buttressed by attitudes of Protestant ascendancy, unworthy electoral practices and unfair discrimination, then its spokesmen were unable to do justice to the real merits of their case and to the undoubted achievements of their regime, both central and local, in bringing prosperity and progress to the people. (Oliver 1978: 68)

'Typically' as Liam O'Dowd has written, 'Oliver does not elaborate the positive philosophy of Unionism any further'

(O'Dowd 1991: 169). The consequences of this fundamental identity crisis is that the unionists have few friends in the media or internationally. In international terms they are excoriated because of their inability to modernise and present themselves in terms acceptable to liberal democratic norms.

Conclusions

The NIO and other official sources cannot always dominate, but official sources have been remarkably effective in influencing media coverage. Alternative sources can and do make an impact, but they tend to be limited by resourcing and credibility problems as well as by official attempts at censorship and intimidation of the media.

The success of a particular media strategy may not mean, and in fact tends not to mean, the domination of news agendas or the reproduction of frameworks of understanding. In general, media strategies focus on more limited goals. Some of the major successes in the media strategies of non-official sources have been successful *in spite* of the fact that media agendas have still operated within parameters set by official sources. It is not always necessary for the media to become oppositional for non-official sources to succeed.

The next chapter examines the content of news reports and shows that the potential of the press to criticise or oppose official views depends on the interaction of a number of identifiable factors, such as format, the policing of the media, and source strategies. It also shows that coverage of Northern Ireland in the US is considerably more open to critical views than that in Britain. Even so, US media coverage still operates predominantly within the official framework. This is the case even in those cases where the British government has felt itself to be losing and the republican movement winning the propaganda war.

4

From 'Terrorists' to 'Freedom Fighters': International Coverage of Northern Ireland

A cursory glance at European or North American newspapers reveals coverage of the conflict in Northern Ireland which is markedly different from that found in Britain. British mainstream news programmes tend to be relatively closed around the official perspective. 'Terrorism' is the ubiquitous description of the activities of the Irish Republican Army. Outside Britain, other, more legitimating, descriptions start to appear. However, this doesn't mean that international coverage tends to favour the 'terrorists'. Comparative analysis of international coverage shows that the way Northern Ireland is reported in Britain is neither 'natural' or immutable, nor is it the only way to cover the conflict in Northern Ireland. Alternative models, even within Western countries, do exist.

Method

In order to examine the ways in which coverage of Northern Ireland varies between different national media systems (even in an age of increasing internationalisation), media types and presentational formats, I will compare British and US press and TV coverage of the killings in Gibraltar in March 1988 and their aftermath. I have chosen the US because it is an ally of Britain and, as we have seen, is regarded as the most important arena of propaganda warfare by both the British and the republicans. The events surrounding the Gibraltar killings are particularly appropriate because they were regarded by the US media as a major story and were one of the increasingly few stories to bring US camera crews to Belfast. Additionally, the killings were the subject of an hour-long documentary on US television, which is something of a rarity.

For Britain I have included all national newspapers as well as main TV news programmes,[1] current affairs and documentary coverage. For the US I concentrate on the three major TV networks -- ABC, NBC and CBS -- as well as a range of the US press -- the *New York Times, Chicago Tribune, Atlanta Constitution, Boston Globe, Christian Science Monitor, Washington Post* and the *Los Angeles Times*. [2] Before we engage in detailed comparisons of the British and US press, I will survey some of the differing ways in which Northern Ireland has been reported around the world.

From 'the Freedom-loving Forces of Northern Ireland' to 'Terrorist Atrocities'

The reporting of Northern Ireland varies in relation to political distance from the conflict, the relationship between the particular media system and the state, and the political complexion of the government. Because all three of these criteria can vary over time and in relation to each other, coverage can evolve and change or even be subject to contradictory pressures or struggles that relate to the exigencies of political power or interest.

The political culture in which journalists operate can heavily influence the way they look at the conflict in Ireland. In the countries of the former Eastern bloc, the political culture was highly critical of British policy in the six counties and this informed reporting by the state-controlled media. But not all of the Eastern European countries covered Northern Ireland in the same way.

At one end of the spectrum of coverage were resolutely oppositional accounts of the conflict. Albania, for example, was one of the most authoritarian of the Eastern European communist countries. In 1984 the Albanian news agency ATA gave its view of the conflict in Ireland: 'The freedom-loving forces of Northern Ireland are responding to the savage violence of the British police and occupying forces with a resolute struggle' (ATA, 17 August 1984, cited in BBC *Summary of World Broadcasts*). The official British view is categorically rejected, as Britain is seen as the cause of the conflict to which the 'freedom-loving forces' only respond. But this report is not straightforwardly supportive of the

IRA. For one thing the language and style reflect the official ideology of 'Marxism-Leninism' more than they do Irish republicanism. Indeed, we can see this report as reflecting the priorities and rationale of the Albanian state in its opposition to the West, rather than simple support of the IRA. The report goes on to explain that the 'savagery' of British policy in Ireland is not simply random but should be seen in the context of Western imperialist interests:

> By implementing its policy towards Northern Ireland, London enjoys the support of American imperialism. During his visit to the Republic of Ireland and Britain this year, Reagan himself condemned the struggle of the people of Northern Ireland, calling it a 'brutal and terrorist violence' ... The support they give each other for their policy of establishing and preserving the hegemonist domination over other peoples is in the interest of both London and Washington. (ibid.)

Soviet reporting was also consistently critical of British policy. McNair argues that until the end of 1987 Northern Ireland was reported 'almost exclusively in terms of "the troubles"' (McNair 1991: 174) and the coverage was predominantly organised within a 'human rights framework' (1991: 176). Soviet journalists routinely and explicitly rejected the British view that the blame for the troubles lies with the 'terrorists'. In 1983, for example, the Young Communist paper *Komsomolskaya Pravda* reported:

> The main cause of the persistent conflict in Ulster, which has already claimed over 2,600 lives, is the human rights situation in the province. To this day London rules Ulster by emergency legislation which quite candidly rides roughshod over the principles and purposes of the UN charter. (*Komsomolskaya Pravda*, 25 August 1983, cited in BBC *Summary of World Broadcasts*, 29 August 1983)

This allowed journalists to describe protest actions in Northern Ireland as *responding* to British 'repression'. On St Patrick's day 1988, for example, the Soviet news agency Tass reported that Northern Ireland: 'again became a scene of spontaneous protest actions against a course of police and military repression imposed upon Ulster by the London Government' (Tass, 17 March 1988, cited in BBC *Summary of World Broadcasts*, 18 March 1988). McNair argues that this tended to result in coverage which was 'sympathetic to and supportive of republican activists, including members of paramilitary organisations' (1991: 176). This seems to be going too far. While much reporting was critical of the British role in Ireland and referred to republican paramilitaries as 'guerrillas' or even 'patriots', there was a coherent strand in the reporting that condemned the activities of 'terrorists' or the killing of non-combatants as counterproductive. In May 1987 Tass reported:

> The progressive forces of Ulster, among them communists, condemn terror as a method of political struggle. Such actions only complicate the situation and offer imperialist circles a pretext for interfering in internal Irish affairs. Indeed, as the press reports, London, taking advantage of another outbreak of terrorism, intends to beef up police forces in Ulster. It sent additional army units there, including units of the SAS which became notorious for their brutality as punitive forces. (Tass, 12 May 1987, cited in BBC *Summary of World Broadcasts*, 14 May 1987)

Following the bombing in Enniskillen in November 1987, the IRA were again condemned. During a long interview the radio announcer asks if 'the latest terrorist act by the IRA has played into the hands of London?' The London correspondent replies: 'Yes, I think this action was deplorable, both from the standpoint of its political effect and in terms simply of the human tragedies it has caused' (Moscow Foreign Service, 20.00 GMT, 10 November 1987, cited in BBC *Summary of World Broadcasts*, 17 November 1987).

Furthermore, the political and institutional context in which different media operate may influence the sources which journalists use. Hence it is very rare for British or US journalists to quote British or Irish Communist Party representatives in their reports. In the Soviet media, however, such sources seem to have been used regularly. Following the Assembly elections in 1982 the *Moscow Home Service* interviewed Moscow Radio's London correspondent, who commented that the elections were a 'cosmetic operation'. This was contrasted with the 'constructive' programme that had been put forward by the Communist Party of Ireland (CPI):

> The election programme of the Communists pointed out the need for a realistic approach to solving Ulster's main problem – guaranteeing real equality between the Roman Catholic population and the Protestants and improving the economy. (Moscow Home Service, 18.02 GMT, 23 October 1982, cited in BBC *Summary of World Broadcasts*, 24 October 1982)

Following the Brighton bombing, which targeted Mrs Thatcher and her cabinet, *Izvestiya* cited the Communist Party of Great Britain (CPGB):

> Democratic circles have resolutely condemned the act of terrorism. As G. McLennan, General Secretary of the Communist Party of Great Britain, pointed out, this act will do nothing to help the Irish people's cause. The bomb and the threat of new attacks play into the hands of those who seek to tie Ireland's just cause and terrorism together in a single knot. (14 October 1984, cited in BBC *Summary of World Broadcasts*, 16 October 1984)

In fact, while the Soviet media was strongly critical of British policy in Ireland, they were also critical of the actions of the IRA and keen to promote the British and Irish Communist parties. A 1982 Soviet TV documentary thus reviewed events in the North and featured interviews with the IRA, [3] politicians, human rights activists and the British army before giving this (somewhat immodest) picture of the CPI: 'Threatened from all sides and made up of only the bravest and most stalwart, the Irish CP supports reunification' ('The Flames of Ulster', Soviet Television, 12 February 1982, cited in BBC *Summary of World Broadcasts*, 15 February 1982).

Soviet media coverage was more complex than McNair's suggestion that it simply supported the IRA. The approach of the Soviets in questioning the legitimacy of the British presence should not be confused with support for what the Soviets themselves regarded as 'terrorism'. The Soviet approach seems to have been echoed by reporting in the newspaper of the French Communist Party, *L'Humanité*, which during the 1981 hunger strikes 'stressed systematically the Republican calls for peaceful demonstrations and condemned the military aspect of their fight. The blame for physical violence is put on the British troops and the Protestant paramilitary groups' (Brennan et al. 1990: 111).

Western News

Reporting on Northern Ireland in Western countries such as France or the US is different from that found in both British and Eastern European media. This is not simply because of the geographical proximity of France or the US to Britain; it is more closely related to ideological criteria. The way terrorism is described is related to who the 'terrorists' are attacking, and how 'politically' proximate they are. Li Causi notes that when Italian television covers political violence outside Italy it tends to provide rational explanation for opposition to the state:

> Foreign terrorism isn't some kind of aberrant spectacle coming from nowhere or out of the heads of third rate ideologists. It has roots, causes, objectives. Its actions can be understood by the television audience, even if not justified. (Li Causi 1982: 231, cited in Schlesinger et al. 1983: 57)

Li Causi has noted that coverage of organisations such as the IRA and UDA on Italian TV is:

> explained in terms of the troubled history of that country, by the centuries-old subjection of Ulster to British rule, and so far as Republican irredentism is concerned, by the economic and cultural oppression of the Catholics by the Protestants, and finally by the presence of the British army. (Li Causi 1982: 226, cited in Schlesinger et al. 1983: 175)

In the French press, a similar pattern is found with a 'pro-Catholic and anti-Protestant, pro-Irish and anti-British' attitude informing the coverage of the right-wing *Le Figaro*. After 1975 this was overlaid by a view of the IRA as 'a terrorist organisation, which was fully integrated into the international terrorist plot' (Brennan et al. 1990: 106–7). Meanwhile, at *Le*

Monde, 'The IRA and later, UDA, activities were not approved. Even if *Le Monde* leaned towards the Irish nationalists, backing the idea of a united Ireland as the best solution in the long term, it never found any good reason to support violence' (Brennan et al. 1990: 118).

As we have seen, the major international target for the public relations activities of both the British state and Irish nationalists is the US. It seems reasonable to suppose that the US is the most pressured space for coverage of Ireland outside of Britain and Ireland. This is because of the media and policy objectives of British, Irish and US organisations (both Irish-American and governmental). It seems clear that successive US presidents have been interested in shoring up the border, whatever their professed views while on the campaign trail to the White House (Cronin 1987). The US is a close ally of the UK and so it might be thought that US coverage would be fairly close to British reporting.

British Guidelines

In Chapter 1 we saw how British broadcasters had progressively tightened their internal rules for covering Northern Ireland, partly as a result of government pressure. The language used to describe the conflict is also subject to close policing. BBC guidelines distinguish between 'terrorists' and 'guerrillas' as follows:

> Members of illegal organisations who bomb and shoot civilians are unquestionably terrorists – they use terror to achieve their objectives. If there are occasions when the term is not appropriate there are always other words available – IRA men, UVF men, killers, murderers, bombers, gunmen. (BBC 1993: 15)

Similarly, in the style book at the *Independent*, on the sparsely populated liberal end of the spectrum of the British press, the advice to journalists is to be cautious about the use of 'terrorist'. But the definition of a 'terrorist' shares key elements with that of the BBC:

> Terrorist is a much abused word that still has a precise meaning. Terrorism is violent action intended to create terror among a civilian population so as to destabilise a government.

> Thus an IRA man who plants a bomb in a public house is acting as a terrorist; one who shoots a British soldier is not ... Resist the unthinking habit of always calling the IRA terrorists. (Keleny 1992: 60–1)

In any case, the distinction between a 'guerrilla' and a 'terrorist' is not applied uniformly, since the IRA is almost uniformly described as 'terrorist' whatever its targets. There is a much more fundamental sense in which the term terrorist is literally 'one-sided'. In the definitions quoted above the 'terrorists' are described not just in terms of targets but also in terms of their relationship to the current political system. Thus for the *Independent* it is groups trying to 'destabilise' a government and for the BBC simply 'illegal' groups that are defined as 'terrorist'. The concept of 'state terrorism' is effectively ruled out. However, some guidelines do not make an explicit distinction between legal and illegal groups or between states or non-state groups. At *The Times*:

> Essentially, the difference should derive from the choice of target or the tactics of that particular violence. Terrorism, in our view, is any act of violence perpetrated willingly or inadvertently against non-military targets. Guerrillas may be guerrillas, but they are terrorists when they attack buses full of civilians. (cited in Taylor 1986: 215)

It is of course equally clear that reference to the state as 'terrorist' is not meant to be within the ambit of such coverage. When the British army kills civilians in Northern Ireland, the British media don't refer to those incidents as 'terrorism'. Similarly words such as 'gunman', 'killer' or 'murderer' are not used to describe government forces. We don't often hear of British 'gunmen' patrolling the streets of Northern Ireland.

BBC guidelines state that journalists should: 'Avoid anything which would glamorise the terrorist, or give an impression of legitimacy. In particular, try not to use terms by which terrorist groups try to portray themselves as legitimate – terms like "execute", "court-martial", "brigade", "active service unit"' (BBC 1989c: 80).

Journalists are even given instructions on the language they can use to describe the relevant territories in Britain and Ireland:

The United Kingdom is made up of Great Britain and Northern Ireland. Northern Ireland is the only correct name for that part. But 'Ulster' (really the name for nine Irish counties of which six are in Northern Ireland) is so widely used as a synonym that it is acceptable. (BBC 1989c: 39)

This is contrasted with the term 'Six Counties', which is not acceptable because it 'has no legal or constitutional basis, and expresses a political viewpoint' (BBC 1989c: 39). It is clear that terms such as 'Northern Ireland', 'United Kingdom' and especially 'Ulster' are no more neutral than 'Six Counties' or 'North of Ireland'. To use the term UK implies an acceptance of current constitutional arrangements, which are of course precisely what are under dispute. Nevertheless the BBC has simply adopted the terminology used by the government as if it were neutral.

BBC World Service

The restrictions on BBC coverage of Northern Ireland meant for consumption in Britain do not apply to the World Service. Operating in a world which does not automatically share the British view of the conflict in Ireland, the World Service tries to protect its credibility by reporting more dispassionately. Its reputation is seen as being premised on how it reports events in Britain in general and in Northern Ireland in particular:

In reporting Britain, we follow the same editorial principles as in reporting the world. A British story must earn its place in our bulletins and current affairs coverage; it must be judged by its news value, not by its effect on Britain's reputation ... We conceal neither the unpleasant nor the positive; we explore both. Indeed, many listeners regard our coverage of the complex and often distressing events in Northern Ireland as a litmus test of our credibility. (BBC World Service 1990)

The problems of covering political violence have resulted in a special appendix in the World Service style book. It describes at length the reasoning that has led the World Service to rule against the use of the word 'terrorist' in its reporting. This 'self-denying ordinance' is justified on the following grounds by World Service news editor David Spaull:

> We too would often like to relieve our feeling of revulsion by using the broadcastable equivalents of 'murdering bastards'. We don't, because we feel that something far more important than our feelings, or the feelings of some of our listeners is at stake. (Spaull 1988: 50)

The debate in the World Service revolves in part around the notion that it is the job of the journalist to 'fight terrorism'. Editorial staff have 'no doubt' that not using the 'T' word enhances their credibility and therefore the fight against 'terrorism':

> If we were to depart from it, our credibility and reputation for impartiality would be badly damaged in the minds of our listeners. Nowhere is this more true than in our reporting of the IRA ... When things do go wrong in the fight against the IRA, as from time to time inevitably they must, there is no better damage limitation in terms of world opinion than the BBC telling the facts without embellishment and without emotive language. (Spaull 1988: 52)

However, World Service editorial policy is not without limits. Journalists are cautioned that only the abbreviation will do when referring to the IRA. 'The IRA is always the IRA -- Irish Republican Army is misleading.' (Brown 1988: 33). The thought that the IRA might be referred to as an army is beyond the limits of objectivity of even the World Service.

Language in the Press

Let us now examine the way guidelines such as these are put into practice in news coverage of the main armed oppositional force in Northern Ireland, the Irish Republican Army. The most common description in both the US and British press was the simple abbreviation IRA (Table 4.1 gives a summary of the most common terms). After this, however, the descriptions diverge markedly. In the British press the ubiquity of the term 'terrorist' is apparent. It was much more commonly used than any other term. In the US press, by contrast, the political distance between the USA and Britain manifested itself in terms like 'member(s)', 'guerrilla(s)' and 'Rebel(s)' which were used more often than the term 'terrorist'.

Table 4.1 Descriptions of Irish republicans in the press

US press		British press	
IRA	399	IRA	163
members	80	terrorists	69
guerrillas	61	members	27
Irish Republican Army	57	bomb squad/gang	26
Sinn Féin, political wing of the IRA	38	Provisionals/Provos	22
rebels	31	paramilitary display/ trappings	18
terrorists	28	gang	17
gunman/men	19	suspected terrorists	15
outlawed	16		
suspects	15		
bombing squad	12		

By way of comparison some of the more favoured and legitimising terminology found in the US press can very occasionally be found in the British media. There was, for example, one reference to 'suspected guerrillas' in *The Times* of 7 March.

The main descriptions of loyalist groups, by contrast were less prejudicial (see Table 4.2). 'Gunman' was the most common description in both countries and other words describing actions, such as 'attacker' and 'assailant', were relatively common in the US. Harder terms for actions, such as 'assassin', 'bomber' and 'killer' were used in the British press.

Table 4.2 Descriptions of loyalist paramilitaries in the press

US press		British press	
gunman/gunmen	22	gunman	77
Protestant paramilitaries	17	UDA	40
attacker	12	assassin	23
Protestant	9	bomber	22
Protestant gunman	8	terrorists	16
Protestant extremist	7	UVF	15
(Protestant) terrorist	7	paramilitary	14
UDA	7	killer	14
assailant	6	fanatic/lunatic/crazed/ kamikazi/psychopathic	12
UDA, loyalist paramilitary group	6	Ulster Defence Association	10
terrorist acts	5		

Loyalist paramilitaries were much more often identified as 'Protestant' in the US than they were in Britain, while the British (tabloid) press more often resorted to the language of irrationality and madness. The main descriptions that transcended the identification of organisations simply with their actions were either the names of the organisations or the term 'paramilitaries'. By comparison, this term was very rarely used to describe republican groups. Descriptions of British forces showed the least variation between the US and British press. Routine terminology included 'British Army', 'troops', 'soldiers', 'military', etc. 'Police' or 'police officers' were the second most common, followed by 'security forces' in both nations (Table 4.3).

It was rare for the British press to include routine negative evaluative information about the RUC, but there were occasional references in the US press to the sectarian makeup of the RUC. There were three references to the RUC as, for example, a 'Mainly Protestant police force' (*Chicago Tribune*, 7 March 1988) or as 'widely perceived not as a traditional police force but as a paramilitary arm of suppression' (*New York Times*, 10 July 1988).

Table 4.3 Descriptions of British forces in the press

US press		British press	
British soldiers/military/ army/troops etc.	376	British soldiers/military/ army/troops	192
Police/detectives/ officers, etc.	251	Police	88
Security forces/chiefs/ services, etc.	52	RUC officers/men	83
Royal Ulster Constabulary, etc.	52	Security forces/services/ personnel	46
British agents/ undercover agents	33	SAS	25
Commandos	19	Royal Ulster Constabulary	19
SAS and descriptions	16	Special Branch/detectives	18
RUC	15		

Comparing the terminology for republicans and British forces in the British press, there are few occasions when the British army is described in the same terminology as the IRA. In the American press it was possible to find the same article referring to British and IRA agents. This recognition in a news account that the IRA and the British army are opposing military forces is very rare in British reporting. Indeed, there were no references in the British sample to republicans as 'agents' and only two to British 'personnel'. On both occasions the term was prefixed with the word 'undercover' and one of these was a description of the beliefs of 'local people'.

The key difference between the descriptions of state and non-state actors, however, is that state actors are rarely described by their actions. In my sample there were no occasions on which British army or RUC personnel were described as 'snipers' or 'killers', though it is clear that the British army has inflicted a substantial proportion of all casualties in the conflict. [4] It is also rare to find state personnel described with evaluative terms such as 'terrorist'. The significant exception to this rule is the use of positive evaluative terms adopted by the state groups themselves. In my sample this was most prominently shown in the use of the labels 'anti-terrorist' and 'Security Forces'.

Formats

Many analyses assume that media reporting is homogeneous, and that there are few noteworthy differences between media types or forms. But, as Bruck has argued, ideological reproduction is not uniform and 'the news media do their work in differing ways at different times, depending, among other things, upon the topic, political circumstances and ... the alternative social and discursive pressures exerted at a given time' (Bruck 1989: 113). It has also been suggested that formats may, in an important sense determine the content of reporting (Altheide 1985, 1987). The rest of this chapter compares and contrasts varying formats in the press and on television to examine such arguments more thoroughly.

News Reports – the Press

On Monday 8 March 1988 the British Foreign Secretary, Geoffrey Howe, announced to the House of Commons that a 'dreadful terrorist act has been prevented' by the actions of 'military personnel' in Gibraltar. [5] He also acknowledged that there had been no bomb in the car belonging to the three IRA members who had been shot and that they had been unarmed. This marked change of story, delivered by a senior government minister in the House of Commons, became the main news angle for some journalists the next day. But editorial judgements in London ensured that although official reports on the killings on the night of 6 March had been so comprehensively wrong, the main news stories in the British press continued to follow the agenda set by official sources rather than exercising critical judgement on the activities of the government. There were no headlines such as the front-page lead in the Dublin *Irish Press*: 'Fury as no bomb found'. Instead, the British press concentrated on other matters, such as the hunt for the alleged fourth member of the IRA squad, with front-page headlines such as 'Fourth IRA Bomber on the Run' (*Guardian*), 'Hunt for Fourth IRA Terrorist' (*The Times*), 'Fourth Terrorist Still at Large', (*Daily Telegraph*), 'Search Continues in Gibraltar for Car Bomb and IRA Terrorist' (*Financial Times*), 'Hunt for IRA Evelyn' (*Sun*) and 'Find Evil Evelyn' (*Daily Mirror*). In these latter tabloid reports, Evelyn Glenholmes was named as being hunted by police throughout Europe over her alleged involvement in the 'Gibraltar Bomb Plot'. [6]

These accounts shared with the government a consensus about the importance of two obviously newsworthy events, accepting that it was more crucial to report the alleged fourth IRA member than question the activities of the government. Some news stories accepted that the account given by Howe was accurate and that the belief in the existence of a car bomb was genuine, if mistaken. Thus the *Star* had 'Find the Real Bomb Car' and the *Daily Telegraph* 'Dreadful Act of Terror Averted Howe tells MPs'.

In the US, by contrast, the headlines centred on the change in the British government story:

British Admit Killing 3 Unarmed Members of IRA (*Atlanta Constitution*)

British Say No Bomb Found in 3 Killings (*Chicago Tribune*)

Britain, in an About-face, says 3 Slain in Gibraltar Hadn't Planted Bomb (*Boston Globe*)

British Amend Account of Killing of 3 in Gibraltar (*New York Times*)

The more routine line in Britain was assigned minority status in the *Los Angeles Times*:

Gibraltar Bomb Sought after IRA Deaths.

These differences in reporting between US and British newspapers are important because they show that front-page stories are not only determined by the intrinsic 'news value' of a particular event or angle. Newspapers in America and in Dublin thought that the more newsworthy story was the change in the British account. The British press, by contrast, thought that the most important story was in following the agenda set by the British government and concentrating on the hunt for the fourth IRA member or the whereabouts of the explosives.

Features

Features are distinguished by a number of formal characteristics. They are longer than news reports, intended to set events in context and are defined as 'soft news' (Bruck 1989: 115). Thus the reporter can more readily include accounts from sources whose credibility is not evaluated on the basis of their authority. 'Colour' can be added by recording anecdotal, bizarre or incidental detail. The 'human', angle on features or backgrounders may allow oppositional perspectives to be aired or alternative information to be presented.

For example, the lead story in the *Daily Mail* on 8 March (in common with the other papers) revealed 'bomber on the run is a woman' with a strap line 'Police link Evelyn Glenholmes with

Gibraltar terror raid'. The story was dominated by official statements from the Spanish police and Geoffrey Howe. Inside the paper, however, a centre-spread started off with the individualised 'soft' news treatment of an eyewitness to the shootings: 'A young mother-of-two watched from her bedroom as the finale of the IRA's attempt to bring mass murder to Gibraltar unfolded before her in the afternoon sunshine' (*Daily Mail*, 8 March 1988). This is a classic introduction to a feature piece. Starting off by personalising the story, it makes clear the vulnerability of the innocent witness about to see an alien scene played out in front of her eyes. She looked, we are told, 'hardly believing what her eyes were telling her'. The witness account of the killings was carried in an almost celebratory way under the headline 'Death in the Afternoon', but nevertheless it was carried at length. It implicitly contradicts the official account given in the House of Commons and on the front page of the *Daily Mail* and every other paper that day. It is worth remembering that, although this eyewitness testimony was available to all the papers, five of the eleven national dailies did not report it. [7] It is possible in news entirely to exclude alternative accounts or information, whereas in features such information is easier to include even if the 'whole structure' of the piece is 'designed to discredit it as a political argument' (Schlesinger et al. 1983: 91).

In American papers feature and background pieces on Northern Ireland (an international story) are particularly appropriate for Sunday newspaper editions, as they can be used as a lens through which to view and contextualise the week's events (this tendency of Sunday newspapers is of course related to the political rhythms of both the US and Britain, where Sunday is 'quiet' in 'hard' news terms). In fact, seven out of the fifteen features on these events were published on a Sunday.

A *New York Times* colour piece, for example, concentrated on the background of Mairead Farrell, one of those shot. It included an extensive contribution from Fr. Raymond Murray, the noted human rights activist, who was also chaplain of Armagh women's prison when Farrell was imprisoned there. Murray's contribution allowed some of the complexities of the debate between the Church and the IRA to be aired. The report opens with a scene-setting description of Murray's preparation of a requiem Mass for Farrell:'It was late, the fire was fading at the rectory hearth and the priest had finished writing his eulogy for Mairead Farrell, an Irishwoman slain in the time-worn rebellion' (*New York Times*, 16 March 1988). The reporter then goes on to describe Farrell in terms unfamiliar to British audiences more used to simple descriptions of IRA members as mindless psychopaths:

> Far from being a romantic enigma Mairead Farrell was a plain spoken adherent of the Irish Republican Army who was involved in a total of two insurgent operations. These were interrupted by 10 years in prison, where Father Murray says he first felt the sharpness of her wit in debate in defending the violent IRA struggle from criticism, particularly the church's. (ibid.)

The report continues, describing Murray's reaction to the prison protests and his very definitely alternative view of the people involved in them:

> 'It destroyed me', he said, describing the death and political struggle of the last 20 years and the militant women he visualises as peaceful leaders in some other time and place. He saw Miss Farrell become the instant leader of scores of women through their darkest days when they held their year long 'no wash' strike in 1980 over the British authorities' withdrawal of their political prisoner status. (ibid.)

The extensive description of Farrell as a human being, with details of her past and testimony from those who knew her, allow for a more rounded picture to emerge. They counteract what Jack Holland has called the 'dehumanising machinery of propaganda' (1988). Such portrayals did not occur in news stories.

The feature form has the potential to allow access to sources, to give personal and individual reactions, and can also allow critiques of official positions to be advanced. While US news coverage often implicitly deviated from official perspectives, it was rare for news to explicitly question the role of the British government, which was predominantly assumed to be a bystander in the conflict. But in a feature one journalist could observe that: 'The London government often leaves nationalists livid by assuming the role of the sad, bewildered referee among these unruly Irishmen' (*New York Times*, 20 March 1988).

Such openness can often leave journalists feeling uneasy and attempting to recoup the lost ground which their interviewees have staked out. The *Christian Science Monitor* was perhaps the closest to official British perspectives of the US papers in this sample. In a background feature highlighting the problems of the police in battling 'deep distrust' amongst Catholics, the London correspondent visited and interviewed residents of Springhill in West Belfast. The discussion starts with the expression by residents of their distrust of the police. One woman argues: 'They're not patrolling to protect us ... They just want to keep an eye on us.' The journalist goes on to frame these responses not as indicating a coherent alternative analysis of the 'troubles' but as a lack of trust which the RUC must overcome to 'improve its reputation as an impartial law enforcement agency' in order that life might 'return to normal'. The attempts made by the RUC to do this are then detailed. Amongst these is the attempt to recruit more Catholic officers, but the failure to do this is put down by the journalist to Catholic distrust. Another resident of Springhill is quoted: 'In all my life in this country there's been no change in the policies of the RUC ... What they say in the papers and what they do on the streets are two different things.'

Although the local people are quoted and their words give an insight into another way of looking at the 'problem', this perspective is not developed and the journalist has to fight to bring the discussion back on to the familiar terrain of the official perspective. In this case he does it by intervening to give his own assessment, saying that the residents of Springhill 'live on the front-line of communal strife and may not have noticed the changes'. This invalidating of the personal experience of ordinary citizens of West Belfast is then backed up by information from a source which has a high credibility – the RUC: 'One positive measure of confidence in the police has been the increased numbers of callers ... to police "hot lines". Police say the numbers have increased by 50 percent in recent months' (*Christian Science Monitor*, 24 March 1988).

While the reporter tried to invalidate the alternative analysis, it is significant that the views of the residents were granted some space. On occasion the 'openness' of the format can allow the reporter simply to record chunks of dialogue without intervention, beyond the selection of the pieces. Towards the end of March the *Boston Globe* ran three features on Northern Ireland. One of these simply recorded extracts of conversation between the reporter and 'ordinary' people, mainly from West Belfast. There were exchanges between the reporter and schoolchildren, one Protestant and one Catholic woman, a Protestant student and a Catholic retired building worker, as well as a republican and former INLA member. There were no interviews with official sources or with spokespersons for any political party. The former member of the INLA explained how he got 'involved' and ended up in prison. He went on to describe his involvement in the shooting of a UDR soldier and then his response to and rationale for his actions:

> Truthfully, I never have any bad dreams about it. Of course, at the same time I don't relish it. It's a sad fact of life. Either they kill you or you kill them. They are legitimate targets in this country. A sectarian force all made up of Protestants who kill unarmed civilians simply because they are Catholic. (*Boston Globe*, 27 March 1988)

In this version, the activities of republican groups are a response to the activities of the state. These perspectives are allowed to continue for five paragraphs and at no point are they contradicted or commented on by the journalist. Instead, the comments of other interviewees stand simply as different views. Such access to the press to explain a republican analysis is uncommon in Britain.

Editorials

Editorials are different from news in that they are the space where a view on the events of the day is taken. On the other hand, editorials are different from columns in that the opinions have the imprimatur of the newspaper rather than that of a named columnist. As we saw in the last chapter, editorial writers are one of the key targets of British information efforts in the USA.

All of the editorials in the US press on the events in March 1988 included critiques of the official view on Gibraltar: 'What chance do reason and justice have to end this mockery of civilisation when even the British, the supposed peacekeepers, shoot first and ask questions later' (*Chicago Tribune*, 21 March 1988). Similarly at the *Boston Globe*:

> Britain, on the one hand, treats the IRA as a criminal rather than a political organisation and strives to maintain the standards of investigation, arrest and trial that are normal in the British system of justice. 'Even-handedness' toward the IRA and the Protestant gangsters and fanatics is the watchword of the police, and to some extent this ideal is achieved. On the other hand, there is the recurrent practice – and perhaps the unstated policy – of treating the IRA as if it really were an army and as if wartime rather than peacetime standards apply. In war, soldiers do not stop to check an enemy's papers or caution him against suspicious moves. They shoot and they shoot to kill. (*Boston Globe*, 16 March 1988)

The underlying model against which all British actions are judged is that promoted by the British government. Editorials in the US press regularly criticised the British position, but the underlying assumption was that Britain is neutral in the conflict, albeit with a tendency to 'overreact' or behave ineptly. A study of US press editorials on Northern Ireland between 1971 and 1981 found a broadly similar pattern: 'The British are very much seen as the "honest brokers" in the dispute. Almost every initiative proposed by the British up to 1981 has been favourably received by the editorial writers' (Artherton 1983a: 20).

By contrast, editorials in British papers mostly supported the shootings in Gibraltar. The *Sun's* view was that: 'The moral for the IRA is a simple one. If they do not want to be killed, they should not try to kill others. Three criminals are dead. Our troops and all the forces on the side of law and order are safe. For us that is a happy ending' (*Sun*, 8 March 1988).

On the other hand there was criticism in the *Guardian*, the *Independent*, the *Observer* and the *Daily Telegraph*:

> It is very rarely that we find ourselves less satisfied with the Government's account of events than the Labour front bench ... There is no doubt of the malevolent intentions of the Irish

group on the rock. But the authorities handling of the affair poses serious questions ... Few British people will mourn the deaths of members of the IRA. But it is an essential aspect of an anti-terrorist policy to maintain the principles of civilised restraint which obtain in a democratic society. A failure to do so argues that terrorism is succeeding in one of it's critical aims, the brutalisation of the society under attack. (*Daily Telegraph*, 8 March 1988)

Comment and Columns

Writing about the background of a story or ruminating on future possibilities allows a certain leeway. Comment pieces and columns allow access to non-institutional sources or personal views. The majority of background and analysis pieces in Britain came from firmly within official or populist perspectives. Norman Tebbit made a trenchant statement of the populist perspective, arguing for the subordination of the rule of law to the war against terrorism:

> There can be no justification for violence to achieve political ends in a democratic system. Such violence or threat of violence must be resisted at all times at all costs ... The fact is that a democratic society which concedes at the point of a gun what cannot be gained through the ballot box, sells out on democracy itself. (*Sunday Express*, 13 March 1988; reprinted in the *Daily Star*, 14 March 1988)

The irrationality of terrorism, a key component of official thinking, means that the terrorists must simply be crushed. In the symbolism of the Vietnam war the village of democracy may have to be destroyed in order to save it:

> If terrorism is to be crushed there must be a twofold commitment. First that no demand is ever conceded under threat ... Second, a commitment that the defeat of terrorism has absolute supremacy over the cause which the terrorists claim to uphold. (*Sunday Express*, 13 March 1988; reprinted in the *Daily Star*, 14 March 1988)

Paul Johnson set out to recoup the ground lost at the Milltown attack, which he saw simply as a 'propaganda victory' for the republicans. In order to do this he reminded readers of who to blame for the killings: 'The origin of yesterday's violence is the IRA. This is the evil force which lies at the root of all the trouble' (*Daily Mail*, 17 March 1988). Here the British are seen as simply reacting to the 'Irish problem'.

By contrast, a guest article by an American academic in the *Los Angeles Times* questioned the notion that violence in Northern Ireland is senseless and included the question of violence by the state, so often left out of comparable discussions in Britain. His recommendations, that the British government make clear to the loyalists that their 'intransigence in the face of genuine efforts of conciliation jeopardises Westminster's willingness to maintain the Union' and the creation of a joint Anglo-Irish peacekeeping force, lead to a conclusion that any backlash from the loyalists would be 'violence' that was: 'truly senseless, which it has not been in political terms thus far' (*Los Angeles Times*, 28 March 1988).

Columns allow more potential space to contest official formulations. But that potential is not always fulfilled. One difference between columnists and outside contributors is that the latter gain access by virtue of a combination of their authoritative status and credibility as an expert or commentator as well as an assessment of what they are likely to say. Regular columnists are either senior journalists or specifically employed writers whose brief may include offering authoritative analysis or polemical views. Either way, the columnist has more latitude to proclaim unpopular or minority views, which may contrast with other parts of the editorial content or even with the editorial line of the paper. Columnists are often used as part of a marketing strategy to advertise the breadth of the paper. Thus the *Mail on Sunday* has run advertising campaigns claiming that it has both left- and right-wing columnists in Julie Burchill and John Junor, respectively. The *Sun* has also employed this strategy with columnists such as Garry Bushell and Richard Littlejohn, as well as Labour MP Ken Livingstone, whom the *Sun* once called 'the most odious man in Britain' for his views on Northern Ireland (*Sun*, 13 October 1981).

In March 1988 columns in the national press were more likely to question official accounts or give voice to alternative views

182

than they were to promote official or populist perspectives. As we have seen, this is in contrast to the coverage in analysis or comment sections of the press. However, columnists in the *Sun*, *Daily Express* and *News of the World* did promote official or populist perspectives. Woodrow Wyatt, for example, argued that:

Last Sunday three IRA terrorists were shot dead in Gibraltar by the British Army. Now Labour appeasers moan. They claim the three ought not to have been shot. They were unarmed so it wasn't legal they say. Unarmed? They had smuggled in a car loaded with explosives. Enough to kill two or three hundred people ... The assassins should have been buried in Gibraltar. Not in Ireland for the IRA to use the funeral for a mass demonstration. It doesn't matter that the individuals weren't carrying arms. (*News of the World*, 13 March 1988) [8]

But there was a sense in which the Gibraltar killings were a step too far in the 'war against terrorism' for some traditionally Conservative writers. Thus the deaths did excite critical comment amongst some columnists in the Conservative press. Auberon Waugh observed that:

What surprised me was the number of saloon bar Britons who reckoned it was all right to gun down the suspected terrorists, even if they were not engaged in terrorist activities at the time. If a majority of Britons feel like this – and my own soundings suggest they do – what is to stop Mrs Thatcher setting up murder squads on the South American model? (*Sunday Telegraph*, 13 March 1988)

This is similar in tone to some of the editorials in the US press, but quite radically different from the editorial written by Peregrine Worsthorne in Waugh's own paper, the *Sunday Telegraph*, the same day. [9] Following the killings at Milltown and Andersonstown, *Daily Mail* columnist Keith Waterhouse questioned the rationale for the British presence in Ireland:

To observe, as one newspaper did yesterday, that 'we have had an horrific foretaste of what would happen if Britain were to pull her troops out of Northern Ireland' seems not quite appropriate to the occasion when the two men mob-lynched on Saturday were themselves British soldiers, and the whole bloody week was precipitated by the SAS action in Gibraltar. For myself, I've always believed that the Army presence tends to aggravate rather than mitigate the situation. That's easy to say and difficult to prove, of course, and those of us who subscribe to this view would feel pretty sick to be proved wrong by hindsight. But it seems to me that recent events are as much an argument of the Army going as for the Army staying. (*Daily Mail*, 21 March 1988)

We can note that such perspectives get some space in the British press, albeit in the margins of the paper. This is potentially important in providing alternative information and perspectives to the British public. Some consequences of this will be discussed in Chapter 5. However, we should remember that such views are a minority even amongst columnists, and are not regularly expressed. Indeed, even columnists who are explicitly employed to have 'views' about contemporary political issues are vulnerable if they express views on Northern Ireland which are too critical of the orthodoxy. Thus the former editor of *Private Eye*, Richard Ingrams, seems to have been sacked as a columnist by the *Sunday Telegraph* because of his writings, and Labour MP Ken Livingstone was a short-lived columnist at Robert Maxwell's *London Daily News* because of his views on Northern Ireland. [10]

If editorials in the US press could be uniformly critical of the official position of the British government and open to the assumptions of alternative perspectives, then the space given to columnists could begin to contest even some of those assumptions. This is not to argue that *all* columns are like this, but there is a different range of information and views available. In the sample period, though, all of the columnists were critical of the official position of the British government. In news reports there were many descriptions of Mairead Farrell, but it was only in a guest column that Sally Belfrage [11] could simply record that for many people in Andersonstown Farrell was 'a much beloved local heroine' (*Los Angeles Times*, 1 May 1988).

She also referred to the possibility of interpreting British views as racist. Her analysis assumes that Britain is intimately involved in the conflict:

Over in London, the people in charge of this mess – whose attitude toward all the Irish, Catholic and Protestant, can be regarded as racist – were searching for expletives in the House of Commons. Having just spoken after the Milltown massacre of the Irish 'plumbing new depths' of savagery and bestiality, the politicians were hard put to come up with new hyperbole when the soldiers were murdered. So they spoke of still *newer* depths of the same being plumbed. Of no concern to Parliament was what had amounted to an execution without trial in Gibraltar: on the contrary, Prime Minister Margaret Thatcher was incensed at Amnesty International for pointing this out. (*Los Angeles Times*, 1 May 1988)

It was also possible to find the killings labelled as murder. The *Boston Globe*'s Mike Barnacle was direct and to the point:

Marvellous! The British celebrated St Patrick's day a bit prematurely last week by killing three unarmed Irish citizens on a street in Gibraltar and you would need a seeing-eye dog to locate an American politician here with even the slightest drop of Celtic blood who dare to label the deed for what it was: simple murder. (*Boston Globe*, 17 March 1988)

The nearest the British media got to such a statement was six weeks after the killings in a guest column in the *Independent*, where Enoch Powell raised the 'possibility' that it was murder in an article itself criticising British media reporting of the Gibraltar incident. Headed 'The questions our muzzled press should be asking on Gibraltar', the article argued that after the killings:

a massive self-congratulation intoned by the Foreign Secretary engulfed the media: it echoed back and forth in Parliament and the papers. Maybe what happened in Gibraltar was perfectly lawful and defensible ... Maybe; but there is another possibility. The possibility that it was deliberate, cold blooded, premeditated murder. (*Independent*, 1 April 1988)

Such sentiments are confined to the margins of the US and British press and in the latter are extremely rare. The endorsement of British disengagement is very rare anywhere in the British media. Only the *Daily Mirror* has endorsed British withdrawal at editorial level and has been attacked by other newspapers for doing so. In twenty-five years there has only been one television documentary devoted to explaining the case for British withdrawal. [12]

Cartoons

The space afforded by cartoons is bounded by the conventions of satire and humour. These are considerably looser than the constraints on factual reporting. Satire allows a huge leeway for comment. The newspaper cartoonist is thought of as being 'creative' and in similar vein to an artist or playwright is given a certain measure of licence not available in other parts of the paper. The liberalising of British television in the 1960s is regularly symbolised by the satirical *That Was The Week That Was* and, in the 1980s, television's *Spitting Image* regularly got away with comment and humour that would be unacceptable in other types of programming.

Indeed, it has been suggested that some of the humour in ITV's *Spitting Image* has been beyond the pale even for comedy. On election night 1987 the programme, screened just after the polls closed, ended with a young blue-eyed boy singing the song 'Tomorrow belongs to me' in a beer garden in a replica of the scene from the film *Cabaret*. In this case, though, the beer garden was populated by puppet members of the Cabinet, beer glasses in hand, who joined in with gusto as the young boy raised his arm in a Nazi salute. This edition of *Spitting Image* shocked the BBC. According to the then Deputy Director-General, Alan Protheroe: 'There was no way the BBC could have put that kind of programme out at that time. As one of my colleagues said, Mrs Thatcher would have ringed Broadcasting House with tanks' (*World in Action*, 1988).

Nevertheless, satire does give a licence for material that would be unacceptable elsewhere. This does not, however, only mean material that is critical of official perspectives, but also material that celebrates official and right-wing populist views.

Here we might also recall the popularity of anti-Irish racism in cartoons in some (especially tabloid) papers. Here, Irish people are drawn as sub-human and ape-like. Explaining this, Michael Cummings, who draws for the *Daily Express*, has said that his cartoons are simply giving expression to a view of Irish people as 'extremely violent, bloodyminded, always fighting, drinking enormous amounts, getting roaring drunk'. Simian caricatures are, he explained, a product of the violence of the IRA, which makes 'them look rather like apes – though that's rather hard luck on the apes' (cited in Curtis 1984b: 83). Kirkaldy has argued that such cartoons have been able to express 'anti-Irish prejudice that in any other form would be publicly unacceptable, even in England' (Kirkaldy 1981: 42).

On the other hand cartoons can provide a more critical space in papers like the *Guardian*, the *Independent* or the *Boston Globe*. The *Independent*'s Colin Wheeler, for example, published a number of cartoons questioning the government line on the killings in Gibraltar including one after the screening of 'Death on the Rock' which implied that the IRA members had been shot after giving themselves up (Figure 4.1).

**Figure 4.1 'Just don't put your hands up, that's all',
Colin Wheeler in the *Independent*, 30 April 1988**

The satirical magazine *Private Eye*, which was one of the strongest critics of the government account of the killings (*Private Eye*, 1989) trod a similar path, devoting one of its covers to the fact that Sean Savage was shot with a large number of bullets (Figure 4.2).

Meanwhile the *Boston Globe* cartoonist Wasserman put it more forcefully, featuring Mrs Thatcher as saying 'We deplore the recent violence in Northern Ireland and will work for a prompt return to law and order. We cannot tolerate the vigilante killing

Figure 4.2 Cover of *Private Eye* during the Gibraltar inquest, 16 September 1988

of unarmed civilians. That's a job for British Commandos' (Figure 4.3). Cartoons as direct as this are rare in the British press, echoing differences between nations in news coverage:

> Of all the factors accounting for the different images of the conflict presented in cartoons, the nationality of the cartoonist is the most powerful. The all-party agreement on Northern Ireland, for example has encouraged a high level of consensus among British cartoonists ... Outside the British Isles, there are clear differences of emphasis between socialist and capitalist countries, but general agreement among all that the issue is essentially to be viewed as a British problem ... Two main explanations for the strong distinction between cartoonists from different settings are the level of their involvement with the issue, and the way in which they perceive their constituencies. (Darby 1983: 115–16)

Figure 4.3 Wasserman in the *Boston Globe*, 20 March 1988

British cartoons are generally more limited than the occasional critiques to be found in the *Guardian* or *Independent*. In the early part of the troubles, according to Darby, 'there was little dispute' in cartoons that Northern Ireland was 'in fact a religious conflict':

> Far from becoming more sophisticated as time passed, this view of the conflict was apparently confirmed by the persistence and intractability of the violence. On the question of blame, too, there was considerable accord among British cartoonists: the roots were firmly planted in Irish bigotry and intransigence. Even when there was a suggestion, as in [Gerald] Scarfe's cartoons, that some of the blame was shared by Britain, it was laid firmly at the door of earlier British administrations. The present governments may make mistakes, but it was generally conceded that their good intentions were above reasonable suspicion. So, although it was uncommon for the Irish to be stereotyped as the subnormal brutes so common in nineteenth century cartoons, many of the analyses were implicitly ethnic. They assumed that the violence arose from qualities inherent in the Irish character – aggression, superstition, unreliability and a kind of unthinking death wish. (Darby 1983: 122–3)

Television News

The first and most obvious point about the US network television news on Ireland is the sheer lack of it. The networks cover Northern Ireland only occasionally and it takes many deaths to spur them to send a camera crew to Belfast. The big events of 1988 and 1989 were the aftermath of the Gibraltar shootings and the twentieth anniversary of the redeployment of British troops. The revolutions in Eastern Europe of 1989/90 forced Northern Ireland off the news pages, with London correspondents either relocated to other parts of Europe or simply assigned to stories in the East. CBS was the first network to cover the story on the nightly news with a report on 7 March. The first ABC report was on 14 March, and it was not until the attack· on the funeral at Milltown on 16 March that NBC introduced the story. If we were to accept the arguments of some journalists and academics

(Altheide 1987) we might expect to find that such lack of time resulted in news that was dominated by official perspectives to an even greater extent than news coverage in Britain. But this is not the case. The stories covered on television news were all event-led updates, some of which were then used as a hook to retell the story of the events of recent weeks. In this respect they were similar to the news briefs and reports in the press.

It is often argued that the British system of public service broadcasting is better able to be independent of the state than a commercial system, such as that in the US. However it is clear that, as with the press, US television is considerably more open than British television. We might recall that under British public service provisions, the BBC and ITN are required by law to produce news which is 'objective', 'unbiased' or 'balanced'. Such legal conventions are routinely violated by British broadcasters.

On US television the IRA has 'members', 'activists' and 'guerrillas'. In contrast, British television used only the term 'members' (Table 4.4). A pattern similar to the press reporting emerges, with perhaps more of an emphasis on the term 'terrorist' on ABC, which accounted for both uses of the term. CBS accounted for all uses of the terms 'guerrilla' and 'activist', while NBC preferred simply using 'IRA', which it did fifteen times.

On British television news there was one mention of an 'IRA Commando Unit', significantly on Channel 4. The word 'commando' is not acceptable on the BBC, even on the World Service, because according to the BBC's 1979 *News Guide*, 'In the 1939–45 war, the word had heroic connotations, and it is still the name of units of the Royal Marines' (cited in Curtis 1984b: 135). The military terminology preferred and used by the IRA, such as 'unit', does occasionally get used. The term 'squad' also has military connotations, but is not used by the IRA. It is used by the broadcasters. Probably on both accounts this is because it links so well with the term 'death' with its connotations of South America. 'Personnel' is occasionally used to describe IRA members, as is the legitimising 'volunteers'. But more often than not British journalists make it clear just how legitimate they think such labels are, as in references to 'so-called volunteers'. For the BBC there is also an issue about using the term 'Provos'. In the sample period it was used four times, all of which were on ITN. BBC news guidelines explicitly state that journalists should *'never'* (their emphasis) use the term 'Provos' because 'we should not give pet names to terrorists' (BBC 1989c: 39.4). Similarly, BBC journalists are advised not to give the IRA 'spurious respectability' by speaking of IRA 'volunteers' because 'we don't know why they joined' (BBC 1989c: 39.9).

Table 4.4 Descriptions of Irish republicans on television

US TV		British TV	
IRA	26	IRA	39
members	12	terrorists	17
Sinn Féin, political wing of the IRA	4	bombers	9
Irish Republican Army	3	members	8
guerrillas	3	gang	4
mob	3	group	4
activists	2	unit	4
leaders	2	Provos	4
sniper	2	squad	3
terrorists	2	what it [the IRA] called/so-called Active Service Unit	2
suspected terrorists	2	paramilitary	2
gunman/men	2		

The use of less pejorative terms such as 'guerrilla' is only part of the story. In the (British) official perspective the IRA are a criminal conspiracy, without political motivation. Their campaign is simply one of terrorism. While there is some room in British broadcasting to contest this proposition, most notably in documentaries and some fictional output, television news remains relatively closed. However, even in the most closed formats of television network news in the US there is a good deal more space to contest key propositions of the official (British) perspective.

Non-news Actuality Coverage

In Britain news coverage of the events of March 1988 was not the only source of television information for viewers. A number of current affairs and documentary programmes covered the killings in Gibraltar and their aftermath. The most critical of these, and the one that caused the most controversy, was an edition of Thames Television's *This Week*, titled 'Death on the Rock', which investigated the killings in Gibraltar and suggested that government accounts of the shootings had, at best, been misleading. In the US, the killings and their aftermath led to the making of a special documentary for the PBS public television network on the life of Mairead Farrell, one of the IRA members killed in Gibraltar. It has been suggested that documentaries are amongst the most potentially open of programme formats in both the US and Britain (Schlesinger et al. 1983; Altheide 1987). It is instructive to compare these two programmes and the reactions to them, as they illustrate the limits of openness in factual television in Britain and the US.

As we saw in Chapter 1, the account given by 'Death on the Rock' directly contradicted the official version. Eyewitnesses interviewed for the programme alleged that there had been no challenge and that the IRA members had made no movements, simply putting their hands up, as if in surrender. Essentially the programme challenged the factual accuracy of the official account, *implying* rather than actually *elaborating* an alternative way of understanding the conflict. The latter approach is very difficult in prime-time British broadcasting.

The 'Death on the Rock' programme makers themselves were very much aware of the limits of covering Northern Ireland. They were conscious that in order to get their programme on to television they would have to include sequences that showed that they were no supporters of 'terrorism'. [13] Indeed the editor, Roger Bolton, who has a long history of involvement in critical programmes on Ireland, made a special request that the programme slot be extended partly so that this material, which 'underlined the hostile editorial stance of the programme towards the IRA and its methods', could be accommodated (Windelsham and Rampton 1989: 22–4). Bolton (1990: 224) has described this insurance policy as putting the investigation 'in context'. The Chairman of the IBA, Lord Thomson, was later to write that he saw no reason to prevent the broadcast of the programme *provided* the criminal record of the terrorists and the enormity of the outrage they planned was made clear' (cited in Bolton 1990: 232, my emphasis). Such precautions are not required in the US.

In America the networks are able to show documentary programmes that simply could not be shown in Britain. In 1980, for example, ABC broadcast a documentary, *To Die for Ireland*, in a peak-time slot. According to press reports British diplomats even complained that it was being shown in America (Glasgow University Media Group 1982: 140–3). [14] The 1989 PBS film on the life of Mairead Farrell – 'Death of a Terrorist' (Cran 1989) – was structured as an investigation into the reasons why a middle-class Catholic girl from Belfast would join the IRA (at the age of 14) and take up arms against the British military. The director, Bill Cran, was keen to show some of the complexities of political violence and organised the film in opposing sections allowing Farrell, and her family and comrades, to present her as an ordinary person and determined, but rational activist. [15] Against this were counter-views which emphasised the official view of the conflict and the suffering caused by IRA actions. As Bill Cran explained:

if you can imagine something like an earthquake meter or something measuring a heart beat, I deliberately plotted it so your sympathies are switching for and against [Mairead Farrell] like she's almost driven into joining the IRA and I sympathise with her but then you know you're confronted with the fact that they're letting off bombs and innocent people get killed. Then she goes to jail, where she's very very brave, and then she comes out and she rejoins. At the end where we reran the news footage of the Gibraltar killings, the funeral, the attack on the corporals and so on we were literally deliberately planning it so that toward the end of the film the oscillations of sympathy start to go off the scale. All the way through the film you're doing small sort of ups and downs until they're absolutely going off the meter at the end. That was deliberately planned. (personal interview, London, May 1990)

The film featured extensive interviews with Farrell, conducted following her release from jail in 1986, as well as with former cellmates and other members of the republican movement. By comparison 'Death on the Rock' did not feature any interviews with either Sinn Féin or the IRA. [16] In sum, the US programme was able to interrogate critically the official picture of Northern Ireland and to show that it is not universally shared. The programme concluded by emphasising the contested nature of definitions of 'terrorism' and leaving to the viewer to decide which version they favoured. 'To some people of the Falls Road she [Mairead Farrell] was a patriot. To the British she was a terrorist. To her family she was a victim of Irish history.' 'Death of a Terrorist' was much more open to alternative views than 'Death on the Rock'. The controversy caused by 'Death on the Rock' compared with the lack of controversy over 'Death of a Terrorist' is indicative of just how close to the limits of British broadcasting the former pushed and of how much looser the limits of US broadcasting are.

In Britain the broadcast of 'Death on the Rock' was subject to an attempt by the Foreign Secretary to have the programme withdrawn. His request to the Independent Broadcasting Authority (IBA) was rejected, and the programme was broadcast as planned. There followed a concerted government attempt to cast (unattributable) doubt on the credibility of the witnesses interviewed and government ministers, including Prime Minister Margaret Thatcher, publicly attacked the programme (Miller 1991). Finally, after a long-running campaign by the government supported especially by Murdoch-owned papers the *Sun* and the *Sunday*

Times, Thames Television were pressured into instituting an independent inquiry into the programme (Windelsham and Rampton 1989). In the US the PBS documentary 'Death of a Terrorist' was not subject to any similar pressures.

The front line for alternative perspectives on the Gibraltar killings in Britain was the raising of questions about the legitimacy of state actions, measured against the standards of democratic government and the rule of law. In America, television was able to go further and consider the reasons why an Irish woman might take up arms against the British state. In other words, questions could be asked about whether the actions of the Irish Republican Army could be seen as legitimate.

US Coverage: Some Strengths and Limits

As the political distance between the media of any country and the political violence on which they are reporting increases, so more open and dispassionate coverage becomes more common. Some have argued that this indicates that such coverage is favourable to 'terrorism'. Weimann, for example, argues that the use of 'positive' labels may allow 'terrorists' to gain 'international recognition and even sympathy' (Weimann 1985: 443). We have seen that the US press is more likely to use more dispassionate terminology in describing non-state actors in Northern Ireland, but this should not be confused with coverage which justifies the 'armed struggle'. On the contrary, while the US coverage from March 1988 tended to be more open than British coverage, it was rare for it to allow unchallenged oppositional views. Moreover, as many researchers have shown (Holland 1989; Artherton 1983a, 1983b; O'Maolchatha 1990; Tan 1987, 1988, 1989; Paletz et al. 1982a, 1982b), US press and television reporting (especially news forms) tends to accept a key element of the 'official' view of the conflict – that the British state is somehow 'above' the fray and holding the ring.

This was certainly the case in the coverage of Gibraltar. The unusual features of the killings (in broad daylight on a public street, outside Northern Ireland where the credibility of witnesses was not automatically suspect) along with the build up of controversial events of early 1988, [17] prompted particularly hostile coverage of British policy in Northern Ireland; coverage is usually far more muted. [18] Yet even in this period the conflict is predominantly conceived of within the parameters of the official perspective. There is criticism of British policy for not matching up to its stated ideals, there are acknowledgements of repressive parts of British policy, there is discussion of the demands and aims of the IRA and there is even some treatment of the IRA and the British army as opposing military forces. But when it comes to characterising the conflict and its causes, official explanations predominate. News from Northern Ireland was predominantly reported in terms of inexplicable acts of continuing violence (cf. Elliot 1977). Where explanations were given or alluded to, irrationality was emphasised. The conflict was sometimes seen as rooted in obscure historical/sectarian/religious passions and sometimes in the 'terrorism', 'guerrilla warfare' or even 'armed struggle' of the IRA. In this period there were nineteen occasions on which the conflict was characterised as 'sectarian' or 'religious' and six where the cause was given as the violence of the IRA. As a corollary loyalist violence was seen as occurring as a *response* to the IRA (for example, 'Protestant paramilitary groups have grown up to fight it [the IRA]', *Atlanta Constitution*, 17 March 1988).

Characterisations of the conflict on US television news also tended to leave the role of the British out of the reckoning. Journalists talked of 'The conflict between Catholics and Protestants in Northern Ireland' (NBC, 16 March 1988), or 'a further escalation of violence between the two communities' (NBC, 19 March 1988), or of the IRA's 'war against the Protestants of the North' (ABC, 23 March 1988). When the *Christian Science Monitor* discusses the 'extremists on both sides' (24 March 1988) it is not referring to the British army. As Ward concluded in his analysis of US network television news coverage of Northern Ireland between 1968 and 1979, the major element missing was an examination of the role of the British government. 'The rationale for the British presence had been discussed in 1969 and was never subsequently contradicted or examined in depth' (Ward 1984: 210).

By contrast, there were only three references in the press that characterised Northern Ireland as a 'British-Irish conflict', [19] and a further three which used the single word 'resistance' to refer to

IRA actions. [20] On only one occasion was the promotion of the 'sectarian conflict' view recognised as a *view* rather than an accepted fact. London correspondent Karen DeYoung wrote:

> Prime minister Margaret Thatcher has seemed particularly prone to the belief that the Irish conflict is intractable and that the citizens of the province, Protestant and Catholic alike, are some sort of alien species locked in arcane warfare and impermeable to civilised reason. (*Washington Post*, 21 March 1988)

This short fragment was the nearest the US press got to referring to the British government as promoting a particular view of Northern Ireland. This compared to the regular references to the value that events would have in 'propaganda' terms for the republicans (cf. Holland 1989; Thomas 1991). Journalists talked of and endorsed the view that IRA or Sinn Féin actions could be measured in terms of their 'propaganda' value. Thus the *Chicago Tribune* reported that 'The IRA, dubbing the dead guerrillas "The Gibraltar Martyrs", has launched a major propaganda campaign' (16 March 1988). Reporting on the killing of three mourners at Milltown Cemetery, the *Washington Post* reported that 'today's events ... are sure to be seen as a major propaganda coup by the IRA' (17 March 1988), while the *Christian Science Monitor* reported that 'some analysts contend' that the IRA and Sinn Féin 'have attempted to turn the Gibraltar setback into a propaganda victory. The elaborate funeral arrangements, they say, aimed to make martyrs of the dead' (17 March 1988). These propaganda gains were then considered to have suffered a setback following the killings of the two British soldiers in Andersonstown three days later. The *New York Times* reported that the IRA 'was seen to have suffered another blow to the image it cultivates of the dedicated defender of the hard-pressed Catholic minority' (23 March 1988). In the only two counter-examples, the *Chicago Tribune* (18 March 1988) referred to 'the movement's traditional salute to its dead' and the *Washington Post* (18 March 1988) reported 'the military display which is traditional at funerals'. CBS echoed this view when it reported that 'IRA men in West Belfast gathered to fire a traditional but illegal honour guard salute' (15 March 1988). In contrast, ABC reported that 'The IRA uses funerals as a propaganda instrument' (ABC, 23 March 1988).

On British television news, however, to accept that the IRA has traditions and perhaps even rules, regulations or a coherent political ideology is beyond the pale of mainstream reporting. The killings in Gibraltar, the return of the bodies, the funeral and the attack on it, the lack of police presence, and finally the killing of the soldiers in Andersonstown were all evaluated in terms of their propaganda value for the republican movement. Thus the *Daily Telegraph* reported 'Sinn Féin to turn IRA burials into publicity stunt' (16 March 1988). [21] Television news also followed this agenda.

It should not be imagined that there are no external limits on US reporting. When journalists become too critical they risk being frozen out by British sources. In a critical commentary on US press coverage, Jack Holland specifically singles out reporting by *New York Times* correspondent Jo Thomas in the mid-1980s as a significant and hopeful exception to the lack of US investigative reporting on Northern Ireland (Holland 1989: 235). Yet Thomas quickly ran into problems with the British government for her revelations about police and army killings:

A senior editor who kept a home in London as well as in New York and who had been enthusiastic about my initial dispatches from Belfast, began telling me to stay out of Northern Ireland. A high-ranking British official, who in the past has had close ties with the intelligence community in Northern Ireland, took me to lunch and suggested I drop my investigation in exchange for a lot of access to the Secretary of State for Northern Ireland as well as an exclusive first look at the Anglo-Irish pact then being negotiated between London and Dublin. I refused. Several American colleagues in London suggested I leave the difficult investigations to the local press: if there really were a story, British and Irish reporters would be on top of it. In fact, they were not – but some of them began treating me as if I were a member of the IRA. Then, too, the mail at my house in London started to arrive opened. In Northern Ireland I was refused access to all official records, even transcripts of inquests and trials that had been open to

the public ... Then in February 1986 I was abruptly ordered
home ... In light of constant complaints that I had been paying
too much attention to Northern Ireland, I suspected this was
the cause, and one senior editor confirmed that this was so.
(Thomas 1991: 123–4)

Clearly, American reporting is vulnerable to pressure.

Conclusions

The contrast between the controversy caused by 'Death on the
Rock' and the lack of response to 'Death of a Terrorist' seems
not to relate to the difference in content of the programmes, but
to factors such as the pressure British sources can apply and the
political closeness of the conflict in Ireland to the British state. [22]
As the head of BBC television news Peter Woon and his deputy
Robin Walsh told Peter Taylor, 'Beirut is a long way away ... We
do work slightly differently when it affects us. Whether subcon-
sciously or consciously we differentiate' (Taylor 1986: 219).

There are clear differences between different forms of actuality
coverage in both the US and the UK. The further you move from
the centre stage of news towards the margins of comment and
satire, the more likely it is that editorial controls will loosen. This
means that there is not only increased space to contest official
perspectives on 'terrorism' but also increased licence to promote
the populism which favours order regardless of the law. There are
also systematic variations between the US and British media
systems. These can be characterised as differences of *range* and
gravity. There is a greater range of coverage in the US, but the
centre of gravity has shifted so that more 'dispassionate' coverage
is the norm.

It is true that news coverage, and especially television news, is
the most limited form of news, but this has less to do with the
shorter length of time news has or with 'natural' formal factors,
than it has with the close policing of news in Britain. News is
not inherently limited to relaying the definitions of the powerful
by its format or other constraints such as time. The limits of the
acceptable for different media formats are not simply given or
determined by the 'Accessibility, visual quality, drama and action'

or the 'thematic unity' of any event (Altheide 1985: 346–7). Rather, decisions made about stories to cover reflect the interests and priorities of contemporary news values and the constraints exerted by source organisations. The comparison of US and British news showed clear differences, not of form or style, but of substantive content – there were a wider range of interviewees and official nostrums could more easily be questioned.

But does this make any difference? What is the relationship between the media and public opinion and belief? It is to this question that the next chapter is devoted.

5

Misinformation and Public Belief:
The Case of Gibraltar

Until one mild March afternoon,
As balmy as an English June,
A Sunday, full of peaceful sounds
And strolling tourists on their rounds,
There came a change of quality.
The game became reality.
At sometime after three o'clock
The Thing they harboured in their Rock
Descended on them; out of the blue –
Slaughter in Winston Churchill Avenue
Panic among the passers-by
As three young Irish people die,
Mown down by men with automatics.
The story goes they were fanatics,
Dangerous terrorists, they said.
Who, the assassins? No – the dead.

But how do we know the intention was
To shoot to kill? we know because
The SAS, to put it straight,
Is that intention incarnate.

Jack Mitchell, *GiB: A Modest Exposure*, 1990

The debate on media coverage of Northern Ireland has continued periodically since the beginning of the current period of
troubles. Most commentary has focused on the 'propaganda
war', the conduct of journalists or the content of what they
write or say. Yet, implicit in almost all that is said are
assumptions about the impact of the media on public belief and
society more widely. For some, the media function as the ally
of the 'terrorists', increasing the support and morale of the

insurgents, spreading fear among their potential victims, gaining the insurgents unwarranted public attention, making it harder for the state to gain support for 'counter-terrorist' measures, and sapping the national will to stay in Ireland. For others, the media are the instrument of the state, demoralising the insurgents, marginalising them to the edges of the public sphere or beyond it, assuring the public that they will be protected, making it easier for the government to bring in repressive measures and ensuring that the public is kept in ignorance of what is happening in Ireland.

In all this debate, which is replicated throughout the extensive literature on 'terrorism' and the media, there is very little direct investigation of public belief (although see Hewitt 1992) and even less on the influence of the media. There is a large and inconclusive body of research on links between violence in the media and violence in society, but this has rarely touched on questions of political violence (Cumberbatch and Howitt 1989).

Design, Method and Sample

This study attempts to examine the processes by which people come to 'make up their minds' about the conflict in Ireland. It seeks to establish what people 'know' and then to trace the sources of this knowledge and belief. This is an approach quite different from that adopted by the bulk of researchers who have examined the reception of media messages. Such approaches have generally involved showing specific programmes to people and then gauging their response, or have simply asked what people 'bring to' the reception process (Morley 1992). In some cases this has meant attempting to measure changes in attitude or knowledge and in others it has been more concerned with examining specific genres of programming rather than specific issues, as in the preponderance of studies of soap opera (Ang 1985; Hobson 1982, 1984; Katz and Liebes 1985; Liebes and Katz 1993).

In contrast, this study asked groups of people to write their own news bulletins using photographic stills taken from actual television programmes. This was to show whether they could recall and reproduce news programmes. The bulletins were then compared with what the groups actually believed to be true and the reasons for their acceptance or rejection of the television message examined by the administration of a small number of questions and then a period of group discussion.

The study was begun in November 1988 and finished in February 1990. At first the research concentrated simply on perceptions of the Northern Ireland conflict in general and a total of nineteen groups – 144 people – took part. Two types of group were selected. Firstly, groups of people who might be expected to have some special knowledge about the conflict in Northern Ireland. These included nationalist and unionist groups living in the North as well as serving British soldiers. The other groups were selected because they were not necessarily expected to have any special knowledge of the conflict. All the discussions were conducted with pre-existing groups of people who work, live or socialise together, chosen to reflect different socio-demographic factors such as age, region, nationality, class and gender. Most of the groups selected were from Scotland. But it was important to include some groups in the South of England for comparative purposes. Accordingly, three groups containing twenty-nine people took part in the general sample. In addition, twenty-nine American students took part in the research (see Appendix D for a full list of groups).

However, it also appeared from comments in some of these groups that it was important to try and investigate beliefs about specific incidents in more depth. An obvious candidate for investigation was the Gibraltar shootings of March 1988. They had received a great deal of publicity and I had already done some research on the media coverage of the events and the propaganda conflict surrounding them (Miller 1991). This made it easier to compare accounts and to trace sources of media information from those given in the groups. So, from mid-September 1989 (nineteen months after the killings) groups were asked to write a news story about Northern Ireland using photographs from the Gibraltar shootings. Eleven further groups (143 people) took part in this second phase of the study, making a total of 313 people (a full list is included in Appendix E). This chapter deals mainly with public belief in relation to the Gibraltar killings.[1]

The Photos

Each group was divided into up to six news teams and given identical sets of photographic stills, taken from actual news bulletins, representing different aspects of routine coverage of Northern Ireland. The photographs included a series of talking heads representing different perspectives on Northern Ireland – British Prime Minister Margaret Thatcher; Labour Party leader Neil Kinnock; a British army spokesperson; Rev. Ian Paisley, MP for North Antrim and leader of the Democratic Unionist Party, and Gerry Adams (then) MP for West Belfast and President of Sinn Féin – as well as other routine news images from coverage of Northern Ireland – a 'riot scene', a republican funeral procession, a helicopter, a fire, RUC personnel (Figure 5.1), an 'Orange [Protestant] walk' (Figure 5.2), a crowd scene (Figure 5.3) and a march preceded by British army personnel carriers. Finally, the groups were also given a photograph showing a scene of folk music being played in a pub (Figure 5.4). This image was included because it was atypical of news coverage of Northern Ireland. Indeed it came from a programme which explicitly attempted to show the 'other side' of life in Northern Ireland.

Figure 5.1 RUC personnel

Figure 5.2 Orange walk

Figure 5.3 Crowd scene

Figure 5.4 Folk musicians in pub

The groups which took part in the research on the Gibraltar killings were given eight pictures specifically about the Gibraltar killings. These were in addition to the 'talking heads', the 'riot' and the funeral the other groups used, but they replaced the other seven scenes detailed above. The Gibraltar shots included an aerial shot of Gibraltar, a TV graphic on which the airport and Government House were marked, a shot of explosives recovered by the Spanish police, a military base on the Rock, and a shot of a military band parading before Government House in Gibraltar (Figure 5.5). There was also a shot of a dead body lying on the ground covered in a blanket and a shot of two further bodies covered with blankets and surrounded by police officers (Figure 5.6). Finally each group was also given an uncaptioned picture of Carmen Proetta (Figure 5.7), one of the key eyewitnesses to the shootings, as she appeared on 'Death on the Rock' and various TV news programmes. [2]

Figure 5.5 Military parade, Gibraltar

Figure 5.6 Dead bodies outside petrol station, Gibraltar

Figure 5.7 Eyewitness Carmen Proetta

The Questions

The questions were asked immediately following the 'presentation' of the news bulletin. All were open-ended and respondents were free to reply as they wanted. The first two questions were about general perceptions of television news:

1. Does the BBC news have a point of view? Does it, for example, favour one political party over another, or is it neutral? Is it biased, unbiased, pro-establishment, anti-establishment, accurate, inaccurate, partial or impartial? How would you describe it?

2. Does ITN operate from a point of view? Do you think it is the same as BBC news or is it different in some way?

These questions were intended to be a general indication of the groups perceptions of TV news and indicated whether television was thought to be biased to the left or right. They were especially useful in providing a tool for investigating the extent to which people believed the news bulletin they had written or whether it was written consciously from a 'television' perspective with which the authors disagreed.

3. How would you feel about going to Northern Ireland?

4. Is life in Northern Ireland mostly violent or mostly peaceful?

5. Does TV news tell you that life in Northern Ireland is mostly peaceful or mostly violent?

6. What is your source of information for questions 3 and 4?

These questions were central to the study. Past academic research and the evidence of this book have shown that the predominant reason for covering Northern Ireland on television news in Britain is violence. I wanted to find out whether people believed this to be the case and whether they also thought that this was a true picture of life in Northern Ireland. Questions 4 and 5 are very similar to the questions asked by Philo in his study of the coal dispute of 1984/5 (Philo 1990). But there is one key difference. Philo asked whether picketing in the strike had been mostly violent or mostly peaceful. In the present case the question is much wider, since it asks about life in Northern Ireland in general. Question 3 was asked as an additional way of asking about perceptions of life in Northern Ireland. It was anticipated that some people might see the picture of Northern Ireland given on television as accurate, but I was also interested in the extent to which people might reject what they saw as the television message. Did they reject television at an intellectual level, but still find the idea of actually visiting Northern Ireland frightening? In the event answers to this question did show marked variations from answers to question 5. It was important to try and find out why people believed or disbelieved television messages about the conflict. Was this because they read other media which gave a different view? Or were there other factors which might cause people to judge that television's account was accurate or inaccurate?

7. Of all the Irish issues that are covered on television what do you think is on TV the most?

8. Of all the things you have seen over the last few years what has stuck in your mind the most? If I say the words 'Northern Ireland' what image or event comes most clearly to mind?

These questions were intended to reveal something of people's perceptions of news coverage and also their own perceptions of the images or experiences that had stuck in their minds in relation to the conflict in Northern Ireland. In practice these questions tended to be answered in relation to the preoccupations and understandings of the groups involved.

9. Which newspaper(s) do you normally read/prefer?

This question was intended partly as an indication of political/ cultural views, but was also useful in tracing information sources. It was especially useful in the part of the study which focused on the killings in Gibraltar, because of the very different coverage available in different parts of the press.

An additional question was asked of the groups taking part in the latter part of the study on Gibraltar. This involved holding up the picture of eyewitness Carmen Proetta, which included a caption with her name on it, and asking the groups 'what is her occupation?' News bulletins written by the groups on Gibraltar tended to deal with the actual events, and it was then possible to ascertain whether they reflected the groups' beliefs about what had actually happened. I was also interested in the extent to which people were aware of the controversy in the media surrounding Proetta's 'character' and reliability, as well as whether they believed the stories printed in the press about her.

The Gibraltar Killings

We have already discussed media coverage of the Gibraltar killings and looked at the furore around the Thames Television programme 'Death on the Rock'. It is, however, probably worthwhile briefly to recall some of the key issues in the public debate around the killings before we proceed, as these in practice were the raw material with which people were working in their reconstructions of television coverage.

The killings took place on 6 March 1988, and were carried out by the SAS in disputed circumstances. First stories from (unattributable) official sources claimed that the IRA members had planted a car bomb and were armed. This quite false story dominated the media for nearly twenty-four hours. The story about the bomb was reported as fact by all British national newspapers and broadcast outlets. It wasn't until the next afternoon that the Foreign Secretary, Sir Geoffrey Howe, revised this version saying in the House of Commons that:

> Near the border they were challenged by the security forces. When challenged they made movements, which lead the military personnel, operating in support of the Gibraltar police, to conclude that their own lives and the lives of others were under threat. In the light of this response they were shot. Those killed were subsequently found not to have been carrying arms ... The parked car was subsequently dealt with by a military bomb disposal team. It has now been established that it did not contain an explosive device. (7 March 1988)

It was later added [3] that the SAS believed that the IRA team could be armed or in control of a radio-controlled detonating device or 'button job'. This was the version which the British government depended on throughout the next year. The alternative case, constructed largely from eyewitness accounts and briefings from Spanish government and police sources, was largely to be found in certain broadsheet papers, television documentaries and more marginal publications such as *New Statesman and Society*. It suggested that there was no challenge to the three IRA members and that they did not make 'movements' which could have been interpreted as reaching for weapons or a 'button job'. Instead, in the words of key witness Carmen Proetta, 'They didn't make any movements – they put their hands up. I believe I've said it before. Yes, they just put their hands up.' Witnesses also saw all three of the IRA members being finished off on the ground.

Writing the News on Gibraltar

When asked to write a news bulletin, groups often protested that they didn't remember anything about Gibraltar or that they knew nothing about the conflict in Northern Ireland. But by using the photographs and working in groups they tended to produce very rapidly a wealth of impressions, half-remembered facts, opinions and views. As one women in Saltcoats put it, 'It comes back to you, mind you, when you think about it. You take in more than you think.'

Interpreting the Photographs

In some cases people found it difficult to write a text that reproduced a news account of the shootings. In general this was because they disagreed with the news version and preferred to give their own analysis of the news coverage and of what had happened in Gibraltar. But in most cases people did produce competent news reports. Sometimes it was evident that these reflected their own views on events in Gibraltar, and in other cases bulletins were produced that gave accounts with which the groups vehemently disagreed. Amongst the groups there was a range of levels of sophistication with which this distancing of the news bulletin from the views of the group was carried out. In some groups there was extremely sophisticated discussion about deadlines, terminology, the state of knowledge at the time they had decided to set the news bulletin, questions about what information would have been released by official and non-official sources, and so on. Such discussions were especially apparent among groups from Northern Ireland. Discussions included whether it was possible to include the names of the three IRA members who had been killed:

1. Should we put the names in?

2. The names haven't been released yet, sure.

(Protestant group, Belfast)

This group also discussed how they should describe the British personnel who carried out the killings:

2. They were believed to be members of the SAS.

1. They were the SAS.

2. Sure, but they wouldn't say by then.

The question of deadlines was also important for the group of serving British soldiers. Three out of the four bulletins they produced were described as news flashes immediately after the shootings. These reports used the speculative language of early reports, including phrases such as 'it is thought' and 'it is also believed'. They also reported that the IRA members were shot as they 'returned towards the border after parking a suspect car bomb'. It emerged that the reason the three groups had done this was in order to avoid the complications of writing a bulletin from the next day. One group concluded their report with a trailer for a later bulletin: 'There will be an in-depth report on this during the 6 o'clock news'. Compare: 'More on that later in our main news on BBC1 tonight at 9 o'clock' (BBC1, 18.25, 6 March 1988). They were quite aware that, as one of them put it, 'a lot of things didn't come to light until three or four days after'. This would have made the story a lot less straightforward from an army perspective, but they did not want to have to deal with that as an issue. They therefore decided to produce a bulletin that fudged the issue of whether the IRA members were challenged or tried to surrender.

The way in which the photographs and group discussion triggered memories and associations resulted in the production of 'news bulletins' that recalled in great detail the key issues in the controversy surrounding the events in Gibraltar. Table 5.1 (see pages 216–7) compares news bulletins written by the groups with actual television news programmes.

All these news bulletins were written by groups between eighteen months and two years after the shootings. They showed remarkable similarities of language and tone with actual television news. The specificity of the details that were remembered is remarkable. All the groups were asked to do was write a news bulletin about the killings of three members of the IRA by the

SAS in Gibraltar using the photos provided. The groups talked of surveillance, of challenges, of attempts to evade capture, of the IRA members carrying guns and of car bombs. Of course, as we have seen, these were all key themes in media coverage about the killings.

The US groups were also able to reproduce journalistic terminology and (especially US) news conventions (see Miller 1994). However, in five out of six cases they were unable to produce news bulletins specifically about the Gibraltar killings. [4] Three groups did general Northern Ireland stories and the other two compiled joke stories which featured drug-running and sex scandals between Irish and British government officials with which the IRA were connected. None of these groups raised issues about whether there was a bomb, about surveillance, challenges, attempted surrender or any of the other debating points found in British and Irish bulletins.

Individual Facts

The photographs provoked a great deal of discussion about what had happened, which almost invariably related to the key terms of the public debate/dispute over Gibraltar. This is interesting because it does show how much people absorb of media information.

There is another issue, which is that all the information about what happened in Gibraltar had come via the mass media. Even in Northern Ireland the only available sources of information in addition to the mainstream media are the alternative and radical papers of each community. In the case of Gibraltar the pre-eminent alternative sources were *An Phoblacht/Republican News*, the weekly paper of the republican movement, and the nationalist weekly *Andersonstown News*. The only people who knew what had happened in Gibraltar first-hand were those that were killed, their killers, the eyewitnesses and (possibly) the other member(s) of the IRA unit. However, the IRA has never publicly acknowledged how many (if any) of its members escaped Gibraltar, nor have their accounts been published. The only option, then was discussion and evaluation of publicly available information from the mass media.

Table 5.1
Bulletins written by groups compared with actual television news

Bulletins written by respondents	Actual television news bulletins
The three dead, two men and a woman, were IRA suspects. A car bomb was found and it is believed that the military parade was the intended target. (Saltcoats WEA group)	British Soldiers in Gibraltar have shot dead three suspected IRA terrorists. It's believed the two men and a woman were on a bombing mission in the British colony. Later a car bomb was found near the Governor's residence. It's thought the target was a British Army parade. The bomb was destroyed with a controlled explosion. (ITN, 21.15, 6 March 1988)
Reports are reaching us of a shooting incident on the Rock of Gibraltar regarding the deaths of three suspected IRA terrorists. It is believed they were involved in planting a bomb which was concealed in a car and planned to go off during a military parade. It is understood that the victims had been under observation for some time by the Spanish Police prior to their entry into Gibraltar. (Ardrossan Senior Citizens)	The target for the IRA bombers were soldiers from the Royal Anglian Regiment on Gibraltar guard duty ... The three Irish terrorists were shot dead on the road back to the Spanish frontier by plainclothed soldiers believed to be from the SAS. The terrorists had been under surveillance from Spanish police in Malaga for several weeks. They crossed into Gibraltar and planted their bomb in the town centre. (ITN, 12.30, 7 March 1988)

Table 5.1 continued
Bulletins written by groups compared with actual television news

Bulletins written by respondents	Actual television news bulletins
Today in Gibraltar three civilians were shot dead by SAS soldiers. Witnesses say they were unarmed. (Saltcoats WEA group)	Witnesses say they were not armed and were shot at close range. (ITN, 12.30, 7 March 1988)
Today in Gibraltar three well known members of the IRA were shot dead by the SAS, while under suspicion of planning a terrorist attack. They had been under surveillance by both Spanish and British authorities since entering Spain and were shot while attempting to open fire on British soldiers. It was however later discovered that at that point they were not armed and an eyewitness claims they were running away from the soldiers rather than towards [them]. (art school students 1989)	The three people who were shot dead in Gibraltar were wellknown to the intelligence services in Belfast, London and Dublin. (BBC1, 18.00, 7 March 1988)

Three people were apparently walking along this road called Winston Churchill Avenue. They were challenged by, it appears, plain-clothed policemen from the Met. Then the shoot-out happened. Two died outside a petrol station, the third one died about 200 yards further into the town. (BBC1, 21.00, 6 March 1988) |
| One of the [IRA] men reached into his jacket and the SAS thought he was reaching for a gun, so they opened fire killing all three of them in a hail of bullets. (SACRO clients 1989) | After being challenged they tried to escape. The woman and one of the men were shot dead immediately. The second man was killed a few hundred yards away. (BBC1, 09.00, 7 March 1988) |

To be sure, there was a range of information available, with a quite clear division in the press between those papers which supported and actively propagandised on behalf of the official view (*Sunday Times, Sun, Sunday Telegraph, Daily Express, Daily Mail, Daily Star* and *Daily Mirror*) and those papers and television current affairs journalists (*Observer, Independent, Guardian, This Week,* BBC Northern Ireland's *Spotlight, Private Eye*) which attempted to investigate the discrepancies in the official line and to come to a judgement about what had happened in Gibraltar. In television news some questions were asked, but the emphasis was on the official version. The question is which version did viewers and readers believe?

The day after every single British national newspaper and television news programme had given their readers and viewers a false account of what had happened in Gibraltar, there were no apologies and no headlines on government misinformation. It was almost as if journalists could not quite believe that they had been so comprehensively misled. Indeed, some journalists found it hard to accept that there was no bomb and continued to produce reports that assumed there was. The *Independent* stated that: 'Army experts then defused the white Renault 5' (8 March 1988). The BBC report following Geoffrey Howe's announcement of the lack of the bomb stated: 'They had planted what was thought to be a car bomb' (BBC, 15.54, 7 March 1988). It is of course impossible to plant or defuse a non-existent bomb. This is not because news values intrinsically inhibit newspapers from accusing the government of lying. Indeed, one newspaper led its front page on 8 March with the headline 'Fury as no bomb found', but this was the *Irish Press*, published in Dublin. In the US the *Boston Globe* headlined 'Britain, in an about-face, says 3 slain in Gibraltar hadn't planted bomb' (*Boston Globe*, 8 March 1988).

In Britain the hunt for the fourth bomber dominated the front pages of most of the newspapers (Miller 1991). Sir Geoffrey's statement to the House of Commons was also prominently reported, but no front-page headlines focused on the false stories from the day before. Instead the *Daily Telegraph* led with 'Dreadful act of terror averted Howe tells MPs' (8 March 1988).

Television news programmes also emphasised the alleged fourth member and the search for the explosives, without explicitly headlining the fact that they had been misled. ITN had 'A fourth terrorist is hunted in Gibraltar as search fails to find IRA's bomb' (ITN, 17.45, 7 March 1988); Channel 4 had 'In Gibraltar, after the killing of the IRA bombers the search for the car with their bomb' (Channel 4 News, 19.00, 7 March 1988). The BBC reported 'The Gibraltar shootings. On the rock police hunt a fourth IRA man and a hundred and forty pounds of explosives' (BBC1, 21.00, 7 March 1988). As Enoch Powell later argued: 'A massive self-congratulation, intoned by the Foreign Secretary, engulfed the media; it echoed back and forth in Parliament and in the papers' (Powell 1988).

The official version as given to journalists by official sources immediately after the shootings, by Sir Geoffrey Howe in the House of Commons and all the way up to the inquest in September, was that the IRA members were challenged. It was evident that the challenge was a key element for the government case, but during the summer official sources started to brief journalists that the shouting of a challenge was of secondary importance (Campbell 1988). Preparing the ground in this way was of key importance for managing public perceptions of the inquest in September. The Crown had the advantage here, because only it was in full possession of the facts (the solicitor for the family was not given all the witness statements) and it was able to determine the order in which the witnesses would appear. When the soldiers who actually shot Farrell and McCann appeared, they were preceded into the witness box by their commanding officer, 'Soldier E', who had not actually been present at the shootings. He nevertheless felt able to say that: 'In both cases the challenge was started ... How far they got in that challenge, I don't know, because I wasn't there ... but I know they started the challenge' (transcript of the Gibraltar Inquest, Day Six, Tuesday 13 September 1988: 34).

The SAS man who started the shooting was not so certain as his superior officer, saying 'I wanted to shout: "Stop". I actually don't know if it actually came out. I honestly don't know.' Nevertheless, the press then felt able to report that the IRA members had been challenged by emphasising the words of the senior SAS officer:

SAS men 'shouted warning' before shooting IRA team (*Independent*, 14 September 1988).

'SAS men tell inquest of warnings' (*Guardian*, 14 September 1988).

SAS 'shouted warnings before they opened fire' (*The Times*, 14 September 1988).

Beliefs

My interest is in exploring the beliefs of the groups and individuals within them about the specific facts of the case and then looking at the way in which particular 'facts' were put together and interpreted against previous knowledge, experience and cultural and political perspectives. I will take each contested detail about the shootings separately and then look in depth at perceptions of the witness Carmen Proetta and her credibility.

Accepting the Message: the Factual Construction of Gibraltar

All 'factual' information on what had happened in Gibraltar was of necessity gleaned from the mass media (including alternative/radical media). Respondents varied in their beliefs about many of the 'facts' of the case and there were sometimes disagreements in the groups about what had happened. But a substantial proportion of respondents did believe the 'factual details' released by official sources which turned out to be false, such as reports that the IRA members had planted a bomb or that they were armed. Some also believed key details of the official case which were contested in parts of the media and turned out to have less factual foundation than the media coverage of them would warrant, such as whether the IRA members were challenged or made movements after such a challenge.

Was There a Bomb?

Most of the serving British soldiers were convinced that there actually was a bomb in the car in Gibraltar when the IRA members were shot. In writing their news bulletin they discussed the weight of the bomb.

Soldier 1. 'What shall we say, how many pounds was there, Semtex?'
Soldier 2. 'Couple of hundred wasn't it?'
Soldier 3. 'You don't need all that Semtex.'
Soldier 2. 'Well, put it this way, the car was packed with it, that's for sure.'

(British soldiers)

It is perhaps unsurprising that many of the soldiers apparently believed, almost two years after the shooting, that there was a bomb, since this was the original story which emerged from official (military) sources on 6 March. Although the story was changed the next day by the Foreign Secretary, government information officers in the Ministry of Defence were still able to write that a bomb had been found. Two weeks later in the government-produced 'magazine of the British Army', *Soldier*, the false story about the bomb was repeated:

An IRA *bomb gang* died when plans to explode a device during a military parade on Gibraltar were foiled by security forces. Soldiers shot dead two men and a woman after they had parked a car *containing the bomb* next to a petrol station not far from the Governor's residence. (*Soldier*, 21 March 1988: 9, emphasis added) [5]

But it wasn't only soldiers that were convinced. One group wrote in their news bulletin: 'The three dead, two men and a woman, were IRA suspects. A car bomb was found and it is believed that a military parade was the intended target' (Saltcoats WEA, September 1989). One of the two women who wrote this bulletin believed that a car bomb was found, while the other thought there was but couldn't 'really remember'. Both said they had gained their impression from television news.

Were Farrell, McCann and Savage armed?

Often members of the groups disagreed on what they thought had actually happened but were nevertheless able to agree on how the news would present it. One bulletin described how the IRA members 'were thought to be carrying arms' (SACRO clients). It

221

then reported eyewitness Carmen Proetta who 'saw the incident from her window', as saying the IRA 'were shot in cold blood'. Then, as 'balance', it continued: 'But the SAS say the IRA started to shoot first.' One group member thought that in reality the members of the IRA had been carrying arms, but he was unsure whether they shot first. He thought that BBC news was one of the 'better news programmes'. Another member of the group disagreed. He thought that both BBC and ITN were biased, saying: 'ITV or BBC never tell you when a British soldier has killed babies or children.' His view was that the IRA members had been unarmed, and he said that he had managed to glean this information from television news. But they had presented the bulletin in this 'balanced' manner because this was how they thought the news would do it.

One young man, a member of another SACRO team, did believe that the IRA members were armed, but that the SAS had shot first. His belief seemed to be innocent of any attempt to justify the actions of the SAS, since he illustrated his answer sheet with a shamrock and the letters IRA – one letter on each leaf – and with the phrase 'up the IRA'.

Did the SAS Think They Were Armed/Had Planted a Bomb?

The motivations of the SAS in shooting McCann, Savage and Farrell were hardly questioned by the groups. Of those who did not believe the IRA members were armed there was wide agreement that the SAS men believed that Farrell, McCann and Savage had planted a bomb and were able to set it off, or were armed. For one of the SACRO groups 'the fact that the terrorists proved to be unarmed created an international incident. But the shooting had taken place in the belief that these people had been armed.'

Another group wrote that the fact that there was no bomb had only been discovered after the shooting: 'Three members of the IRA were shot dead in Gibraltar, suspected of placing a bomb in a car. When the bomb disposal unit set off a controlled explosion there was no bomb' (Paisley retired women).

Even groups that were otherwise very critical of the shootings appeared to believe that the lack of a bomb was only discovered after the shooting: 'After the bomb disposal team were called in to search the car in which the three had parked it was discovered that there were no explosives in the car' (nationalist group, West Belfast). This particular group also believed that the explosives found two days later in Spain had been planted there by the British army to cover up what the group termed 'their mistake'. This is a distinctly alternative view of the actions of British army personnel. It should be noted that neither the British media, the British government, or the IRA has ever suggested that this was the case.

Were They Challenged/Did They Make Movements?

There was less unanimity on the question of whether the IRA members were challenged or made movements which might be interpreted as reaching for concealed weapons or attempting to detonate a bomb (a 'button-job' as the SAS dubbed it). One of the teams believed that the IRA members had made movements: 'One of the [IRA] men reached into his jacket and the SAS thought he was reaching for a gun, so they opened fire killing all three of them in a hail of bullets' (SACRO clients).

Some groups produced apparently contradictory reports, which echoed the assumptions of some news programmes: '... were shot while attempting to open fire on British soldiers. It was however later discovered that at that point they were not armed' (Art School Students).

The IRA members could not, of course, have attempted to open fire on the SAS because they were unarmed. One of the soldiers had a very detailed memory of how the shooting had started:

> In fact, what started [it] off was one of them had been like compromised as such that they were following them, the guy turned round, spotted them being followed and then they started to leg it and that's what made them open fire, that's what started it, and then they thought well right now their aims obviously changed there but they had to stop them before they detonated it so really their options ran out at that point ... that came up in court in the end when the soldiers were being cross examined. (British soldiers)

This account is strikingly similar to that given at the inquest by the SAS men, as well as to that pioneered by the *Sunday Times* following official briefings:

As the terrorists approached the junction, and crossed the road, the SAS men, still following on foot, saw Savage peel off ... and head back to town. Farrell and McCann continued walking North. Just why Savage backtracked is not known ... Then, it is believed, Farrell and McCann somehow realised that they were being followed. The SAS men had closed up in the busy street so that they could keep the terrorists in sight and, if anything went wrong, have a clear line of fire. They believed they had been rumbled and, shouting a challenge, one SAS man reached behind him and pulled a Browning 9mm automatic pistol from the waistband of his jeans. (*Sunday Times*, 8 May 1988)

Rejecting the Official Version of the Shootings

Although it was more common for respondents to believe key elements of the official case than details associated with alternative explanations, some respondents did reject official 'facts' and believed instead in alternative versions. In general these 'alternative facts' had also been gleaned from the mass media. Two key areas included reading alternative information in the press and culling details and fragments from television news accounts. We have already seen that some official 'facts' were rejected in favour of others. In particular, this related to a rejection of the initial discredited story about a bomb having been planted and the IRA members being armed. This was often replaced with subsequent official 'facts' about the IRA members making movements and the army 'discovering' that there was no bomb and that they were not armed.

However, it should not be thought that government impression management was altogether successful in building up an empirical picture of what had happened in Gibraltar. There were two particular areas in which alternative understandings gained some hold. The question of surveillance and the testimony of eyewitnesses were areas in which people were more likely to hold critical views.

Were They Under Surveillance?

There was almost unanimous agreement among the groups in both their news bulletins and spoken comments that the IRA members had been under surveillance. None of the groups questioned this detail. Indeed, from the time of the shootings until mid-summer 1988 this was common ground between Ministry of Defence briefers, the Spanish police and Interior Ministry and critical journalists and was routinely reported in the mainstream media. By the time of the inquest the official version had changed (cf. *Private Eye* 1989). Now it was said that the Spanish police had 'lost' McCann, Farrell and Savage soon after they arrived on the Costa del Sol on 4 March. This change in story had the advantage that it allowed British sources to claim that they did not know when the three would arrive on the Rock so it was not possible to arrest them at the border. [6]

The assertion that the three had been 'lost' was reported as the truth in those papers that supported the official version, but it did not gain the prominence of the headlines on the bomb, the question of eyewitness testimony or the character of one of those witnesses. It appears that this detail had entirely passed the groups by, although it was crucial for the government case at the inquest. It seems that this was a key area in which official attempts at impression management conspicuously failed. It was not only information managers at the Ministry of Defence who noticed that accepting the surveillance story potentially damaged their case. Some of the respondents in the groups noticed too: 'The question I as a Welsh guardsman would like to ask is why were the IRA permitted to cross into Gib. There are police and customs at the barrier to prevent the entry of such people' (Ardrossan senior citizens). This evaluation of the actions of the SAS came from a person who read the *Daily Express*, thought BBC news had a 'leftish tinge' and that Carmen Proetta was a 'part-time hostess', yet he had evaluated the information available to him and seen the potential contradiction in the government case.

Surrender?

A few of the groups reproduced the tenor of eyewitness accounts featured in parts of the press and most notably on 'Death on the Rock'. The central allegations were that there had been no challenge, that Farrell and McCann put their hands up as if in surrender, and that all three were shot again on the ground.

An eyewitness says that one woman and two men were gunned down in the street directly below her flat window for no apparent reason. She went on to say that one of them raised his hands as if to surrender but was still shot four times in the stomach. (art school students)

In this account, which expressed the reservations of members of the group about the actions of the SAS, the accounts of eyewitnesses are emphasised. There were also a handful of other discussions and presentations which cited witnesses as saying no warning was given. In such cases people were often unsure about which version to believe. There is a further key factor which affected how people judged the killings and especially the eyewitness testimony. This is the assault on the credibility of key witness Carmen Proetta.

Carmen Proetta

Perhaps the most bitter of the information battles fought out over the Gibraltar killings was that for the reputation and credibility of key eyewitness Carmen Proetta. Following Proetta's appearance on 'Death on the Rock', official sources in Gibraltar and one government minister [7] provided journalists with information which resulted in a series of defamatory stories about Proetta.

The headlines included: 'Shamed! Drug and sex secrets of wife in SAS telly storm' (*Daily Mirror*), 'Trial by TV Carmen is Escort Girl boss' (*Daily Express*) and the 'The Tart of Gib' in the *Sun* (30 April 1988). The *Sun* alleged that Proetta 'used to be a prostitute'. The *Daily Mail* claimed that she was 'a director of a Spanish escort agency'. The *Daily Mirror* alleged of the supposed escort agency that 'police say it is just a cover for vice'. The *Star* went so far as to claim that Carmen Proetta 'campaigns for Spanish rule in Gibraltar'. The *Daily Telegraph* alleged that 'several residents of the colony, who would not be named, had claimed she was one of only forty-four Gibraltarians to vote to end British Rule in the 1967 referendum'. [8] All these allegations were untrue. Carmen Proetta issued writs against seven national newspapers all of which ended with apologies and substantial damages to Carmen Proetta. [9] The first to settle was the *Sun*, which:

agreed to pay damages to Mrs Carmen Proetta and apologised to her for ... highly defamatory and unfounded allegations ... It accepted that Mrs Proetta had given an honest account of what she remembers seeing and that she neither hated the British nor was she guilty or involved in the other misconduct described. (*Sun*, 17 December 1988)

All the apologies were of much less prominence than the original stories, appearing on inside pages and taking up no more than a few sentences in a single column. [10]

Prostitute?

As we have already seen from extracts from news bulletins produced by the groups, there were many references to an eyewitness or eyewitnesses. It was comparatively rare for the groups to actually refer to the allegations against Proetta in their news bulletins. Only in one bulletin did a group describe Proetta straightforwardly as a 'prostitute' in their news bulletin (SACRO clients), although several others referred to allegations about Proetta being of 'doubtful character'. However, it was clear that people were actually discussing the allegations within the groups. During the writing of the news bulletins there was often laughter and joking about the allegations when the picture of her was being discussed. It seemed that part of the reason for this was that the groups did not believe the television news would repeat such allegations. But there was also a sense in which many participants were reluctant to discuss openly the topic of prostitution, although many of them knew or remembered that it was a factor in the story. This behaviour made it especially important for me to ask directly about their views on Carmen Proetta's occupation. Sometimes when I did this there was literally a roar of embarrassed laughter, especially among older participants (for example, the pensioners group in Ardrossan). None of them had mentioned in their bulletins that the 'character' of the eyewitness might be an issue, but when I asked directly about Proetta's occupation, the vast majority were clear that it had been raised in the media. Even then the answers they gave to the question were couched in ambiguous and evasive language such as 'entertainer in a nightclub', 'flamenco dancer', 'part-time hostess', 'nightclub hostess', 'a lady of leisure', 'a lady of easy virtue – it's a national pastime', 'naughty girl', 'model', 'model with sideline', 'she had a fancy man', 'perhaps a street-walker'. Not one of the respondents in this group used the word 'prostitute'. Indeed, some were reluctant to even hint that they believed that Proetta was a prostitute. One put down that Proetta was a 'house agent'. On asking what this meant the respondent said that she believed Proetta was a prostitute but that 'I didn't like putting it down'. It is likely, then, that the number of people who were prepared to state that they believed Proetta to be a prostitute is an underestimate.

In fact, 30 per cent of the general Gibraltar sample did feel able to say they believed Proetta to be a prostitute or similar and a further 15 per cent put that she was possibly a prostitute. [11] This is in itself a remarkable finding, given that the stories discrediting Proetta appeared almost exclusively in the press, mainly in the English tabloids, and were wholly false. There were similar stories discrediting Proetta in the *Sunday Times, Daily Telegraph* and *Sunday Telegraph*, but by and large television news stayed clear of recycling damaging information about Proetta. The majority (twenty-seven out of thirty-eight) of those who thought Proetta was or was possibly a prostitute read English or Scottish tabloids (*Sun, Mirror, Daily Express, Daily Record*[12]), but the remainder were readers of broadsheet papers (only one of which listed a paper which had repeated the allegations against Proetta – the *Sunday Times*). This suggests that there can be an additional circulation of salacious stories which become big enough to be known, repeated and circulated among a wider population than those who read (or admit to reading) popular papers.

There is a sense in which people monitor what is the correct thing to say, but it also seems that doubts and alternative explanations, interesting details or salacious gossip lurk below the 'acceptable' responses. An interest in such gossip is one of the strong selling points of newspapers such as the *Sun*. There was a striking example of this in the nationalist group from West Belfast. Five out of the eight participants said that they read English tabloids, predominantly the *Sun*. But the majority of the group (six out of eight) also listed other papers such as the nationalist *Irish News, Andersonstown News* and Sinn Féin's *An Phoblacht/Republican News*. All eight members of this group thought that television news was 'pro-British', 'anti-Irish' or 'tells lies about the Irish'. In all the other groups in the Gibraltar study people tended to answer the question about Carmen Proetta by either giving an occupation (or a possible occupation) or saying that they did not know. The West Belfast group went further, many of them indicating that they were aware of media stories about Proetta, but that they did not believe them. Five of the eight included comments such as, 'She got the blame for being a prostitute. I don't believe it'; 'We were told by the British news and papers that she was a prostitute, which I do not believe.'

Their awareness of the stories about Proetta had been discussed during the news-writing exercise accompanied by laughter and jokes. This resulted in one woman believing that other members of the group thought that Proetta was a prostitute. In fact, one other member of this four-person team did believe that Proetta was a prostitute. He had listed the papers he read as the *Sun*, the *Star* and the *Irish News*. However, the other two members of the team rejected the idea that she was a prostitute although they had taken part in the joking during the writing of the bulletin. It could be argued that this is an illustration of the way in which a strong sense of political identity can override an otherwise keen interest in sex scandals. It seems likely that there was also an element of giving the 'correct' answer of people from nationalist West Belfast as their part in the propaganda war. The rejection by the bulk of this group of the Proetta 'story' is testament to the power of political ideology in withstanding propaganda assaults. But it is also clear that even when political identity is a strong part of everyday life it is possible for elements of propaganda messages to be accepted. One of the group did believe that Proetta was a prostitute even though he also stated that 'we want the British soldiers off our streets and we want our nationality back'.

Rejecting the Message

A large number of respondents said that they did not know Proetta's occupation (45 per cent). A much smaller number volunteered that they were aware of attempts to discredit her. On asking what her occupation was one simply wrote that she was 'a victim of pressure to change her evidence' while another put that 'lies were told about her'. Proetta was in fact a bilingual legal secretary. Only two people out of the entire Gibraltar sample came anywhere near this, saying she was a 'bilingual secretary' or 'interpreter'. Both of these women were in the Saltcoats WEA group. One had heard the other say it, while the latter had remembered it from watching 'Death on the Rock'. This woman had Irish (Catholic) parents and had watched 'Death on the Rock' with interest. The fact that her sister also did the same job as Proetta had acted as an *aide-mémoire*. These two participants were also aware of the story about prostitution, but did not believe it. As one of them put it, 'A couple overheard the shooting. The press and media called them liars and the woman was later called a prostitute.'

The belief that Carmen Proetta was a prostitute or was possibly a prostitute was widespread among the groups between sixteen to twenty-two months after the stories had been printed. The success of the story was probably boosted by the way it tapped into popular images and conceptions of femininity. The fact that Proetta was a woman and also that she was Spanish may have increased the believability of the stories about her. Good propaganda has to 'fit' with public preconceptions such as the idea that working in the sex industry makes a person less credible. This was particularly evident in the assumption that some of the American students made about the photograph of Carmen Proetta. They had not actually seen any of the coverage of the Gibraltar shootings, since they had only arrived in Britain a couple of months before the session took place in February 1990. They were unable to reconstruct Proetta's allegations and did not know that she was an eyewitness. Nevertheless, it emerged in their answers that a small number of them (four out of twenty-four) thought that Proetta's sexual reputation might in some way be in question.[13] I was surprised at this response, since the only evidence they had been given was the photographic still of Proetta (Figure 5.7). It emerged that they had made this assumption because of her physical appearance (she appeared to be wearing make-up) and because of their familiarity with US media coverage of sex scandals. Women wearing make-up, they reasoned, only get on the news in relation to their (alleged) sexual behaviour.

DM. You said something about her being made up?
Female 1. Yes, she was very harsh looking I thought, very glamorised.

Female 2. I'd say not a prostitute but a woman who was sleeping with one of the men involved in the scandal. That's what came to my mind, a mistress.

DM (to Female 1). You thought she was a prostitute because she was made up?

Female 1. Yeah.

Male 1. That's an American impression. I'll back you up on that point.

[...]

Male 1. You look at all the people who were supposedly ... mistresses.

Female 2. Fawn Hall and Tammy Baker ... Who was the chick that was in the news, the large chest in the video?

Male 2. Jessica Hahns ... She's like Miss Made-Up. But I don't think it's justified just because somebody's made up to think they're a prostitute either.

Female 1. I would confirm that -- it was just a first impression. She could be a nice lady.

(US Students, Manchester)

But whether Proetta was a 'nice lady' or not, many of the participants in this study were also convinced that she was or was possibly of dubious reputation and therefore credibility.

Liar? Changed evidence?

In addition to perceptions of Proetta as a prostitute there was a wider current of opinion within the groups about her credibility, which seemed in part to be related to the stories about her in the press we have already discussed. Although perceiving Proetta as a prostitute did not necessarily lead to scepticism about her evidence or truthfulness, such perceptions did have their role to play. It is plausible to argue that the stories about prostitution set the context for further attempts to undermine her credibility. Many of those who thought that Proetta was a prostitute also believed that she had withdrawn her account or given a different version at the inquest.

For example, news teams in the Ardrossan pensioners' group believed both that Proetta was a prostitute and that she had changed her evidence. As one member of a team said:

There were no members of the press present when it happened so any reports must of necessity be based on hearsay and conjecture, especially as an eyewitness's testimony vastly varied on the first and subsequent occasions when she was interviewed. (Ardrossan senior citizens)

In another team the picture of Proetta was held up by one participant, who asked the rest of the team 'is she the witness?', to which another replied to general assent 'yes, she retracted her evidence'. Some of the ex-prisoners at SACRO were also convinced that Proetta had retracted. One news team wrote: 'An eyewitness saw the whole view of what happened and said the SAS just pulled guns out and shot them without warning. But later on when she was being interviewed by police she denied all knowledge' (SACRO clients). The other team echoed this: 'She said the SAS shot them down in cold blood, but later on in the inquiry she said that she made it up' (SACRO clients).

These groups had mostly believed that Proetta was a prostitute but were otherwise very critical of the actions of the SAS in the killings. In one of the Saltcoats teams there was some dispute about whether Proetta was telling the truth and about whether she had retracted. [14] This resulted in a long argument about whether Proetta could have heard or seen the shootings since she was 'quite far away'.

In all these examples the people who believed Proetta had retracted also believed she was a prostitute. But there were also some groups who believed she had retracted even though they did not believe that she was a prostitute. The retired women in the Paisley group were critical of the shootings and did not believe that Proetta was a prostitute. They were, however, confused about what had happened in Gibraltar primarily because they had become doubtful about Proetta's testimony. As one of the women in the group put it, 'Can we believe in the integrity of the eyewitnesses? Through the newspapers we were led to believe that at least one was of doubtful character and not always truthful.' Perhaps more surprisingly, some of the participants in the nationalist group in West Belfast accepted that Proetta had changed her evidence. They had explicitly rejected the story about prostitution, but they believed, as one put it, that 'she said one story, then she said another'.

But not all those who thought that Proetta had changed her story believed that what she had originally said was false. One news bulletin done by three clients of SACRO reported that Proetta had changed her evidence. The groups believed this to be true but also believed that she had changed her evidence 'because she was scared' of the police and the SAS.

Media Coverage of Proetta at the Inquest

How are we to explain the fact that some people did not believe Proetta to be a prostitute, yet thought that she had changed her evidence at the inquest or that she had retracted her story? In addition to the allegations of prostitution, official sources briefed journalists that her evidence was 'wrong' from immediately after the broadcast of 'Death on the Rock' until the inquest. [15] Reports also emerged from official sources that Proetta would refuse to attend the inquest. [16] Proetta commented that this 'looked like another attempt to smear her by implying that she was hesitant about her evidence' (*Independent*, 30 May 1988).

When Proetta gave evidence she held firmly on to her testimony under cross-examination by lawyers for the Crown and the SAS. The Crown case was that Proetta had either not seen the shooting at all or had only seen its aftermath. There were two key areas on which the lawyers for the Crown and the SAS tried to shift Proetta: first, the question of whether Farrell and McCann were surrendering and second, whether she could actually be sure that the shots she heard were coming from the guns pointed at the IRA members. Asked if Farrell and McCann were giving themselves up, she said: 'That's the impression I got, but they weren't given a chance', to which the Crown lawyer responded 'Were they surrendering, yes or no?' and Proetta replied: 'For me, the signal of hands up can mean surrendering, it can mean shock, or it can mean something else.' We can note that Proetta continued to maintain that Farrell and McCann had their hands up when they were shot.

Pressed on the question of whether she had seen the shots, she said:

If you see people with guns, you presume it's coming from them. You don't get guns in people's hands every day in

Gibraltar ... I didn't see the smoke, I didn't see the fire. I gathered the shooting was done through those guns that these men were carrying. (transcript of the Gibraltar Inquest, 23 September 1988: 87 and 89)

This was reported in most of the press as indicating a major revision of evidence or a total retraction. The *Daily Mirror* headlined, 'I could have got it wrong, says Carmen' (24 September 1988), the *Sun* front-page lead had 'Carmen admits doubts on SAS' (24 September 1988) and the *Daily Record* reported 'her story fell apart' (24 September 1988). *Today* reported that Proetta had 'agreed that the shots she heard while they [Farrell and McCann] were lying on the ground could have been those which killed the third gang member, Sean Savage, at the back of her flat' (24 September 1988). The *Sunday Times* added a bit more detail: 'In court she said, "I didn't notice where the shots came from. I have no idea where they came from. I didn't see any trace of smoke and firing"' (25 September 1988). The press reporting of Proetta's appearance at the inquest followed much the same pattern as previous reporting about her credibility. A different view was given in papers such as the *Guardian*, which had 'Carmen sticks to story on Gibraltar shootings' (24 September 1988). What was different about the coverage was that television news also reported that Proetta had significantly changed her evidence: 'The inquest has also heard from a woman who appeared in 'Death on the Rock'. Carmen Proetta indicated that she no longer was sure that the terrorists had tried to surrender' (BBC1, 18.00, 23 September 1988). [17]

A few days later it became clear that Proetta could not have seen flashes or smoke as the SAS members fired their guns. A Scotland Yard forensic expert, David Prior, gave evidence that

the bullets used by the four soldiers who shot the three IRA members were of the new smokeless propellant variety. He [Prior] agreed with ... Mr McGrory that on a clear March day it was quite possible for someone to see the shooting but miss both the flash and the smoke. (*Irish Times*, 28 September 1988)

But this fragment of information was not reported in any of the tabloid papers. Indeed it was very hard to find anywhere in the British press, with only the *Daily Telegraph* printing it as a fragment of an extensive report on inside pages of the paper. Interestingly, the *Sunday Times* journalists who wrote the book *Ambush* also fail to mention that the SAS men were using smokeless bullets. They also reported Proetta as 'not so sure' (Adams et al. 1988: 182). Although Adams, Morgan and Bambridge were not in Gibraltar for the inquest, it was not lack of information that resulted in their interpretation of Proetta's evidence. The *Sunday Times* had journalists at the inquest filing verbatim transcripts of the proceedings back to Wapping.

There is an additional factor which might explain the large number of people who believed that Proetta had retracted her evidence. This is that Proetta gave evidence on the same day as another eyewitness, Kenneth Asquez, who had told 'Death on the Rock' that he had seen Sean Savage 'finished off' on the ground. He appeared to retract what he had told the television programme although, as Roger Bolton has said, 'A close reading of the court transcript makes it clear that by the end of his two sessions in the Gibraltar witness box, the coroner was not sure if what Mr Asquez now said in court was the truth' (*Late Show*, BBC2, 25 January 1989). [18] Nevertheless, most papers and television news programmes accepted at face value that Asquez's original account was false. The BBC reported: 'The headlines tonight. A witness at the Gibraltar inquest, Kenneth Asquez, has admitted he was lying' (BBC1, 18.00, 23 September 1988). The relevance of this is that many of the papers the next day had front-page headlines which referred to a witness 'lying' without specifying which one:

'Death on the Rock' witness lied for TV (*The Times*, 24 September 1988).

Lies on the Rock (*Daily Mail*, 24 September 1988).

Death on Rock 'witness' admits he was lying (*Daily Telegraph*, 24 September 1988).

Why I lied by TV trial witness (*Daily Express*, 24 September 1988).

It was lies says Provo shootings witness (*Daily Record*, 24 September 1988).

The most prominent picture used by both the *Daily Express* and the *Daily Record* to accompany their headlines was one showing Carmen Proetta. It is perhaps less surprising, then, that so many people in the groups were apparently convinced that Proetta had changed her story even though some did not believe that she was a prostitute.

Questioning the Killings

It was not necessary to disbelieve each and every official fact in order to believe that the action of the SAS was illegitimate. In fact various members of the SACRO groups believed that the IRA members had been armed, had 'made movements' as though going for a gun, that Carmen Proetta was a prostitute and that she had changed her evidence. Given this, one team still felt able to title their news bulletin in a reflection of their own sentiments: '3 murdered in cold blood by the SAS'.

One of the nationalist teams from West Belfast produced what they called a 'Falls News'. [19] This gave a view radically different from that found on British television:

Three volunteers of the Provisional Irish Republican Army were shot dead in Gibraltar early today by the SAS as they were holidaying on the rock. The British government claimed they were attempting to blow up the bandsmen. Eyewitnesses claimed the two were shot in the back as they passed the garage and two of the volunteers were riddled with bullets. The third volunteer named Sean Savage who was 40 yards behind tried to make his escape and was wounded. Then eyewitnesses said they saw an SAS man putting his foot on the volunteers back and shot him in the head. After the bomb disposal team were called in to search the car, in which the three had parked, it was discovered that there were no explosives in the car. The explosives were found two days later after the British Army had planted them in a car to cover their mistake. [20]

Here, in contrast to British news, the IRA is the 'Provisional Irish Republican Army', its members are 'volunteers' not 'terrorists'. While this bulletin clearly expressed a point of view, the group also attempted to insert some tones of 'balance' by using the term 'claimed' for both the British version and that of the eyewitnesses. In that respect this news bulletin can be seen as a mirror image of actual television news, delivered from a different perspective.

It was evident that the political culture, background and experience of these respondents had made them very critical of the news. They had (with one or two exceptions) rejected most of the 'facts' promoted by British sources and elaborated a consistently oppositional perspective. In many respects they had very successfully resisted the message. This finding supports other research, which has found that people in Northern Ireland are more resistant to media coverage about Northern Ireland than people who live in Britain (Nolan 1993; Wober 1981).

On occasion the background and experience of some of the groups proved to overwhelm not only news coverage but also their memories. Some groups seemed to indulge in a little wishful thinking. For example, one of the teams of soldiers included a Sinn Féin comment in their news bulletin to the effect that the three IRA members were tourists. This reflected their view of republican propaganda and their desire to discredit the republican movement. In another example one of the women in the Saltcoats group had referred to the three as 'holidaymakers' in a bid to further delegitimise the shootings. In fact the IRA acknowledged on the evening of the shootings that the three were volunteers attached to a special 'General Headquarters Unit' and that they were on active service.

In groups where people did not have strong political views on Northern Ireland or alternative political identities, official information could structure how people thought about the killings. But alternative information could also make people uneasy in their acceptance of the legitimacy of the actions of the SAS. Thus one of the teams of pensioners in Ardrossan had become worried about the actions of the SAS. They read the *Daily Record* or the *Daily Express*, and four out of five thought that television news was unbiased or objective with one thinking the BBC news was biased towards 'Eire'. Four of the five thought Carmen Proetta was a prostitute, and yet they sounded a note of caution at the end of their news bulletin: 'Was the army right to shoot? We must leave that for future generations to decide. Nobody has sympathy for the IRA but in the shooting at Gibraltar had we taken a leaf from their book?'

This questioning and uncertainty was echoed in a large number of groups, in particular amongst participants who were very critical of the government on other political topics. For them the chief effect of the assault on the credibility of Carmen Proetta was to make them unsure of what had happened in Gibraltar.

Gibraltar conclusions

The groups showed a great deal of familiarity with the details of the killings in Gibraltar. But it was striking that the original (false) story about armed IRA members and a car bomb seemed to have such an impact on people's beliefs. Ministry of Defence public relations specialists have long recognised the importance of getting the story out first. Royal Marines Officer Alan Hooper has written that journalists 'are prisoners of current events – a weakness which is exploited by the skilful propagandist – hence the impact of the initial "story"' (Hooper 1982: 139). Colin Wallace, the ex-army press officer who specialised in disinformation in the 1970s, has also commented on the ability of official public relations attempts to set the agenda of public understanding: 'The important thing is to get saturation coverage for your story as soon after the controversial event as possible. Once the papers have printed it the damage is done. Even when the facts come out, the original image is the one that sticks.' [21]

It was also clear, however, that a number of people had picked up the revised version as set out by the Foreign Secretary Sir Geoffrey Howe and subsequently developed by official sources in briefings to sympathetic journalists. The believability of this version of the shootings was seriously weakened by the eyewitness accounts given in 'Death on the Rock', but it seems to have been bolstered by the smear campaign against the credibility of key witness Carmen Proetta. This story was widely believed among the groups in the study, even amongst some people who didn't read the papers in which the allegations were carried.

There were, however, some cracks in the edifice of the official propaganda campaign, such as over the question of surveillance and the question of whether the IRA members were challenged or tried to surrender.

Beliefs About Media Portrayals of Violence [22]

British news coverage of Northern Ireland has often been criticised for reporting violence at the expense of context, background and explanation (Curtis 1984a; Elliot 1977, 1980, 1982; Schlesinger et al. 1983). But does it matter? For some, the constant flow of television images 'goes in one ear and out the other', leaving people with little memory or knowledge about the events covered each night. For others, such coverage is worth little since people 'actively' make sense of television and other media.

So do people know what television news covers or do they (more or less) randomly decide what they have seen? In my own research there was a very high degree of agreement that television news mostly showed violence. Overall a total of 96.9 per cent (222 people out of 229) [23] thought that television showed Northern Ireland as mostly violent. [24] Five people (2.2 per cent) referred to reporting as 'just news'. [25] One person (0.4 per cent) didn't know and one (0.4 per cent) thought that the news was not 'all violent'. Not a single person in this study thought that television news showed Northern Ireland as 'mostly peaceful'. There was, then, remarkable unanimity about the question of violence in television coverage of Northern Ireland. This compares with opinion poll data such as those obtained by BARB in 1990. Using a sample of 3,217 they found that 80 per cent and 81 per cent agreed or strongly agreed that television portrayed Northern Ireland as 'An extremely difficult place to live a normal life' and 'A dangerous place to live' respectively (BARB 1990).

Beliefs About Violence in Northern Ireland

While perceptions of television coverage of violence were quite uniform, beliefs about real life in Northern Ireland were more complex. Many people had rejected the media picture as inaccurate, at least at an intellectual level. In the general British sample a total of 77 people (53.8 per cent) believed that life in Northern Ireland was mostly peaceful, 21 people (14.7 per cent) believed that the violence tended to be confined to particular areas (Belfast, Derry and the border were all mentioned here), or particular times of the year, and a further 6 (4.2 per cent) that Northern Ireland was more violent than other places.

Twenty-two people (15.4 per cent) believed that life in Northern Ireland was mostly violent, with a further seventeen (11.9 per cent) hazarding that it was 'probably' mostly peaceful. This latter category were all very doubtful about it being mostly peaceful.

Among the groups who either lived in Northern Ireland or were in the British army there were marked difference in perceptions of violence. Amongst the army group 27 (69.2 per cent) believed that life in Northern Ireland was mostly peaceful, 4 (10.3 per cent) thought it was mostly violent and a further 8 (20.5 per cent) that it depended where you were. Amongst groups living in Northern Ireland 75 per cent thought that life in Northern Ireland was mostly peaceful, one person thought it was mostly peaceful with the constant threat of violence, two people said that it 'depends what you want' or 'life is as you make it' and six people (12.5 per cent) put that it depended where you lived. There were three people (6.25 per cent) who thought that life where they lived was mostly violent.

These findings are broadly similar to other research in the area. In 1981 Wober found that viewers in Yorkshire were less likely than viewers in Northern Ireland to agree with the statement 'In real life Northern Ireland is not as violent as TV suggests'. Sixty-two per cent of Northern Ireland viewers agreed, but only 29 per cent of Yorkshire viewers did so. Thirty-one per cent of Yorkshire viewers disagreed, compared with 17 per cent of Northern Ireland viewers (Wober 1981). [26]

Would They Go?

The high number of people who wrote that Northern Ireland was mostly peaceful appeared to reject what they saw as television's message, at least at an intellectual level. However, when asked how they would feel about going to Northern Ireland a much more even split occurred. Fifty people (35 per cent) indicated that they would have no problem going to Northern Ireland, 14 (9.8 per cent) said they would be wary but would go and 12 (8.4 per cent) said they would go but only to certain places, or at certain times. In some cases people said that they would go but, as one wrote, 'only if I had reassurance about my welfare'. By contrast sixty (42 per cent) people said that they would not go. Many of the people who said that they would not go were quite emphatic that they would not set foot in Northern Ireland, writing comments such as 'no way', 'Not B. likely' and 'Never'. Their lack of desire to visit seemed not to stem from lack of interest, [27] but from a quite palpable fear. Comments ranged from 'terrified', 'scared', 'frightened', 'I wouldn't go to Ireland as a visitor because you would be a British target for terrorists' (SACRO clients), 'No thank you – why tempt fate?', to 'Very wary because of the news coverage' (hospital staff). A small number of respondents who said they would not go related this not to a wariness of being shot by 'terrorists' or to fear instilled by the media, but to their own political perspective. One respondent seemed to be operating his own cultural boycott in the style of the Anti-Apartheid Movement. He said that he would not go to Northern Ireland because to do so would condone the British view that Northern Ireland was part of the 'UK'.

There was a very high degree of consensus that television showed life in Northern Ireland as mostly violent, but more than half of the respondents rejected this as a factual picture of life in Northern Ireland. However, a large proportion of respondents (42 per cent) were unwilling to visit Northern Ireland, almost all because they were scared of the threat of violence. It seemed that, at a deeper level, many respondents' critique of the news was quite insecure. Two questions arise from these quantitative findings. First, why do so many people believe that Northern Ireland is mostly violent or are scared to visit, and second, what were the reasons for the rejection of the television message evident among a high proportion of respondents?

Sources of Information

Of those who thought it was mostly violent, the majority (seventeen out of twenty-two), cited television, the press or the media in general as their only source of information. Five others also cited evidence from friends, acquaintances or family. Of the 60 people who would not go to Northern Ireland 31 gave the media as their only source of information, with a further 15 citing the media and another source. Two gave non-news media, 6 had some critique of the news, 3 had compared the TV with other accounts, 16 listed friends and acquaintances and 2 the personal experience of visiting Northern Ireland. [28]

Of the 77 people who believed it was peaceful there was a less heavy dependence on the media as the only source of information (11 gave only the media as a source and a further 22 gave the media and another source). Eight gave alternative media information, 12 a critique of the news, and 6 said they had compared Northern Ireland with other parts of the world or that their view was based on assessments of people in Northern Ireland. The biggest category (58 people) by far was direct and indirect experience. Seven gave family, 34 mentioned people from NI or acquaintances who had visited NI and 17 cited the direct experience of living in or visiting Northern Ireland as their reason for rejecting what they saw as the television message.

Media Influence

The clearest reason why people accepted that life in Northern Ireland was mostly violent was because of media (especially television) coverage of the conflict. Such imagery had evidently informed what respondents said about life in Northern Ireland. Some commented explicitly that 'Because of what I hear on TV I believe it to be very violent' (Harrow victims support group), while others regarded media coverage as a transparent reflection of life in Northern Ireland (cf. Richardson and Corner 1986), as in 'TV news seems to be merely reporting the facts' (Harrow victims support group).

Such coverage seemed also to have had a greater impact on the willingness or desire of respondents to visit Northern Ireland, as in the comment from one State Enrolled Nurse who thought that life in Northern Ireland was 'very violent': 'I would feel very wary because of the news coverage it gets. I would feel very unsafe.'

The two most obvious factors which resulted in their rejection of the media account of violence in Northern Ireland were, first, contact (through family, friends or acquaintances with people who had been to Northern Ireland or had lived there) and, second, direct experience of personally visiting Northern Ireland.

Memories and Beliefs

If there was a high level of agreement about the meanings of news coverage of violence, there was also a spread in the memories given by respondents as having had the most impact on them. The responses to this question were highly socially patterned. The first and most striking difference was the recollection of personal experiences as being the most important. Such recollections were mostly absent among British groups. The key memories they gave had mostly been experienced through the media.

The most commonly mentioned key memories of the British groups were related either to general descriptions of violence: 'funerals', 'bombings', 'killings', 'deaths', etc. were mentioned thirty-seven times. Particular atrocities were also mentioned. The bombing at Enniskillen in November 1987 was cited most often (by twenty-seven people). The killings of 'innocents' or 'children' or of people in front of their families were cited by ten people and the killings of two British soldiers who drove into an IRA funeral cortege were mentioned specifically by three people. Such references tended to reflect the respondents' political identity. By contrast, there were a few references from respondents who were critical of government policy on Ireland or who came from a Catholic background or Irish extraction: 'Bloody Sunday', 'British oppression' and 'that the British don't call it a war' were all mentioned once, as were 'integrated education' and the 'ecumenical movement' from people who had religious convictions. Scottish respondents tended to mention events in Ireland as key memories rather than bombings in Britain. This was not the case for respondents in the South East of England, who referred to the bombing of the Horseguards' Parade and the 'deaths of English soldiers' as having a strong impact.

It is clear that these responses are socially patterned and that in the case of the British groups the responses are mainly sourced with the media. Such responses are often seen as negotiations of the meaning of media messages, but it seems clear that the comments relate to events (mediated or not) which have had the most impact (or been the most poignant) for them. These responses are related in part to what people 'bring to' the media in the form of prior political perspectives, identities and ideological baggage. But there is a difference between reactions to a programme and perceptions of it. The content of media coverage has a clear empirical content, which was not negotiated by my respondents.

Conclusions

The clearest reason for rejecting the message of television was the actual experience of going to Northern Ireland of the nineteen people in the general sample who had direct experience of Northern Ireland, none believed life there was mostly violent. The Northern Ireland groups were the most emphatic in rejecting the message. This finding supports other research, which has found that people in Northern Ireland tend to be very critical of the way in which the media cover the conflict.

In a study of responses among people living in Northern Ireland to a BBC Northern Ireland programme sponsored by the Community Relations Council,[29] Nolan found that judgements on the programme were closely linked with nationalist or unionist perspectives or with other political identities. However, groups from both communities did share some evaluations of the content of the programme:

> While, in an obvious sense, the readings made from a nationalist and a unionist perspective oppose each other, the alienation described by both communities seems to stem from a common source, or at least to converge to a common point. This might best be described as a vexation with the tendency of television to exclude the more authentic voices of Belfast's communities in order to promote a safe and reassuring view of the city's sectarian divisions ... The broadcasters are seen to be instrumental in promoting an establishment view – dissembling, complacent, and unwilling to make space for dissident voices. For the Catholics and Protestants from the troubled parts of the city interviewed in this study, the mirror that is held up by television succeeds in rendering them invisible. It is ironic that a programme which set out to explore the reality of a divided

city only served to confirm them in that belief. (Nolan 1993: unpaged)

In a series of research projects (Cairns 1983, 1984, 1987, 1990; Cairns et al. 1980, 1981, which will be discussed in the next chapter) examining the impact of televised coverage of the Northern Ireland conflict on children's conceptions of life in Northern Ireland, Cairns concludes, in apparent surprise, that:

> Despite all this exposure to violence ... the evidence is that children in Northern Ireland have not become totally over-whelmed by the troubles. That is, they have not absorbed Northern Ireland's media image to the extent where the very names 'Northern Ireland' or 'Belfast' conjure up nothing but thoughts of death and destruction. Indeed, despite the media concentration on violent death in Northern Ireland children have apparently been able to retain a perspective which allows them to understand that in most years since 1970 more people in Northern Ireland have died in road accidents than have died as a result of the 'troubles'! (Cairns 1987: 43)

The same cannot be said for many of those people in Britain whose only source of information is television. We will consider some of the theoretical issues raised by these findings in the next chapter.

6

Conclusion:
Winning the Information Battle

It is evident that the media are regarded as a very important element in the struggle for power and resources in Northern Ireland by most if not all of the participants in the conflict. That is why public relations are central parts of the campaigning and legitimating strategies of those organisations. But there remains a profound dispute about the precise role played by the media in the Northern Ireland conflict. In part this is in itself an intimate part of the propaganda war. For some the media are all-powerful and act on behalf of either the state or the insurgents, while for others the media are less important and have minimal impacts on, for example, public opinion or public policy. This chapter reviews some contemporary debates about the power of the media and concludes by making an assessment of that power.

The Powerful Media: Ally of the Insurgent?

For many of the counterinsurgency theorists and 'terror experts', the media are guilty of hampering the 'fight against terrorism'. Sometimes it is argued that because the 'terrorists' want publicity it must be in their interests and for that reason alone media personnel should not allow themselves to be 'hijacked' by 'terrorists'. For Walter Laqueur, 'The media are the terrorist's best friend. The terrorist act by itself is nothing, publicity is all' (Laqueur 1976: 104; see also Clutterbuck 1981; Wright 1990). Yet such theorists implicitly accept that gaining media coverage is not the only goal of any insurgent organisation. The point of publicity is not only publicity, it is the impact which it is feared/hoped will flow from media coverage that concerns the 'anti-terrorism' theorists. We might think of such impacts as being directly on the government or indirectly via 'public

246

opinion'. Leading US ideologue Norman Podhoretz has put it as follows:

> The publicity that has been accorded the terrorist groups has had the effect of habituating the public mind to the kind of action – the murders, the kidnappings, the hijackings – that once seemed so horrible as to be virtually unthinkable ... We become habituated, we lose the sharpness of our sense of outrage, we lose the clarity of our moral judgement. This is the first way in which the publicity that terrorism has received helps to further the aims of the terrorist. (Podhoretz 1980: 85)

Alternatively, there is a fear that publicity may boost the morale of the 'terrorists' or that media coverage may result in the contagion of 'terrorism'. Some writers have held that the imitative effect applies specifically to tactics and know-how as well as, or instead of, providing the impetus to violence in the first place. We have seen that counterinsurgency theorists tend not to examine media coverage or the process by which it emerges, directly and empirically, but when we turn to the impact of media coverage of political violence there is almost no published research on the impact of media coverage of terrorism on public opinion or of the impact of public opinion on government. The literature on contagion is not based on the direct investigation of public belief or on the beliefs and motivations of the 'terrorists', but on a host of other approaches or 'methods'.

The Contagiousness of International Terrorism?

In counterinsurgency doctrine the media encourage terrorism. For Norman Podhoretz, 'one of the main reasons and possibly the most important reason, for the use of these terrorist tactics in advancing the political aims of the organisations involved is treatment by the media' (Podhoretz 1980: 85). In a similar vein, leading 'terror expert' Yonah Alexander has written that 'terrorism, however local, is by its very nature a world-wide theatrical attraction, it tends to encourage angry and frustrated groups beyond a particular country to undertake similar acts as a way out of their helplessness and alienation' (Alexander 1978: 47). British terrorologist Paul Wilkinson has stated that: 'the recent history of terrorism in many democratic countries vividly demonstrates that terrorists thrive on the oxygen of publicity' (Wilkinson 1990: 30). But the evidence given for such hypotheses is remarkably slight, being based almost entirely on anecdotes and comparisons between the use of apparently similar tactics by differing groups (Dobkin 1992). As Schlesinger et al. have put it:

> It is characteristic of this argument and of the way it is mobilised in official thinking, that it constantly detaches events from their specific historical and political contexts and regroups them as part of the same general phenomenon because they look the same, employ the same techniques, or occur together in time. In doing so it glosses over crucial differences between them and the situations from which they spring. (Schlesinger et al. 1983: 141)

In fact remarkably few studies have attempted to examine the relationship between non-state political violence and the media by empirical rather then rhetorical means, as Picard has noted:

> As one reviews the literature it becomes shockingly clear that not a single study based on accepted social science methods has established a cause-effect relationship between media coverage and the spread of terrorism. Yet public officials, scholars, editors, reporters, and columnists continually link the two elements and present their relationship as proven. The dearth of evidence associating the two variables is not the result of conflicting studies or arguments over interpretation of evidence, but rather the absence of research on the subject. At times some scholars have attempted to overcome that problem or to place the pallor of respectability over their opinions by 'borrowing' conclusions from the literature on the effects of televised violence and crime on viewers and then projecting similar effects to coverage of terrorism. (Picard 1986: 387)

The 'evidence' which has been presented (Berkowitz 1973; Heyman and Mickolus 1981; Holden 1986; Mazur 1982; Midlarsky 1970, 1978; Midlarsky et al. 1980; Stoil and Brownell 1981; Weimann and

Brosius 1989) is entirely at the level of correlation, which is then mistaken for causation. In one of the more recent studies, Robert Holden claims to have developed a 'mathematical model' of contagion, which he applies to aircraft hijackings in the United States between 1968 and 1972. He argues that 'analyses show that successful hijackings in the United States did generate additional hijacking attempts of the same type' (Holden 1986: 874). He goes on to say that:

> Even though it was not possible to show statistically that media coverage was responsible for the stimulating effects, the results tend to support the common belief that hijacking had stimulating effects is consistent with previous studies showing that violent acts are more likely to be imitated if they are seen to be rewarded. (Holden 1986: 902)

Although Holden goes on to note that: 'The finding is more consistent with the assumption that most hijackers were rational than that they were irrational' (Holden 1986: 902), it is hard to resist the temptation to view the 'terrorists' as pathological. This is because, as with all the other research in this tradition, 'terrorist' acts are wrenched out of their social, political and historical context.

'Terrorists' are pictured as being provoked into hijacking by virtue simply of watching television. But Holden then comes close to acknowledging the weakness of his case by stating that the contagion effects he had observed

> might be more consistent with spurious contagion than with causal connections between events. That is, exogenous factors may have raised the hijacking rate over certain long periods, yielding dependence between counts of events at time points within those periods. Of course, contagion and exogenous causation are not mutually exclusive, and it is possible that both types of effects occurred. The findings of the present research should not be dismissed because of the mere logical possibility that a completely exogenous rate process exists. (Holden 1986: 901–2)

If it is the case that other factors may be at work and that 'contagion' is not necessarily the only or most important factor, the entire case for 'contagion' as direct and powerful media effects collapses. [1]

'Terrorism' and the 'Effects' of the Media

There is one partial exception to the failure amongst 'terror' writers to investigate the impact of the media on public beliefs about terrorism. Gabriel Weimann, alone among 'terror' experts (as far as I am aware), has attempted to study media effects in this area. Like other 'terror experts', Weimann has argued that:

> Press attention appears to be sufficient to enhance the status of the people, problem, or cause behind a terrorist event. Terrorists' success in attracting media attention may then guarantee world-wide awareness and recognition of the political, racial, or, religious problem that caused the event. (Weimann 1983: 44)

In a later study he concluded that his results 'provide abundant evidence to the agenda-setting and status conferral functions of media coverage' (Weimann 1990: 23). According to Weimann 'what is surprising' is the 'image improving effect' of media coverage. Weimann talks of the 'world-wide recognition' of the problems which cause 'terrorism' and the improvement of image which results from media exposure, yet his research singularly fails to provide support for such statements. This is largely because of his slippery use of concepts such as 'image' and 'recognition' and inadequate conceptualisation of the field of study.

Weimann carried out two separate studies with 80 undergraduates from the University of Haifa, and 'a random sample of 200 Israelis, all adult Jews' (Weimann, 1983, 1990). He asked both sets to complete a questionnaire on attitudes to 'terrorism', then in the case of the undergraduates split them into 'matched groups' (1983: 40). One was designated the control group for the first of two case studies and the other control for the second. The events used were the hijacking of a Dutch train by South Moluccans in 1975 and the hijacking of a TWA plane by Croatians in 1976. The research groups were given a selection of press cuttings from an Israeli daily newspaper, which 'paralleled everyday coverage by providing the full account of the sequence of events' (1983: 40). The two case-study 'terrorist' events were selected to be 'remote in time, location and socio-political distance' from the respondents (Weimann 1983: 40). The second study was largely similar except that it also exposed respondents to television reporting of the two 'terrorist' events and asked the research and control groups additional questions about perceptions of the incidents.

As Edward Herman has pointed out, the clippings given to the groups were not a random set and were from only one newspaper:

> Weimann does not even claim that they were either complete or randomly selected. They seem to have been selected for information coverage. But many media comments are emotional rather than factual. Without a random set, the method is biased and without scientific value. (Herman 1988: 63)

Weimann assumes that the media promote the cause of the terrorists by explaining it in news reporting. He writes that 'media coverage of terrorist events must explain the motive' of the 'terrorists' (Weimann 1990: 27). In fact this is simply wishful thinking for which he has no evidence. It is clear that television news does not regularly explain the causes of those groups which it defines as terrorist. Indeed the major critique of television news and press coverage of political violence has been that it tends to concentrate on violence at the expense of background and context. In a study of the *New York Times* and the London *Times*, Kelly and Mitchell conclude, in a far from unique statement, that news reports were 'sapping terrorism of its political content' and that 'less than 10 percent of the coverage in either newspaper dealt in even the most superficial way with the grievances of the terrorists' (Kelly and Mitchell 1981: 287; see also Dobkin 1992; Elliot 1977; Knight and Dean 1982; Paletz et al. 1982a, 1982b).

Following exposure to the press cuttings and TV reports the experimental groups were consistently more likely than the control groups to agree with statements such as 'the problem which caused the terrorist act is important'; 'the problem should have been covered by the mass media': 'the problem should be solved by international institutions'; 'people should know about this event and its causes'; 'I would like to know more about this subject'. From this Weimann concludes that 'the observed difference between the [experimental and control] groups provide abundant evidence to the agenda-setting and status conferral functions of media coverage' (Weimann 1990: 23). Later he refers to the 'image-improving effect' which his studies reveal (1990: 26). This is a radical overstatement of his findings.

Weimann's use of terms such as 'image' and 'recognition', 'enhance the status' is problematic. To 'recognise' the name of a 'terrorist' group such as the IRA is not the same thing as granting them 'recognition' as legitimate entities. The recognition of the PLO at the United Nations as the 'sole legitimate representative' of the Palestinians which so exercises Weimann, as an Israeli academic, is quite simply not the same as recognising that the people who took over a Dutch train are from South Molucca. As Herman has put it:

Weimann confuses status conferral and initial recognition ... An image must be changed if one never heard of a group previously and now reads of it's existence and actions. The image is reorganised from a blank to a something, even if that something is negative. (Herman 1988: 63)

It is perfectly clear that regarding the 'problem which caused the event' as important is not at all the same thing as being in sympathy or support of the organisation which carried out the hijacking. Nor is recognising the existence of a group or believing that the problem which caused its existence should be solved the same as supporting that group or of understanding the ideology and objectives of the organisation in the way that the group, itself, would wish (Schlesinger 1981). Such slippery thinking is common amongst counterinsurgency thinkers in Britain and the US (cf. Alexander 1979). It also appears to exist within the ranks of liberal Israeli social scientists. [2]

The most fundamental question is, if the media have an image improving effect on 'terrorists', why is it that Western public opinion appears to be overwhelmingly opposed to organisations defined in the media as 'terrorist'? (Hewitt 1992).[3] Moreover, Weimann's respondents were 'very homogenous' in their views on 'terrorism' and they mostly 'objected' to 'terrorism' (Weimann

1983: 42) both before and after the experiment. The question that then arises is, if the media have such a strong improving effect on the image of 'terrorists', why do his respondents have such a negative view of them in the first place? Unless they can come up with better evidence and clearer thinking such writers ought to desist from making statements about media influence and cease their lobbying for repression of the media. [4]

Terrorism as Communication

Underlying much of this debate is a key conceptual problem. The use of violence is held to be a 'communicative strategy'. In this view the function of terrorism is to communicate through the media of mass communications. This leads some to the radical position that, without the media, terrorism would cease to exist. This is part of the underlying assumption of the concept of the 'oxygen of publicity' advanced by Margaret Thatcher. Lord Chalfont, terror expert, and now chair of the Radio Authority in Britain, has put this view: 'the first point to be grasped is that terrorism would be impotent without publicity. It depends for its effect upon dramatic impact in order to compel and hold public attention (Chalfont 1990: 18). [5]

But not all adherents of the 'oxygen of publicity' thesis would accept this. Paul Wilkinson, for example, has rejected such an explanation as simplistic:

> the media are often held up to be in some sense 'responsible' for terrorism. If these acts were not publicised it is argued, how could the terrorist achieve his purposes? Superficially this is a plausible theory and, not surprisingly, has been readily taken up by those who find it convenient to blame the media for every social evil. However, close analysis of the links between terrorism and the media suggests that the relationships are in reality a far greater complexity. (Wilkinson 1978: 2)

Nevertheless the idea that 'terrorism' depends on or is mainly oriented towards the media is widespread amongst counterinsurgency theorists. For example, Brian Jenkins has argued that:

terrorist attacks are often carefully choreographed to attract the attention of the electronic media and the international press. Taking and holding hostages increases the drama. The hostages themselves often mean nothing to the terrorists. Terrorism is aimed at the people watching not the actual victims. Terrorism is theatre. (Jenkins 1975: 4)

More significantly, the dependence of the 'terrorists' on the media is also maintained by liberal and critical scholars. The most notable contribution here is that of Alex Schmid and Janny DeGraaf, who argue that 'terrorism can best be understood as a violent communication strategy ... violence to become terroristic requires witnesses' (Schmid and DeGraf 1982: 15).

Here it is assumed that one of the primary aims of 'terrorist' organisations is to gain media coverage. Therefore, when the media do cover acts of retail political violence they are in effect playing the terrorists' game. Naturally the solution to this problem is for the media to stop covering terrorism.

For some critics the impact of bombings and killings on real people is unimportant; publicity is all. Yet is it true to say that the armed struggle of the IRA has had no material impact outside of publicity? The presence of thousands of British troops, the commitment of an annual subvention of around £2 billion and the deleterious effect of the conflict in Ireland on civil liberties in Britain argues otherwise. In the early 1970s the IRA conducted what it called an economic bombing campaign in the North of Ireland and in the early 1990s it has tried to do the same in Britain. The effect of this latter campaign prompted widespread publicity and, it is true, that publicity was more widespread than for similar bombings in Ireland. Yet the bombing of Bishopsgate in the City of London in 1993 also caused billions of pounds of damage and resulted, amongst other things, in the government stepping in to pick up the tab for future insurance bills. Whatever the symbolic value of such attacks, which, it can not be doubted, is huge, they also have real material consequences. Indeed it is very difficult to separate the symbolic and material importance of such bombings. They are intimately related, as indeed are the symbolic and material aspects of government action.

Whether the material effects of any political action by non-state insurgents, or by governments, are noticed by the media or the public, those effects are real. However, it is also the case that the effects of any action on public opinion and public policy can be substantially affected by the way its symbolic dimensions are characterised. This is why all 'terrorists', pressure groups and governments engage in public relations.

Consider a government which hosts press conferences and stage-manages appearances by its personnel. We would be justified in thinking that the government's aim is to get publicity, and possibly good publicity, from such appearances, but it would be absurd to argue that the reason that governments engage in press conferences is simply so that they can gain media coverage. The object of a press conference is indeed to obtain media coverage and even favourable coverage but it also functions to help the government carry out its political objectives. In counterinsurgency theory it is forgotten that the aim of non-state 'terrorist' groups is the resolution of a particular grievance (be it a ransom demand, the release of prisoners, a change in government policy or state power). The attempt to use the media may be one part of this process, but public relations, whether used by government or 'terrorists' (or by a government which practices 'terrorism'), is never an end in itself. If it were the case that all the IRA wanted was favourable coverage in the media, we could have peace in Ireland simply by giving the airwaves over to the Republican Press Centre in Belfast. In reality, though, the aims of the republican movement are much more substantial than the regular appearance of Gerry Adams on *News at Ten*.

In the view of the counterinsurgents, the irresponsibility of the media needs to be countered by increasing controls over the media. In the 1970s the predominant approach was to emphasise voluntary agreements between the broadcasters and the state (see Wilkinson 1978), although there was some advocacy of tightening the law to force journalists to reveal their sources (Institute for the Study of Conflict 1978; Wilkinson 1980 cited in Schlesinger et al. 1983). But Wilkinson was an early advocate of the approach adopted in the south of Ireland, where interviews with Sinn Féin and the IRA were banned in the 1970s. As early as 1977, Wilkinson was advocating this as a response to the IRA campaign in Britain (Wilkinson 1977: 167).[6] He repeated this view at a conference in 1988:

Experience in the Republic of Ireland certainly shows that such a ban can be operated smoothly and efficiently for many years without in any way threatening parliamentary democracy. Few observers pointed out that even in a free society, no freedom of expression is totally unlimited. Most of us believe for example that pornography should be banned from TV and radio. Inviting terrorists on TV to crow about their latest atrocity is the ultimate pornography of violence. Banning them will prevent causing real distress to hundreds of relatives bereaved by terrorist murderers. It will also help to protect the far more basic democratic freedoms of life and liberty by helping to defeat the terrorist murderers. (Wilkinson 1990: 33)

This was eight months before the Home Secretary did indeed announce the introduction of the ban discussed in Chapter 1. Such calls are issued in tandem with demands that the broadcasters abandon impartiality and declare an open commitment to the state in covering political violence. For Lord Chalfont, the media tend

to search for some kind of bogus intellectual objectivity and to regard the terrorist on the one hand, and the police officer or soldier on the other, as two sides of a morally symmetrical confrontation. In publications of otherwise impeccable respectability, the phrase 'state of violence' is used to describe military or police action against violent subversives and terrorists. This language often results from the sheer incapacity to distinguish between an attack by a violent minority on the institutions of a democratic state and the right of that state to defend itself against such an attack. This absence of differentiation is demonstrated by the frequent television appearances of terrorists and the spokespeople of the organisations that sponsor them, who are allowed to disseminate their violent propaganda with the same freedom as a candidate for parliament addressing his or her constituency. (Chalfont 1990: 19)

This tendency to interview 'terrorists' is of course entirely fictional. But there can be little doubt that such attacks have had their effect on the broadcasting institutions (see Chapter 1).

The Powerful Media: Instrument of the State

In contrast, tighter censorship is opposed by writers from a variety of critical perspectives. They see the media quite differently from the counterinsurgents, as being in a subordinate relationship with the state. First, there is the body of research associated with George Gerbner and 'Cultivation Analysis'. Second, there is the structuralist conception common to much critical media studies in the 1970s, especially the Birmingham Centre for Cultural Studies, and third, there is the 'propaganda model' advanced by Noam Chomsky and Edward Herman. In all three cases the media end up being seen as instruments of the state. For Gerbner and his colleagues, the continual flow of television imagery cultivates compliance with society as presently structured and can even win consent for an increase in repression:

> My argument is simply that symbolic uses of violence tend to benefit those who control them, usually states and media establishments. Isolated acts of small scale insurgencies or bold strikes of a few individuals may force media attention and convey a public message of outrage and defiance. But in the last analysis, that challenge is often made to seem even more outrageous and serves to enhance media credibility ... and to mobilise support for repression, often on a higher scale than warranted by the threat, as in the form of wholesale state violence and terror or military action, which is presented as justified by the provocation. (Gerbner 1991: 3)

The cultivation approach has been criticised for ruling out the possibility of contradictory messages across different programme types and within particular programmes (Schlesinger et al. 1983: 161–2; Wober and Gunter 1988: 2–14) and, in common with much other work on television impacts, for neglecting the specific meanings communicated in particular programmes. Cultivation analysis assumes that compliance is cultivated by the sheer amount of television that some viewers watch, the result being a 'television bias' in public perceptions of the world. In relation to violence this might have a marked effect on assessments of risk and safety:

In the portrayal of violence there is a relationship between the roles of the violent and the victim. Both roles are there to be learned by the viewers. In generating among the many a fear of the power of the few, television violence may achieve its greatest effect. (Gerbner et al. 1979: 180)

In Northern Ireland people tend to watch more television programmes about Northern Ireland than people in Britain (Wober 1992) and yet in my research (cf. Wober 1981) I found that people who lived in Northern Ireland felt a greater sense of safety in walking the streets of Belfast than did people in Britain. This raises another criticism of 'cultivation analysis' which is that there has been little attempt to investigate the sources of public belief about vulnerability to violence. It is as if the public have perceptions about violence and safety which don't interact with their own social experience of the world, not to mention other sources of information and experience. Gerbner's work at least has the merit of trying to engage with the real world of thinking, acting subjects. The other two approaches have not carried out any empirical work on public belief.

In the structuralist conception most often associated with the work of Stuart Hall and his colleagues (1978) the media are seen as subordinated to the 'primary definers' of the state. I have already argued that this model misconceives the relationship between the media and the state because it sees the output of the media as guaranteed in advance by the structural relationship between the media and official sources (cf. Miller 1993b).

In the 'propaganda model' outlined by Chomsky and Herman, the media are regarded essentially as 'instruments' of the state and media output is constrained by five major filters. The model:

traces the routes by which money and power are able to filter out the news fit to print, marginalise dissent, and allow the government and dominant private interests to get their messages across to the public. The essential ingredients of our propaganda model, or set of news 'filters', fall under the following headings: (1) the size, concentrated ownership, owner wealth, and profit orientation of the dominant mass-media firms; (2) advertising as the primary income source of the mass media; (3) the reliance of the media on information provided by government, business, and 'experts' funded and approved by these primary sources and agents of power; (4) 'flak' as a means of disciplining the media; and (5) 'anti-communism' as a national religion and control mechanism. (Herman and Chomsky 1988: 2)

The model is based on the operations of the US media and seems to be less applicable to the British media system. For example, taking each filter in turn, the continued existence of a public service broadcasting system in Britain does make a substantial difference in the spaces it can open up for dissent. This means that the BBC, for example, has not been owned by private capital, nor has it relied on advertising for revenue. Although it does tend to rely on 'official' sources, it is also expected to foster a consensual national identity, which for much of the 1980s was out of kilter with Thatcherism, and this means that critical voices were heard. 'Flak' is certainly used in Britain as a means of disciplining the media, as we saw in Chapter 1. However, the extent to which ideology is simply imposed from the top as a control mechanism is open to dispute. If this were the case in Britain it would be hard to explain the consistent majority in favour of British withdrawal from Northern Ireland. The idea that there might be active struggle over definitions is characterised by Herman and Chomsky as a pluralist approach or is dismissed as irrelevant. Yet some of the evidence in this book suggests that there are conflicts between different sources, within the state and within the media, and that there is not a straightforward relationship between the media and public opinion. This does not mean that the media are independent of the state or that they are not vulnerable to use in propaganda campaigns, but it does mean that the media are not simply instruments of the state.

The most relevant point for our present purposes is that such writers have not empirically examined the relationship between public belief and the media. Instead, much of their writing has assumed the media have powerful and direct effects on public beliefs. [7] In some ways the public are therefore seen as victims of the media. Cohen, for example, talks of 'mass delusions' (Cohen 1972). [8] But there is little acknowledgment that the material interests that some sections of the population in Western countries bring to the media are likely to mean that there is little incentive to question television representations of Nicaragua, Panama or Iraq. My suggestion is that there is perhaps too much emphasis on the power of the media, which almost inevitably results in an instrumentalist perspective.

Learning from Television

There are a variety of studies that have examined the impact of television coverage of Northern Ireland (or other conflict situations) on public perceptions and have concluded that television has a relatively weak impact on belief. Many of these and similar studies are prompted by concerns about the deleterious effects of televised violence on the perceptions, particularly of 'vulnerable' groups, such as children. These studies tend to be prompted by concerns about the strong impact of television and researchers are often surprised or disappointed that their research shows the media to be less powerful than they had anticipated (Cairns et al. 1980).

Such findings have inspired theories with scientific-sounding names such as 'knowledge gap effect' and 'information processing'. These emerge from psychological traditions of research. Information processing, for example, is closely linked with the study of memory and comprehension. In the variety of information processing studies, television is seen as a relatively ineffective means of communicating information. Television news information is forgotten or misunderstood – TV news is, as Robinson and Levy have put it, 'beyond comprehension' (1986: 232). In their survey of the research in the area Robinson and Davis conclude that:

> there is no question that people *perceive* that they obtain most of their information from TV. However these perceptions do not seem to match very well [with] more direct studies, [which] examine what people actually learn from the news ... But our results and those of others ... clearly suggest that whatever televisions impact, it may be short lived. As news events unfold and additional contextual information becomes available television news influence pales in comparison to that of other news media. (Robinson and Davis 1990: 117, original emphasis)

These conclusions are drawn from a series of studies, many funded by the broadcasters themselves, which appear to indicate that people either miscomprehend much of the news (Robinson and Levy 1986), or forget it (Collett and Lamb 1985; Findahl and Höijer 1985; Gunter 1987). The conventional wisdom is that television news is an ineffective communicator and that news information goes in one ear and out the other. However, in my own research it was clear that people had retained a very high level of 'knowledge' and information about the conflict in Ireland, and especially about the killings in Gibraltar. One explanation for these differences is that in my research I was interested not in how much of the total content of news bulletins was lost but on how much was retained about a specific topic. There are, however, some similar findings. In my own research (as with Philo 1990) I did find that there was a high degree of forgetfulness about details such as names, dates and places; however, this was complemented by the reproduction of key explanatory news themes. What is being measured in information processing research is an abstract count of the percentage of information recalled. It does seem unlikely that a one-off event happening in another country would have the same impact as the prolonged coverage of the conflict in Ireland. Yet such research makes no distinctions between different events, treating all news as discrete lumps of information. In measuring retention, 'information processing' research assumes, in the candid acknowledgement of Robinson and Davis, 'that the recall of certain specific information can provide a useful initial index of overall understanding' (Robinson and Davis 1990: 113). However, as Philo has argued:

> It is important to analyse the process by which news information may be located within the political perspectives which are promoted and contested in the development of social ideologies. Methods and analysing news comprehension are inadequate if they treat the content of news (events, places, causalities) as discrete units, irrespective of the processes by which the news is generated. It is not enough simply to assess how many of these different 'units' are retained in the memory. (Philo 1990: 176)

A second approach from within the 'learning from television' perspective is the 'knowledge gap effect'. First hypothesised by Tichenor and his colleagues (Tichenor et al. 1970), it has been applied to many topics (Ettema and Kline 1977; Ettema et al. 1983; Shingi and Mody 1976). The hypothesis is that:

> as the infusion of mass media information into a social system increases, segments of the population with higher socio-economic status tend to acquire this information at a faster rate than the lower status segments, so that the gap in knowledge between these segments tends to increase rather than decrease. (Tichenor et al. 1970: 160)

The methods used are rather similar to those employed by researchers in the information processing tradition, in that they attempt to assess the assimilation of information provided by television. Two pieces of research that examine television coverage of Northern Ireland have been published examining the knowledge gap hypothesis. The first one, with respondents in Britain and the north and south of Ireland, examined learning from one episode of *Ireland: a Television History*. [9] The authors concluded that their evidence supported the knowledge gap hypothesis (Rawcliffe-King and Dyer 1982). The author of the other study, however, concluded that his evidence from children in the north and south of Ireland provided 'virtually' no support for the hypothesis (Cairns 1984: 36). The methodology of both studies involved asking a set of questions about aspects of Irish history or politics and is vulnerable to the same charge as the information processing theorists: or confusing memory for understanding. More fundamentally, though, the evidence from my own research suggests the opposite of the knowledge gap hypothesis. Those who relied on television as a source of information to the exclusion of other sources were much more likely to believe the picture presented by the news than were respondents who had drawn upon other sources of information. Conversely, those who had more complex perceptions about the conflict in Northern Ireland were those who actually lived there. Far from learning the most from television they actively rejected what they saw on television as untrue. This highlights the most fundamental problem with the psychological approaches reviewed here, which is that the concept of learning from television tends to assume that television gives a truthful account of social conflict.

Violence on Television

There is a further, somewhat idiosyncratic, approach which has emerged from the social psychological tradition of studying the effect of televised violence on children. Ed Cairns and his colleagues at the University of Ulster have carried out a number of projects examining the perceptions, particularly of children, in Northern Ireland. In their earliest and most interesting work the researchers compared groups of children living in Northern Ireland with groups in Scotland. Younger children (aged 5–6) were shown line drawings of a train crash or a house on fire and asked to say what had happened, while older children (aged 7–8) were asked to write a short essay to begin 'Here is the news ...'.

Children from Northern Ireland were much more likely to mention bombs or explosions in stories than children in Scotland who 'virtually never' mentioned such things. However, Cairns and his colleagues found some groups of children in the west of Scotland who, at the time (1976–77), could only receive television from Northern Ireland. These children mentioned violence more often than the other Scottish groups (Cairns et al. 1980). Cairns concludes from this that: 'The evidence presented here thus appears to confirm the conclusions reached by other investigators – that television news can distort perceptions of reality – and to extend this finding to children as young as 5 years' (Cairns et al. 1980: 6).

Cairns's work is, however, vulnerable to a number of criticisms. The first is that there is a failure in the research to distinguish between children's conceptions of television and children's conceptions of reality. As Wober and Gunter have argued:

for children living in Northern Ireland the necessary analytic and empirical distinction which should have been made is between the nature of television news and that of life 'outside'; for children in Scotland (when receiving Northern

Ireland television) the distinction needed is three fold between the nature of television news, that of life in Northern Ireland and that of life in Scotland. (Gunter and Wober 1981: 73)

It's not clear whether the responses of the younger children to the drawings reflect their view of television coverage, their view of life in Northern Ireland or their view of life in their own area. However, Cairns' use of essays and line drawings was genuinely innovative. It showed that even young children can absorb and reproduce the themes of television news coverage. The news bulletin produced by one respondent is particularly telling: 'a bomb has just gone off in Belfast and that is the end of the news' (Cairns et al. 1980: 5). If even young children are able to reproduce the essential themes and ways of understanding of television news, the next questions that need to be asked relate to beliefs and the television sources. Do children, or indeed adults, believe that life in Northern Ireland is as violent in reality as they perceive it to be on the news; and what are the sources of belief or disbelief about the predominance of violence?

In fact Cairns went on to ask about perceptions of real violence, as have other researchers (Cairns 1987: 41–3 and 64–70; McWhirter et al. 1983). Cairns found that 'despite possible exposure to a daily diet of Northern Ireland violence in the media children, happily, have the violence rather more in perspective than might have been expected' (Cairns 1987: 41–2). McWhirter and her colleagues concluded that:

The present data indicate a heightened awareness of the phenomenon of death amongst young Belfast children but there is no evidence of a preoccupation with violent death. Overall, death was attributed more often to sickness than to accidents *or* violence. On a more specific level, just as many children cited heart disease or old age as explosions or shootings and more children ascribed death to road accidents and cancer than to violence related specifically to the Northern Ireland conflict. In short the children's per-ceived realities quite accurately reflect the objective situa-tion. (McWhirter et al. 1983: 91, original emphasis)

As we have seen, these results with children in Northern Ireland are broadly in line with the findings of my own research that people in Northern Ireland are likely not to believe news accounts as simple descriptions of events in Northern Ireland. But Cairns goes on to make a seemingly opposite point, arguing that perceptions of violence (described by McWhirter as 'quite accurate' and by Cairns himself as 'happily ... in perspective') are actually a manifestation of a psychological process of 'denial'. Citing a study of 3,000 schoolboys carried out in 1971/2 (Russell 1973), together with his own research on children (Cairns 1982; cited in Cairns 1987: 67) and adults (Cairns and Wilson 1984), he argues that 'obviously there are various ways in which this information can be interpreted, but one is that at least some of the children questioned in both 1971 and 1981 were denying that a lot of violence had occurred in their area' (Cairns 1987: 68). Turning to the adults views he concludes that 'the majority ... denied there had been a lot of trouble in their district even when the statistics on violence told a different story' (Cairns 1987: 68–9). Cairns concludes that 'it would appear that a convincing case may be building up that denial is indeed at least one of the important coping mechanisms being used by both children and adults in Northern Ireland' (Cairns 1987: 69). This quite clearly contradicts his earlier conclusions, but he appears not to notice. From the perspective of media reception we can note that a limitation of researching perceptions about the real world and perceptions about television separately is a difficulty of linking the two together in any meaningful way. The concern in my own audience research was to assess public perceptions about news portrayals of reality and about reality itself, and then to ask them why those perceptions were identical or why there was a disjunction between them. As we saw, there was a very high degree of agreement on what television showed together with a substantial variation in perceptions of reality. The question which then needs to be asked is what are the sources of public belief in this area? This is a particularly relevant point when we consider research on changes in perception of students from outside Northern Ireland between their arrival and a period one year later. After the students had been in Northern Ireland for a year 'mentions of violence had almost disappeared from their impressions. Instead they concentrated on the more normal aspects of life' (McIvor 1981: 8, cited in Cairns 1987: 66). For a researcher so interested in the impact of the media, it is odd that Cairns doesn't think to ask the obvious question about why students from outside Northern Ireland perceived it as being so violent.

In a subsequent study with 520 children in various 'low', 'medium' and 'high' violence towns in the north and south of Ireland, Cairns found that children's estimates of the level of violence in their areas 'corresponded at least in rank order terms, to the rank order of the areas in terms of actual levels of violence' (Cairns 1990: 449). Cairns also found that children in the more violent towns reported watching the news more often than others. This is not surprising, since it is well known that the media consumption of people in Northern Ireland is higher than in Britain (Wober 1992). However, it is necessary to do more than simply demonstrate correlation between media consumption and perceptions of everyday reality.

That Cairns's findings suggest that television is less powerful than had been expected is largely a function of inadequate methodology and conceptualisation. But this doesn't stop Cairns from concluding in two separate articles that 'one possible effect is that overexposure to news about violence may lead to the perception of violence as more usual and also more acceptable' (Cairns et al. 1980: 6; 1983: 122). While this may be 'possible', Cairns's own evidence points in the opposite direction. As with the work of Gerbner referred to above, one of the key problems of this type of argument is a failure to attend to the actual meanings conveyed by the media. Curiously enough, many of the problems with this type of psychological research have been replicated by much recent 'critical' analysis of media reception.

The Weak Media and the 'Active' Audience: Is a Television a Toaster?

The predominant trend in recent audience research in media and cultural studies has been a move away from the power of the media and towards demonstrating the power of the audience. At the methodological level, such work has moved away from analysing the content of television programmes or press reporting and towards the analysis of audience activity and resistance to

television messages. Such resistance is held to invalidate concerns about the power of television. Indeed, as Corner has noted, some reception analysts seem to regard the analysis of media content as indicating an attachment to 'naive' notions of media power (Corner 1991: 281). [10]
For the theorists of the active audience, the meaning of any given message is not determined by the productive ideological labour that goes into construction, but by the encounter between the audience and the text. As one of the most influential theorists, John Fiske, puts it: 'Meanings are determined socially: that is, they are constructed out of the conjuncture of the text and the socially situated reader' (Fiske 1987: 80). [11]
This leads on to a conception of the relation between television and its audience as essentially interactive: 'Television and its programs do not have an "effect" on people. Viewers and television interact' (Fiske 1987: 19, cited in Seaman 1992: 306). This is more than saying that each of us have the ability to interpret what we see. For some reception analysts people are actively engaged in the 'creation' of meaning, as if there was an almost unlimited potential for people to 'read' any 'meanings' at will from a given 'text'. Such studies have, as Corner and his colleagues have pointed out, tended to operate with slippery concepts of 'meaning':

> The investigation of meaning in reception studies needs to differentiate analytically between 'understanding' and 'response', however interfused these may be in practice. For it is of course entirely possible for viewers to agree as to how to understand an item but to disagree in their responses to it. (Corner et al. 1990: 50)

In the research reported here there was a very high degree of agreement that television news was mostly violent. If a large proportion of respondents had said that they thought that television news showed mainly scenes of beautiful countryside in its coverage of Northern Ireland, we would not speak of this as a 'negotiated reading' of television. Instead of accepting this as an act of resistance to be celebrated, we would more straightforwardly describe this as a 'misreading'. In a critique of the celebration of audience 'resistance', Gitlin has argued that the active audience theorists have all but given up engaging with the world of actual political resistance:

> Resistance, meaning all sorts of grumbling, multiple interpretation, semiological inversion, pleasure, rage friction, numbness, what have you – 'resistance' is accorded dignity, even glory, by stamping these not so great refusals with a vocabulary derived from life-threatening work against fascism – as if the same concept should serve for the Chinese student uprising and cable TV grazing. (Gitlin 1991: 336)

Instead of engaging with the conditions under which real political resistance is fostered and real political dominance maintained, some cultural theorists have drifted off into celebrations of consumer culture. This is the politics of defeat.

There is a second trend in contemporary research on the 'active audience' which seems to go further than finding that audiences are able to exert cultural power over television messages. This is the study of the use of television (and other communication technologies). One of the first was David Morley's study *Family Television* (1986), followed by his work with Roger Silverstone (Morley and Silverstone 1990, 1991; Silverstone 1990) and the writings of others such as James Lull (1990) and Ien Ang (1991). Lull takes the American functionalist tradition to task for its obsession with quantification and suggests that the use of ethnography is the way ahead for audience research on 'the empirical life-worlds of audience members' (Lull 1990: 20). Much of this research examines the extent to which the use of television technology is gendered. Key areas of interest include the exercise of control by men over which programmes are watched. Such research does not of course tell us very much about the formation of public belief, but it is conceivable that it might reveal the impact of gender roles on which media products are consumed and why. However, this would only be the first stage in investigating the implications of consumption patterns for the messages to which people are exposed and their interaction with the beliefs of family members. Unfortunately the question of the consequences of viewing is routinely ignored. Silverstone identifies three 'key issues' for anthropological audience research to tackle amongst which he does include the issue of 'consequences'.

But he elaborates on this by referring first to the impact of television technology on the 'boundary around the household [and] the links between home and school; home and work; home and leisure opportunities' (Silverstone 1990: 188); and second to the impact of television consumption on the formation in the home of 'age and gender identities' and 'its significance as an ameliorator or prompter of conflict' (Silverstone 1990: 188). The question of the content of television messages and whether people believe them is plainly not part of the agenda. Such lack of interest is echoed in Morley's most recent work (1993) and in the work of Ien Ang. Ang, who has a fondness for suggesting that active audience research opens the way for 'radical' new departures in ways of conceptualising the audience, argues that the key issue is not the analysis of the meanings promoted by particular types of programming. Instead it is the uses to which television technology is put in the home:

> Morley's research enables us to begin to conceive of 'the ideological operations of television' in a much more radical way than has hitherto been done. The relation between television and audiences is not just a matter of 'negotiations' between texts and viewers. The process of television consumption, and the cultural positioning of television as such, have created new areas of constraints and possibilities for structuring social relationships, identities and desires. If television is an 'ideological apparatus,' to use that old-fashioned sounding term, this is not so much because its texts transmit certain 'messages' as because it is a cultural form through which those constraints are negotiated and those possibilities take shape. (Ang 1991: 110)

For Lull, Silverstone, Morley, Ang and others there is a reluctance even to pose questions about the impact of television and other media messages on public belief, as if this would in some way be elitist. This is a flight not only from the text as a meaningful construction but also from the specifics of audience interpretation. Such theorists don't seem interested in the construction of public belief and the success (or failure) of information management activities in shaping public belief and facilitating the exercise of power in one direction or another. The view of the 'radical' theorists of the agenda for audience research ends up being more or less the same as the old uses and gratifications research. Or, as Curran has put it, 'old pluralist dishes being reheated and presented as new cuisine' (Curran 1990: 151). Some researchers have even gone so far as to rule out the investigation of the effects of the media and thus rule out finding any effects. In a straightforward statement of that position, Elihu Katz has argued that 'what interests us, however, is not what people take from television but what they put into it' (cited in Kubey, forthcoming : 14).

In the end the supposedly 'radical' approaches of the new audience theorists is largely indistinguishable from the study of the consumption of any other item of modern household technology. There is very little sense in any of this work of the consequences not of television as a technology but precisely as a *message-bearing* technology. For this school of theorists there seems to be no analytical difference between a television and a toaster.

The Efficiency of British State Information Management

It could be argued that the success of government information management about Northern Ireland is limited by a number of factors. First, Ireland is very close to Britain. It is not only the access of the media to Northern Ireland that makes it different from the insurgencies in Malaya, Cyprus or Aden or to information management attempts in relation to the Falklands or Gulf wars. There are a very large number of people living in Britain who are of Irish descent. People in Britain have families in the north or south of Ireland, people go to Northern Ireland on business or holiday. There are, therefore, many people who have channels of communication with people living in the north of Ireland and do not only have to rely on the media for information about the conflict. Obviously such channels will be more or less frequently used or more or less direct. As we have seen, direct communication with people from Northern Ireland can be enough to undermine media-based perceptions, but it does not always do so. Indeed, we can see that the impact of personal channels that undermine mainstream media messages can be limited by the relatively small number of channels and the cohesiveness of expatriate communities. We must also remember that the content of the information and interpretation offered by people coming to Britain is likely to differ substantially not only between nationalist and unionist identifications but in relation to class, gender and rural/urban splits, etc.

There was also a second limit to official public relations attempts in relation to public belief on the Gibraltar killings. This was in the formation of overall judgements on whether the SAS action was justified. Judging the 'facts' of what happened in Gibraltar was clearly influenced by political and cultural identities, personal experience, prior knowledge and values of the groups. But beliefs about the facts were not endlessly elastic. Thus participants could acknowledge the weakness of their case in a particular area. For example, the soldiers who were reluctant to acknowledge that there had, in fact, been no bomb in Gibraltar had avoided the difficulty by writing a newsflash set on a date before the facts damaging to their case had become known. People do share information and may acknowledge weaknesses in their own arguments by trying to avoid discussing them. There is an extent to which people protect themselves and their sense of identity from damaging information, be it government propaganda or uncomfortable facts about the state. But such identities are not inviolate. They are constantly reconstructed (sometimes in the same way or sometimes in a new direction) as people deal with new information or experience. Sometimes that information comes from the media.

In some ways it would be surprising if a single incident such as the Gibraltar killings overturned long-held opinions or impressions, since there are many 'incidents' in Northern Ireland every year. Gibraltar was exceptional in the amount of coverage it attracted and in the fact that the case against the government was more credible for the media and, it seems, parts of the public. It is interesting to find that people might not reject particular beliefs even though they are key parts of the evidence used by an opposing frame of reference. So it is possible to find people of republican sympathies who have absorbed key elements of the propaganda of the British government. My suggestion is that people do not exist inside sealed, ideologically correct bubbles. They can maintain contradictory or seemingly contradictory beliefs simultaneously. Pieces of information, impressions, tastes, beliefs and memories may never be evaluated against each other, or may be different for varying situations. But it also means that they can on occasion very effectively undermine even strongly held political identifications.

For some people who were otherwise quite critical of the government the most obvious result of the propaganda campaign on Gibraltar was that they became confused about what had happened. It is not unreasonable to conclude that their confusion represented a considerable victory for government information management attempts to muddy the waters.

In some ways the Carmen Proetta story was a very crude form of propaganda. It was easy for liberal broadsheet papers (such as the *Guardian* and the *Independent*) to print opposing stories pointing out the propagandistic coverage in other papers. On the other hand, the use of a smear does not require that everyone wholeheartedly believes it, just that it raises doubts about past activities or motivations. The impression management engaged in by British official sources after the allegations of prostitution against Carmen Proetta can be seen as more sophisticated, in that it had a less sensational and broader impact on the press. It was even reported as fact on television, in marked contrast to the allegation of prostitution. The fact that Proetta had not withdrawn her story at the inquest was not widely pointed out in the media. This, together with the question mark over her 'reputation', made it more difficult for the public to believe alternative information.

Good propaganda has to fit with what is already known and what seems plausible. The assault on the credibility of Carmen Proetta made great use of popular assumptions and prejudices about femininity and sex workers. It is often said that women have one of two roles in public life: virgin or whore. Discrediting Carmen Proetta by labelling her as a prostitute clearly worked with many respondents, although it did not always overrule other views on the killings even when it was believed.

It is important to note that the extent to which nationalist and unionist groups rejected the general picture of life in NI portrayed by the news was much greater than that with which they rejected specific details of the Gibraltar story. It seems likely that this has something to do with the very specificity of the question of Gibraltar, even though there were clearly very deep and detailed memories about what had happened. My argument is, however, that a key reason for the success of some messages about Gibraltar was the fact that all information had to be gleaned from the mass media, whereas for stories occurring in Northern Ireland other channels are routinely available. This brings us to another point, which is that the killings in Gibraltar gained a larger amount of coverage than any of the other controversial special forces killings in Northern Ireland which have occurred throughout the troubles. This meant that the details of the killings, and especially the alternative case, were more easily available in Britain than in most of the other cases. Accordingly, people in Britain are likely to know more details about Gibraltar than about the killings in 1990 on the Falls Road or at Cullyhanna for example. This in turn means there is likely to be less British public concern about killings in Ireland. Part of the reason that the Gibraltar killings gained such prominence was the fact that they did not occur in Ireland and that the official cover story was so quickly changed by the Foreign Secretary himself. An additional factor was that the witnesses to the killings did not lack credibility for journalists, as do witnesses in Ireland. The witnesses in Gibraltar were not Irish and had no obvious link with particular perspectives on Northern Ireland. Indeed the very Britishness of Gibraltar boosted the credibility of such witnesses (at the same time as making it unlikely that more would come forward – see Jack 1988). This does point to the importance of a wide range of publicly available information if the British public is sensibly to make up its collective mind about what should happen in Northern Ireland.

What is the Role of the Media in the Conflict in Ireland?

The ability of the British state to manage opinion is *potentially* limited by a number of factors which have been highlighted throughout this book. First of all, a large number of differing interests and rivalries exist and coexist within a given state organisation as well as between different state organisations. Thus we find there are divisions between administrative civil servants and information officers in the NIO, between the police and the civil service, between the police and the army and between the various branches of the intelligence services. Such divisions are part of serious and ongoing struggles for resources and power: they are not always, and indeed are rarely, fundamental. Even then, however, this does not divest divisions within the state of importance, for they can have material effects on resourcing pattern and on government policy (Miller 1993b).

The resources available to the institutions of the state cannot be matched by any of the other participants in the conflict. The financial resources available for public relations, and the security and authority of state institutions, allow them huge inbuilt advantages over other organisations. The use of the law and intimidation are perhaps the most obvious ways in which such resources can be mobilised. We saw in Chapter 1 that the pre-eminent forms of intimidation of the broadcast media often involve nothing more than telephone calls to senior broadcasters, together with briefings to the press. This is not to say that more energetic forms of intimidation are not used. Journalists and photographers have been shot with plastic bullets, hit with truncheons, beaten up, arrested and harassed by the army and police, but the more authorised forms of intimidation are much more likely to be successful. Threatening journalists is much less sophisticated than taking them to lunch. Thus republican PR was less sophisticated in the early 1970s. In 1971 the IRA blew up the *Daily Mirror*'s printing plant in Belfast, and in November 1974 two *Mirror* journalists were kidnapped by the IRA for around four hours. More recently, in 1988 two BBC journalists were threatened by callers claiming to be from the IRA in order to prevent them giving evidence in court. [12] Thames television researcher Eamon Hardy was also threatened in 1988 and told to leave Belfast (Bolton 1990). In general, however, it is unionists who have more often and more severely attempted to intimidate journalists (Moloney 1988). In 1984 Jim Campbell of the *Sunday World* was shot by loyalists in his home in Belfast (Campbell 1985; 1991). In October 1992 a bomb was planted in the offices of the *Sunday World* by the UVF and in November of that year death threats were made to *Sunday World* staff by the UFF. As a result journalist Martin O'Hagan left Northern Ireland and editor Jim Campbell worked for a period from the Republic of Ireland (*Index on Censorship* 1993a; 1993b).

Official organisations have superior resources but necessarily compete with other sources for media space and are not always successful in doing so. Thus the attempt by the British government to criminalise the republican movement in the 1970s foundered when the republicans' response of hunger strikes gained public sympathy, and then when Sinn Féin successfully entered the electoral arena in the early 1980s.

A further major limit on the ability of official sources to dominate the media is the disjunction between the state strategy of containing the troubles and the operational imperatives of journalism. The drive towards maximising audiences, whether in print or broadcast media, together with the legitimation of journalism as a 'public service' or 'fourth estate', means that the priorities of the media and the government can be quite distinct. But we should not come to the conclusion that the media and especially television are therefore independent of the state. The differing motives, ideologies and priorities of the media often overlap or coincide with those of the state. Similarly the priorities of the republicans, the unionists and others may also on occasion overlap with those of the media. But such coincidences are less numerous and much more marginal than those between the media and the state.

It is true that critical voices in Ireland have been pushed progressively to the margins of the media over the last twenty years. One of the most marked impacts of official policing in the late 1980s on the forms of television was the turn towards the drama-documentary (Kerr 1990). As the ability to make factual programmes decreased journalists turned to dramatisations, which offer increased space for dramatic licence and make it easier to represent events without requiring informants to appear on television.

It is also true that a significant public service ethos remains in broadcasting and that the ideology of the 'fourth estate' remains in parts of the press, although there are very clear limits on the practice of a watchdog role. In addition, the operation of contemporary news values causes difficulties for the government strategy of emphasising 'good news'. But the definition of good news is itself not a neutral category. If the state has tried and largely succeeded in dominating 'bad news' about Northern Ireland, it has also succeeded in dominating the good news which does appear. Nevertheless, news values have proved fairly resistant to good news, as have some individual reporters who perceive the campaign for good news as a propaganda exercise. [13]

There is a sense in which the role of the media is contradictory. On the one hand, the media are vulnerable to the propaganda of the state and can perform functionally in legitimating the activities of the state. On the other hand news values and the remnants of public service ideology can be at the least inconvenient and at times a major obstacle to official actions.

The routine repetition of official misinformation when state violence occurs can enhance the capacity of the RUC or the army literally to get away with murder. The reporting of Northern Ireland in terms conducive to the official view of the conflict dissipates public pressure on the government to try to end the conflict and legitimates the introduction of ever more repressive legislation. There can be little doubt that the 'field dressing' (Elliot 1976) supplied by the British media following the Birmingham and Guildford bombings in 1974 eased the passage of the 'draconian' Prevention of Terrorism Act and helped to convict the Maguire family, the Guildford Four and the Birmingham Six for bombings they did not commit. These events conform quite well to an instrumental model which emphasises the drift to a strong state accomplished by the mechanism of 'moral panic' (e.g. Hall et al. 1978).

However, it explains the subsequent release of the Guildford Four and Birmingham Six less well. In the Guildford and Birmingham cases it is clear that television played a role in forcing an acknowledgement that the convictions were unsafe, by helping to 'move the counter discourses enunciated in Republican and Left publications from the periphery to the centre of the public sphere' (Murdock 1991: 112). Both Granada's *World in Action* and Yorkshire's *First Tuesday* made a series of documentaries between 1984 and 1987, followed by Granada's drama-documentary 'Who Bombed Birmingham' (in 1990) which ended by naming the men allegedly responsible for the bombings. The programmes and associated books (Kee 1986; McKee and Franey 1988; Mullin 1987) questioned the safety of the convictions and eventually led to the cases being sent back for appeal and subsequently to the release of all the defendants. Let us remember that this was in the teeth of opposition from the very highest officials in government and the legal system, especially the judiciary.

The media cannot simply be described as instruments of any side in the conflict. Major-General Richard Clutterbuck, for example, has written that the television camera is 'a weapon lying in the street available for either side to pick up and use' (1981: xv). Nor are the media the mythical 'fourth estate'. It is simply fanciful to describe the release of the Guildford Four as the victory of a 'free media', as Abraham Miller has done (Miller 1990). The media operate within a set of constraints in which power is clearly skewed towards the state. The major constraints on the media are those imposed by the economic context of media production, the use of the law, government intimidation, direct censorship and self-censorship. Journalists continue to mistake authority and status for credibility and are oriented towards the state in their work practices and their reportage. However, the extent to which the state or the government comes in for criticism from the media is variable. It depends among other things on the balance of political forces at any time. If the government is weak or divided then it will be easier for journalists to criticise and for the broadcasters to resist pressure and intimidation. The media provide an arena in which battles for definition are fought out. The institutions of the state command the greatest resources in this area, and this means that media institutions are, in general, oriented towards the state. But they can, on occasion, be harnessed by non-governmental organisations, especially if the state is divided.

In traditional democratic models the media are supposed to oil the wheels of democracy by supplying the population with enough information to make up its collective mind. Yet it is evident from the research presented in this book that many people in Britain have a quite distorted picture about violence in Northern Ireland or believed false propaganda distributed by the government. Nonetheless it is apparent that the bulk of the British public do not draw the same conclusion as the media from such reporting in terms of what should be 'done' about Northern Ireland.

In almost every poll since 1971 a majority has favoured some form of British withdrawal from Ireland. However, withdrawal is hardly seriously discussed in the mainstream media. It seems that only two papers have advocated British withdrawal. Under the influence of leader writer Joe Haines, the *Daily Mirror* adopted an editorial policy of advocating British military withdrawal from 1978 until Haines's departure from the *Mirror* after the death of proprietor Robert Maxwell in 1991. [14] The policy was not matched by any significant difference in the news reporting of Northern Ireland, which remained on a par with other mass-market tabloids. The only other paper to advocate a British withdrawal was the *Sunday Times*. [15] In the ideology of consumer sovereignty adhered to by many in journalism, the content of the media only reflects the wishes of the consumer, since if it didn't sales would plummet. If this were so we might expect to see at least half of the British press adopting a policy of 'troops out'. In reality, however, newspapers give their readers a substantial proportion of what the newspaper proprietor or editor wants them to hear.

It doesn't seem unreasonable to suppose that the decontextual-ised coverage of violence which so predominates British news coverage should lead people to the conclusion that the British army can perform no useful role in Northern Ireland. Such sentiments appear to include both those who want to let the Irish fight it out amongst themselves and those who see the British presence as part of the problem. Opinion polls indicate that there is a fairly even split on the preferred constitutional status of Northern Ireland and on the role of the British army in the conflict. [16]

According to counterinsurgency theorists, the media favours the 'terrorists' by providing the oxygen of publicity, yet a close examination of opinion poll data together with the audience research reported in Chapter 5 indicates that media coverage of dramatic republican attacks tends to push public opinion into greater support for government policy. [17]

First of all, it should be noted that a very small number of people in Britain are prepared to say that they regard the IRA as 'freedom fighters' (3 per cent in 1977 and 1983 – De Boer 1979; Hewitt 1992). This is hardly consistent with unrelenting favour-able coverage for the republican movement. The most important finding here is that media coverage of republican paramilitaries can shift public opinion in the government's favour. Although most polls show a majority in favour of British withdrawal there are a few significant exceptions to the pattern. As early as

September 1971 a total of 59 per cent said they favoured withdrawal (cited in Curtis 1988). This seems to have dropped to 39 per cent by October following 'widespread violence' (Flackes and Elliot 1989: 2) at the tail end of September in the aftermath of internment (Rose et al. 1978). The next clear majority against withdrawal came in August 1972, when a record low of 34 per cent favoured withdrawal. This followed hard on the heels of the twenty-six bombs exploded in Belfast by the IRA on 'Bloody Friday', as a result of which eleven people died. Following this all the opinion polls I have been able to trace between 1974 and 1986 showed more than 50 per cent of the British population in favour of withdrawal. With three exceptions this also applies to all polls since 1986. These three results followed closely on the heels of two major IRA attacks in which civilians were killed. In November 1987 the percentage favouring British withdrawal fell under 50 per cent for the first time in fifteen years. The poll was taken between 20 and 24 November, only eleven to fifteen days after the IRA had exploded a bomb at the Enniskillen Remembrance Day ceremony killing eleven civilians. After the bombing, television news carried an emotional account of the last exchange of words by one of the injured, Gordon Wilson, with his daughter, as her life slipped away under the wreckage caused by the bomb. It seems likely that the coverage of this was an important element in allowing British people to identify with the experiences of victims of violence. Certainly, Enniskillen was the most prominent memory among British people in the audience research reported in Chapter 5. In 1987, support for British withdrawal dropped from 61 per cent in January of that year to 40 per cent by November. Enniskillen appears to have had a marked impact because by January 1988 the proportion favouring withdrawal had risen to only 44 per cent. However, the Birmingham Six appeal, the announcement of no prosecutions in the Stalker/Sampson inquiry, the killing of civilian Aidan McAnespie by a British soldier and the SAS killings in Gibraltar were amongst the events between that poll and the next one carried out between 11 and 15 March 1988. It showed 50 per cent in favour of withdrawal. The only other occasion when support fell below 50 per cent was in March 1993, when 45 per cent said they were in favour. This poll was taken between 25 and 26 March, barely a week after the Warrington bombing in which Jonathon Ball (aged

3) and Tim Parry (aged 12) died. Because it happened in England, the coverage of this bombing was much more extensive and emotional than comparable deaths in Ireland (Greenslade 1993a).

This suggests that media coverage can function to decrease the number of people in favour of a British withdrawal. This fits with evidence from BBC research carried out at the time of the interview with an INLA representative in 1979. As a result of watching the programme a majority of respondents felt a little or a lot more sympathetic to the British army (65 per cent) and a little or a lot more hostile to both the INLA (74 per cent) and the IRA (67 per cent). However, a total of 80 per cent of respondents also felt it was right to show the programme (BBC 1980a).

If the strategy of the IRA is to 'sicken' the British public out of Ireland, then it seems that there is a double sense in which it has been mistaken. First, IRA operations that kill civilians seem to result in British public opinion moving in favour of the British military presence. Second, the British government has shown itself perfectly able to ignore the wishes of the electorate when it comes to Ireland.

According to some commentators, British public opinion cares little for what happens in Northern Ireland. This is credited in some accounts to the activities of the IRA and the long-lasting nature of the conflict. Mark Urban argues that public opinion in Britain is 'desensitized by years of terrorism' and therefore 'tends to care little for the lives of its perpetrators' (Urban 1992: 243). But if it is true that the British public cares little for what happens in Ireland, then we ought to ask how they came to care so little. It is precisely the objective of British government public relations to contain the Northern Ireland conflict and thus isolate it from mainstream British politics. In that sense the desensitization of the British public owes something to successful official information management. But it seems likely that the partial success of the strategy of containment has meant that the conflict in Northern Ireland has never been a popular war. The consistent majorities in favour of British withdrawal contrast markedly with the sizable, though not majority, support for the British interventions in the Falklands/Malvinas (Glasgow University Media Group 1985) and the Gulf. What is different about those conflicts is the active construction of the Argentine government and Saddam

Hussein as popular hate figures to legitimate military intervention (Philo and McLaughlin 1992). By contrast the British government preferred the Northern Ireland conflict to recede from the front pages and sink into obscurity. No British elections were won with the aid of military success in Northern Ireland. Despite consistent public opposition to the policy of successive British governments, it has never been the policy of any mainstream British party to implement the popular will. Although the media do tend to benefit the government it is also true that they have some beneficial effects for the 'terrorists'. The media do play a role in setting the political agenda.

However, counterinsurgency theorists misconceptualise the power of the media. The media in Britain do not and have not supported the Provisional republican movement. Indeed, both Sinn Féin and the IRA have been consistently excoriated in the mainstream media. In addition British public opinion has not, as a result of media coverage of 'terrorism', fallen in behind the IRA. As we have seen, opinion surveys show very low levels even of expressed 'sympathy' for the insurgents. It is evident that the media have a central part to play in the process by which some problems emerge onto the political agenda and come to be seen as important. This is why both the British government and the republican movement have regarded public relations as a central part of their respective strategies.

There is a political and practical dilemma at the root of the arguments advanced by the counterinsurgents. This concerns how a political system which claims to be democratic reacts to challenges to its democratic credentials by an armed attack on their legitimacy. In practice, it would be possible to counter the limited use that the insurgents are able to make of the media. Such moves would have to include much stricter censorship, including banning the reporting of Sinn Féin as once obtained under Section 31 in the Republic of Ireland. It would also be necessary to go further and prohibit all reporting of the actions of both Sinn Féin and the IRA and indeed all mentions of their existence not only in broadcasting, but in the press as well. An attempt to do this was made in the Irish Republic in the middle years of the twentieth century, but it failed when the term 'illegal organisation' became known as a synonym for the IRA (Horgan 1984). Paramilitary actions would have to be kept secret even if the Northern Ireland Secretary or the entire cabinet were taken hostage or assassinated by the 'terrorists'. In fact, such an approach was recommended by Labour Northern Ireland Secretary Roy Mason in the 1970s (see Curtis 1984a: 162), but no serious attempts were ever made to introduce such a measure. If it were, international journalists would have to be kept out of Northern Ireland and attempts by the Republican Press Centre to communicate with the outside world would have to be checked.

These measures would, however, be ineffective without introducing legal changes such as the banning of Sinn Féin (and any successor) to prevent them taking part in elections. Such a move has in fact been recommended by Paul Wilkinson (1990).

However, even these measures would not ensure the defeat of the 'terrorists'. The 'armed struggle' would continue, but it would not have the same capacity to put the Northern Ireland problem on the political agenda. Sweeping legal changes such as these would also give the government a much freer hand to 'root out' the 'terrorists' away from the spotlight of the media in a manner reminiscent of some Central American states. Such a course of action might be hampered by an increased human rights interest in Northern Ireland, and conflict with international organisations, which might lead to government action to curtail the activities of human rights activists in Northern Ireland and Britain.

Were we to adopt such a course, the democracy that such measures were alleged to defend would have disappeared in the effort to decouple law from order. The fundamental value question that remains is: do we want to go any further down that road?

There is, at first sight, a disjunction between media coverage and public opinion. The editorial position of almost all of the press is in favour of the British presence, yet a majority of the British public favour withdrawal. On closer inspection, however, it is apparent that it is only very rarely that papers spell out their view on the British presence. When they do, they are usually found in editorials or columns. There has in fact been no campaign in the British media to convince the public specifically that the British presence is necessary. Instead the dominant themes in British news coverage have been the portrayal of the IRA as criminals and terrorists and the British army as peacekeepers. The main rationale for coverage has been violence covered without context or explanation. Although official sources would prefer that Northern Ireland drifted into obscurity, it is clear that the portrayal of 'terrorists' and 'peacekeepers' fits well with official media management strategies. Furthermore, the audience research reported in this book indicated that such themes dominate British public understandings. Key aspects of the official story on the Gibraltar killings were also believed by a large proportion of people in my sample. What this suggests is that public opinion can be vulnerable to propaganda offensives by official sources. However, it is clear that the impact of the media is variable, depending, amongst other things, on other sources of information available, prior beliefs, views and experience. Nevertheless, the most important conclusion of this book is that the media can, under certain circumstances, have a strong influence on public perceptions of contemporary political issues and allow the powerful to legitimate their actions.

Postscript

As this book was about to go to press (September 1994) the IRA declared a unilateral 'total cessation' of military activity. Even if this leads to peace in Ireland, the process is unlikely to be smooth or short. Since the emergence of the Hume–Adams process and the revelation of government contacts with the republican movement, media reporting has entered a new phase. Many of the old certainties for British journalists were undermined as the British government markedly changed its policy on Northern Ireland. We can remember the 'we will never talk to terrorists' formulation and the 'IRA is a criminal phenomenon' formulation. Such statements of principle are now utterly devalued. Although many in the media contrived not to notice the changes, there was a real sense in which coverage changed. Northern Ireland became an attractive news story once again as journalists descended on the first real political developments since the 1970s.

One key change in government strategy is a move from trying not to mention the war to the presentation of intense diplomatic activity and the attempt to use the media as part of the negotiation process, in a sort of megaphone diplomacy. This has become possible only because there is real negotiation going on and the other participants, particularly the Dublin government, Sinn Féin and the SDLP have joined the public toing and froing in the media.

Unionism has continued to speak only the language of sell-out. If the loyalist paramilitaries do not join the peace process, then we will see an increasing attempt (already begun by official sources) to marginalise and demonise loyalist 'terrorists' in the media. In this respect propaganda and secrecy will be as important as ever for the government.

But if the peace process develops further we can expect a much freer atmosphere. Where previously information was jealously guarded as ammunition in the propaganda war, we may find that previously hidden aspects of the secret war will be revealed as now 'retired' participants emerge into public roles. Such a process will make us look back in wonder at the covert actions of the past. But we should beware the comforting view from the present which confines illegitimate activities only to memory. The propaganda fixers of central government do not retire just because one insurgency comes to a close. Their attention is even now being drawn to other spheres of conflict.

Appendix A

Unattributable Briefing Documents issued by the Foreign and Commonwealth Office, 1980–93

1980

Hunger Strikes *Greyband Brief,* October
Protest Campaign in Northern Ireland Prisons *Greyband Brief,* October (revised)

1981

Protest Campaign in Northern Ireland Prisons *Greyband Brief,* February (revised)
Northern Ireland and Anglo–Irish Relations *Greyband Brief,* February
Non-Jury (Diplock) Courts in Northern Ireland *Greyband Brief,* May
Comment on Northern Ireland *Greyband Brief,* May
Overseas Comment on Northern Ireland *Greyband Brief,* July
Northern Ireland: Intimidation *Greyband Brief,* August
Hunger Strikes *Greyband Brief,* August (revised)
Irish Terrorism's Overseas Supporters *Greyband Brief,* October
Comment on Northern Ireland *Greyband Brief,* October
The Provisional IRA's Support in Ireland *Greyband Brief,* November
Noraid and the financing of the Provisional IRA *Greyband Brief,* December (revised)

1982

Human Rights in Northern Ireland *Greyband Brief,* February (revised)
Irish Terrorist contacts in Europe and the Third World *Greyband Brief,* May

1983

1984

The Provisional Republican Movement: Sinn Féin *Greyband Brief,* February
Northern Ireland: Emergency Legislation *Greyband Brief,* May
Libya and Irish Terrorism *Background Brief,* June
Human Rights in Northern Ireland *Greyband Brief,* June
The Provisional Republican Movement: The IRA *Greyband Brief,* July
Libya's Foreign Relations *Background Brief,* August
Human Rights in Northern Ireland *Greyband Brief,* September (revised)
The Provisional IRA and Noraid *Greyband Brief,* September

1985

The Attitude of the churches to Irish terrorist activities *Greyband Brief,* February
Risk Control and Baton Rounds in Northern Ireland *Greyband Brief,* May
Northern Ireland: The Economy and Employment *Greyband Brief,* July
The Provisional IRA's Punishment Tactics *Greyband Brief,* September
The Security Forces in Northern Ireland: Controversial Incidents *Greyband Brief,* November
Northern Ireland: The Extreme Republican Vote *Greyband Brief,* November
Non-Jury (Diplock) Courts in Northern Ireland *Greyband Brief,* December

1986

International Reaction to Terrorism *Background Brief,* January
The Anglo–Irish Agreement, 1985 *Greyband Brief,* January
Libya: Second International Conference against Imperialism *Background Brief,* April

Libyan State Terrorism *Background Brief,* April
Gadaffi and Irish Terrorism *Greyband Brief,* April
Unionist reaction to the Anglo–Irish Agreement *Greyband Brief,*
May
International Terrorism: The European Response *Background Brief,* June
The Provisional Movement and Noraid *Greyband Brief,* October
The Anglo–Irish Agreement: One Year Later *Greyband Brief,*
November
The Provisional Republican Movement: The IRA *Greyband Brief,*
November

1987

Riot Control and Baton Rounds in Northern Ireland *Greyband Brief,* January
The Security Forces in Northern Ireland: Controversial Incidents *Greyband Brief,* January
Northern Ireland: Accountability of the Security Forces to the Law *Greyband Brief,* February
Northern Ireland: Transfer of prisoners *Greyband Brief,* February
Sinn Féin: Abstentionism and the Irish General Election *Greyband Brief,* March
Northern Ireland: The Economy and Employment *Greyband Brief,* April
Northern Ireland: Converted Terrorists *Greyband Brief,* May
Northern Ireland: The extreme Republican vote *Greyband Brief,* June
Northern Ireland: Accountability of the Security Forces to the Law *Greyband Brief,* June (revised)
The Irish National Liberation Army *Greyband Brief,* July
Human Rights in Northern Ireland *Greyband Brief,* August
The Provisional Republican Movement: Sinn Féin *Greyband Brief,* September
Comment: Enniskillen Remembrance Day Atrocity *Greyband Brief,* November
Northern Ireland: Finance for Terrorism *Greyband Brief,* December

1988

The Provisional IRA: International contacts outside the United States *Greyband Brief,* January

Northern Ireland: The Background and the Facts *FCO Briefing,* January

Northern Ireland: The Economy and Employment *Greyband Brief,* January

Northern Ireland since the Anglo–Irish Agreement *Greyband Brief,* February

Non-jury (Diplock) courts in Northern Ireland *Greyband Brief,* May

Recent atrocities by the Provisional IRA *Greyband Brief,* August

Libya: External Relations and Activities *Background Brief,* October

Fair Employment in Northern Ireland *Greyband Brief,* October

The Provisional Republican Movement: Sinn Féin *Northern Ireland Brief,* November (revised)

'Loyalist' Paramilitary Organisations in Northern Ireland *Northern Ireland Brief,* November

Northern Ireland: Emergency Legislation *Northern Ireland Brief,* December

1989

Northern Ireland: Accountability of the Security Forces to the Law *Northern Ireland Brief,* June

Recent civilian victims of the Provisional IRA *Northern Ireland Brief,* June

Northern Ireland: The Economy and Employment *Northern Ireland Brief,* August

Riot control and baton rounds in Northern Ireland *Northern Ireland Brief,* October (revised)

1990

Northern Ireland: The Background and the Facts *FCO Briefing,* January

Northern Ireland: The Economy and Employment *Northern Ireland Brief,* April

Northern Ireland: Accountability of the Security Forces to the Law *Northern Ireland Brief,* June (revised)

Fair Employment in Northern Ireland *Northern Ireland Brief,* October

1991

The Provisional IRA's Campaign of Terror: Comment and selected chronologies *Northern Ireland Brief,* January

Northern Ireland Prisons *Northern Ireland Brief,* February

Education in Northern Ireland: A new direction *Northern Ireland Brief,* March

Northern Ireland: The Background and the Facts *FCO Briefing,* April

Community Relations in Northern Ireland *Northern Ireland Brief,* June

Northern Ireland: Emergency Legislation *Northern Ireland Brief,* September

Fair Employment in Northern Ireland *Northern Ireland Brief,* October (revised)

'Loyalist' Paramilitary Organisations in Northern Ireland *Northern Ireland Brief,* December

IRA and Sinn Féin Propaganda *Northern Ireland Brief,* December

1992

The Urban Regeneration of Northern Ireland *Northern Ireland Brief,* January

The Tourist Industry: Northern Ireland's growing asset *Background Brief,* February

The Provisional IRA's Campaign of Terror: Comment and selected chronologies *Northern Ireland Brief,* April

Northern Ireland: The Protection of Human Rights *Northern Ireland Brief,* May

Northern Ireland: The Economy and Employment *Background Brief,* June

Northern Ireland: The Royal Irish Regiment *Northern Ireland Brief,* June

Northern Ireland: The Background and the Facts *FCO Briefing,* June

Northern Ireland: The Sinn Féin vote *Northern Ireland Brief,* June

Education in Northern Ireland: A new direction *Background Brief,* July

Northern Ireland: Opportunities for Investment *Background Brief,* August

Northern Ireland and the European Community *Background Brief,* October

'Loyalist' Paramilitary Organisations in Northern Ireland *Northern Ireland Brief,* December

1993

Northern Ireland: Compensation for criminal damage and criminal injuries *Northern Ireland Brief,* January

Northern Ireland: The MacBride Principles Campaign *Northern Ireland Brief,* January

Fair Employment in Northern Ireland *Northern Ireland Brief,* January (revised)

Non–jury (Diplock) courts in Northern Ireland *Northern Ireland Brief,* February

Northern Ireland Prisons *Northern Ireland Brief,* April

Northern Ireland: The Protection of Human Rights *Northern Ireland Brief,* May

The Provisional IRA's Campaign of Terror: Comment and selected chronologies *Northern Ireland Brief,* August

Northern Ireland: The Background and the Facts *FCO Briefing,* September

Appendix B

Cost of press, public relations, advertising and marketing by official bodies in Northern Ireland (£)

	NIO press and PR	NIO advertis-ing	NIO total press, PR & advertsng	Army Inform-ation Services	NI Tourist Board	Industrial Develpmnt Board [1]
1969/70	–	–	184,100	–	–	–
1970/71	--	–	--	--	–	–
1971/72	–	–	–	--	–	–
1972/73	–	432,638	–	--	--	–
1973/74	111,000	753,952	864,952	--	--	–
1974/75	–	833,543	--	–	–	--
1975/76	–	343,467 [2]	--	–	–	–
1976/77	–	--	584,565 [3]	–	–	–
1977/78	–	–	–	–	–	–
1978/79	--	--	–	--	–	–
1979/80	615,397 [4]	1,900,209	2,515,606	–	--	–
1980/81	715,502	1,556,528	2,272,030	–	–	–
1981/82	883,079	2,206,899	3,089,978	–	909,998	--
1982/83	1,027,492	3,157,901	4,185,393	–	1,252,813	782,000
1983/84	1,222,094	5,765,690	6,987,784	216,000	1,216,314	3,145,000
1984/85	1,800,124	5,405,516	7,205,640	230,000	1,356,344	2,924,000
1985/86	2,300,482	7,638,743	9,939,225	240,000	1,194,574	3,785,000
1986/87	2,714,909	7,216,478	9,931,387	122,000	1,471,509	4,372,000
1987/88	5,675,209	4,028,259 [4]	9,703,468	130,000	1,864,659	4,455,000
1988/89	9,184,086	4,606,655	13,790,741	140,000	2,031,817	5,071,000
1989/90	11,464,663	5,227,759	16,692,422	–	2,300,666	5,234,000
1990/91	12,713,869	5,886,796	18,600,665	--	2,761,955	5,626,000
1991/92	5,701,719	7,387,167	13,088,886	–	1,684,129	5,481,000
1992/93	6,048,241	7,988,100	14,036,341	–	3,515,498	4,490,000

	RUC FCIC *Staff costs*	RUC *Advertising*
1985/86	1,500,000	--
1986/87	1,550,000	--
1987/88	1,840,000	47,000
1988/89	1,230,000	37,000
1989/90	1,380,000	22,000
1990/91	1,630,000	49,000
1991/92	1,285,000	23,000
1992/93	2,185,000	30,000

Note: These figures are compiled in the main from *Hansard* (and for 1970/71, the *Stormont Hansard*). They are only as accurate as the civil service makes them. In particular, the figures given for NIO spending on Press and PR work have often been contradicted by data given elsewhere in *Hansard*. Figures on PR spending between 1979/80 and 1990/91 are obtained by adding the separate departmental spends given in *Hansard*, 2 April 1990: 451–2. These figures are plainly inaccurate between the years 1979/80 and 1983/84 because they leave out all spending at the London and Belfast Offices of the NIO. Clearly the NIO Information Service in London and Belfast did not run on nothing in this period. In addition figures given in 1986 which do not match those given in 1990, are also inaccurate, since they are only slightly different. I have tried to use figures which are most consistent with each other, although when there was a straight contradiction, I have used the higher figure. According to Sir Patrick Mayhew (in a letter to Frank Dobson MP, 31 January 1994) inconsistencies in figures given for advertising between 1986 and 1990 were due to 'an oversight'. However, Mayhew writes that, 'officials are unable to throw any definitive light on the apparent discrepancies in the NIO public relations figures provided in 1986 and 1990 ... Unfortunately, Departments do not normally keep advice on the preparation of draft answers for more than two years, and they cannot say for certain why there are differences'.

Figures for RUC spending on PR work are only available in the form of staff costs (including, according to Sir Patrick Mayhew, 'travel and uniform etc' (ibid.)) for FCIC as a whole.

1. The Industrial Development Board was formed in 1982.
2. This figure covers 1 January 1975 to 31 December 1976, rather than the financial year (*Hansard*, 16 July 1976: 94).
3. This figure is unlikely to be accurate since it is less then the total spent on advertising alone in 1974/75.
4. Figures in this column from 1987/88 do not include spending on advertising by the Northern Ireland Office in London and Belfast. In 1986/87 this amounted to £3,428,850 of total NIO spending.

Appendix C

PR staffing levels in official bodies in Northern Ireland

	NIO total information officers	NIO total staff	Army	RUC police staff	RUC civilian staff
1969			2	1	1 [1]
1970	12				
1971			40 [2]		
1972	14				
1973					
1974	33 [3]				
1975	27	62			
1976	26	60	40 [4]		
1977	26	57		12	3
1978	27 [5]	60			
1979	24 [6]	56			
1980	25	54			
1981	20	43	21 [7]		
1982	20	41		14 [8]	4
				60 [9]	
1983	19	39			
1984	19	38	4		
1985	19	38		58 (59) [10]	7
1986	19			55 (58)	7
1987	19	37		58	7
1988				63 (58)	7
1989		50 (52)	3	61 (56)	7.5
1990		54 (61)		61 (56)	7.5
1991		58 (60)	4	48 (46)	13.5
1992		58.5		42 (40)	13
1993				38 (37)	13

1. Letter to the author from Bill McGookin, RUC, 26 June 1991.
2. 'at least' (Foot 1990: 9).
3. In March, during the power sharing Executive. By October, after its fall, there were 25.
4. In February (Curtis 1984a: 253).
5. On 1 January. By July there were 24.
6. On 1 January. By 1 May there were 25.
7. Curtis 1984a.
8. Before the creation of FCIC (Murtagh 1982).
9. After the creation of FCIC (Hamilton-Tweedale 1987).
10. Figures in brackets refer to authorised posts. They are included only where there is a difference between authorised and filled posts.

Appendix D

Groups taking part in the general audience study

	Number of groups	Number of participants
General Scottish groups		
SACRO clients	1	8
Society of Telecom Executives	1	4
Glasgow School of Art, 2nd Year students	1	5
Bruntsfield Hospital staff, Edinburgh	1	14
Total	4	31
General English groups		
Harrow Victims Support Group	1	10
Chislehurst Neighbourhood Watch	1	7
Pensioners Keep Fit, Shepherds Bush	1	12
Total	3	29
Soldiers		
Redford Barracks, Edinburgh	1	19
Total	1	19
Nationalist groups in Northern Ireland		
Cromac Street	1	2
Lower Ormeau Road Women	1	2
Turf Lodge, West Belfast	1	5
Suffolk Community Services Group	1	4
Total	4	13
Unionist groups in Northern Ireland		
Shankill Womens Group	1	8
Dee Street Community Centre	1	6
Total	2	14
Mixed group		
Farset	1	8
Total	1	8
American Students	1	26
Totals	20	140

Appendix E

Groups taking part in the Gibraltar study

	Number of groups	Number of participants
General Scottish groups		
Saltcoats Workers Educational Association	1	7
SACRO clients	1	15
Glasgow College of Technology		
2nd Year Communication Studies students	1	9
Ardrossan Senior Citizens	1	32
Paisley retired women	6	
Glasgow School of Art 2nd year students	1	14
Total	6	83
Soldiers		
Redford Barracks, Edinburgh	1	20
Total	1	20
Northern Ireland groups		
West Belfast Parent Youth Support Project	1	8
(nationalist)		
Suffolk Community Services Group	1	4
(unionist)		
Total	2	12
American Students		
US Students at Manchester University	1	24
US Students at Glasgow University	1	4
Total	2	28
Totals	11	143

Notes

Introduction

1 Glover was the author of the 1978 secret intelligence report *Northern Ireland Terrorist Trends* which was leaked to the press. In it he concluded that:

> The Provisionals' campaign of violence is likely to continue while the British remain in Northern Ireland ... We see little prospect of political development of a kind which would seriously undermine the Provisionals' position ... PIRA will probably continue to recruit the men it needs. They will still be able to attract enough people with leadership talent, good education and manual skills to continue to enhance their all round professionalism. The movement will retain popular support sufficient to maintain secure bases in the traditional Republican areas. (reproduced in Faligot, 1983: 241)

Chapter 1

1. There is still some dispute over whether Eden intended to 'take over' the BBC during the crisis (see Grisewood 1968; MacKenzie 1969).

2. See *The Times*, 1 January 1987

3. See Cockerell et al. 1984: 90–6; Hennessy 1985:17–29. My thanks to Peter Goodwin for supplying some of the information on which the following section is based.

4. Minute 632, 'Programmes Relating to Atomic and Hydrogen Bombs' 20 December 1954.

5. HO 256/360 minute by Sir Kenneth Cadbury, 17 August 1956.

6. PREM 11/2226, 16 June 1958

7. The first, the 'Fourteen Day Rule' prevented the discussion of any matter likely to be debated in parliament in the succeeding fortnight. The second prohibited the broadcast of party political broadcasts on behalf of any political party

other than those arranged with the main political parties and primarily affected the Scottish National Party and Plaid Cymru (Miller 1990).

8 *Independent*, 7 May 1988.

9. Chataway's further comment that 'nobody wants propaganda substituted for truthful reporting' was, of course, somewhat less than the whole truth. By late 1971 the 'Information Policy' unit was in operation at Army HQ in Northern Ireland. Its whole purpose was propaganda and misinformation.

10. See Schlesinger 1987, Chapter 8 for the most detailed account of this episode.

11. Conversation with John McCormick, Controller, BBC Scotland, 10 March 1993.

12. The current Secretary to the Committee, like all his predecessors, is a high-ranking military official, Rear Admiral W. A. Higgins CB, CBE. He can be reached at the MoD Main Building in Whitehall or on 071–218 2206.

13. It should also be noted that the Broadcasting Act 1990 extends both the Obscene Publications Act and incitement to hatred legislation to broadcasting. In the case of incitement to hatred, senior police officers have the power to demand access to film, photographs, tape or documents if they suspect that an offence has been or is likely to be committed (McBride 1990: 132).

14. Although a number of 'IRA voices' have been heard on the screen. These have been either interviews carried out abroad (as in the case of the Channel 4 documentary *Ireland: The Silent Voices*, broadcast in 1983), or short audio clips not originally recorded by broadcasters and used as documentary evidence rather than as an interview (such as the short clip of the voice of Mairead Farrell in the Thames film 'Death on the Rock'). Mairead Farrell could also be seen speaking when Channel 4 broadcast Derry Film and Video's *Mother Ireland* in its 'banned' season in 1991. Her interview was subtitled because of the broadcasting ban. Farrell was not interviewed as a member or representative of the IRA, and it was only her death in Gibraltar at the hands of the SAS which revealed that she had been a member. The idea of broadcast journalists approaching the IRA for an interview

about IRA policy or strategy is now simply a non-starter.

15. See Bolton 1990 for an account of this.

16. A further casualty of this heightened sensitivity was Lieutenant Colonel Michael Dewar, whose book *The British Army in Northern Ireland: An account of the Army's fight against the IRA* (Dewar 1985) was due to be published towards the end of October. The typescript had been cleared by the army, but the Northern Ireland Secretary refused the author clearance for a visit to Belfast to promote the book and ordered him not to discuss the work with reporters or on television or radio. According to the publishers, Arms and Armour Press, 'The Government does not want any ballyhoo at present about the army's role. For the sake of the talks they are trying to play this down and emphasise the role of the police.' (John Ezard, 'Minister bans Ulster army author' *Guardian*, 7 October 1985).

17. This was in part due to the appointment of governors favourable to the Thatcher government. According to Assistant Director-General Alan Protheroe, 'there was a new style of relationship between the two boards, between the Governors and the management, there was a heightened tension and it became more difficult to get one's point across, there was less discussion and more argument, it was this building up of tension' (*World in Action* 1988).

18. Sinn Féin contested elections from 1982 following the victory of Bobby Sands in the 1981 Fermanagh/South Tyrone by election. By 1985 it had gained a total of fifty-nine council seats with 11.8 per cent of the total vote and 35 per cent of the nationalist vote (Flackes and Elliot 1989).

19. See Ying Hui Tan 'Law Report – Press ordered to produce photos' *Independent*, 4 November 1986; *Guardian*, 15 October 1986 and 17 October 1986.

20. See Wilson, 1990a for some little-known examples.

21. See Taylor, 1991: 142–3 for comment on the editorial judgement involved in the decision to publish and a reproduction of one of the most explicit photographs.

22. It does now.

23. See Michael Zander, 'From Aberfan to Gib', *Guardian*, 7 May 1988.

24. At this stage Thames Television were not aware of Howe's

phone calls (Windelsham and Rampton 1989; Bolton 1990). The Foreign Office claimed it called the press conference because Thames had started to leak the story. According to Roger Bolton this was 'a straight lie' (Bolton 1990).

25. Some Conservatives sought to use the row to impose further controls on the IBA or even close it down. Some government briefings also raised the possibility of extending the powers of the nascent Broadcasting Standards Council (BSC) from monitoring sex and violence to having a power to preview and possibly veto politically sensitive broadcasts. However, the government was not prepared to go quite that far and the Prime Minister's press secretary confirmed that the BSC would not gain extra powers on 4 May (*Independent*, 5 May 1988).

26. The full transcript of the programme can be found in Windelsham and Rampton 1989: 28–68.

27. Such doubts about the official story were not laid to rest following the inquest on the killings in September 1988, which delivered a majority verdict of lawful killing. In the view of human rights and civil liberties organisations the inquest was an inadequate forum for examining whether the killings were extra judicial executions and the question therefore remained open (see Amnesty International 1989; Bonnechère 1988; Kitchin 1989; Tweedie 1988).

28. These will reflect various alliances and priorities among different sections of the state.

29. Incidentally, senior management at the BBC deny that Mrs Thatcher's performance had any bearing on the decision to broadcast the programme. One senior executive involved in the decision making commented to the author that 'that is just ridiculous. It does not work like that' (personal interview, London, February 1993).

30. This contrasts quite markedly with the analysis of Owen's immediate superior at the time of the controversy, Colin Morris, the Controller Northern Ireland. He put it as follows:

It was perfectly proper for government ministers to appeal to the BBC and Thames Television not to transmit their programmes – talk about Ministerial blackmail and arm-twisting is nonsense. But it was also perfectly proper for the broadcasting authorities, once they had made sure they were acting within the law, to go ahead - which they did only after the most searching deliberation, for these are grave matters, and any appeal from Ministers of the Crown must be treated with great respect and earnest consideration. So we went ahead ... this time to the Government's discomfiture. But next time, should our commitment to the truth lead us to support the official position in a contentious issue, then our account will have added authority because we have been consistent in the exercise of our impartiality. Had we withdrawn a programme we conscientiously believed should be transmitted, why should the public have any faith next time round that our impartiality is still intact? (Morris 1988b: 4).

31. Interview with senior BBC executive, London, February 1993. In an interview with the author in May 1993, Owen declined to comment on these events.

32. Thanks to Martin Stott at the Channel 4 Press Office for supplying me with press cuttings and associated information on this episode.

33. Reported in Mary Kelly, 'C4 asked for murder evidence', *Belfast Telegraph*, 3 October 1991, David Watson, 'Annesley hits out at TV "slur"', *Belfast Telegraph*, 4 October 1991

34. There has been remarkably little comment on these powers which have a very wide potential application in relation to the media. The text of the relevant parts of Section 17 is as follows:

(2) Where in relation to a terrorist investigation a warrant or order under Schedule 7 to this Act has been issued or made or has been applied for and not refused, a person is guilty of an offence if, knowing or having reasonable cause to suspect that the investigation is taking place, he: (a) makes any disclosure which is likely to prejudice the investigation; or (b) falsifies, conceals or destroys or otherwise disposes of, or causes or permits the falsification, concealment, destruction or disposal of, material which is or is likely to be relevant to the investigation.

There are two defences available in law. Firstly, lack of knowledge that the investigation is taking place or that the disclosure is likely to cause prejudice; and secondly that the defendant had 'lawful authority' or 'reasonable excuse' for making the disclosure. It is not at all clear (to me at any rate) what would constitute lawful authority or who is in a position to grant it. Does it for example exempt the RUC press office and any journalist who reveals proceedings acting on information from the RUC?

35. For a personal account of the story see McPhilemy 1992.

36. See David Pallister, 'BBC to intensify gag on Ulster broadcasts', *Guardian*, 2 October 1992 and the response from John Wilson of the BBC, 'Censorship and the BBC', *Guardian*, Letters to the Editor, 5 October 1992. See also Bernadette McAliskey's own account 'Silenced', *Weekend Guardian*, 5 September 1992.

37. It is only Sinn Féin which is being referred to here, as no other political party with elected representatives is deemed to have associations with illegal/paramilitary groups.

38. Information from interview with senior BBC executive, London, February 1993.

39. This was described by the then Assistant Director-General Alan Protheroe in the Preface in the following manner: 'The *News and Current Affairs Index* is not a "classified" document. Neither is it a document for distribution to the public' (BBC 1987: 7). As well as being a welcome break with tradition, the decision to publish the guidelines in 1989 also allowed the BBC to get rid of the kind of double-talk passed off by Protheroe as reasoned argument.

Chapter 2

1. There is some potential for such organisations to pressure the media by political or violent means, but such actions represent the actions of the relatively powerless.

2. This is not to suggest that O'Neill was a moderniser in terms of economic or social policy. According to Bew et al., 'modernisation' under O'Neill was concerned largely with 'symbols' of progress which were a 'blatantly cosmetic' marketing exercise (Bew et al. 1979: 153 and 155).

3. Letters to the author from Bill McGookin, RUC Force Control and Information Centre, 31 May 1991 and 26 June 1991.

4. Even although they were motivated by a desire not to get

'sucked into' what Home Secretary Callaghan called the 'Irish bog'. (Callaghan 1973:15)

5. This is agreed upon by both investigative journalist Duncan Campbell (1990: 16), the one-time Head of Information Policy Maurice Tugwell (Tugwell 1980: 223) and David Charters, a colleague of Tugwell's. For Charters this problem was due to failings of political leadership and the failure to invest in psyops sooner:

> The British government, for its part, showed a complete lack of understanding of the power (for good and evil) of propaganda. Apart from letting itself get trapped into propaganda disasters such as internment, the Government does not appear to have made a conscious effort to 'sell' the British case either to the people of the province or to the rest of the United Kingdom. Nor was there, until 1972, an organised plan to counter IRA propaganda or to discourage bad journalism: until that time the IRA held the initiative in the propaganda war. (Charters 1977: 26)

6. It should be remembered that Tugwell was Head of Information Policy in the early 1970s.

7. This official story was somewhat doubtful since it was Wallace's job to leak confidential information. Wallace maintains that he was removed for attempting to put a stop to official dirty tricks, including undermining the Labour government (see Dorril and Ramsay 1991; Foot 1990; Leigh 1988).

8. According to Anne McHardy: 'The Northern Ireland Office is now adamant that "dirty tricks" will not be used again, neither will any form of propaganda not based strictly on the truth. All army statements are therefore vetted by Mr Mason's staff at Stormont Castle' (*Guardian*, 26 February 1977, cited in Hamilton-Tweedale 1987: 333). Andrew Stephen echoed this:

> Since these embarassing episodes, there has been a much tighter control over what the Army press officers are allowed to say to journalilsts. In effect the Northern Ireland Office tells them what they can and cannot say; the Army has to obtain Northern Ireland Office permission to issue statements with even the remotest political ramificatiions. (*Observer*, 29 February 1976)

9. This point was acknowledged by David Charters, a colleague of Maurice Tugwell, in the *Royal United Services Institute Journal*. Written in 1977 his article is unusual in that it openly debates psychological operations and intelligence matters:

> The Army's counter insurgency doctrine, evolved over 25 years of fighting insurgency in the Empire, was difficult to apply in Ulster because the doctrine was not designed for domestic use ... The restrictions and harsh measures which had made a successful campaign possible in Malaya could not be applied readily in Britain, with its long tradition of individual liberty and freedom of the press. In Malaya, thousands of miles away from home, operations beyond the jungle fringe could be conducted in almost complete secrecy; in Ulster, the daily movements of a patrol may be seen on TV that evening in Belfast and in London. Moreover, because Northern Ireland is constitutionally part of the United Kingdom, the problem is a domestic one, and politicians in London are more inclined to intervene directly in the actual conduct of security policy and operations. (Charters 1977: 25–6)

   Of course, part of the reason why politicians were more likely to intervene (to the chagrin of the Army) was that the media was covering the conflict.
10. According to one broadsheet journalist, Hermon had a 'deep distrust of the press ... He didn't understand the media, he was frustrated with them and his instinct was to pretend that they didn't exist of if they did exist he would keep them at arms length' (personal interview, Belfast, August 1990).
11. *Sunday Tribune*, 26 August 1990.
12. In 1976/7 the PR budget of the NIO was £584,665; by 1979 it had risen to £1,431,237 plus £344,181 for advertising (see Appendix 2 for known details of funding for the NIO and RUC).
13. Drumm, Vice-President of Sinn Féin, was shot dead while in the Mater hospital as a patient.
14. Interview with Míceál Holden, Sinn Féin press officer, Belfast, July 1989. Morrison was arrested and imprisoned shortly after this (see Sinn Féin International Publicity and Information Committee 1990a; 1990b for a Sinn Féin view on this).

15. Information from telephone interview with Richard McAuley, May 1991.

Chapter 3

1. It is nevertheless true that security considerations can hamper the efforts of the information manager. In the view of one director of the NIIS: 'If you had a totally free hand obviously you would be dragging it out for weeks and days in advance, sending out invitations and all that sort of thing. Stimulating people to be there, especially if it was a good story of a factory opening or jobs or something like that' (personal interview, Belfast, July 1990).
2. COI, 1989: 23.
3. Information from the NIIS, August 1989.
4. Although it is paid for by the Information Dept of the FCO, OVIS was, until 1990, part of the COI, with a staff complement of 43 in London (COI 1990b) plus a visits officer in each of the regional offices in Newcastle, Leeds and Bristol as well as one at the Welsh Office, three at the Scottish Office and two at the Northern Ireland Office (COI 1990c: 32–4). In the year 1988–9 OVIS organised a total of 900 programmes for 2,500 visitors from 132 countries. (COI 1989: 23) In 1989–90 there were 926 visits for 2,600 people. (COI 1990a:24). In addition there is the London Correspondents Service with a staff of six (COI 1990b) which organises visits for journalists resident in Britain. Table 3.1 gives available data on trips organised by the Tourist Board and the Industrial Development Board.

Table 3.1 Number of visits by journalists to Northern Ireland paid for by the NITB and and the IDB, 1982–93.

	NITB	IDB
1982/83	130	n/a
1983/84	>140	n/a
1984/85	200	n/a
1985/86	140	n/a
1986/87	200	47
1987/88	300	83
1988/89	400	96

	NITB	*IDB*
1989/90	300	83
1990/91	>300	61
1991/92	300	108
1992/93	250	70

Key: n/a = not available. Sources: *NITB Annual Report and Accounts*, Vol. 39, 1986/87: 11; Vol. 40, 1987/88: 8; Vol. 41, 1988/89: 9; Vol. 41, 1989/90: 9; *IDB Annual Report and Accounts* 1990/91: 89; 1991/92: 27; 1992/93: 33

5. These papers, all produced by the Information Department of the Foreign Office, come in two main series: *Background Briefs* about all aspects of government and foreign policy and *Greyband Briefs* (after 1988, titled *Northern Ireland Briefs*) which are specifically about Northern Ireland. Each of the briefs bears the legend 'this paper has been prepared for general briefing purposes'. On the *Background Briefs* are the additional words 'it is not and should not be construed or quoted as an expression of government policy'. The first Greyband brief I have been able to trace appeared in October 1980 and dealt with the ongoing prison protests (Foreign and Commonwealth Office 1980). The *Background Briefs* go back as far as 1978. Significantly, this is the year the Information Research Department in the Foreign Office was disbanded and replaced by the Overseas Information Department. This in turn was replaced by the Information Department in the early 1980s. IRD was a covert propaganda department of the Foreign Office with close links to the intelligence community (Bloch and Fitzgerald 1983; Fletcher 1982; Dorril and Ramsay 1990; Smith 1979). IRD officials were also seconded to the Information Policy Unit in Lisburn in the early 1970s to help with this information work (Foot 1990). During that period, IRD produced several 'briefing documents' on Northern Ireland such as *The IRA: Aims, Policy, Tactics*. Briefings produced by the Information Department during the 1980s are the direct descendants of such material.

6. An updated version of *Northern Ireland Chronicle* was made after the signing of the Anglo–Irish Agreement in 1985 and is still (in 1993) on the catalogue of the London Television

Service at the COI, which produces films for the FCO to distribute overseas.

7. These figures are calculated from a compilation of published information to be found in Appendix C. The total does not include any of the staff in the COI or the MoD in London or the home and overseas branches of the diplomatic service, especially in the US, who spend large proportions of their time on information work on Northern Ireland. Nor does it include the personnel of advertising agencies and public relations consultants working on NIO advertising or, writing 'good news' about Northern Ireland.

8. This was Trevor Hanna, who went on to become the Belfast correspondent for the *Sun*.

9. Information from conversation with senior former member of the SDLP, June 1993.

10. On harassment of journalists by republicans, loyalists and British forces see Bolton 1990: 219–20; Campbell 1985; Curtis 1984: 251–3; 'The Mirror and the IRA', *Daily Mirror*, 23 November 1974: 1; *Journalist*, July/August 1991: 6–7; Conway 1989; Hanvey 1990; *Index on Censorship*, 1993a; 1993b.

11. The question is when is a mistake not a mistake? I have tried to give as accurate an account of this incident as possible; however, this is not to say that all 'mistaken' disclosures of information are actual mistakes, nor should it be assumed that genuine mistakes do not on occasion have some beneficial payoffs.

12. See Foot 1990, for some examples. See also 'Black Propaganda in Ulster admitted, *The Times*, 31 January 1990.

13. See, for example, Chris Ryder, Neil Darbyshire and Ben Fenton, 'Yard Minutes on the IRA are leaked', *Daily Telegraph*, 22 April 1992; Duncan Campbell, Richard Norton-Taylor and Owen Bowcott, 'Yard plays down IRA leak', *Guardian*, 23 April 1992; Richard Norton-Taylor, 'MI5 and Met in anti-terror showdown', *Guardian*, 23 April 1992; Richard Norton-Taylor and Duncan Campbell, 'MI5 wins fight to take on IRA', *Guardian*, 9 May 1992; David Rose, 'MI5 will take over more police work', *Observer*, 21 June 1992.

14. In the event the DPP advised against prosecution.

15. As opposed to those civilians who are by implicit contrast labelled as culpable. In particular these include members of the nationalist community who are shot by the 'security forces'. In the official view the notion of a guilty civilian is further complicated by the fact that members of illegal paramilitary groups are deemed to be civilians for the purposes of official statistics, but when they are shot dead by British forces, they are 'terrorists'.

16. It is this point that has so often exercised the ire of counter insurgency writers and Northern Ireland ministers. However they conveniently tend to ignore the other factors outlined here (see, for example, Clutterbuck 1981; Rees 1985: 338–45; Wilkinson 1977).

Chapter 4

1. BBC1, 21.00, ITN, 22.00, C4 News and BBC2's *Newsnight*.

2. These papers were chosen largely for ease of access. In 1990 the *Los Angeles Times* became the biggest selling paper in the US (*UK Press Gazette*, 14 May 1990) and it should be understood that the tabloid/broadsheet split is not nearly so marked in political terms in the US as it is in Britain.

3. This is significant because, as we have noted, the IRA have not been interviewed on British television since 1974.

4. Between 1969 and 30 June 1989 British forces inflicted 11.8 per cent of total casualties (Irish Information Partnership 1990).

5. See Chapter 1 for a summary of the events in Gibraltar.

6. Glenholmes was Fleet Street's 'most wanted terrorist' for several years in the 1980s. She was first named by Scotland Yard in 1984, appearing in the papers as the 'Terror Blonde in jeans' (*Daily Mail*, 13 November 1984) and the 'Blonde Bomber' (*Evening Standard*, 12 November 1984). After an unsuccessful extradition attempt in Dublin in 1986 the papers obtained several photographs of 'Evil Evelyn' which replaced the artist's impression released by the police two years earlier. They showed, among other things, that Glenholmes was not, in fact, blonde. These photographs have been appearing periodically ever since, for example, with the caption 'Angel of Death' in the *Star* of 11 January 1988. They resurfaced on 8 March 1988. Their significance was

illustrated when *Irish Press* columnist John McEntee reported witnessing the 'creation of a little bit of history' in Gibraltar's Holiday Inn, 'the invention of Evelyn Glenholmes as the missing fourth IRA member in Gibraltar'. McEntee asked a 'colourful colleague if he believed the theory of the fourth man. "Oh, it's a woman and we are saying it's Evelyn Glenholmes", this craggy veteran explained. Why on earth, I wondered aloud, was he saying it was Glenholmes. "Because", he replied, "we have a nice picture of her and she won't sue"' (*Irish Press*, 16 March 1988).

7. We can contrast this with the feature pieces carried in the *Mail* during the Gibraltar inquest. All of these, written by 'special feature writer' Geoffrey Levy, were polemical accounts of the inquest or attacks on the merest whiff of alternative evidence or perspective. This suggests that analysing media content to locate variation rather that domination needs to be tempered by a very sensitive attention to what is at stake for dominant explanations in the appearance of alternative views or information. The extent to which official sources are briefing hard and are able to anticipate developments may have a decisive impact on the actual visibility of alternative sources or explanations even within more open formats.

8. Incidentally, Wyatt seems to have got a bit confused here. The explosives were not of course smuggled into Gibraltar.

9. Under the heading 'Liberals cry wolf over Gibraltar shootings', Worsthorne wrote:

When it comes to the issue of terrorism, particularly of IRA terrorism, there seems to be little doubt that reason and morality are both on the side of the reactionaries rather than the liberals – unless, that is, one starts from the premise that the IRA ought to be allowed to win, which most of the disapprovers claim not to do. In fact, they almost all start off by declaring that they detest the IRA, before going on to condemn the use of the only methods that are proving at all effective in defeating the IRA, thereby demonstrating themselves to be humbugs of liars. fighting terrorism is not like fighting any other type of crime. Terrorists are the enemies of the state, just as the Germans were during the World War II. The primary aim, therefore, is to defeat them. (*Sunday Telegraph*, 13 March 1988)

10. Ingrams 'wrote a column for the *Sunday Telegraph*, but was soon sacked for his un-tory views on Northern Ireland' (Lynn Barber 'Lord Gnome's Mid-Life Crisis' *Independent on Sunday Review*, 16 February 1992: 9). Ingrams himself had earlier written 'I felt certain that the reason was some remarks of mine about the IRA and the late Airey Neave that were considered undiplomatic' (*Observer*, 13 March 1988). Robert Maxwell terminated Livingstone's contract following the MP's maiden speech in the House of Commons which dealt with intelligence activities in Northern Ireland. Maxwell was reportedly 'appalled' by the speech and said that was no place in any paper of his for such 'reckless' material: 'Your engagement to write for the *London Daily News* is terminated forthwith' he wrote ('People Diary', *Guardian*, 16 July 1987).

11. Author of *The Crack: A Belfast Year*, 1988.

12. 'Pack up the Troubles', *Critical Eye* Channel 4, 24 October 1991.

13. Personal interview with *This Week* reporter Julian Manyon, February 1989. In Britain concerns such as these are not confined to news programmes. Although the use of language can be somewhat relaxed in a documentary or current affairs programme, broadcast institutions do police language closely. For example, Peter Taylor recalls arguing with BBC Deputy Director-General Alan Protheroe about how to describe the killing of Airey Neave:

> The film showed two men walking in Phoenix Park, Dublin, where a century earlier some forerunners of the IRA ... had assassinated Lord Frederick Cavendish, the new Chief Secretary for Ireland. The point of comparison was that the men now seen in the Park were former members of the INLA which had 'assassinated' Airey Neave. Alan Protheroe ... saw the film prior to transmission and said that the word should be 'murder' not 'assassination'. I said I had used the word deliberately to draw the parallel between that and the incident which had happened one hundred years before at the same spot. Mr Protheroe took the point but insisted that 'murder' was 'the more precise and accurate word'. So 'murder' was used. (Taylor, 1986: 219).

14. Such films are quite rare. According to the Vanderbilt Television News Archive at Vanderbilt University, Nashville, Tennessee, there were a total of six documentary reports on Northern Ireland between 1980 and 1989 on the ABC and PBS networks. These included a showing of an edition of the BBC *Real Lives* programme, 'At the Edge of the Union' which is discussed in Chapter 1.

15. According to Cran, the use of the word 'Terrorist' in the title of the film was intended to be a question (personal interview, London, May 1990).

16. Interviewing members of the republican movement is difficult on British television. *This Week* did interview Gerry Adams of Sinn Féin for 'Death on the Rock' but decided not to use the interview because it 'would give the IRA a propaganda platform that could not be justified' (Windelsham and Rampton: 20). The programme did feature a short audio taped clip of Mairead Farrell's voice.

17. The rejection of the Birmingham Six appeal, the shooting, in suspicious circumstances, by the British army of a civilian, Aidan McAnespie, the release and return to service of Private Ian Thain after serving only two years of the first murder sentence ever imposed on a member of the British army in Ireland since 1969.

18. A British Information Services (BIS) press officer told Paul Artherton that 'any sort of initiative we suggest is pretty well assured of favourable coverage' (Artherton 1983a: 20).

19. All the examples of this short phrase were found in the *New York Times*, 13 March 1988, 17 March 1988 and 20 March 1988.

20. These references were all on 20 March from the pen of a *New York Times* journalist whose copy was used by both the *Atlanta Constitution* and the *Chicago Tribune*.

21. One correspondent for a British tabloid related how a republican funeral in the early 1980s was viewed by his paper:

I was told by my people to see what it was like and if it was a stunt to write it as a stunt. So I said 'What do you mean?' And they replied: 'Well, if the IRA turn up and fire gunshots over the coffin, we want all that, we must have how the IRA hijacked the funeral' ... I was told to write a story saying that this was the IRA turning a man's funeral into a propaganda stunt. (cited in Hamilton-Tweedale, 1987: 390)

22. I am not arguing that US television generally takes a line critical of Western governments on issues of political violence or that it is the fourth estate watchdog that some commentators maintain. There is abundant evidence to suggest that the role of the US media in reporting political violence, carried out by governments or sub-state groups opposing US foreign policy imperatives, is in many respects quite similar to the role of British broadcasting in reporting Northern Ireland. (See Andersen 1988; Chomsky 1989; Hallin 1987 and Herman and Chomsky 1988 for contrasting critical views.) Just as British television could, in the 1980s, report *relatively* dispassionately on El Salvador or Nicaragua, compared to the US media, so the US media can frame the conflict in Northern Ireland in looser terms than in Britain. This relates largely to the *political* distance of the conflict in Ireland from the immediate exigencies of US foreign policy.

Chapter 5

1. Other parts of the study are reported in Miller 1994.
2. In fact I took captioned photos of Proetta, Ian Paisley and Gerry Adams to all groups in case people could not identify them. I gave them uncaptioned photos in the first instance, as I was interested in whether they would be recognised and assigned to the correct party and political/religious allegiance. If there was real uncertainty as to who the people were, this was noted and then the captioned photos were introduced. In practice this was done very rarely since most of the groups (with the significant exception of some of the American students) were able to recognise both Adams and Paisley. With Proetta, the identification of her name was not important, but it was interesting to see how many groups would recognise or use her in their accounts as an eyewitness.
3. Primarily in briefings to the *Sunday Times*.
4. The one group that was able to produce a bulletin on the Gibraltar shootings included one person who had seen the American documentary 'Death of a Terrorist' on the life and

death of Mairead Farrell and was able to construct the bulletin from his memory of that programme (see Chapter 4; Miller, 1994).

5. *Soldier* is published by the Ministry of Defence.

6. The original of the statement made by a Spanish police officer allegedly to the effect that the three had been lost has never been disclosed to the press or to the lawyers for the families. There are, however, at least seven separate statements from various Spanish police and governmental sources, which all agree that the IRA members were followed to the Gibraltar frontier. See John Hooper and Peter Murtagh, 'Questions linger over Rock shooting' (*Guardian*, 25 March 1989: 2).

7. According to Michael Cockerell one government minister 'rang the political correspondents of three different newspapers with defamatory allegations' against Proetta (Cockerell, 1989: 341).

8. This was repeated by the *Sun, Today* and the *Sunday Telegraph* (1 May 1988).

9. The papers were the *Sun, Star, Daily Express, Daily Mail, Mail on Sunday, Daily Mirror* and *Sunday Times*.

10. Two sentences in the *Daily Mail* (1 February 1989) and the *Daily Express* (27 February 1989).

11. The group of soldiers were if anything slightly less convinced that the general population. groups. A total of seven respondents (35 per cent) believed Proetta was or was possibly a prostitute. The numbers involved here are too small to compare properly.

12. The *Daily Record* is the sister paper of the *Daily Mirror* in Scotland. Throughout the coverage of the events in Gibraltar news coverage in the *Record* was mostly simply selected from copy used by the *Mirror*.

13. They wrote 'night club singer', 'I have no idea! Perhaps a prostitute!', 'prostitute (I don't know)' and 'secretary/Mistress'.

14. Both members of the other team believed that she had retracted her evidence.

15. See for example, John Keegan, 'Army questions TV version of Gibraltar deaths', *Daily Telegraph*, Saturday 30 April 1988.

16. See for example, *Mail on Sunday*, 29 May 1988. As the inquest approached, the *Sunday Telegraph* reported 'It is still not clear whether Mrs Carmen Proetta will be among the witnesses' (4 September 1988).

17. The reports from Gibraltar went on:
    She told the documentary that from her window overlooking the scene she saw four men get out of a police car, jump over a barrier and shoot McCann and Farrell. They had their hands raised. They were giving themselves up. But in court today she said she didn't see men firing guns. She heard the shots and presumed they came from them. Michael Hucker: 'Were McCann and Farrell really surrendering? Yes or No?' Mrs Proetta: 'For me, having your hands up can mean surrender or shock or something else'. 'I'm suggesting you were totally mistaken. You didn't see these people shot'. 'That's your opinion, not mine.' (BBC1 18.00, 23 September 1988)

18. Auberon Waugh, not normally noted for his defence of investigative journalism, wrote that Asquez:
    claimed that the lie was told in response to pressure from Thames Television. It is normal practice when a witness admits to having lied, to ask what reason there is to believe his revised version – whether he might not now be giving false evidence in response to pressure from another source. At very least, his evidence tends to be taken with a pinch of salt. But not, it would appear, by the poodles. (Waugh 1988)

19. The Falls Road is the main thoroughfare through West Belfast.

20. They went on to write that: 'Gibraltar Airlines have refused to take bodies back to Belfast for their burial as a protest against the freedom fighters of Ireland.' This was interesting because it showed a very detailed level of memory which seemed to be related to their own experience and concerns. This fact seemed to have stuck because they regarded it with disdain. No other group remembered this detail.

21. Quoted in *What the Papers Say*, Channel 4, 11 March 1988.

22. The data upon which this chapter draws are the groups taking part in the general study as well as those taking part in the Gibraltar study.

316

23. Not including the American Students.
24. A total of 95.9 per cent of the general British sample.
25. For three of the five this was related to a recognition that news values meant that violence was newsworthy. They did not, however, believe that Northern Ireland was mostly violent in reality. The other two did believe that Northern Ireland was mostly violent and that this was faithfully reflected on television.
26. Forty per cent of Yorkshire and 20 per cent of Northern Ireland viewers replied that they 'didn't know'. The sample size was 300 in each area.
27. In fact only five people said they would not go because they were 'not interested' or had 'no inclination'.
28. One had been as a soldier and didn't want to go back, and the other didn't want to return because she had been there with her father when he was in the army.
29. The Community Relations Council is a government-funded body which is charged with helping to improve 'community relations' and in the long term ease the conflict. See Miller 1993d for a discussion of this project as a government strategy.

Chapter 6

1. Schlesinger et al. (1983) noted the same limitation in the work of Berkowitz and his colleague Macaulay (Berkowitz 1973; Berkowitz and Macaulay 1971). One 'exogenous' factor that Holden and others fail to note is that the increase in hijacking attempts also correlates with the increase in international air travel.
2. According to Bruck 'Weimann considers himself on the left of the political spectrum in his country, has contacts with, and sympathy for, such movements as *Peace Now* and is quite aware of the imperatives for a progressive political practice' (Bruck 1988a: ix).
3. Hewitt cites a 1983 poll in which only 3 per cent of the sample admitted to considering the IRA as 'freedom fighters' (Hewitt 1992: 201).
4. Weimann has claimed that his suggestions for media control do not involve 'repression'. He says 'there is a call for

guidelines and policies – all created and adopted by the media on a voluntary basis and not for dictates, censorship and repression' (Weimann 1988b: 84). As we saw in Chapter 1, such 'voluntary agreements' have indeed resulted in censorship, and guidelines, or the threat of them, are enough to severely constrain the media.

5. Former Israeli Foreign Minister (and current (in 1994) leader of the opposition), Benjamin Netanyahu, has expressed this in his characteristically forthright way. He has argued that:

   today's terrorists in fact, frighten not thousands but millions. But they could not achieve this result without the free press. Unreported, terrorist acts would be like the proverbial tree falling in the silent forest. Even if passed by word of mouth, news about terrorist outrages would hardly command the attention of government leaders, the public at large, and indeed, as often happens, the centre of the international stage. The press has become the unwilling – and in some cases, willing – amplifier of the terrorists' publicity campaign. (Netanyahu 1986: 109)

   It is of course the case that if enough of the proverbial trees fell unobserved in the rainforests, and this was not reported by the news media, the first thing we would know about it would be when the oxygen started to run out.

6. Although his views appear to have softened by the following year when he recommended voluntary agreements between broadcasters and the government (Wilkinson 1978).

7. Ironically this is one of the (justified) criticisms Herman makes of the work of liberal American media academics: 'Gatekeeper analyses usually do not provide any extended treatment of actual media performance and impact on ideology and opinion. They also offer little in the way of dynamics that would show how the media mobilise public opinion, or are manipulated (or co-operate) in mobilisation by others' (Herman 1986: 174).

8. For a critique of moral panic theory see Miller and Reilly 1994.

9. This was the BBC's 13-part documentary on the history of Ireland, first broadcast in 1981.

10. See for example Brunt 1992, and the exchange between Brunt and Janice Radway after her paper. Here there is a

recommendation that analysts should not 'return to the text' as if it is possible to research the impact of media messages without knowing what those messages are.

11. See also Fiske, 1991. Such formulations can be found widely in the literature. Peter Dahlgren, for example, writes: 'By "meaning" I refer here to the processes of making sense of the world around us. It has to do with a general coherence in our lives, of establishing an order in which to anchor our existence ... Meaning is negotiated; it resides in the forcefield between the givenness of the programmes and the sense-making of the viewers' (Dahlgren 1992: 203 and 205).

12. Although, Sinn Féin said they could find no evidence that the calls were authorised and one of the journalists subsequently returned to work in Northern Ireland.

13. At least one British newspaper's correspondent in Belfast has refused on principle to write 'good news' stories (telephone interview, May 1990). Similarly, Kevin Cullen of the *Boston Globe* has reported coming under pressure to do 'good news' pieces about Northern Ireland, particularly about integrated education, following reportage of his which the British Consul General in Boston told him was 'extraordinarily negative' (telephone interview, January 1991).

14. Although the *Mirror* had called for a withdrawal as early as 1972 in the aftermath of Bloody Sunday (Curtis 1984: 315).

15. In 1981 it suggested that such a move might be a prelude to the establishment of an Independent 'Ulster'. This position changed with the appointment of right wing editor Andrew Neil in 1983.

16. A 1976 NOP poll found that 32 per cent would prefer the British government to withdraw and leave the Protestants and Catholics to their own fate while 25 per cent thought the government should encourage the North and South to unite into one country. These findings are matched by the split throughout the 1980s between those favouring an independent Northern Ireland and those who preferred a united Ireland. Between 1980 and 1984 there was between 30 and 37 per cent support for the former and between 18–25 per cent for the latter. By 1991 the figures for these questions were at level pegging at 25 per cent each (MORI 1991). In 1991 MORI also found that only 17 per cent thought the British

presence had been helpful to the political situation in Northern Ireland, with 37 per cent saying it made no difference. By contrast, 36 per cent of people thought that British troops had made the political situation worse (MORI 1991).

17. Unless otherwise stated, opinion poll data in the following section is taken from Curtis 1988; MORI 1991; Rose et al. 1978; Wilson 1988 and successive editions of the *Gallup Political Index 1981–1992*.

Bibliography

Adams, Gerry (1986) *The Politics of Irish Freedom*, Dingle, Co. Kerry: Brandon.

Adams, Gerry (1988) *A Pathway to Peace*, Cork: Mercier.

Adams, Gerry (1990) 'Presidential Address' at 85th Sinn Féin Ard Fheis, Mansion House, Dublin, Saturday 3 February, Dublin: Sinn Féin.

Adams, James, Morgan, Robin and Bambridge, Anthony (1988) *Ambush, The War between the SAS and the IRA*, London: Pan.

Alali, A. Odasuo and Eke, Kenoye Kelvin (eds) (1991) *Media Coverage of Terrorism: Methods of Diffusion*, London: Sage.

Alexander, Yonah (1978) 'Terrorism, the Media and the Police', *Police Studies*, June: 45–52.

Alexander, Yonah (ed.), (1979) 'Terrorism and the Media: Special Issue', *Terrorism*, 2 (1 and 2) New York: Crane Russak.

Alexander, Yonah and Latter, Richard (eds) (1990) *Terrorism and the Media: Dilemmas for Government, Journalists and the Public*, Washington: Brassey's.

Alexander, Yonah and Picard, Robert, G. (eds) (1991) *In the Camera's Eye: News Coverage of Terrorist Events*, Washington: Brassey's.

Altheide, David and Johnson, John M. (1980) *Bureaucratic Propaganda*, Boston, MA: Allyn and Bacon.

Altheide, David (1985) 'Impact of Format and Ideology on TV News Coverage of Iran', *Journalism Quarterly*, 62, Summer: 346–51.

Altheide, David (1987) 'Format and Symbols in TV Coverage of Terrorism in the United States and Great Britain', *International Studies Quarterly*, 31: 161–76.

Amnesty International (1988) *United Kingdom: Northern Ireland: Killings by Security Forces and 'Supergrass' Trials*, AI Index: EUR 45/08/88, June, London: Amnesty International.

Amnesty International (1989) *United Kingdom: Investigating Lethal Shootings: The Gibraltar Inquest*, AI Index: EUR 45/02/89, April, London: Amnesty International.

Amnesty International (1990) *United Kingdom: Killings by Security Forces in Northern Ireland: Update*, AI Index 45/02/90, April, London: Amnesty International.

Amnesty International (1991) *United Kingdom: Human Rights Concerns*, AI Index: EUR 45/04/91, June, London: Amnesty International.

Andersen, Robin (1988) 'Visions of Instability: US television's law and order news of El Salvador', *Media, Culture and Society*, 10 (2): 239–64.

Anderson, Alison (1991) 'Source Strategies and the Communication of Environmental Affairs', *Media, Culture and Society*, 13 (4): 459–76.

Ang, Ien (1985) *Watching 'Dallas'*, London: Methuen.

Ang, Ien (1991) 'Wanted: Audiences: On the politics of empirical audience studies', in Ellen Seiter, Hans Borchers, Gabrielle Kreutzner and Eva-Maria Warth (eds) (1989), *Remote Control: Television, Audiences and Cultural Power*, London: Routledge.

Artherton, Paul (1983a) *Editorial Treatment of the Northern Ireland Conflict in Selected American Newspapers, 1971–1981*, Penn State University: unpublished dissertation.

Artherton, Paul (1983b) 'The American Press Connection', *Fortnight*, September: 7.

Arthur, Max (1987) *Northern Ireland Soldiers Talking: 1969 to Today*, London: Sidgwick and Jackson.

Arthur, Paul (1987) 'The Media and Politics in Northern Ireland', in Jean Seaton and Ben Pimlott (eds), *The Media in British Politics*, Aldershot: Avebury.

BARB (Broadcasters' Audience Research Board Ltd), *Audience Reaction Report*, ITV National Report for Week Ending Sunday 2nd December (BARB Week 48), Produced by BBC Broadcasting Research Department, London: BARB.

Barker, Martin (1992) 'Stuart Hall, *Policing the Crisis*', in Martin Barker and Anne Beezer (eds), *Reading into Cultural Studies*, London: Routledge.

Barzilay, David (1973) *The British Army in Ulster, Vol. 1*, Belfast: Century Services.

BBC (1956) *BBC Handbook, 1956*, London: BBC.

BBC (1966) *BBC Handbook, 1966*, London: BBC.

BBC (1980a) 'The INLA Interview on *Tonight*: 5 July 1979',

Annual Review of BBC Audience Research Findings, 1978/79, No. 6: 88–106.

BBC (1980b) *News and Current Affairs Index,* October, London: BBC.

BBC (1984) *News and Current Affairs Index,* 2nd edn, January, London: BBC.

BBC (1987) *BBC News and Current Affairs Index,* 3rd edn, March, London: BBC.

BBC (1989a) *Annual Report and Accounts,* London: BBC.

BBC (1989b) *BBC Producers Guidelines,* London: BBC Information.

BBC (1989c) *Guidelines for Factual Programmes,* December, London: BBC.

BBC (1993) *Style Guide for News and Current Affairs Programmes,* London: BBC.

BBC World Service (1990) *Editorial Standards: A Guide for Staff,* London: BBC.

Belfrage, Sally (1988) *The Crack: A Belfast Year,* London: Grafton.

Bell, Robert, Johnstone, Robert and Wilson, Robin (eds) *Troubled Times: Fortnight Magazine and the Troubles in Northern Ireland 1970–91,* Belfast: Blackstaff.

Berkowitz, L. (1973) 'Studies of the Contagion of Violence', in H. Hirsch and D. Perry (eds), *Violence as Politics,* New York: Harper & Row.

Berkowitz L. and Macauley J. (1971) 'The Contagion of Criminal Violence', *Sociometry,* 34 (2): 238–60.

Bew, Paul and Patterson, Henry (1985) *The British State and the Ulster Crisis: From Wilson to Thatcher,* London: Verso.

Bew, Paul, Gibbon, Peter and Patterson, Henry (1979) *The State in Northern Ireland 1921–1972,* Manchester: Manchester University Press.

Billig, M., Deacon, D., Golding, P. and Middleton S. (1993) 'In the Hands of the Spin Doctors: Television, politics and the 1992 General Election', in Nod Miller and Rod Allan (eds), *It's Live, But is it Real?,* London: John Libbey.

Birt, John (1988a) 'Sinn Féin Ban: Giving the Full Picture', *Aerial,* 9 November.

Birt, John (1988b) 'Gagging the Messenger', *Independent,* 21 November.

Birt, John (1989) 'Time to tell the whole Ulster story', *Daily Telegraph,* 16 October.

Birt, John (1990) 'Media and the Police: A Conflict of Public Interests', Speech to the Autumn Conference of the Association of Chief Police Officers, 3 October.

Birt, John (1992) 'Let us hear their apologies', *Independent*, 19 October: 19.

Bloch, Jonathon and Fitzgerald, Patrick (1983) *British Intelligence and Covert Action*, London: Junction Books.

Bolton, Roger (1986) 'The Problems of Making Political Television: A Practitioner's Perspective', in P. Golding, G. Murdock and P. Schlesinger, *Communicating Politics: Mass Communications and the Political Process*, Leicester: Leicester University Press.

Bolton, Roger (1989) 'Fact and Friction', *The Listener*, 3 August: 4–5.

Bolton, Roger (1990) *Death on the Rock and Other Stories*, London: Optomen/W. H. Allen.

Bonham-Carter, Mark (1989) 'Broadcasting and terrorism', *Index on Censorship*, 2: 7–33.

Bonnechère, Michèle (1988) *The Gibraltar Inquest on the Deaths on 6 March 1988, of the Irish Nationalists Mairead Farrell, Daniel McCann and Sean Savage: The IADL Judicial Observer's Report*, Brussels, Belgium: International Association of Democratic Lawyers.

Brennan, Paul, Goldring, Maurice, Deutsch, Richard and Gaudin, Elizabeth (1990) 'The Northern Ireland Conflict in the French Press: *Le Figaro*, the Left-Wing Press, *Le Monde*, and the Religious Press', in John Darby, Nicholas Dodge and A.C. Hepburn (eds), *Political Violence: Ireland in a Comparative Perspective*, Belfast: Appletree Press.

Briggs, Asa (1965) *The Golden Age of Wireless: The History of Broadcasting in the United Kingdom Vol. 2*, London: Oxford University Press.

Briggs, Asa (1970) *The War of Words: The History of Broadcasting in the United Kingdom Vol. 3*, London: Oxford University Press.

Briggs, Asa (1979) *Governing the BBC*, London: BBC.

Brown, Mike (1988) *BBC Bush House Newsroom Guide and Style Book*, BBC, London.

Bruck, Peter (1988) 'Preface: News Media and Terrorism', in Peter Bruck (ed.), *The News Media and Terrorism*, Discussion Document Series, Ottawa, Canada: Centre for Communication, Culture and Society, Carleton University.

Bruck, Peter (1989) 'Strategies for Peace, Strategies for News Research', *Journal of Communication*, 39 (1), Winter: 108–29.

Brunsdon, Charlotte (1991) 'Text and Audience', in Ellen Seiter, Hans Borchers, Gabrielle Kreutzner and Eva-Maria Warth (eds) (1989), *Remote Control: Television, Audiences and Cultural Power*, London: Routledge.

Brunt, Rosalind (1992) 'Engaging with the Popular: Audiences for Mass Culture and What to Say About Them', in L. Grossberg, C. Nelson and P. Treichler (eds), *Cultural Studies*, London: Routledge.

Bunyan, Tony (1977) *The History and Practice of the Political Police in Britain*, London: Quartet.

Burns, Jimmy (1990) 'Japanese still wary of Ulster's troubled image', *Financial Times*, 29 June: 8.

Butler, David (1991) 'Ulster Unionism and British Broadcasting Journalism, 1924–1989', in Bill Rolston (ed.), *The Media and Northern Ireland: Covering the Troubles*, London: Macmillan.

Cairns, Ed (1983) 'The Political Socialisation of Tomorrow's Parents: Violence, Politics and the Media', in Joan Harbison (ed.), *Children of the Troubles: Children in Northern Ireland*, Belfast: Stranmillis College Learning Resources Unit.

Cairns, Ed (1984) 'Television News as a source of Knowledge About the Violence for Children in Ireland: A Test of the Knowledge-Gap Hypothesis', *Current Psychological Research and Reviews*, Winter: 32–8.

Cairns, Ed (1987) *Caught in Crossfire: Children and the Northern Ireland Conflict*, Belfast: Appletree Press.

Cairns, Ed (1990) 'Impact of Television News Exposure on Children's Perceptions of Violence in Northern Ireland', *Journal of Social Psychology*, 130 (4): 447–52.

Cairns, Ed, Hunter, Dale and Herring, Linda (1980) 'Young Children's Awareness of Violence in Northern Ireland: The Influence of Northern Irish Television in Scotland and Northern Ireland', *British Journal of Social and Clinical Psychology*, 19: 3–6.

Cairns, Ed, Hunter, Dale and Herring, Linda (1981) 'Adult

Perceptions of Reality: A Reply to Gunter and Wober', *British Journal of Social Psychology*, 20: 74–5.

Cairns, Ed and Wilson, R. (1984) 'The Impact of Political Violence on Mild Psychiatric Morbidity in Northern Ireland', *British Journal of Psychiatry*, 145: 631–5.

Callaghan, James (1973) *A House Divided*, London: Collins.

Campaign For Free Speech on Ireland (1979) *The British Media and Ireland: Truth the first casualty*, London: Information on Ireland.

Campbell, Duncan (1980) 'The D Notice quangette', *New Statesman*, 4 April: 502–3.

Campbell, Duncan (1988) 'Panic in the Street', *New Statesman and Society*, 17 June: 11.

Campbell, Duncan (1990) 'Still Dark in Paranoia Gulch', *New Statesman and Society*, 9 February: 15–17.

Campbell, Jim (1985) 'Northern Ireland: Shoot the Journalist', *Index on Censorship*, 14 (5), October: 2 and 30.

Campbell, Jim (1991) 'Reporter that Loyalists guns couldn't silence', *Journalist*, July/August: 6.

Cathcart, Rex (1984) *The Most Contrary Region: The BBC in Northern Ireland 1924–1984*, Belfast: Blackstaff.

Cathcart, Rex (1988) 'Hearing no Evil', *Fortnight*, 267, November: 7.

Central Office of Information (1989a) *Overseas Radio Services*, November, London: COI.

Central Office of Information (1989b) *Annual Report and Accounts, 1988–89*, London: COI.

Central Office of Information (1990a) *Annual Report and Accounts, 1989–90*, London: COI.

Central Office of Information (1990b) *COI Directory*, January, London: COI.

Central Office of Information (1990c) *Information and Press Officers in Government Departments*, December, London: COI.

Chalfont, A. (1990) 'Terrorism and International Security', in Y. Alexander and R. Latter (eds), *Terrorism and the Media: Dilemmas for Government, Journalists and the Public*, Washington: Brassey's.

Charters, David (1977) 'Intelligence and Psychological Warfare Operations in Northern Ireland', *RUSI Journal*, 122 (3), September: 22–7.

Chibnall, Steve (1977) *Law and Order News*, London: Tavistock.

Chomsky, Noam (1989) *Necessary Illusions: Thought Control in Democratic Societies*, London: Pluto.

Chomsky, Noam (1991a) *Pirates and Emperors: International Terrorism in the Real World*, Montreal: Black Rose Books.

Chomsky, Noam (1991b) 'International Terrorism: Image and Reality', in Alexander George (ed.), *Western State Terrorism*, Cambridge: Polity.

Chomsky, Noam (1992) *Deterring Democracy*, London: Vintage.

Clutterbuck, Richard (1981) *The Media and Political Violence*, London: Macmillan.

Cockerell, Michael (1989) *Live From Number 10: The Inside Story of Prime Ministers and Television*, London: Faber and Faber.

Cockerell, Michael, Hennessy, Peter and Walker, David (1984) *Sources Close to the Prime Minister*, London: Macmillan.

Cohen, Akiba A., Adoni, Hanna and Bantz, Charles R. (1990) *Social Conflict and Television News*, Newbury Park, CA: Sage.

Cohen, Stan (1972) *Folk Devils and Moral Panics*, London: McKibbon and Kee.

Collett, P. and Lamb, R. (1985) *Watching People Watch Television*, London: IBA.

Committee on the Administration of Justice (1991) 'Human Rights in Northern Ireland', *Submission to the United Nations' Human Rights Committee*, February.

Committee on the Administration of Justice (1992) *Inquests and Disputed Killings in Northern Ireland*, CAJ Pamphlet No. 18, January.

Committee on the Administration of Justice (1993) *Submissions on the killings of Pearse Jordan, Gerard Maginn and Patrick Finucane to the United Nations Special Rapporteur on Summary or Arbitrary Executions*, October, Belfast: Committee on the Administration of Justice.

Committee on the Administration of Justice (forthcoming) *The Use of Lethal Force by Security Forces in Northern Ireland*, CAJ Pamphlet, Belfast: Committee on the Administration of Justice.

Commons Expenditure Committee (1973) *First Report from the Expenditure Committee: Accommodation and Staffing in Ottawa and Washington*, 22 November, HC 29, London: HMSO.

Conway, John (1989a) 'Pressure and Practicality', *Aerial*, 24 January: 7.

Conway, John (1989b) 'Orange Alert', *Edinburgh International Television Festival Programme*: 16–20.

Cook, Timothy (1989) *Making Laws and Making News: Media Strategies in the US House of Rpresentatives*, The Brookings Institution: Washington DC.

Corner, John (1991) 'Meaning, Genre and Context: The Problematics of "Public Knowledge" in the New Audience Studies', in James Curran and Michael Gurevitch (eds), *Mass Media and Society*, London: Edward Arnold.

Corner, John, Richardson, Kay and Fenton, Natalie (1990) *Nuclear Reactions: Form and Response in Public Issue Television*, John Libbey, London.

Cran, Bill (1989) 'Death of a Terrorist', *Frontline*, WGBH Boston for the PBS network.

Crelinsten, R.D. (1987a) 'Terrorism as Political Communication: The Relationship between the Controller and the Controlled', in P. Wilkinson and A. Stewart (eds), *Contemporary Research on Terrorism*, Aberdeen: Aberdeen University Press.

Crelinsten Ronald D. (1987b) 'Power and Meaning: Terrorism as a Struggle over Access to the Communication Structure', in P. Wilkinson and A. Stewart (eds), *Contemporary Research on Terrorism*, Aberdeen: Aberdeen University Press.

Crilly, Anne (1988) *Mother Ireland*, Derry Film and Video Workshop, 1 Westend Park, Derry, Ireland.

Cronin, Sean (1987) *Washington's Irish Policy, 1916–1986*, Dublin: Anvil Press.

Cullyhanna Justice Group, *Cullyhanna: Report of the Public Inquiry into the killing of Fergal Caraher and the wounding of Miceál Caraher in Cullyhanna, Co. Armagh on 30th December 1990*, Dublin: Irish National Congress/Cullyhanna Justice Group.

Cumberbatch, Guy and Howitt, Dennis (1989) *A Measure of Uncertainty: The Effects of the Mass Media*, London: John Libbey.

Curran, Charles (1979) *A Seamless Robe: Broadcasting — Philosphy and Practice*, London: Collins.

Curran, James (1990) 'The New Revisionism in Mass Communication Research: A Reappraisal', *European Journal of Communication*, 5: 135–64.

Curran, James (1991) 'Rethinking the Media as a Public Sphere', in P. Dahlgren and C. Sparks (eds), *Communication and Citizenship*, London: Routledge.

Curran, James and Seaton, Jean (1991) *Power Without Responsibility: The Press and Broadcasting in Britain*, 4th edn, London: Routledge.

Curtice, John and Gallagher, Tony (1990) 'The Northern Irish Dimension', in Roger Jowell, Sharon Witherspoon and Lindsay Brook (eds), *British Social Attitudes: The 7th Report*, Aldershot, Hants: Gower.

Curtis, Liz (1982) *They Shoot Children: The Use of Rubber and Plastic Bullets in the North of Ireland*, London: Information on Ireland.

Curtis, Liz (1984a) *Ireland: The Propaganda War*, London: Pluto.

Curtis, Liz (1984b) *Nothing but the Same Old Story: The Roots of Anti-Irish Racism*, London: Information on Ireland.

Curtis, Liz (1986) *'The British Media and Ireland'*, in J. Curran, J. Ecclestone, G. Oakley and A. Richardson (eds), *Bending Reality: The State of the Media*, London: Pluto.

Curtis, Liz (1988) 'The North of Ireland: British Government Misinformation', *Information on Ireland Briefing*, September, London: Information on Ireland.

Curtis, Liz (1989) 'Update: Incidents Following the Broadcasting Ban on Ireland', *Information on Ireland Briefing*, London: Information on Ireland.

Curtis, Liz and Jempson, Mike (1993) *Interference on the Airwaves: Ireland, the Media and the Broadcasting Ban*, London: Campaign for Press and Broadcasting Freedom.

Dahlgren, Peter (1992) 'What's the Meaning of this? Viewers' Plural Sense-making of TV News', in Paddy Scannell, Philip Schlesinger and Colin Sparks (eds), *Culture and Power: A Media, Culture and Society Reader*, London: Sage.

Daly, Bishop Edward (1989) 'Terrorism, Violence and the Media: The Christian Responsibilities of the Media', Paper given at Cleraun Study Centre seminar on *The Christian Responsibilities of the Media*, Dublin, 19 November.

Darby, John (1983) *Dressed to Kill: Cartoonists and the Northern Ireland Conflict*, Belfast: Appletree Press.

Deacon, David and Golding, Peter (1991) 'When Ideology Fails:

The Flagship of Thatcherism and the British Local and National Media', *European Journal of Communication*, 6 (3): 291–314.

De Boer, Connie (1979) 'The Polls: Terrorism and Hijacking', *Public Opinion Quarterly* 43: 410–18.

Derry Film and Video Workshop (1988) *Press Release*, 1 November, Derry Film and Video, 1 Westend Park, Derry, Ireland.

Dewar, Michael (1985) *The British Army in Northern Ireland: An account of the Army's fight against the IRA*, London: Arms and Armour Press.

Dickson, Brice (1990) 'The Powers of the Police', in Brice Dickson (ed.), *Civil Liberties in Northern Ireland: The C.A.J. Handbook*, Belfast: Committee on the Administration of Justice.

Dillon, Martin (1988) *The Dirty War*, London: Hutchinson.

Dillon, Martin (1992a) *Killer in Clowntown: Joe Doherty, the IRA and the Special Relationship*, London: Hutchinson.

Dillon, Martin (1992b) *Stone Cold: The True Story of Michael Stone and the Milltown Massacre*, London: Hutchinson.

Dobkin, Bethami A. (1992) *Tales of Terror: Television News and the construction of the Terrorist Threat*, New York: Praeger.

Dobson, Christopher and Payne, Ronald (1982) *Terror! The West Fights Back*, London: Macmillan.

Docherty, David, Morrison, David and Tracey, Michael (1988) *Keeping Faith: Channel Four and its Audience*, London: John Libbey.

Doornaert, Mia and Larsen, Hans (1987) *Censoring 'The Troubles': An Irish Solution to an Irish Problem?*, Report on an IFJ fact-finding mission to Ireland in January (1987, Brussels:International Federation of Journalists.

Dorril, Stephen (1993) 'Conspiracy to Conceal', *Free Press*, No. 73, March/April: 3.

Dorril, Stephen and Ramsay, Robin (1990) 'In a Common Cause: The Anti-Communist Crusade in Britain, 1945–60', *Lobster*, (19), May: 1–8.

Dorril, Stephen and Ramsay, Robin (1991) *Smear! Wilson and the Secret State*, London: Fourth Estate.

Downing, John (1986) 'Government Secrecy and the Media in the United States and Britain', in Peter Golding et al. (eds),

Communicating Politics: Mass Communications and the Political Process, Leicester: Leicester University Press.

Downing, Taylor (ed.) (1982) *The Troubles: The Background to the Question of Northern Ireland*, 2nd edn, London: Thames Television Ltd/MacDonald Futura.

Dugdale, John (1990) 'Proscribed Treatment', *The Listener*, 15 November: 9–10.

Elliot, Philip (1976) 'Misreporting Ulster: News as a Field-dressing', *New Society*, 25 November.

Elliot, Philip (1977) 'Reporting Northern Ireland: A Study of News in Britain, Ulster and the Irish Republic', in UNESCO (ed.), *Media and Ethnicity*, Paris: UNESCO.

Elliot, Philip (1980) 'Press Performance as Political Ritual', in Harry Christian (ed.), *The Sociology of Journalism and the Press*, Keele: University of Keele.

Elliot, Philip (1982a) Media Performances as Political Rituals, *Communication*, 7: 115–30.

Elliot, Philip (1982b) 'Intellectuals, the "Information Society" and the Disappearance of the Public Sphere', *Media, Culture and Society*, 4: 243–53.

Ericson, Richard (1989) 'Patrolling the Facts: Secrecy and Publicity in Police Work', *British Journal of Sociology*, 4 (2): 205–26.

Ericson, Richard, Baranek, Patricia and Chan, Janet (1989) *Negotiating Control: A Study of News Sources*, Milton Keynes: Open University Press.

Ettema, James S. and Kline, F.G. (1977) 'Deficits, Differences and Ceilings: Contingent Conditions for Understanding the Knowledge Gap', *Communication Research*, 4: 179–202.

Ettema, James S., Brown, James W. and Leupker, Russell V. (1983) 'Knowledge Gap Effects in a Health Information Campaign', *Public Opinion Quarterly*, 47: 516–27.

Evelegh, Robin (1978) *Peace-Keeping in a Democratic Society: The Lessons of Northern Ireland*, London: Hurst and Co.

Ewing, K.D. and Gearty, C. (1990) *Freedom under Thatcher: Civil Liberties in Modern Britain*, Oxford: Clarendon.

Faligot, Roger (1983) *Britain's Military Strategy in Ireland: The Kitson Experiment*, London: Zed Books, Dingle, Co. Kerry: Brandon.

Farish, Stephen (1990) 'RUC Ransacks Press Office' *PR Week*, 11 January: 1.

Farrell, David M. (1982) 'RTE: A Path of Serfdom', *New Exchange*, Spring: 28–34.

Findahl, O. and Höijer, B. (1985) 'Some Characteristics of News Memory and Comprehension', *Journal of Broadcasting and Electronic Media*, 29 (4).

Fiske, John (1987) *Television Culture*, London: Methuen.

Fiske, John (1991) 'Moments of television: Neither the text nor the audience', in Ellen Seiter, Hans Borchers, Gabrielle Kreutzner, and Eva-Maria Warth (eds) (1989), *Remote Control: Television, Audiences and Cultural Power*, London: Routledge.

Flackes, W. D. and Elliot, Sydney (1989) *Northern Ireland: A Political Directory, 1968–88* (3rd edn), Belfast: Blackstaff Press.

Fletcher, Richard (1982) 'British Propaganda Since World War II – A Case Study', *Media Culture and Society*, 4: 97–109.

Foot, Paul (1990) *Who Framed Colin Wallace?*, London: Macmillan.

Foote, Donna (1988) 'A Shadow Government', *Newsweek*, 12 September: 37–8.

Foreign and Commonwealth Office (1980) revised 'Protest Campaign in Northern Ireland Prisons', *Greyband Brief,* October.

Foreign and Commonwealth Office (1988) 'The Provisional IRA: International Contacts Outside the United States', *Background Brief,* January.

Forgan, Liz (1992a) 'A Court Order that could Kill', *Independent on Sunday*, 3 May.

Forgan, Liz (1992b) 'A Law to Silence Whistle-blowers', *The Independent*, 6 August.

Fortnight (1991a) 'Events Diary', *Fortnight*, January: 20–22.

Fortnight (1991b) '"Troubles" Chronology', *Fortnight*, September: 26–9.

Francis, Richard (1977) *Broadcasting to a Community in Conflict – The Experience in Northern Ireland*, London: BBC.

Francis, Richard (1981) 'The Journalist Cannot Survive as an Informer, Except When ...', *The Listener*, 12 February: 206–7.

Gaffikin, Frank and Morrissey, Michael (1990) *Northern Ireland: The Thatcher Years*, London: Zed Books.

Gandy, Oscar (1980) 'Information in Health: Subsidised News', *Media, Culture and Society*, 2: 103–15.

Garnham, Nicholas (1986) 'The Media and the Public Sphere', in P. Golding, G. Murdock and P. Schlesinger (eds), *Communicating Politics: Mass Communications and the Political Process*, Leicester: Leicester University Press.

Gearty, Conor (1991) *Terror*, London: Faber.

George, Alexander (ed.) (1991a) *Western State Terrorism*, Cambridge: Polity.

George, Alexander (1991b) 'Introduction', in Alexander George (ed.), *Western State Terrorism*, Cambridge: Polity.

Gerbner, George (1991) 'Symbolic Functions of Violence and Terror', in Y. Alexander and R.G. Picard (eds), *In the Camera's Eye: News Coverage of Terrorist Events*, Washington: Brassey's.

Gerbner, G., Gross L., Signorelli, N., Morgan, M. and Jackson-Beeck, M. (1979) 'The Demonstration of Power: Violence Profile No. 10', *Journal of Communication*, 29: 177–96.

Gill, Peter (1980) 'TV Reporting of Northern Ireland', letter to the editor, *The Times*, 19 December.

Gilliland, David (1983) Speech to *Meeting of the Belfast Chamber of Commerce and Industry*, Forum Hotel, Belfast, 31 January.

Glasgow University Media Group (1982) *Really Bad News*, Writers and Readers: London.

Glasgow University Media Group (1985) *War and Peace News*, Milton Keynes: Open University Press.

Golding, Peter and Murdock, Graham (1991) 'Culture, Communications and Political Economy' in James Curran and Michael Gurevitch (eds), *Mass Media and Society*, London: Edward Arnold.

Gormally, Brian, McEvoy, Kieran and Wall, David (1993) 'Criminal Justice in a Divided Society: A Case Study of Prisons in Northern Ireland', unpublished paper, Belfast: NIACRO.

Gosling, Mick (1991) 'Anomalies in the Unbanning of Mother Ireland', Letters Page, *Guardian*, 20 April.

Grattan, Alan (1988) 'Protestants, the Press and the Anglo-Irish Agreement', Paper presented to Media, Culture and Society International Colloquium, Polytechnic of Central London, October.

Greene, Sir Hugh (1969) *The Third Floor Front: A View of Broadcasting in the Sixties*, London: Bodley Head.

Greenslade, Roy (1993a) 'The Forgotten Tragedy', *Guardian*, 12 April: 12.

Greenslade, Roy (1993b) 'Belfast, Beautiful Belfast', *Guardian*, 6 December: 16–17.

Greer, Herb (1990) 'When Television gets away with Murder', *Sunday Telegraph*, 22 April.

Grisewood, Harman (1968) *One Thing at a Time*, London: Hutchinson.

Gunter, Barrie (1987) *Television and the fear of crime*, London: John Libbey.

Gunter, Barrie and Wober, Mallory (1981) 'Children's Perceptions of TV News and Reality: A Response to Cairns et al', *British Journal of Social Psychology*, 20: 73–4.

Hall, Stuart, Critcher, Chas, Jefferson, Tony, Clarke, John and Roberts, Brian (1978) *Policing the Crisis: Mugging, the State and Law and Order*, London: Macmillan.

Hallin, Daniel C. (1987) 'Hegemony: The American News Media From Vietnam to El Salvador, A Study of Ideological Change and its Limits', in David Paletz (ed.), *Political Communication Research: Approaches, Studies, Assessments*, Ablex, Norwood, NJ.

Hamilton-Tweedale, Brian (1987) *The British Press and Northern Ireland: A Case Study in the Reporting of Violent Conflict* University of Sheffield: unpublished Ph.D.

Hanvey, Bobbie (1990) 'Is this the defence of Ulster?', *Fortnight*, October: 35.

Harbinson, J.F. (1973) *The Ulster Unionist Party, 1882–1973*, Belfast: Blackstaff Press.

Hardy, Eamon (1983) *'Primary Definition' By the State: An Analysis of the Northern Ireland Information Service as Reported in the Northern Ireland Press*, Queens University, Belfast: unpublished dissertation.

Harris, Eoghan (1987) *Television and Terrorism*, 15 November, Dublin: Irish Television Producers Association.

Harris, Robert (1990) *Good and Faithful Servant: The Unauthorised Biography of Bernard Ingham*, London: Faber.

Hattersley, Roy (1988) 'Read My Lips', *The Listener*, 15 December: 18–19.

Hawthorn, Jeremy (ed.) (1987) *Propaganda, Persuasion and Polemic*, London: Edward Arnold.

Hawthorne, James (1988) 'The Fragrant Harbour's Electric Platform', *The Listener*, 7 July: 6–8.

Hearst, David (1989) 'Hurd's Gag begins to Tighten: Sinn Féin Seems to be Losing its Gift for Manipulating the Media', *Guardian*, 8 May.

Helsinki Watch (1993) 'Freedom of Expression in the United Kingdom: Recent Developments', *Helsinki Watch: The Fund For Free Expression*, 5 (3), March.

Henderson, Lesley, Miller, David and Reilly, Jacqueline (1990) *Speak No Evil: The British Broadcasting Ban, The Media and the Conflict in Ireland*, Glasgow: Glasgow University Media Group.

Hennessy, Peter (1985) *What the Papers Never Said*, London: Portcullis Press.

Hennessy, Peter (1987) 'The Quality of Political Journalism', *Journal of the Royal Society of Arts*, November: 926–34.

Herman, Edward S. (1982) *The Real Terror Network: Terrorism in Fact and Propaganda*, Boston, Mass: South End Press.

Herman, Edward S. (1986) 'Gatekeeper versus Propaganda Models: A Critical American Perspective', in P. Golding, G. Murdock and P. Schlesinger, *Communicating Politics: Mass Communications and the Political Process*, Leicester: Leicester University Press.

Herman, Edward S. (1988) 'The Use and Abuse of Terrorism – A Comment', in Peter Bruck (ed.), *The News Media and Terrorism*, Discussion Document Series, Ottawa, Canada: Centre for Communication, Culture and Society, Carleton University.

Herman, Edward S. and Chomsky, Noam (1988) *Manufacturing Consent: The Political Economy of the Mass Media*, New York: Pantheon.

Herman, Edward S. and O'Sullivan, Gerry (1989) *The 'Terrorism' Industry*, New York: Pantheon.

Herman, Edward S. and O'Sullivan, Gerry (1991) '"Terrorism" as Ideology and Cultural Industry', in Alexander George (ed.), *Western State Terrorism*, Cambridge: Polity.

Hermon, Sir John (1990) 'The Police, the Media and the Reporting of Terrorism', in Yonah Alexander and Richard Latter (eds), *Terrorism and the Media: Dilemmas for Government, Journalists and the Public*, Washington, DC: Brassey's.

Hess, Stephen (1981) *The Washington Reporters*, Washington DC: Brookings Institution.

Hewitt, Christopher (1992) 'Public's Perspectives', in David L. Paletz and Alex P. Schmid (eds), *Terrorism and the Media: How Researchers, Terrorists, Government, Press, Public, Victims View and Use the Media*, London: Sage.

Heyman, Edward and Mickolus, Edward (1980) 'Observations on "Why Violence Spreads"', *International Studies Quarterly*, June: 299–305.

Hickey, Neil (1976) 'Terrorism and Television: The Medium in the Middle', *TV Guide*, 7 August: 10–13.

Hickey, Neil (1981) 'The Battle for Northern Ireland: How TV Tips the Balance', *TV Guide*, 26 September: 8–27.

Hill, Charles (1964) *Both Sides of the Hill*, London: Heinemann.

Hill, Charles (1974) *Behind the Screen*, London: Sidgwick and Jackson.

Hillyard, Paddy and Percy-Smith, Janie (1988) *The Coercive State: The Decline of Democracy in Britain*, London: Collins/Fontana.

Hobson, Dorothy (1982) *Crossroads: The Drama of a Soap Opera*, London: Methuen.

Hobson, Dorothy 'Soap Operas at Work', in Ellen Seiter, Hans Borchers, Gabrielle Kreutzner and Eva-Maria Warth (eds) (1989), *Remote Control: Television, Audiences and Cultural Power*, London: Routledge.

Höijer, Birgitta (1990) 'Studying Viewers' Reception of Television Programmes: Theoretical and Methodological Considerations', *European Journal of Communication*, 5: 29–56.

Holden, Robert T. (1986) 'The Contagiousness of Aircraft Hijacking', *American Journal of Sociology*, 91 (985): 874–902.

Holland, Jack (1988) 'When English Eyes are Jaundiced ...', *Irish Echo*, Saturday 23 April.

Holland, Jack (1989) *The American Connection: US Guns, Money and Influence in Northern Ireland*, Poolbeg, Swords, Co. Dublin, Ireland.

Holroyd, Fred with Burridge, Nick (1989) *War Without Honour*, Hull: Medium Publishing Co.

Hooper, Alan (1982) *The Military and the Media*, Aldershot: Avebury.

Hooper, David (1988) *Official Secrets: The Use and Abuse of the Act*, London: Coronet.

Horgan, John (1984) 'State Policy and the Press', *The Crane Bag*, 8 (2): 51–8.

Houston, P. (1992) 'Government Information Service', Introduction to *INF files*, Public Record Office of Northern Ireland, 25 February, Belfast: PRONI.

Howitt, Dennis and Cumberbatch, Guy (1989) *A Measure of Uncertainty: The Effects of the Mass Media*, London: John Libbey.

Independent Broadcasting Authority (1979) *Television Programme Guidelines*, London: IBA.

Independent Broadcasting Authority (1985) *Television Programme Guidelines*, April, London: IBA.

Independent Television Commission (1991) *The ITC Programme Code*, July, London: ITC.

Index on Censorship (1993a) 'Index Index', 22 (2): 38

Index on Censorship (1993b) 'Index Index', 22 (3): 38

Industrial Development Board, Northern Ireland (1985) *Encouraging Enterprise: A Medium Term Strategy for 1985–1990, A Summary*, Belfast: Industrial Development Board.

Industrial Development Board, Northern Ireland (1990) *Annual Report and Accounts 1989–1990*, Belfast: IDB.

Ingham, Bernard (1991) *Kill the Messenger*, London: Harper Collins.

Institute for the Study of Conflict (1978) *Television and Conflict*, London: ISC.

Irish Information Partnership (1990) *Irish Information Agenda*, 6th edn, London: Irish Information Partnership.

Irvin, Cynthia (1992) 'Terrorists' Perspectives: Interviews', in David Paletz and Alex Schmid, *Terrorism and the Media: How Researchers, Terrorists, Government, Press, Public, Public, Victims View and use the Media*, London: Sage.

Jack, Ian (1988) 'Gibraltar', *Granta*, 25: 14–86.

Jenkins, Brian (1975) *International Terrorism*, Santa Monica, CA: Rand Corporation.

Jenkins, Simon and Sloman, Anne (1985) *With Respect Ambassador: An Inquiry into the Foreign Office*, London: BBC.

Journalist (1991) 'Northern Ireland: "A Price Too High"', July/ August: 6–7.

Jowett, Garth and O'Donnell, Victoria (1992) *Propaganda and Persuasion* (2nd edn), Beverly Hills: Sage.

Katz, Elihu and Liebes, Tamar (1985) 'Mutual Aid in the Decoding of *Dallas*: Preliminary Notes from a Cross-Cultural Study', in P. Drummond and R. Patterson (eds), *Television in Transition*, London: BFI.

Keane, John (1991) *Media and Democracy*, Cambridge: Polity.

Kee, Robert (1986) *Trial and Error: The Maguires, the Guildford Pub Bombings and British Justice*, London: Hamish Hamilton.

Keleny, Guy (ed.) (1992) *The Independent Style Book 1992*, London: The Independent.

Kellner, Douglas (1992) *The Persian Gulf TV War*, Boulder, CO: Westview.

Kelly, Michael J. and Mitchell, Thomas H. (1981) 'Transnational Terrorism and the Western Elite Press', *Political Communication and Persuasion*, 1: 269–96.

Kerr, Paul (1990) 'F for Fake? Friction over Faction', in Andrew Goodwin and Garry Whannel (eds), *Understanding Television*, London: Routledge.

Kirkaldy, John (1981) 'English Cartoonists; Ulster Realities', *Eire-Ireland*, 16 (3): 27–42.

Kitchin, Hilary (1989) *The Gibraltar Report: Inquest into the Deaths of Mairead Farrell, Daniel McCann and Sean Savage*, London: National Council for Civil Liberties.

Kitson, Frank (1971) *Low Intensity Operations*, London: Faber & Faber.

Kitzinger, Jenny (1990) 'Audience Understandings of AIDS Media Messages: A Discussion of Methods', *Sociology of Health and Illness*, xii (3): 319–35.

Kitzinger, Jenny (1993) 'Understanding AIDS: Media messages and what people know about Acquired Immune Deficiency Syndrome', in Glasgow University Media Group (eds), *Getting the Message*, London: Routledge.

Kitzinger, Jenny and Miller, David (1992) '"African AIDS": The Media and Audience Beliefs', in P. Aggleton, P. Davies and G. Hart, *AIDS: Rights, Risk and Reason*, London: Falmer Press.

Knight, G. and Dean, T. (1982) 'Myth and the Structure of News', *Journal of Communication*, Spring: 145–61.

Kubey, Robert (forthcoming) 'On Not Finding Media Effects: Conceptual Problems in the Notion of an Active Audience' (with a Reply to Elihu Katz), in L. Grossberg, J. Hay and

E. Wartella (eds), *Toward a comprehensive theory of the audience*, Boulder, CO: Westview Press.

Kuhn, Annette (1988) *Cinema, Censorship and Sexuality 1909–1925*, London: Routledge.

Laqueur, Walter (1976) 'The Futility of Terrorism', *Harper's*, March: 99–105

Laqueur, Walter (1978) *Terrorism*, London: Abacus.

Leapman, Michael (1987) *The Last Days of the Beeb* (rev. edn), London: Coronet.

Leigh, David (1980) *The Frontiers of Secrecy*, London: Junction Books.

Leigh, David (1988) *The Wilson Plot: The Intelligence Services and the Discrediting of a Prime Minister 1945–1976*, London: Heinemann.

Li Causi, Luciano (1982) 'Il terrismo degli altri: movimenti politici illegali in contesti stranieri', in *Terrorismo e TV: Italia, Gran Bretagna, Germania Occidentale, 2* Introduction by Franco Ferrarotti, Turin: ERI.

Liebes, Tamar and Katz, Elihu (1989) 'On the Critical Abilities of Television Viewers', in Ellen Seiter, Hans Borchers, Gabrielle Kreutzner and Eva-Maria Warth (eds) (1989), *Remote Control: Television, Audiences and Cultural Power*, London: Routledge.

Liebes, Tamar and Katz, Elihu (1993) *The Export of Meaning: Cross-Cultural Readings of Dallas*, 2nd edn, Cambridge: Polity.

Loftus, Belinda (1980) 'Images for Sale: Government and Security Advertising in Northern Ireland, 1968–1978', *Oxford Art Journal*, October: 70–80.

Loftus, Belinda (1982) *Images in Conflict: Visual Imagery and the Troubles in Northern Ireland 1968–1981*, University of Sheffield: unpublished Ph.D.

Lull, James (1990) *Inside Family Viewing: Ethnographic Research on Television's Audiences*, London: Routledge.

Lyon, Alison and McEvoy, David (1991) 'A Question of Ulster?', in Markey Research Society, *Market Research Society 34th Annual Conference*, London: Market Research Society.

McBride, Steve (1990) 'Freedom of Expression', in Brice Dickson (ed.), *Civil Liberties in Northern Ireland: The C.A.J. Handbook*, Belfast: Committee on the Administration of Justice.

Mac Conghail, Muiris (1984) The Creation of RTE and the Impact of Television, in Brian Farrell (ed.), *Communications and Community in Ireland*, Cork: Mercier.

McCormack, Gerry (1990) 'Access to Information', in Brice Dickson (ed.), *Civil Liberties in Northern Ireland: The C.A.J. Handbook*, Belfast: Committee on the Administration of Justice.

McGarvey, Paddy (1988) 'Getting away with Murder on the Box', *UK Press Gazette*, 31 October: 17 and 19.

McGuire, Maria (1973) *To Take Arms: A Year in the Provisional IRA*, London: Quartet.

McIvor, M. (1981) 'Northern Ireland: A Preliminary Look at Environmental Awareness', paper presented at the *Sixth Biennial Conference of the International Society of the Study of Behavioural Development*, Toronto.

McKee, Grant and Franey, Ros (1988) *Time Bomb: Irish Bombers, English Justice and the Guildford Four*, London: Bloomsbury.

MacKenzie, F. R. (1969) 'Eden, Suez and the BBC – A Reassessment', *The Listener*, 18 December.

McKittrick, David (1990) 'Web of intrigue spun on black propaganda', *Independent*, 3 February: 5.

McNair, Brian (1991) *Glasnost, Perestroika and the Soviet Media*, London: Routledge.

McPhilemy, Sean (1992) 'Dispatches Court Ruling Creates a No-go Area', *Broadcast*, 7 August: 8.

McWhirter, Liz (1982) 'Northern Irish Children's Conceptions of Violent Crime', *The Howard Journal*, 21: 167–77.

McWhirter, Liz, Young, Valerie and Majury, Juanita (1983) 'Belfast Children's awareness of violent death', *British Journal of Social Psychology*, 22: 81–92.

Margach, James (1979) *The Abuse of Power: The War Between Downing Street and the Media*, London: W. H. Allen.

Mazur, Allan (1982) 'Bomb Threats and the Mass Media: Evidence for a Theory of Suggestion', *American Sociological Review*, 47, June: 407–11.

Michael, James (1982) *The Politics of Secrecy: Confidential Government and the Public Right to Know*, London: Penguin.

Midlarsky, Manus (1970) 'Mathematical Models of Instability and a Theory of Diffusion', *International Studies Quarterly*, 1 (1), March: 6084.

Midlarsky, Manus (1978) 'Analyzing Diffusion and Contagion Effects: The Urban Disorders of the 1960s', *American Political Science Review*, 72: 996–1008.

Midlarsky, Manus I., Crenshaw, Martha and Yoshida, Fumihiko (1980) 'Why Violence Spreads: The Contagion of International Terrorism', *International Studies Quarterly*, 2 (2): 262–98.

Miller, Abraham H. (1990) 'Preserving Liberty in a Society under Siege: The Media and the "Guildford Four"', *Terrorism and Political Violence*, 2: 305–23.

Miller, David (1990) 'The History Behind a Mistake', *British Journalism Review*, 1 (2): 34–43.

Miller, David (1991) 'The Media on the Rock: The Media and the Gibraltar Killings', in Bill Rolston, *The Media and Northern Ireland: Covering the Troubles*, Basingstoke: Macmillan.

Miller, David (1993a) 'The Northern Ireland Information Service and the Media: Aims, Strategy, Tactics', in Glasgow University Media Group, *Getting the Message*, London: Routledge

Miller, David (1993b) 'Official Sources and Primary Definition: The Case of Northern Ireland', *Media, Culture and Society*, 15 (3), July: 385–406.

Miller, David (1993c) 'Why the Public Needs to Know', *Index on Censorship*, 22 (8 and 9), September–October: 5–6.

Miller, David (1993d), 'The New Battleground? Community Relations and Cultural Traditions in Northern Ireland', *Planet: The Welsh Internationalist*, 102, December/January: 74–9.

Miller, David (1993e) 'Lip Service', *Fortnight*, 323, December: 10.

Miller, David (1994) 'Understanding "Terrorism": US and British Audience Interpretations of the Televised Conflict in Ireland', in Meryl Aldridge and Nicholas Hewitt (eds), *Controlling Broadcasting: Access, Policy and Practice in North America and Europe*, Manchester: Manchester University Press.

Miller, David and Reilly, Jacquie (1994) *Food and the Media: Explaining Health 'Scares'*, Glasgow: Glasgow University Media Group.

Miller, David and Williams, Kevin (1993) 'Negotiating HIV/AIDS Information: Agendas, Media Strategies and the News', in

Glasgow University Media Group, *Getting the Message*, London: Routledge.

Milne, Alasdair (1988) *DG: The Memoirs of a British Broadcaster*, London: Coronet.

Ministry of Defence (1969) *Land Operations: Volume III – Counter Revolutionary Operations*, London: MoD.

Mitchell, Jack (1990) *GiB: A Modest Exposure*, Dublin: Fulcrum Press.

Moloney, Ed (1988) 'The Media: Asking the Right Questions?', in Michael Farrell (ed.), *Twenty Years On*, Dingle, Co. Kerry: Brandon.

Moloney, Ed (1990a) 'Raiders were "Finished Off by Army Hitman"', *Sunday Tribune*, 14 January: 1 and 3.

Moloney, Ed (1990b) 'Shadows and the Gunmen', *Sunday Tribune*, 14 October.

Moloney, Ed (1990c) 'Leaking of RUC Report seen as Attempt to Influence DPP', *Sunday Tribune*, 16 December.

Moloney, Ed (1991a) 'Closing Down the Airwaves: the Story of Broadcasting Ban', in Bill Rolston (ed.), *The Media and Northern Ireland: Covering the Troubles*, London: Macmillan.

Moloney, Ed (1991b) 'The Coagh Killings Up Controversial Deaths to 67', *Sunday Tribune*, 9 June: 6.

MORI (1991) *British Attitudes to Northern Ireland*, research conducted on behalf of Northside Productions, 21–24 March 1991, London: MORI.

Morley, David (1980) *The 'Nationwide' Audience, Structure and Decoding*, London: BFI Publishing.

Morley, David (1986) *Family Television: Cultural Power and Domestic Leisure*, London: Comedia.

Morley, David (1991) 'Changing Paradigms in Audience Studies', in Ellen Seiter, Hans Borchers, Gabrielle Kreutzner and Eva-Maria Warth (eds), *Remote Control: Television, Audiences and Cultural Power*, London: Routledge.

Morley, David (1992) *Television, Audiences and Cultural Studies*, London: Routledge.

Morley, David and Silverstone, Roger (1990) 'Domestic Communication', *Media, Culture and Society*, 12 (1): 31–56.

Morley, David and Silverstone, Roger (1991) 'Communication and Context: Ethnographic Perspectives on the Media Audience', in K.B. Jensen and N.W. Jankowski (eds), *A Handbook of*

Qualitative Methodologies for Mass Communication Research, London: Routledge.

Morris, Colin (1988a) 'Lives on the Line in Northern Ireland', *Guardian*, Monday 4 April: 9.

Morris, Colin (1988b) 'Tip-Toeing through the Minefield: Tracking the Truth in Northern Ireland', *University of Ulster Convocation Lecture*, University of Ulster, Jordanstown, 18 May, Belfast: BBC.

Morrison, Danny (1979) 'Censorship at Source', in Campaign for Free Speech on Ireland (ed.), *The British Media and Ireland: Truth the First Casualty*, London: Information on Ireland.

Morrison, Danny (1985) 'Danny Morison', in Martin Collins (ed.), *Ireland After Britain*, London: Pluto with Labour and Ireland.

Morrison, Danny (1989) *Ireland: The Censored Subject*, April, Belfast: Sinn Féin Publicity Department.

Morton, Brig Peter (1989) *Emergency Tour: 3 Para in South Armagh*, Wellingborough, Northamptonshire: William Kimber.

Mowlana, Hamid, Gerbner, George and Schiller, Herbert I. (1992) *Triumph of the Image: The Media's War in the Persian Gulf – A Global Perspective*, Boulder, CO: Westview.

Mullin, Chris (1987) *Error of Judgement: The Truth About the Birmingham Bombings* (rev. edn), Swords, Co. Dublin: Poolbeg.

Murdock, Graham (1989) 'Critical Inquiry and Audience Activity', in Brenda Dervin, Lawrence Grossberg, Barbara J. O'Keefe and Ellen Wartella (eds), *Rethinking Communication: Volume 2, Paradigm Exemplars*, Newbury Park/London: Sage, published in cooperation with the International Communication Association.

Murdock, Graham (1991) 'Patrolling the Border: British Broadcasting and the Irish Question in the 1980s', *Journal of Communication*, 41: 104–15.

Murphy, David (1991) *The Stalker Affair and the Press*, London: Unwin Hyman.

Murray, Raymond (1990) *The SAS in Ireland*, Cork: Mercier Press.

Murtagh, Peter (1982) 'RUC Press Office to Change Soon', *Irish Times*, 4 August.

National Union of Journalists (1990) *Death on the Rock*, Ethics Council Report, March.

Netanyahu, Benjamin (ed.) (1986) *Terrorism: How the West Can Win*, New York: Farrar, Straus, Goroux.

Nolan, Paul (1993) *Screening the Message: A Study of Community Relations Broadcasting*, A report for the Central Community Relations Unit, Northern Ireland Office, Stormont, Belfast.

Northern Ireland Information Service, (no date), *Northern Ireland Observed*, Belfast: NIIS.

Northern Ireland Information Service/Arts Council of Northern Ireland (1985) *Images: Arts and People in Northern Ireland*, March, Belfast: NIIS/Arts Council.

Northern Ireland Office (1980a) *H-blocks: The Facts*, October, Belfast: NIO.

Northern Ireland Office (1980b) *H-blocks: The Reality*, November, Belfast: NIO.

Northern Ireland Office (1981a) *Day to Day Life in Northern Ireland Prisons*, March, Belfast: NIO.

Northern Ireland Office (1981b) *Scope for Further Improvements in Prison Life*, July, Belfast: NIO.

Northern Ireland Office (1981c) *H-blocks: What the Papers Say*, July, Belfast: NIO.

Northern Ireland Office (1981d) *The Tragedy of Terrorism*, October, Belfast: NIO.

Northern Ireland Office (1985a) *Life Sentence Prisoners in Northern Ireland: An Explanatory Memorandum*, January, Belfast: NIO.

Northern Ireland Office (1985b) *Armagh Prison Strip Searching: The Facts*, Belfast: NIO.

Northern Ireland Office (1989) *'The Day of the Men and Women of Peace Must Surely Come ...'*, July, Belfast: NIO.

Northern Ireland Tourist Board (1990) *Annual Report (1989)*, 42, Belfast: NITB.

Odling-Smee, James (1989) 'Making Histories', *Fortnight*, September: 14–15.

O'Dowd, Liam (1991) 'Intellectuals and Political Culture: A Unionist–Nationalist Comparison', in Eamonn Hughes (ed.), *Culture and Politics in Northern Ireland 1960-1990*, Milton Keynes: Open University Press.

O'Dowd, Liam, Rolston, Bill and Tomlinson, Mike (1980)

Northern Ireland: Between Civil Rights and Civil War, London: CSE Books.

O'Dowd, Liam, Rolston, Bill and Tomlinson, Mike (1982) 'From Labour to the Tories: The Ideology of Containment in Northern Ireland', *Capital and Class*, 18, Winter: 72–90.

O'Leary, Brendan (1992) 'Public Opinion and Northern Irish Futures', *Political Quarterly*, 62 (2): 143–70.

Oliver, John (1978) *Working at Stormont*, Dublin: Institute for Public Administration.

Ó Maoláin, Ciaran (1989) *No Comment: Censorship, Secrecy and the Irish Troubles*, London, Article 19.

O Maolchatha, Aogan (1990) *Accounting For Death: Press Coverage of the 1981 Northern Irish Hunger Strike*, Dekalb, Illinois: Northern Illinois University, unpublished thesis.

O'Neill, Terence (1972) *The Autobiography of Terence O'Neill, Prime Minister of Northern Ireland 1963–1969*, London: Rupert Hart-Davis.

Owen, Arwel, Ellis (1989) 'The Anglo–Irish Agreement – A Broadcaster's Experience', *Guardian Lecture*, Nuffield College, Oxford.

Paletz, David, Ayanian, John and Fozzard, Peter (1982a) 'Terrorism on TV News: The IRA, the FALN and the Red Brigades', in William C. Adams, *Television Coverage of International Affairs*, Norwood, NJ: Ablex.

Paletz, David, Peter A. Fozzard and John Z. Ayanian (1982b) 'The IRA, the Red Brigades and the FALN in the New York Times', *Journal of Communication*, 32 (2), Spring: 162–71.

Palmer, Alasdair (1984) 'The History of the D-Notice Committee', in Christopher Andrew and David Dilks (eds), *The Missing Dimension: Governments and Intelligence Communities in the Twentieth Century*, London: Macmillan.

Philo, Greg (1990) *Seeing and Believing: The Influence of Television*, London: Routledge.

Philo, Greg and McLaughlin, Greg (1992) *The British Media and the Gulf War*, Glasgow: Glasgow University Media Group.

Picard, Robert (1986) 'News Coverage as the Contagion of Terrorism: Dangerous Charges Backed by Dubious Science', *Political Communication and Persuasion*, 3 (4): 385–400.

Picard, Robert (1993) *Media Portrayals of Terrorism: Functions and Meaning of News Coverage*, Ames, Iowa: Iowa State University Press.

Pilger, John (1992) *Distant Voices*, London: Vintage.

Podhoretz, Norman (1980) 'The Subtle Collusion', *Political Communication and Persuasion*, 1: 84–9.

Ponting, Clive (1990) *Secrecy in Britain*, London: Basil Blackwell.

Powell, Enoch (1988) 'The Questions our Muzzled Press Should be Asking on Gibraltar', *Independent*, 1 April.

Private Eye, (1989) *Rock Bottom: The Gibraltar Killings, Government and Press Cover-up*, London: Private Eye.

Protheroe, Alan (1985) 'Wanted – More Thought, Less Rhetoric', *The Listener*, 15 August: 5–6.

Raboy, Marc and Bruck, Peter (eds) (1989) *Communication For and Against Democracy*, Montreal: Black Rose Books.

Rawcliffe-King, Anne and Dyer, Nadine (1982) 'The Knowledge Gap Reconsidered: Learning from "Ireland: A Television History by Robert Kee"', in BBC (ed.), *Annual Review of BBC Broadcasting Research Findings*, 8, 1981/82, London: BBC.

Rees, Merlyn (1985) *Northern Ireland: a Personal Perspective*, London: Methuen.

Richardson, Kay and Corner, John (1986) 'Reading Reception: Mediation and Transparency in Viewers' Accounts of a TV Programme', *Media, Culture and Society*, 8: 485–508.

Robertson, Geoffrey and Nicol, Andrew (1992) *Media Law* (3rd edn), London: Penguin.

Robins, Kevin, Webster, Frank and Pickering, Michael (1987) 'Propaganda, Information and Social Control', in Jeremy Hawthorn (ed.), *Propaganda, Persuasion and Polemic*, London: Edward Arnold.

Robinson, John P. and Davis, Dennis K. (1990) 'Television News and the Informed Public: An Information Processing Approach', *Journal of Communication*, Summer: 106–19.

Robinson, John P. and Levy, Mark R. (1986) *The Main Source: Learning from Television News*, Beverly Hills, CA: Sage.

Rolston, Bill (1991) 'Containment and its Failure: The British State and the Control of Conflict in Northern Ireland', in Alexander George, *Western State Terrorism*, Cambridge: Polity.

Rose, Richard, McAllister, Ian and Mair, Peter (1978) 'Is there a

Concurring Majority About Northern Ireland?', *Studies in Public Policy*, 22, Glasgow: Centre for the Study of Public Policy, University of Strathclyde.

Rudin, Michael (1985) '"At the Edge of the Union" – Censorship and Constitutional Crisis at the BBC', *Journal of Media Law and Practice*, 6 (3): 277–300.

Russell, James (1973) 'Violence and the Ulster School boy', *New Society*, 26 July: 204–6.

Ryder, Chris (1977) 'Army Plans to Stress "Successes"', *Sunday Times*, 27 February.

Ryder, Chris (1989) *The RUC: A force under fire*, London: Methuen.

Sadler, Rex and Hallyar, Tom (eds) (1985) *Senior Drama*, South Melbourne, Australia: Macmillan.

Sahin, Haluk, Dennis K. Davis and John P. Robinson (1982) 'Television as a Source of International News: What Gets Across and Why', in William C. Adams (ed.), *Television Coverage of International Affairs*, Norwood, NJ: Ablex.

Scannell, Paddy and Cardiff, David (1991) *A Social History of British Broadcasting vol. 1*, Oxford: Basil Blackwell.

Schlesinger, Philip (1981) '"Terrorism", the Media and the Liberal-Democratic State: A Critique of the Orthodoxy', *Social Research*, 48, 1: 74–99.

Schlesinger, Philip (1987) *Putting 'Reality' Together: BBC News* (2nd edn), London: Methuen.

Schlesinger, Philip (1990) 'Rethinking the Sociology of Journalism: Source Strategies and the Limits of Media-Centrism', in Marjorie Ferguson (ed.), *Public Communication: The New Imperatives*, London: Sage.

Schlesinger, Philip (1991) *Media, State and Nation: Political Violence and Collective Identities*, London: Sage.

Schlesinger, Philip, Dobash, R. Emerson, Dobash, Russell P. and Weaver, C. Kay (1992) *Women Viewing Violence*, London: British Film Institute.

Schlesinger, Philip, Murdock, Graham and Elliot, Philip (1983) *Televising 'Terrorism': Political Violence in Popular Culture*, London: Comedia.

Schlesinger, Philip, Tumber, Howard and Murdock Graham (1991) 'The Media Politics of Crime and Criminal Justice', *British Journal of Sociology*, 42 (3), September: 397–420.

Schmid, Alex and De Graaf, Janny (1982) *Violence as Communication: Insurgent Terrorism and the Western News Media*, London: Sage.

Seaman, William (1992) 'Active audience theory: pointless populism', *Media, Culture and Society* 14 (2), April: 301–11.

Seiter, Ellen, Borchers, Hans, Kreutzner, Gabrielle and Warth, Eva-Maria (eds) (1989) *Remote Control: Television, Audiences and Cultural Power*, London: Routledge.

Seiter, Ellen, Borchers, Hans, Kreutzner, Gabrielle and Warth, Eva-Maria (1989) '"Don't Treat us like we're so Stupid and Naïve": Towards an Ethnography of Soap Opera Viewers', in Ellen Seiter, Hans Borchers, Gabrielle Kreutzner and Eva-Maria Warth (eds), *Remote Control: Television, Audiences and Cultural Power*, London: Routledge.

Shingi, P.M. and Mody, B. (1976) 'The Communication Effects Gap', *Communication Research*, 3 (2): 171–90.

Silverstone, Roger (1990) 'Television and Everyday Life: Towards an Anthropology of the Television Audience', in Marjorie Ferguson (ed.), *Public Communication: The New Imperatives*, London: Sage.

Simon, Stuart (1982) 'How Britain is Losing the Irish Argument', *The Listener*, 108, 2 December: 5–6.

Sinn Féin (1987) *A Scenario for Peace: A Discussion Paper*, May, Dublin: Sinn Féin Ard Chomhairle.

Sinn Féin (1990) *Brooke Talks - A Sinn Féin Response*, internal briefing paper for PROs, Belfast: Sinn Féin.

Sinn Féin International Publicity and Information Committee (1990a) *Sinn Féin publicity director imprisoned on false charges: Neutralising political opponents*, briefing paper, January, Belfast: Sinn Féin Foreign Affairs Bureau.

Sinn Féin International Publicity and Information Committee (1990b) *British Agent Implicates Sinn Féin Activists*, briefing paper, Belfast: Sinn Féin Foreign Affairs Bureau.

Smith, Anthony (1972) Television Coverage of Northern Ireland, *Index on Censorship*, 1 (2), Summer: 15–32.

Smith, Lyn (1979) 'Covert British Propaganda: The Information Research Department: 1947–1977', *Millenium: Journal of International Studies*, 9 (1): 67–83.

Smyth, Jim (1987) 'Unintentional Mobilisation: The Effects of the 1980-81 Hunger Strikes in Ireland', *Political Communication and Persuasion*, 4 (3): 179–89.

Spaull, David (1988) 'Appendix, Newsroom Policy on Neutral Language and Terrorism', in Mike Brown, *BBC Bush House Newsroom Guide and Style Book*, London: BBC.

Stalker, John (1988) *Stalker*, London: Penguin.

Sterling, Claire (1981) *The Terror Network*, New York: Holt, Rhinehart and Winston/Reader's Digest.

Stoil, Michael J. and James R. Brownell, (1981) 'Research Design for a Study of Threat Communication and Audience Perception of Domestic Terrorism', *Political Communication and Persuasion*, 1 (2): 209–15.

Stuart, Charles (ed.) (1975) *The Reith Diaries*, Glasgow: Collins.

Sunday Times Insight Team, (1972) *Ulster*, London: Penguin.

Tan, Zoe C.-W. (1987) *Mass Media and Insurgent Terrorism: The Case of Belfast, 1916–1986* University of Michigan: unpublished Ph.D.

Tan, Zoe C.-W. (1988) 'Media Publicity and Insurgent Terrorism: A Twenty Year Balance Sheet', *Gazette*, 42: 3–32.

Tan, Zoe C.-W. (1989) 'The Role of Media in Insurgent Terrorism: Issues and Perspectives', *Gazette*, 44: 191–215.

Taylor, Ian (1988) 'The Analysis of Television Coverage of Political Violence – Comments on Weimann's Paper', in Peter Bruck (ed.), *The News Media and Terrorism*, Discussion Document Series, Ottawa, Canada: Centre for Communication, Culture and Society, Carleton University.

Taylor, John (1991) *War Photography*, London: Routledge.

Taylor, Peter (1979) 'Reporting Northern Ireland' in Campaign for Free Speech on Ireland, *The British Media and Ireland: Truth: The first casualty*, London: Information on Ireland.

Taylor, Peter (1980) *Beating the Terrorists? Interrogation in Omagh, Gough and Castelreagh*, London: Penguin.

Taylor, Peter (1986) 'The Semantics of Political Violence', in P. Golding, G. Murdock and P. Schlesinger (eds), *Communicating Politics: Mass Communication and the Political Process*, Leicester: Leicester University Press.

Taylor, Peter (1990a) 'Inside the Maze', *Observer Magazine*, 18 November: 16–24.

Taylor, Peter (1990b) 'Getting into the Maze', *Omnibus*, 1 (1): 22–5.

Tiffen, Rodney (1989) *News and Power*, Sydney: Allen and Unwin.

Thackrah R. (1987) 'Terrorism: A Definitional Problem', in P. Wilkinson and A. Stewart (eds), *Contemporary Research on Terrorism*, Aberdeen: Aberdeen University Press.

Thompson, Brian (1989) 'Broadcasting and Terrorism', *Public Law*: 527–41.

Thompson, Brian (1991) 'Broadcasting and Terrorism in the House of Lords', *Public Law*: 346–53.

Thomas, Jo (1991) 'Toeing the Line: Why the American Press Fails', in Bill Rolston (ed.), *The Media and Northern Ireland: covering the troubles*, London: Macmillan.

Thornton, Peter (1987) *The Civil Liberties of the Zircon Affair*, London: National Council for Civil Liberties, 11 February.

Thornton, Peter (1989) *Decade of Decline: Civil Liberties in the Thatcher Years*, London: Liberty (National Council for Civil Liberties).

Tichenor, P.J., Donohue, G.A. and Olien, C.N. (1970) 'Mass Media Flow and Differential Growth in Knowledge', *Public Opinion Quarterly*, 34 (2): 159–70.

Tracey, Michael (1982) 'Censored – The War Game Story', in Crispin Aubrey (ed.), *Nukespeak: the media and the bomb*, London: Comedia.

Tracey, Michael (1983) *In the Culture of the Eye: Ten Years of Weekend World*, London: Hutchinson.

Trethowan, Sir Ian, (1989) 'Foreword by Sir Ian Trethowan Chairman, Thames Television', in Windelsham and Rampton, *The Windelsham/Rampton Report on Death on the Rock*, London: Faber.

Tugwell, Maurice (1973) 'Revolutionary Propaganda and the Role of the Information Services in Counter-insurgency Operations', *Canadian Defence Quarterly*, 3, Autumn: 27–34.

Tugwell, Maurice (1980) *'Revolutionary Propaganda and Possible Counter Measures'*, unpublished Ph.D, March, King's College, University of London.

Tugwell, Maurice (1981) 'Politics and Propaganda of the Provisional IRA', *Terrorism*, 5, (1–2): 13–40.

Tugwell, Maurice, (1986) 'Terrorism and Propaganda: Problem and Response', *Conflict Quarterly*, 6, Spring: 5–15.

Tugwell, Maurice (1987) 'Terrorism and Propaganda: Problem and Response', in P. Wilkinson and A. Stewart, *Contemporary Research on Terrorism*, Aberdeen: Aberdeen University Press.

Tweedie, June (1988) *The Gibraltar Inquest Report: A Report into the Deaths of Mairead Farrell, Daniel McCann and Sean Savage, Gibraltar Coroners Court, September 1988*, London: Inquest.

Urban, Mark (1992) *Big Boys' Rules: The SAS and the Secret Struggle Against the IRA*, London: Faber.

Verrier, Anthony (1983) *Through the Looking Glass: British Foreign Policy in the Age of Illusions*, London: Jonathan Cape.

Walker, Clive (1992) *The Prevention of Terrorism in British Law* (2nd edn), Manchester: Manchester University Press.

Walters, Ian (1984) 'Despite Its Bad Media Image, Northern Ireland Proves To Be A Good Place To Do Business', *Business America*, 23 July: 12–14.

Ward, Ken (1984) 'Ulster Terrorism: The US Network News Coverage of Northern Ireland 1968–1979', in Y. Alexander and A. O'Day (eds), *Terrorism in Ireland*, London: Croom Helm.

Watt, Nicholas (1993) 'Wires Crossed over Two Faces of Northern Ireland', *The Times*, 20 August: 6.

Waugh, Auberon (1988) 'Why don't the Poodles of the Press ask the Main Gibraltar Question?', *Spectator*, 1 October.

Weaver, Russell L. and Bennet, Geoffrey (1989) 'The Northern Ireland Broadcasting Ban: Some Reflections on Judicial Review', *Vanderbilt Journal of Transnational Law*, 22 (5): 1119–60.

Weaver, Russell L. and Bennet, Geoffrey (1992) 'Banning Broadcasting – A Transatlantic Perspective', *Media Law and Practice*, June: 179–87.

Weimann, Gabriel (1983) 'The Theatre of Terror: Effects of Press Coverage', *Journal of Communication*, 33 (1): 38–45.

Weimann, Gabriel (1985) 'Terrorists of Freedom Fighters? Labelling Terrorism in the Israeli Press', *Political Communication and Persuasion*, 2 (4): 433–45.

Weimann, Gabriel (1987) 'Conceptualizing the Effects of Mass-Mediated Terrorism', *Political Communication and Persuasion*, 3: 213–16.

Weimann, Gabriel (1987) 'Media Events: The Case of International Terrorism', *Journal of Broadcasting and Electronic Media*, 31 (1), Winter: 21–39.

Weimann, Gabriel (1988a) 'Mass Mediated Theatre of Terror - Must the Show Go On?', in Peter Bruck (ed.), *The News Media and Terrorism*, Discussion Document Series, Ottawa, Canada: Centre for Communication, Culture and Society, Carleton University.

Weimann, Gabriel (1988b) 'Critics in the Theatre of Terror – Weimann's Reply' in Peter Bruck (ed.) *The News Media and Terrorism*, Discussion Document Series, Ottawa: Centre for Communication, Culture and Society, Carleton University.

Weimann, Gabriel (1990) '"Redefinition of Image": The Impact of Mass-Mediated Terrorism', *International Journal of Public Opinion Research*, 2 (1): 16–29.

Weimann, Gabriel and Hans-Bernd Brosius (1989) 'The Predictability of International Terrorism: A Time-Series Analysis', *Terrorism*, 11: 491–502.

Whelan, Leo J. (1992) 'The Challenge of Lobbying for Civil Rights in Northern Ireland: The Committee on the Administration of Justice', *Human Rights Quarterly*, 14 (2), May: 149–70.

White, Robert W (1988) 'Commitment, Efficacy and Personal Sacrifice among Irish Republicans', *Journal of Political and Military Sociology*, 16, Spring: 77–90.

Wilkinson, Paul (1977) *Terrorism and the Liberal State*, London: Macmillan.

Wilkinson, Paul (1978) 'Terrorism and the Media', *Journalism Studies Review*, June, 3: 2–6.

Wilkinson, Paul (1987) 'Can a State be Terrorist?', *International Affairs*, 57: 467–72.

Wilkinson, Paul (1990) 'Terrorism and Propaganda', in Y. Alexander and R. Latter (eds), *Terrorism and the Media: Dilemmas for Government, Journalists and the Public*, Washington: Brassey's.

Wilson, John (1990a) 'The Police and Journalistic Material', *IPI Discussion Papers*, A special report for the British executive of the International Press Institute, 17 September.

Wilson, John (1990b) 'Long Arm of the Law', *Journalist's Week*, 21 September: 7.

Wilson, Robin (1988) 'Poll Shock for Accord', *Fortnight*, 261, April: 6–8.

Wilson, Robin (1990) 'Troops Shot Small-time Thief 12 Times', *Independent on Sunday*, 12 August.

Winchester, Simon (1974) *In Holy Terror: Reporting the Ulster Troubles*, London: Faber and Faber.

Windelsham, Lord and Rampton, Richard (1989) *The Windelsham/ Rampton Report on Death on the Rock*, London: Faber.

Wober, Mallory (1981) 'Broadcasting and the Conflict in Ireland: Viewers' Opinions of Two Series and Their Context', *IBA Research Paper*, London: Independent Broadcasting Authority.

Wober, Mallory (1992) 'Xenovision: Images of Life in Northern Ireland Through Its Portrayals on Screen', *ITC Research Reference Paper*, February, London: Independent Television Commission.

Wober, Mallory and Gunter, Barrie (1988) *Television and Social Control*, Aldershot: Avebury.

Woodman, Kieran (1985) *Media Control in Ireland 1923–1983*, Carbondale and Edwardsville: Southern Illinois University Press.

Woolf, Lord Justice and Pill, Mr Justice (1992) *In the matter of an application for orders under order 52 rule 9 of the rules of the supreme court and/or writs of sequestration, between The Director of Public Prosecutions and Channel Four Television Company Limited and Box Productions Limited*, In the High Court of Justice, Queens Bench Divisional Court, CO/689/92, 31 July.

World in Action (1988) 'The Taming of the Beeb', ITV, 29 February.

Wright, Joanne (1991) *Terrorist Propaganda: The Red Army Faction and the Provisional IRA, 1968–86*, London: Macmillan.

INDEX